The Emerging European Union

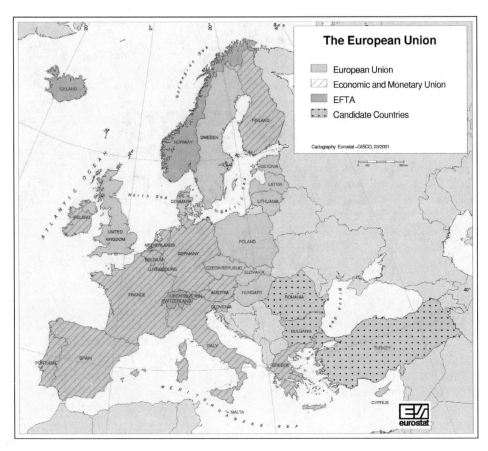

The European Union and Candidate Countries

The Emerging European Union

THIRD EDITION

David M. Wood

University of Missouri—Columbia

Birol A. Yeşilada

Portland State University

PEARSON
Longman

New York   Boston   San Francisco
London   Toronto   Sydney   Tokyo   Singapore   Madrid
Mexico City   Munich   Paris   Cape Town   Hong Kong   Montreal

Vice President/Publisher: Priscilla McGeehon
Executive Editor: Eric Stano
Senior Marketing Manager: Megan Galvin-Fak
Production Manager: Eric Jorgensen
Project Coordination, Text Design, and Electronic Page Makeup:
    UG / GGS Information Services, Inc.
Cover Design Manager: John Callahan
Cover Design/Illustration: Keithley & Associates, Inc.
Manufacturing Manager: Dennis Para
Printer and Binder: Courier Corporation
Cover Printer: Coral Graphics Services, Inc.

Map facing title page adapted from (http://www.eurunion.org/legislat/agd2000/adg2000.htm). Copyright
of the map is owned by the European Commission but reproduction is authorized.

Library of Congress Cataloging-in-Publication Data

Wood, David Michael, 1934–
    The Emerging European Union / David M. Wood, Birol A. Yesilada.—3rd ed.
        p. cm.
    Includes bibliographical references and index.
    ISBN 0-321-15996-9
    1. European Union.   2. European federation.   3. European Union countries—Economic policy.
    4. European Union countries—Foreign relations.   I. Yesilada, Birol A.   II. Title.

JN30.W66 2003
341.242'2—dc21

                                                            2003051688

Visit us at http://www.ablongman.com

ISBN 0-321-15996-9

2 3 4 5 6 7 8 9 BKM BKM   09876543

For Mary and Susan

Contents

Preface

The Emerging European Union (third edition) is a political science text designed for upper division college courses in three fields: (1) comparative European politics, (2) international political economy, and (3) international organizations. It can be used as well for more specialized courses on individual European political systems, particularly those of the United Kingdom (UK), France, and Germany, and on the European Union (EU) and the process of European integration.

Substantial revisions in the third edition include recent theoretical advances in the study of EU institutions, the recent constitutional convention, eastern enlargement and its implications, the state of the transatlantic relations following the war on terrorism and Iraq, and thorough discussion of major developments in the growing policy agenda of the EU.

For comparative politics courses the book draws the attention of students to how membership in the EU and its predecessor, the European Community (EC), has affected and been affected by the domestic politics of the member countries. In Chapters 1 and 3–6, we highlight the roles played in European integration at various times in the past and especially in the 1990s by the governments of the three largest countries. In Chapter 5 the discussion of the constitutional convention involves institutional changes affecting the relative voting weights of large and small and of old and new members in the Council of Ministers and the possibility of an elected president of the council.

From the standpoint of international relations and political economy, we treat the EU as the product of fundamental systemic and regional changes that had profound impact on member states. How this has occurred historically is one of the themes we address in Chapter 2 on the evolution of regional integration theory, in which economic and political explanations have periodically been stimulated by unexpected developments in European integration. Discussions in Chapters 3–5 demonstrate how the international political economy influenced this history. Chapters 7–12 examine policy responses of the EU to changes in the international political economy. In these chapters we examine the enlargement process (Chapter 7), economic and monetary policies (Chapter 8); the Common Agricultural Policy (CAP) (Chapter 9);

cohesion, environmental, and industrial policies (Chapter 10); external economic relations (Chapter 11); and foreign and domestic security policies (Chapter 12). Among
the topics of recent importance are the creation of the euro and the European Central
Bank, fiscal and monetary policy coordination mechanisms in the Union, the stability
pact, the budget problems, efforts at reforming the Common Agricultural Policy,
changes in the cohesion policies, the external economic relations and trade problems
with the U.S., problems associated with a single Common Foreign and Security Policy, challenges facing transatlantic relations in the aftermath of the Iraq war and different trade conflicts between the E.U.-U.S., and harmonization of member states'
policies in areas of home and justice affairs.

For international organizations courses, the EU serves as the unique case of a regional organization that has moved beyond the strictly intergovernmental format of
the typical international organization. In every chapter of the book, we examine the
ways in which the EU has pushed the concept of an international organization to the
limit by combining intergovernmental and supranational features.

In designing and writing the book, we have been conscious of the fact that the
study of the EU does not fit neatly into the traditional substantive breakdowns of political science curricula. In targeting the previously mentioned types of courses, we
have tried to include enough substantive material to satisfy instructors looking for a
main text on European integration, without going into so much depth that the text
will not fit the specifications for a supplementary text. We believe we have produced
a text that will effectively cover this variety of needs.

The authors wish to acknowledge the intellectual contribution of colleagues, including William Fisch, Robin Remington, Herbert Tillema, and Walter Johnson at the University of Missouri-Columbia; Leon Hurwitz at Cleveland State University; and Emil
Joseph Kirchner at the University of Essex. The European Union Center at the University of Missouri-Columbia and its former Director, Andrew Balas, and Associate Director, Kelly Shaw, have been of great assistance, as has the European Union Studies Association (EUSA), and the Delegation of the European Communities in Washington, D.C.

We would also like to thank the following individuals who reviewed the manu-
script for the first, second, or third edition and provided helpful suggestions:

Philip P. Baumann, Moorhead State University

Laura Brunell, Gonzaga University

Patrick Conge, University of Arkansas

Desmond Dinan, George Mason University

William M. Downs, Georgia State University

Robert Evans, Bologna Center, Johns Hopkins University

Richard B. Finnegan, Stonehill College

Gary P. Freeman, University of Texas

Norman Furniss, Indiana University

Arthur B. Gunlicks, University of Richmond

Louis D. Hayes, University of Montana

James F. Hollifield, Southern Methodist University

Steven Lewis, University of Wisconsin

Anthony M. Messina, Tufts University

Anthony Mughan, Ohio State University

Jorgen Rasmussen, Iowa State University

Martin Slann, Clemson University

David S. Wilson, University of Toledo

Stephen Wright, Northern Arizona University

DAVID M. WOOD
BIROL A. YEŞILADA

Abbreviations

ACP	African, Caribbean, and Pacific Countries (Lomé states)
ACP–EC PA	ACP–EC Partnership Agreement
AMS	Aggregate Measure of Support
ASEAN	Association of South East Asian Nations
Benelux	Belgium, the Netherlands, Luxembourg Customs and European Union
BSE	Bovine Spongiform Encephalopathy
CAP	Common Agricultural Policy
CCP	Common Commercial Policy
CDU/CSU	Christian Democrats (Germany)
CEDEFOP	European Center for the Development of Vocational Training
CEEC	Central and Eastern European Countries
CFSP	Common Foreign and Security Policy
CMO	Common Market Organization
COR	Committee of the Regions
COREPER	Committee of Permanent Representatives
CSCE	Conference on Security and Cooperation in Europe
CU	Customs Union
DG	Directorate General
DGXIV	Directorate General XIV of the European Commission
DM	Deutsche mark (Germany)
EAGGF	European Agricultural Guidance and Guarantee Fund
EAP	Environmental Action Programs
EBRD	European Bank for Reconstruction and Development
EC	European Community
ECB	European Central Bank
ECJ	European Court of Justice
Ecofin	Council of Economic and Finance Ministers
ECSC	European Coal and Steel Community
Ecu	European currency unit
EDC	European Defense Community
EDF	European Development Fund
EEA	European Economic Area
EEC	European Economic Community
EES	European Economic Space
EFTA	European Free Trade Association
EIB	European Investment Bank
ELDR	European Liberal Democrats and Republicans (EP group)
EMI	European Monetary Institute

EMS	European Monetary System
EMU	Economic and Monetary Union
EP	European Parliament
EPC	European Political Cooperation
EPP	European People's Party (Christian Democratic EP group)
ERM	Exchange Rate Mechanism
ERRF	European Rapid Reaction Force
ESC	Economic and Social Committee
ESCB	European System of Central Banks
ESDI	European Security and Defense Identity
ESDP	European Security and Defense Policy
ESF	European Social Fund
ESPRIT	European Strategic Program for Research and Development in Information Technologies
EU	European Union
EUA	European Unit (currency) of Account
Euratom	European Atomic Energy Community
Euro	EMU single currency
EUT	European Union Treaty
FDP	Free Democratic Party (Germany)
FIFG	Financial Instrument for Fisheries Guidance
GATT	General Agreement on Tariffs and Trade
GDP	Gross domestic product
GDR	German Democratic Republic (former East Germany)
GMP	Global Mediterranean Policy
GNP	Gross national product
GSP	EU's General System of Preferences
IEPG	Independent European Program Group
IFOR	Multinational military implementation force (in Bosnia-Herzegovina)
IGC	Intergovernmental Conference
IGO	Intergovernmental Organization
IMF	International Monetary Fund
ISPA	Instrument for Structural Policies for Pre-accession
JHA	Justice and Home Affairs
JRC	Joint Research Center
KFOR	International security forces in Kosovo
KLA	Kosovo Liberation Army
MCA	Manadatory compensatory account
MEDA	Financial instrument for the Euro-Mediterranean partnership
MEP	Member of the European Parliament
MFN	Most favored nation
MITI	Ministry of International Trade and Industry (Japan)
MP	Member of Parliament (Britain)

MRP	Popular republican Movement (French Christian Democrats)
MTR	Mid-term review
NAFTA	The North American Free Trade Agreement
NATO	North Atlantic Treaty Organization
NCB	National Central Bank
NMBC	Nonmember (OEU) Mediterranean Basin Countries
NTA	New Transatlantic Agenda
OCT	Overseas Countries and Territories
OECD	Organization for Economic Cooperation and Development
OSCE	Organization for Security and Cooperation in Europe
PCF	French Communist Party
PES	European Socialist Party (Socialist EP group)
PHARE	Technical Assistance for Central and Eastern Europe
QMV	Qualified majority voting
R&D	Research and development
RPR	Rally for the Republic (French Neo-Gaullists)
SAPARAD	Special Accession Program for Agricultural and Rural Development
SCVPH	Scientific Committee of Veterinary Measures Relating to Public Health
SDR	Special drawing rights (of the IMF)
SEA	Single European Act
SPD	Social Democratic Party (Germany)
STABEX	Commodity Export Earnings Stabilization Scheme (of Lomé)
SYSMIN	Mineral Accident Insurance System (of Lomé)
TACIS	Technical Assistance in Confederation of Independent States
TEU	Treaty on European Union (Maastricht Treaty)
TRNC	Turkish Republic of Northern Cyprus
TSE	Total support estimate
UDF	Union for French Democracy
UK	United Kingdom
UN	United Nations
UNMIK	United Nations mission in Kosovo
UNPROFOR	United Nations Peacekeeping Forces in the former Yugoslavia
UNSCR	United Nations Security Council Resolution
USSR	Union of Soviet Socialist Republics
VAT	Value-added tax
VER	Voluntary export restraint
WEAG	Western European Armaments Group
WEU	Western European Union
WTO	World Trade Organization

About the Authors

David M. Wood is professor emeritus of Political Science at the University of Missouri—Columbia. He received his doctorate from the University of Illinois in 1960. Among his publications are two coauthored books, *Comparing Political Systems: Power and Politics in Three Worlds*, Fourth Edition, and *Back from Westminister: British Members of Parliament and Their Constituents*; and numerous articles in scholarly journals. He specializes in the study of European political systems, including the EU, and comparative legislative behavior.

Birol A. Yeşilada is professor of Political Science and International Studies and holder of the Contemporary Turkish Studies Endowed Chair at Portland State University. He received his doctorate from the University of Michigan in 1984. Among his publications are one edited book, *Comparative Political Parties and Party Elites: Essays in Honor of Samuel J. Eldersveld*; two co-edited books, *The Political and Socioeconomic Transformation of Turkey* and *Agrarian Reform in Reverse: The Food Crisis in the Third World*; and articles and chapters in scholarly journals and research books. He specializes in the EU policies of integration and enlargement, international political economy, integration of global financial markets and democratic reforms, decision-making and conflict resolution, and Turkish politics.

1

Introduction

The subject of this book is the European Union (EU), which superceded the European Community in 1993, when the Treaty of European Union (TEU) came into effect. Each significant development in the evolution of European integration has involved the pooling of some governmental functions and powers by the Western European member states. During the 1950s, three regional European organizations were formed: the European Coal and Steel Community (ECSC), the European Economic Community (EEC), and the European Atomic Energy Community (Euratom). Initially, six states were involved in the formation of these organizations: Belgium, France, Italy, Luxembourg, the Netherlands, and the German Federal Republic. Today there are 15 members and prospects that more will join in the current decade (see Map 1).

In this introductory chapter we provide a brief overview of the European Union from two points of view: (1) how the EU governing institutions collectively make policies to be uniformly implemented in the 15 member states; and (2) how the domestic politics of the member states are related to the politics of the EU.

THE FRAMEWORK OF THE EUROPEAN UNION

The European Union is emerging as something more than an organization of regional economic integration. It is both an economic and monetary union (EMU) and a political union. The EMU, which is in its third and final stage of development, has opened the way for the creation of macroeconomic policy—common fiscal and monetary policy for all member states. A common central banking system akin to the U.S. Federal Reserve system now exists for member states, and on January 1, 1999, 11 of the 15 EU members adopted the euro as their common currency, replacing the separate currencies of the states. A twelfth EU member, Greece, was admitted to EMU at the beginning of 2001. Coins and bills in euro denominations were introduced into circulation at the beginning of 2002. The policy implications of the EMU are hotly debated by EU member states, especially the three that decided not to join the EMU in the third stage: Britain, Denmark, and Sweden.

The meaning of political union is a combination of what the EU is at present after over 40 years of evolution and of what are aspirations for future political integration on the part of those who advocate the creation of a European federated state. Currently, political union takes the form of specific institutions that are either intergovernmental or supranational in character. This is similar to the distinction between a confederation and a federation. A *confederation* makes decisions through a process of intergovernmental bargaining, whereas a *federation* has decision-making bodies that are independent of the member states. For example, one of the legislative bodies of the EU is the European Parliament, whose members are elected by the voters in the member states, in much the same way as the U.S. Congress is elected. But the other legislative body, the Council of Ministers, consists of ministers of the governments of the 15 EU countries. The Parliament is a supranational body, whereas the Council of Ministers is an intergovernmental one. Decision making is a balancing act in the EU, which operates sometimes as a confederation and sometimes as a federation. Supranational bodies can act independently of individual national governments, but they can be overridden by intergovernmental bodies. However, it is not necessarily easy to override supranational decisions, and, if accomplished, it may give rise to new supranational decisions with intended effects similar to those earlier rejected.

Intergovernmental bodies bring together political leaders or delegates of the 15 member governments. The principal intergovernmental body is the *Council of Ministers;* 15 ministers meet to adopt policy measures applicable to all member states. At its apex is the *European Council*, which consists of heads of state and government. This body meets four times a year to make the EU's most important decisions, setting the agenda for other legislative bodies to implement. When new institutional arrangements, the admission of new members, or major departures in EU policy are under consideration, the European Council will find the unanimous consensus to give direction to the Council of Ministers, or the new steps will not be taken. Leadership (called presidency) of the Council of Ministers is rotated to a new member state every 6 months, ensuring that each of the 15 members will preside once every 7 1/2 years. While the presidency has some agenda-setting powers, decisions are made by the Council as a collective body. Intergovernmental conferences are held from time to time; these function somewhat like constitutional conventions to consider revisions of the treaties on which the EU is based. Intergovernmental conferences (IGCs) preceded the four major revisions of the Rome Treaty, in 1985, 1991, 1996–1997, and 2000. Currently, a constitutional convention, with wider ranging membership than is found in IGCs, is meeting to consider a further revision of the treaties, potentially amounting to a constitution for the EU (see Chapters 5 and 6).

Supranational bodies bring together nationals of the member states who are not accountable to their governments but deliberate in the name of the European citizenry or the EU as a whole. The principal supranational institutions follow the threefold separation of powers familiar to students of U.S. government. The *Commission* is the executive body. It consists of 20 commissioners who are nominated by the governments of the member countries (two commissioners for each of the five largest members—Britain, France, Germany, Italy, and Spain—and one for each of the smaller members), and then formally chosen by the Council of Ministers, which also elects one of the commissioners president. The president assigns responsibilities to the other commissioners. The European Parliament can reject the proposed Commission as a whole but cannot stop the appointment of commissioners on an individual basis.

The other two supranational bodies are the *European Parliament* (EP) and the *European Court of Justice* (ECJ). The 626 members of the European Parliament are directly elected by voters in "Euro elections" every 5 years. The formal powers of the EP have been growing steadily since the 1970s, but it shares its legislative power with the Council of Ministers. The Court of Justice has 15 judges who, like the commissioners, are nominated by their member governments and formally chosen by the Council of Ministers. The ECJ interprets the treaties of the EU and has established its authority to declare actions of EU bodies and member states in violation of EU law. Its power is akin to the judicial review exercised by the U.S. Supreme Court.

This, then, is a brief outline of the EU's principal institutions. In Chapter 6 we will examine the respective powers of these institutions and the degree to which they collectively meet the criteria for a democratic system of governance. We will also assess the extent to which the EU represents a departure from a confederal mode of power sharing and is moving toward a federal pooling of sovereignty.

The European Council and the Council of Ministers act as 15-member intergovernmental bodies which try to find common ground among all member states before making decisions. But in the 1980s and 1990s the practice grew, with the encouragement of three treaty revisions, to decide matters in the Council of Ministers by "qualified majority vote" (QMV)—that is, a weighted vote of more than 71 percent.[1] As QMV advances, the sovereign independence of the member states recedes, and the European Union becomes increasingly a supranational arrangement of institutions. The Commission, the Court of Justice, and the European Parliament are supranational bodies, but they remain dependent upon the intergovernmental bodies to register the consensus among member states necessary to move the EU ahead. Clearly, the member states, individually as well as collectively, are major actors in the EU political process. But some are more "major" than others, and there are important differences between them that are relevant to the ways they act at the European level.

THE MEMBER STATES

Each of the 15 member states encompasses a political system with its own set of laws, governing institutions, political parties, elections, interest groups, and subnational levels of government. Increasingly, developments within the EU affect these domestic political systems. For example, with the evolution of the European Council as the EU's principal agenda-setting body, the influence of heads of state and government in their own national political systems has grown at the expense of other elected officials.[2] Summit meetings generate a great amount of media attention, so national-level political actors are dependent upon the president or prime minister to negotiate effectively with other heads on behalf of the member country's interests. Successful negotiations of European Community (EC) package agreements in the 1980s added to the stature of German chancellor Helmut Kohl, French president François Mitterrand, and British prime minister Margaret Thatcher, all of whom cultivated an image of toughness combined with tactical adroitness in knowing when to make concessions while retaining the principal advantage. Such image management at the EU level undoubtably contributed to the remarkable longevity in office of all three of these national leaders. However, as we will see in Chapter 5, the more difficult decisions on the EU agenda in the 1990s and the opening years of the twenty-first century have made it harder for current leaders to elevate their prestige through the bargains struck in high-level intergovernmental negotiations.

In 10 of the 15 member states, the domestic government operates within a parliamentary system (Table 1.1). In such a system the head of government and the ministers (department heads and/or cabinet members) chosen by the head of state are responsible to a majority in the legislative body, or parliament. If the government in power loses a vote of confidence in parliament, it means that they no longer have the support of the majority, and they must resign in order to allow the parliament to choose a new government. In some parliamentary systems, such as Britain, they may instead call new elections in order to get the support of the electorate for a new parliament with a favorable majority.

Britain is usually cited as the classic example of a parliamentary system. British voters choose between candidates of political parties in single-member districts. The winner of the most votes (*plurality*) in each district gains a seat in the House of Commons. The leader of the party which gains a majority of seats in the Com-

TABLE 1.1   Systems of Government among EU Member Countries

Country	Year Joined	System of Government
Austria	1995	Premier, weak president
Belgium	1958	Parliamentary
Denmark	1973	Parliamentary
Finland	1995	Premier, strong president
France	1958	Premier, strong president
Germany	1958	Parliamentary
Greece	1981	Parliamentary
Ireland	1973	Premier, weak president
Italy	1958	Parliamentary
Luxembourg	1958	Parliamentary
Netherlands	1958	Parliamentary
Portugal	1986	Premier, formally weak president
Spain	1986	Parliamentary
Sweden	1995	Parliamentary
United Kingdom	1973	Parliamentary

mons becomes the prime minister. He or she then chooses a cabinet from among the elected members to govern the country with the support of the House of Commons majority. The party that wins the election stays in power until defeated in a subsequent election or in a vote of no confidence. The two main parties in Britain, the Conservative Party and the Labour Party, together win most of the parliamentary seats in each election. One of them almost always has a clear-cut majority of seats, and because party members rarely break ranks, the ruling party can usually stay in power for a full 5-year term, or call new parliamentary elections sooner if the prime minister judges that it would be to the ruling party's advantage to hold new elections.

With some specific differences, the 10 EU members that have pure parliamentary systems operate under similar rules. The main distinguishing feature of the British system is that one or the other of its two main parties is strong enough to win a majority in its own right. In this it is helped by the single-member district plurality electoral system, which encourages voters not to waste their votes on smaller parties, but instead to vote for the candidates of parties with a chance of winning a majority of seats, enabling them to form a government. British voters know that the parties that do not get a majority of the seats in Parliament will be on the outside looking in as far as policymaking is concerned. In other European parliamentary systems coalition governments are usually formed because it is rare for one party to have a majority. In all of the parliamentary EU countries other than Britain the electoral system is one or another variant of proportional representation, which gives parties shares of seats in parliament roughly proportional to their shares of the popular vote. Such electoral systems do not penalize voters for voting for smaller parties, although there are thresholds to keep out very small parties, such as the 5 percent barrier in Germany.

Britain is one of a minority of member countries in which issues relating to the EU have been sufficiently divisive that they can affect political contests at the national level. In Chapters 3 to 5 we discuss some of the British debates over Europe that have occurred over the past 40 years. From the mid-1950s to the mid-1970s the fights were over the question of whether or not Britain should join or, later, stay in the EC. Since the late 1980s debate has centered on the main elements of the Maastricht Treaty: the EMU and political union. Most British politicians prefer that the EU remain essentially an intergovernmental union, and they oppose any further extension of the powers of supranational bodies. EMU involves a substantial transfer of economic policymaking capability from the member states to a supranational institution, the European Central Bank (ECB). The Labour government of Tony Blair, when elected in 1997, put off a decision on whether Britain will give up the pound for the euro, while most (but not all) Conservatives oppose British membership in the EMU.

By contrast, in another parliamentary member country, Germany, EU politics has not produced many serious domestic political divisions. Unlike Britain, Germany has more than two political parties with a reasonable chance of sharing governmental power. Also unlike Britain, it is very rare for one party to have a majority of seats in the Bundestag, which is comparable to the British House of Commons. This is because Germany uses a system of proportional representation in translating votes into seats. There are two large parties, the Christian Democrats (CDU/CSU) on the right and the Social Democrats (SPD) on the left. The smaller Free Democratic Party (FDP) joined with the CDU/CSU to form a coalition government under Chancellor Helmut Kohl (CDU leader) from 1982 to 1998. Then a new coalition of Social Democrats and Greens came to power with Social Democratic leader Gerhard Schröder as chancellor. This coalition won a narrow victory for a second term in the September 2002 elections. Issues that distinguished the two coalitions do not include German policy toward the European Union.

Among the other member countries with parliamentary systems, Denmark and Sweden have shown the greatest interparty and public disagreement over the question of EU powers. As in Britain, the Maastricht Treaty proved particularly divisive in Denmark; the voters failed to ratify the treaty in a 1992 referendum. But a year later, when the Social Democrats, who had opposed Danish ratification in 1992, were back in power, they supported ratification; the voters were again consulted, and the treaty was ratified. It was likewise uncertain whether voters would ratify Swedish accession to EU membership in 1994, but as in Denmark, when the Social Democrats returned to power shortly before the referendum, they supported Swedish entry, and their voters provided the necessary votes for ratification. However, Denmark, Sweden, and Britain have remained outside of the EMU as it consolidates its third stage. In September 2000 the Danish Social Democratic government asked voters whether Denmark should join the EMU. In a very closely watched referendum, Danish voters said no, 53 percent to 47 percent. This result was seen as a factor further delaying attempts by the Swedish and British governments to seek voter support for EMU membership. In the remaining purely parliamentary countries, Italy, Spain, Greece, the Netherlands, Luxembourg, and Belgium, support for political union and for the EMU is strong enough that it is unlikely to have a decisive effect on domestic politics. However, in two of those, Spain and Greece, enlargement of the EU to include countries of central, eastern, and southeastern Europe has produced opposing opinions on economic grounds in Spain and political grounds in Greece (see Chapter 7).

The remaining five EU member countries—Austria, Finland, France, Ireland, and Portugal—do not have pure parliamentary systems of government. Nor are they presidential systems like the United States. They have mixed features, elements of both presidential and parliamentary systems, or what Matthew Shugart and John Carey have called "premier-presidential" systems.[3] All of them have directly elected presidents, more like the U.S. president. They also have premiers who, like the British prime minister, rely on the support of majorities in directly elected legislative bodies. In the four smaller premier-presidential countries the president plays a relatively passive role, allowing executive authority to be wielded by the premier and cabinet. At times of political deadlock the president is available to step in and resolve conflicts, but parties in Austria, Finland, Ireland, and Portugal prefer to work out their differences in the Parliament rather than letting the president play a stronger role. In three of these four countries, EU issues have not been sufficiently divisive to affect the normal political process. Austria has proved to be the exception because of the rise of the right-wing Freedom Party, which opposes EU enlargement to the east, because it is seen as likely to increase immigration into Austria. In October 1999, the Freedom Party, led by the charismatic Jörg Haider, finished second and, after months of negotiation, was brought into a coalition government with the center-right People's Party. The president, who happened to be of the opposition Social Democratic Party, cautioned against the coalition but did not have the formal power to prevent it. (See Chapter 5 for a discussion of the effect upon the EU of this Austrian development.)

The formal institutional arrangements in France are unique among EU members. France has had the mixed premier-presidential form since the formation of the Fifth Republic in 1958. The first president of the Fifth Republic, General Charles de Gaulle (1958–1969), played a strong role in ending the Algerian War, which had brought on the fall of the Fourth Republic; he also took upon himself as president the formulation of French foreign policy, as well as its policy as a member of the original European Economic Community (see Chapter 2). He determined who would be his prime minister, a practice followed by his successors until the mid-1980s. This meant that the president was ultimately in control of domestic as well as foreign policy. If he or she allowed the premier to make decisions, they had to be decisions that followed the president's general policy lines. When conflicts occurred between president and premier, the latter would have to yield or be replaced by someone more compliant with the president's wishes.

De Gaulle wanted France to control the development of the European Community; otherwise he would not cooperate with the other member governments.[4] He approved of the economic benefits France gained from membership, but he did not want the EC to infringe upon French sovereignty in more politically sensitive areas. After de Gaulle left office in 1969, his successors gradually became more cooperative with EC partners while continuing to exercise leadership, usually in tandem with Germany. By the mid-1980s the European Community had virtually ceased to be a major issue among French politicians. Public opinion polls showed that the initially skeptical French populace had become comfortable with France's role in the EC.

But an inherent contradiction within the premier-presidential system surfaced in 1986. Prior to the parliamentary elections in March of that year, the Socialist Party of President François Mitterrand, the leading left-of-center party, had a solid majority in the National Assembly, the popularly elected lower house of Parliament. The election proved to be a serious setback for Mitterrand's Socialists. The two principal opposition right-of-center parties, the Union for French Democracy (UDF) and the Rally for the Republic (RPR), gained a bare majority of seats, enough to make it impossible for Mitterrand to appoint his own person as premier. He was forced to choose the leader of the "neo-Gaullist" RPR, Jacques Chirac, who then formed his own right-of-center government. Mitterrand and Chirac therefore found themselves locked in what was quickly termed "cohabitation," meaning that a president of the left and a premier of the right were required to live together. This happened because the president was elected for a 7-year term, but Parliament's term is only 5 years, so the elections did not coincide. It also happened because the Constitution of the Fifth Republic contains the normal parliamentary provision that a majority of the Assembly can vote the premier out of office: if the president named one of his own supporters premier, he would be inviting repudiation of his choice by the National Assembly.

Two other cohabitation periods have occurred: one in Mitterrand's second term, when he shared power with Gaullist Edouard Balladur from 1993 to 1995, and the other from 1997 to 2002, when President Jacques Chirac was forced to give up much of his power to Premier Lionel Jospin, a Socialist. During cohabitation periods, the consensus across left and right over European policy matters has prevented deadlocks between president and premier. Both have attended meetings of the European Council, but the president has been generally recognized by the other leaders around the table as the legitimate spokesperson for France.

Before the French presidential and parliamentary elections were scheduled to take place in the spring of 2002, the Constitution of the Fifth Republic was amended to reduce the President's term of office from 7 to 5 years. The terms of both President Chirac, elected in 1995, and the National Assembly with its left majority, elected in 1997, came to an end in the same year. It was agreed between Chirac and Socialist prime minister Lionel Jospin that the presidential election would precede the legislative election. In the first ballot of the presidential election there were so many candidates cutting into the votes of the two principal candidates, Chirac and Jospin, that Jospin finished third and Chirac outdistanced Jean-Marie Le Pen, the right-wing second-placed candidate, by only 3 percent of the vote. But Le Pen gained little further ground in the runoff against Chirac two weeks later, when Chirac won 82 percent of the vote.

When there is cohabitation in France, presidential powers recede, but when a president is elected along with a parliamentary majority, the president becomes the preeminent leader. This has been true of President Chirac, who has taken a firmer hold of French foreign and EU policy, as well as domestic policy, since his election in June 2002. It has not been the case in Austria, Finland, Ireland, or Portugal. In these countries the premier is the chief policymaker, but the president's role as a sort of "conscience" of the government is important.

This brief discussion of the political institutions of the European Union and its leading member states has been designed to demonstrate that the politics of the EU goes on simultaneously at two levels; what happens on one level has an important effect on the other. Contrary to the formal definition of a federal system, the transfer of powers from the national level to the institutions of the EU has not meant that the national governments have ceased to be involved in deciding how they will be used.[5]

In Chapter 2 we will review the leading theories of European integration, presenting them in their historical context. Chapters 3, 4, and 5 provide a historical overview of the development of the European Union from its origins in the Schuman Plan of 1950 to the end of 2002. Chapter 3 outlines the growing political coordination between the member states in the 25-year period up to the mid-1970s, when the European Council was established, a development that represented a turning point in the process of political integration. Chapter 4 focuses on the steps toward growing economic and political integration within the EC later in the 1970s and during the 1980s. Chapter 5 traces the steps leading to the agreement at Maastricht in December 1991, as well as the struggle to ratify the treaty in 1992–1993, the follow-up Treaty of Amsterdam, and the two principal projects that have followed it: entry into the third stage of EMU and preparations for further enlargement of the European Union.

Chapter 6 outlines the roles played by the principal agenda-setting and decision-making institutions of the EU: the European Council, the Council of Ministers, the Commission, the European Parliament, and the European Court of Justice. It also considers the extent to which an EU "public" is taking shape, capable of influencing the course of European integration independent of the wishes of political leaders. In this light, the June 1999 European Parliament elections are reviewed. The enlargement of the EU is at the top of the EU's agenda early in the first decade of the 21st century. A separate chapter (Chapter 7) is devoted to it.

Chapters 8 through 12 look at policy areas in which the European Union has either taken over functions previously belonging to the member governments or served as a forum for efforts to coordinate policies remaining primarily in members' hands. Chapter 8 examines the developing macro-level economic policy coordination that took place in the European Monetary System, including the exchange rate mechanism that controlled monetary fluctuations among member country currencies and that has been strengthened under the Economic and Monetary Union with its single currency, the euro.

Chapters 9 and 10 analyze important EU internal policies that are necessitated by problems created or made worse by poor economic performance: the common agricultural policy in Chapter 9 and regional, social, industrial, and environmental policies in Chapter 10.

Chapter 11 examines external economic policies of the EU, an important feature of the European Community since its inception; and Chapter 12 discusses foreign and security policy. Under the Maastricht Treaty, foreign and defense policies constitute the second pillar of the European Union. It is separate from the "EC pillar," or what might be considered the domestic policy of the EU, and it does not as yet fully involve some of its members. The steps taken in the Maastricht Treaty have produced better planning and more systematic approaches to crises such as those in the Balkans, the Middle East, and Central Asia, but it will remain more squarely within an intergovernmental framework than economic policy coordination. Finally, the third pillar, internal security, is outlined at the end of Chapter 12. We present our overall conclusions in Chapter 13.

ENDNOTES

1. Votes of the member states in the Council of Ministers are weighted roughly according to the sizes of the members' populations. To pass a motion by a qualified majority requires combining slightly more than 71 percent of the weighted votes.
2. Fritz W. Scharpf, "The Joint-Decision Trap: Lessons from German Federalism and European Integration," *Public Administration* 66 (Autumn 1988): 268.

3. Matthew Soberg Shugart and John M. Carey, *Presidents and Assemblies: Constitutional Design and Electoral Dynamics* (Cambridge: Cambridge University Press, 1992), p. 41.

4. Andrew Moravcsik, *The Choice for Europe: Social Purpose and State Power from Messina to Maastricht* (London: UCL Press, 1999), chap. 3.

5. Robert D. Putnam, "Diplomacy and Domestic Politics: The Logic of Two-Level Games," *International Organization* 42 (1988): 427–460; Emil Joseph Kirchner, *Decision-Making in the European Community: The Council Presidency and European Integration* (Manchester, England, and New York: Manchester University Press, 1992).

2

Theories of European Integration

In this chapter we will review the major theories of regional integration that have been formulated during the half-century since European integration became more than just a gleam in the eyes of European visionaries. The student should be given two warnings before we begin. First, theories of international integration, like all political theories, are produced in order to better understand ongoing political events and solve distressing problems that preoccupy political leaders. Thus, they follow the times, and they compete with one another to set the trend. Those theories that get the most attention are "fashionable"; they are not necessarily the ones that will continue to provide inspiration for political thinkers a half-century, or even a decade, later. In this chapter several theories with varying degrees of staying power will be reviewed. None of them is sufficient to fully understand where the European Union (EU) is today or how it got that way. But we will draw upon those that are general enough and strong enough to give us part of the explanation.

Second, political theorists attempt to do three things: explain, predict, and prescribe. All the theories we will discuss in this chapter have done a better job of explaining what has happened than predicting what will happen. If they had been better at predicting, they might have stayed in fashion longer. As for prescribing, it is safe to say that they are often directed toward outcomes that are the same as those they predict. For example, if the theorist wants to see a European federal state created, then the theory will be constructed so as to show how that outcome will be achieved, both by highlighting recent trends that have already moved Europe in the right direction and by showing how a continuation of those trends will lead to the predicted outcome. In this chapter and the next three we will concentrate on the explanatory and predictive elements of most of the theories, but there will be hints of the prescribed outcomes as well. We will also compare theory with practice over time.

REALISM AND IDEALISM

Why would nation-states like France or Germany give up any of their sovereign powers to a regional collectivity? To do so would be to do away with flexibility in dealing with unforeseen problems; it would also make the nation-state subject to collective decisions and actions that might not be in the best interests of its own citizens. Adherents of the *realist school* of international relations insist that the governments of nation-states usually act rationally on behalf of their citizens, carefully weighing the likely consequences of their decisions on the societies they govern. From this perspective, national governments will not generally do things that run counter to the national interest. Hans Morgenthau, the founder of this post–World War II school of international relations, defined a "national interest" in the most general terms as the power that governments must protect in order to achieve their objectives. Nation-states, according to Morgenthau, are the most powerful actors on the international scene.[1]

How do we know that nation-states act rationally? Because they constantly seek to maintain and enhance their power, say the realists. But how do we know that states will always act this way? What if they make mistakes or their leaders get swept up in some "irrational" sentiment, like the urge to help others (altruism) or find the Holy Grail (idealism)? The realists' answer tends to be that "governments don't do such things." Even though some of their decisions may turn out to have been ill-advised, the leaders have calculated that they are in the nation's best interest—that is, they will enhance the power of the nation-state. Marshall Plan aid after World War II may have looked to some Americans like incredible generosity emanating from Washington, with the flow of benefits going entirely in the direction of Europe. But realists insist that the United States obtained political benefits far in excess of the economic costs, and that, in fact, within a decade, the economic benefits to the United States outweighed the original economic costs as well.[2] On the other hand, the series of decisions made in the 1960s as the United States became more embroiled in the Vietnam War were seen at the time by many critics, and later by historians, to have been misguided, but they too were based on the government leaders' assessments of the "best interests" of the United States. "Realistic" calculations superceded whatever other premises might have prevailed.

The *idealist school* of international relations, more recently labeled *liberal internationalism*, acknowledges that nation-states sometimes seek to protect or expand their relative power positions. But this tendency is what leads them to commit acts of aggression and to attempt to strengthen themselves in ways that are likely to provoke countermeasures on the part of other nation-states. This school both hopes and predicts that nation-states will give up such uncivilized habits and learn to live with one another peaceably without arming to the teeth. They argue that there is a higher rationality than the egoistic quest for power and that nation-states can improve the welfare of their citizens more certainly by burying their short-term differences and reaching accords with one another designed to promote their *mutual* well-being over the longer run. Proponents of the idealist school ask if it is rational for states to distort the economic division of labor within their societies by building up stores of arms and conscripting young citizens out of the domestic workforce. Such policies, they insist, will increase the likelihood that much of the economy and population will be destroyed or left in a weakened position because the mobilization, even if justified on the grounds of defense, has led eventually to war. Further, war will disrupt international trade, adversely affecting the economies of many countries. Finally, they believe that institutions of national governments and international organizations can be improved through democratization and the spread of the rule of law, in such a way that the temptation to go to war will be held in check.[3]

Europeans, more than Americans, experienced the destruction and deprivation of world war. Europeans perceived the danger of Soviet expansion, but as individual states they lacked the capacity to build up their power to meet the threat. In the period following World War II, their economies were in such shambles that the immediate task of each government was to rebuild a peacetime economy. No military buildup could occur otherwise. So they chose to rely on the United States for military protection and a jump start on the way to economic reconstruction and modernization.

In the dangerous circumstances of the late 1940s, there was general recognition in Europe that states could not simply abandon the effort to protect themselves. But it was also recognized that they could not each do so apart from the others. Their common tragic experience in the 1930s and early 1940s also suggested that World War II itself might have been prevented had the European states more closely coordinated their efforts to deter Hitler's aggression. In the early postwar period European idealists and realists alike saw the need to create regional international organizations to cope with common problems, especially economic problems.

FEDERALISM, FUNCTIONALISM, AND "MONNETISM"

Two plans that were gaining support in the late 1940s were federalism and functionalism. The former attracted the support of nongovernmental organizations and movements led by prominent public figures; the latter was pursued more quietly by governmental officials.

Federalists believed that the vulnerable states of Western Europe should join together in a political union in which they could exercise mutual self-help in the face of threats to their common security. By forming a federation of once-sovereign states, they could pool their individual capacities to organize their defenses, mobilize their resources and industrial strengths, and guide their economies in the direction of modernization and economic growth. The basic thrust was political. The purpose of federation would be to concentrate the power of the federating states in a central authority. The authority would be given control over certain economic levers in order to better accomplish its overriding objective of providing for the collective security of the member states. The states would retain control over those aspects of their domestic affairs that were not seen to be vital for the common effort. But the pooling of sovereignty in the "federal government" would be substantial, and once having given up this sovereignty, each state would be bound to abide by common decisions.[4] As idealists, they believed that political leaders would simultaneously recognize that wars could only be prevented if nations pooled their military resources in a political union dedicated to resolving conflicts among them peaceably.

The closest Western Europe came to attaining such a political union was the European Defense Community (EDC), which was agreed upon in 1952 and was to include the six original members of the future EU: France, West Germany, Italy, Belgium, the Netherlands, and Luxembourg. The EDC would bring the armed forces of the six countries under a single multinational command structure. A political community was also envisioned at that time, to provide institutions for democratic political control over the multinational defense structure.[5] But these plans fell by the wayside in 1954 when the ratification of the EDC treaty was rejected by the French National Assembly. Further concrete steps toward European integration did not follow the federalist blueprint.

Unlike the federalists, the *functionalists* did not outline plans for an elaborate division of political responsibilities. They were pragmatists, concentrating on the immediate economic needs of the survivors of World War II.[6] The leading functionalist theorist was David Mitrany, who produced the main writings on the subject during and immediately after the war.[7] He was interested not in the functional integration of European nations per se, but in the creation of international organizations to fulfill certain specific needs. These might include organizing relief efforts for war refugees, regulating air traffic, formulating and enforcing international health and safety standards, or promoting more efficient agricultural methods. According to Mitrany's vision, several such organizations might come into being for different purposes, and comprise different sets of member states, sometimes including members from different continents and subregions around the globe. They would not all involve a given set of members found in a particular region. That is, they would not gradually become a collective statelike territorial entity in their own right. Mitrany rejected federalism on the grounds that it would replace the old states with a new, larger one, without necessarily reducing human misery.[8]

Yet Mitrany is generally regarded as a forerunner of a movement for *European* functional integration, which actually did go on to achieve the first real success in that direction: the European Coal and Steel Community (ECSC). This was the brainchild of a Frenchman, Jean Monnet, who had served in the League of Nations before its collapse on the eve of World War II; as a liaison figure between France, Britain, and the United States during the war; and as head of the French economic planning commission after the war. Monnet had always concentrated on finding very practical solutions to immediate problems, usually problems of an economic nature. Like Mitrany, Monnet believed that, when faced with their own inability to solve problems that could only be solved by international cooperation, states would, albeit reluctantly, relinquish limited elements of their sovereignty and pool their efforts in international organizations.

Monnet was optimistic about nation-states and their leaders. He believed that government leaders could be persuaded to move from a narrow, short-run definition of the national interest to one that acknowledged the long-term benefits of joining forces. And Monnet was a very persuasive individual. Throughout his career he had accumulated a rich network of contacts in many countries, people who shared elements of his ideas and were willing to support his goals.[9] He drew these contacts—many of whom occupied positions of governmental authority in Western Europe in the 1950s—into his Action Committee for a United States of Europe. The group successfully mobilized elite support in Western Europe for the creation of the European Economic Community (EEC), the forerunner of today's EU.[10] In the final analysis, Monnet was committed to a regionally specific set of countries joining together in what would eventually become a European federation. But his method of attaining it was indirect. Federalism was essentially a political goal for Monnet, ultimately involving a common foreign and security policy, which is sometimes called "high politics."[11] But Monnet preferred to begin by attaining consensus among a limited number of states to cooperate in "low politics," essentially policies for regulating production and trade.

The concrete problem with which Monnet began was that of overproduction in the European coal and steel industries and the necessity for production to be publicly regulated to avoid the likelihood of a severe depression in these sectors that would drive producers out of business and threaten the security of the region by diminishing reserve productive capacity. If governments of the affected countries could come together to regulate production—a common goal that was limited in scope but strategically crucial—market failure could be avoided. Monnet's plan was popularly known as the Schuman plan, after Robert Schuman, the French foreign minister who publicly initiated it in 1950. The "European six"—France, West Germany, Italy, Belgium, the Netherlands, and Luxembourg—agreed to form the ECSC with surprising rapidity, and it came into being less than two years later. The six nations invited Britain to join, but the Labour government was suspicious of what looked like longer-run federalist objectives, and Britain stayed out.[12]

Monnet was a pragmatist. While he envisioned a United States of Europe along federal lines, after the defeat of the European Defense Community in 1954, he refocused his attention upon more immediately achievable goals.[13]

Government leaders of the Monnetist persuasion formulated a new agenda for the European six in the mid-1950s. The result was the creation, in 1958, of the European Atomic Energy Community (Euratom) and the European Economic Community. Euratom achieved only modest results, largely because of the unwillingness of governments, especially the French, to give up their sovereign control of what was considered a vital element of national interest. In contrast, the EEC achieved remarkable success as a customs union[14] during the first decade of its life. Yet by the end of that decade, its chances of achieving a full fledged *political* union still appeared to be visionary. (See Chapter 3 for a fuller discussion of these developments.)

THE RISE AND DECLINE OF NEOFUNCTIONALISM

The attainment of economic goals through political means lies at the heart of the scholarly revision of functionalism that came to be called *neofunctionalism*. Its founder was Ernst B. Haas, an American political scientist who had witnessed at first hand the emergence of a new European agenda in the 1950s. Haas was sufficiently impressed by Monnet's strategy and tactics to put them into a theoretical framework that was more elaborate and academic in nature.[15] Haas argued that functional integration would most likely occur if influential and powerful elites were motivated to take decisive steps toward it. These must include government and other political leaders; but the politicians could not be expected to take action unless pressure was exerted by opinion leaders and special interest groups, especially those in the economic sector— business, labor, and agricultural leaders. He was more skeptical about the potential impact of the European federalists. He did not disagree with their goal, at least as an ideal, but he felt that mass opinion was likely to be too passive to be moved directly by groups promoting idealistic causes, and political elites were too hardheaded to risk their careers by single-mindedly supporting objectives that were not high on the national agenda.[16]

Haas introduced a number of neofunctionalist concepts to help explain the steps toward regional integration that had already occurred, as well as elucidating any further steps that might occur. Two central concepts were *spillover* and *supranationalism*.[17] By "spillover" Haas meant that, if the tasks of a regional organization were to expand, it would occur as a result of experiences with the tasks the organization was already performing. The ECSC had positive achievements that invited emulation in other spheres; it also had some unintended consequences that had to be addressed. Hence, the EEC, which came on its heels, was an attempt both to produce the same advantages in other sectors and to deal with some of the ECSC's side effects.

But Haas emphasized that there was nothing automatic in spillover. Task expansion by the regional organization would require political initiative. What we now call "cross-national networks" were becoming more frequent and broader. This process of communication made it possible for elites to address common problems in concrete terms and to discover an "upgraded common interest." The communications net corresponded to neither a federal nor a confederal framework; instead it was supranational.[18] Although the principal actors were nationally based, they came together predisposed to find common solutions to their mutual problems, and their method of arriving at decisions was by unanimous consent, avoiding votes, vetoes, and subsequent expressions of antagonism. The bias, Haas found, was in favor of reaching agreements.[19] This was the spirit in which Monnet had operated.

It was also the spirit that guided Walter Hallstein, the West German politician and administrator who became the first president of the EEC Commission. Under Hallstein's leadership, the EEC developed a method of decision making that refused to acknowledge the absence of consensus. In the early 1960s midnight deadlines were imposed upon meetings of the Council of Ministers and the clock was stopped at a minute before, with the meetings continuing on into the next day or days until agreement could be reached.[20]

With the publication of his later study of the International Labor Organization,[21] Haas gave greater attention to the importance of leadership as a part of his conception of supranationalism. The executive leaders of international organizations can play an important role in upgrading the common interest if they use their skills to (1) define an organizational ideology, (2) build a bureaucracy committed to that ideology, and (3) build coalitions of national actors supporting the leadership and its ideology.[22] Haas saw these attributes as necessary for the organization to be able to expand its functions.

In 1965, EEC President Hallstein attempted to force spillover from the economic to the political realm by presenting the Council of Ministers with a plan that would provide for a greater transfer of revenues from the national governments to the EEC. This would have strengthened the organization's economic impact. President Charles de Gaulle of France objected to Hallstein's plan and pulled his ministers out of the Council for what turned out to be a period of six months, from July 1965 to January 1966. Ultimately Hallstein and the governments of the other five countries had to withdraw the budget expansion proposal and concede to France informally, and counter to the spirit of supranationalism, that when a member government considered very important interests of its country to be at odds with a given proposal to be voted on in the Council, it could insist on the unanimity rule and thereby exercise a veto.[23]

The earlier supranational assumption that consensus would be reached and action would be taken whenever the Council met to decide an issue began to wither away with this French-imposed "empty-chair" crisis (see Chapter 3). Although further items on the original Rome Treaty agenda were adopted and implemented later in the 1960s, spillover was no longer taking place; new agenda items were not being taken on board in response to the effects of policies already adopted.

By the early 1970s, neofunctionalists were no longer as optimistic as they had been a decade earlier. Leon Lindberg and Stuart Scheingold conceded that the nation-state had reoccupied the political high ground and that progress toward regional integration that had been made in the 1950s and early 1960s had been confined to the low politics realm of economic, especially trade and agricultural, policy.[24] By the mid-1970s Ernst Haas observed that "global turbulence" was destroying the coherence of the European Community (EC) and other regional economic organizations.[25]

A PAINFUL LEARNING EXPERIENCE

Global Economic Interdependence

As Chapters 3 and 4 will show in greater depth, the 1970s were difficult years for regional integration in Europe. Important economic changes were taking place that would be better understood in the following decade. Advanced industrial countries in the 1970s experienced a slowing down of economic growth, which had been unusually rapid for most of them in the preceding 20 years. Along with slower growth came greater monetary instability. The U.S. dollar ceased to be a reliable anchor for other currencies, which gained substantially in value relative to the dollar during the 1970s, requiring adjustments in the world monetary order. European Community growth was more sluggish than that of Japan and other East Asian economies. The Pacific Rim countries were competing in product areas where Western Europeans had held a comparative advantage before the 1970s. European Community member countries were finding it more difficult to control unemployment, inflation, adverse trade balances, and monetary instability. Then came the oil crisis of 1973–1974. Domestic economies were being hit by a multitude of international shocks.

Because he was writing about an organization in the early years of its development, Ernst Haas had focused on the dynamic elements of the process of integration. More recent students of European integration have pointed to the continuity of an organizational complex that is now a half-century old. What is more noticeable today is the ability of existing European institutions to maintain the momentum of this complex of organizations by adapting to changing circumstances through continual modification of the institutions' agendas for decision and implementation. This is still a dynamic process, but it proceeds along many paths at different speeds, without any necessary spillover. Member states continue to play a vital role. Heads of government, foreign ministers, ministers of finance and economic affairs, and other governmental officials play leading roles in setting the numerous agendas and moving them along. "Supranational" actors play major roles as well. Any analysis of these processes has to take into account the institutional complexity.

Intergovernmentalism

By the early 1980s, many analysts felt that the EC had become, at bottom, an intergovernmental organization. In this period, the Commission was no longer looked to for leadership. Most major policy issues were decided in the European Council in negotiations between governmental leaders. Even obligatory decisions, like the EC annual budget or farm prices under the Common Agricultural Policy (CAP), could be held up without decision in the Council of Ministers by an intransigent government. Such deadlocks had to await resolution at the next meeting of the European Council, where the heads of state and government could make commitments to one another that their ministers could not. Member states had come to dominate the EC and had reduced the supranational Commission to a subordinate role.[26]

On the other hand, realists of an earlier day might have been surprised at the extent to which, even at the height of the economic turbulence in the mid-1970s, the governments of the EC member countries had come to regard themselves as partners in a community in which armed conflict between them could no longer be imagined. This had freed them to concentrate on the economic problems that separated them and to cooperate in seeking solutions. Though major decisions were reached with great difficulty, they were made collectively through consultation and bargaining. When disagreements could not be resolved, decisions were postponed.

Light at the End of the Tunnel

At the June 1985 Milan summit meeting, the European Council accepted a white paper that called for making the EC institutions more efficient to facilitate completion of the Common Market through adoption of a Single European Act (SEA). The

SEA was ratified two years later. At this point it should be noted that earlier theories of regional integration were unable to predict that the members of the EC would conclude that a more thoroughgoing removal of trade barriers among themselves would be needed in order to cope with competition from more efficient and technologically up-to-date competitors. This was not a neofunctionalist spillover from one policy domain to another. Instead, it involved returning to an already existing policy domain and improving EC performance in line with the original Rome Treaty objectives. It was prompted by changes in the world in which the EC found itself, rather than by processes internal to the EC, as neofunctionalists would have anticipated.

Theorists sought to explain the Single European Act in terms of some of the various formulations we have thus far discussed in this chapter, or combinations of them. Neofunctionalist arguments were used in part, especially in placing emphasis on the leadership of the EC Commission. But the argument was also made that economic interdependence had superseded the efforts of EC nations or the EC itself to exercise effective economic regulation.[27] Nevertheless, theorists were generally in agreement that member states, pursuing their own interests, had to reach some convergence of interest in order for the major departure to take place.[28] The latter point of view was highlighted by the study of the SEA by Andrew Moravcsik, who argued that it was achieved through an intergovernmental process of bargaining, in which the Commission and even the Commission's president played roles that were secondary to those of the governments of the leading states, France, Britain, and West Germany. Changes in the domestic political configurations of these countries, especially of France, had cleared the ground for the SEA, according to Moravcsik.[29]

Yet, by the early 1980s an institutional pattern was emerging in which the member governments as well as the Commission and other supranational actors shared in both the setting of the EC's agenda and the choices made between alternative policies.[30] This institutional pattern was continued through the 1980s and 1990s. To a considerable extent, analysis of institutional processes and adaptations has replaced the broader perspectives of theories derived from the debate between neofunctionalists and neorealists that stemmed from arguments between idealists and realists in the study of international relations. Today, analytical tools developed in the field of comparative politics have become important alongside those of international relations in the study of the institutional framework and dynamics of the European Union.[31]

In 1988, the president of the EC Commission, Jacques Delors, resurrected plans originally outlined in 1970 for an Economic and Monetary Union. In 1990, two intergovernmental conferences were instituted that developed separate parts of a Treaty on European Union that was adopted at the Maastricht summit of December 1991. The two parts were (1) Economic and Monetary Union, which entailed a European central bank, closer economic and monetary policy coordination, and a common EC currency; and (2) political union, which provided for steps toward establishing common foreign and security policies for what was to be called the "European Union," extended the principle of qualified majority voting to new policy realms, and added further to the powers of the directly elected European Parliament.

These steps, taken in the early 1990s, moved well beyond what neofunctionalism might have predicted as realizable in such a short period of time. They were much more than an incremental accretion of low-politics functions. That they sought European Union before allowing time to absorb the single market or even to begin the stages envisaged for Economic and Monetary Union was due primarily to the events in Eastern Europe, which dramatically altered the stable security equation of the Cold War and, in particular, presented them in 1990 with the imminent achievement of German unification. Global political change served as a stimulus to integration. This "great leap forward" to European Union seemed to resemble the blueprints of the old discarded European federalism: seize the opportunity when it arrives because it may not come again soon! Yet, early in the next decade (and century), similar misgivings and questions are being raised among theorists and practitioners about the EU's longer-term directions and next steps.

REGIONAL INTEGRATION THEORY TODAY

Most students of European integration today, including the authors of this text, have concluded that no single theoretical framework can hope to account for the phenomena they study. This is the case for two reasons.

First, major economic and political events that are beyond the control of the EU as an organization or any of its members acting singly or jointly continue to occur in defiance of any EU efforts to pursue a stable course of action. The member states are not only dependent upon one another, but if they are to plan ahead for their mutual security and economic well-being, they are dependent upon the rest of the world to "stay still" long enough for them to agree on and carry out coherent courses of action. Broad theories of international interdependence help us to understand the dilemmas the EU faces,[32] but they do not provide answers as to what will occur when and with what effects.

Second, as a decision-making mechanism, the EU has become much too complex to be captured by any simplifying framework drawing upon familiar ideas that political scientists commonly accept. The EU is a multilevel and polycentric set of institutions.[33] Different theories discussed previously can all find levels or niches within this organizational complexity that "work" the way the theories tell us they should. The EU permits a variety of equally coherent definitions of existing relationships, explanations of how they got that way, and predictions of where they are going, every one of which is plausible if one accepts the beginning assumptions.

A process of intergovernmental decision making is not incompatible with a willingness to concede sovereignty on important matters if mutual benefits can be perceived by all member governments and what is given up does not offend the deeply held values and norms of member states' citizens. Thus outcomes may be supranational in the neofunctionalist sense, even though decision processes are not. To understand how these decisions are made we can still find theories of international relations useful. But once the decisions are made, there follows a process that involves supranational decision-making institutions within domains about which there is already longer-standing agreement and where affected interest groups may be brought into agreement. Another way of saying this is to suggest a two-step process: (1) intergovernmental bargaining produces the transfer of new powers to supranational institutions, which in turn (2) make decisions in ways similar to how their counterparts at national levels make them. There is a legislative process in the EU that bears some similarity to legislative processes nationally; likewise, there is an executive wielding executive powers and a judiciary exercising judicial powers (see Chapter 6).

Today, writers employing the intergovernmental perspective in the study of the European Union place emphasis on the trading that takes place between member states, each pursuing its own interests but recognizing that it cannot prevail without making concessions on issues where it has less to lose than what it will gain if the agreement is reached.

Andrew Moravcsik has developed a "liberal intergovernmental" view of the process,[34] according to which the member states are primarily motivated by economic interests when they decide to propose, accept, or reject compromises on EU policy issues. Governments, according to Moravcsik, act "on the basis of goals that are defined domestically," with foreign policies "varying in response to shifting pressure from domestic social groups, whose preferences are aggregated through political institutions."[35] These are national political institutions headed by national political leaders: "Whereas neo-functionalism stresses the autonomy of supranational officials, liberal intergovernmentalism stresses the autonomy of governmental leaders."[36] For Moravcsik, governments can be persuaded to pursue cooperation within the European Union framework for economic objectives, but it will be because they cannot attain their objectives unilaterally, not because they have been maneuvered into giving up their best interests by supranational policy entrepreneurs. There will be no automatic spillover from fulfilling one policy commitment to reaching agreement on another. The process is controlled by the member governments coordinating their own agendas, with very limited help from the Commission.

Moravcsik's view of how EU decisions are made could, without too much trouble, be converted into a version of what is called "rational-choice institutionalism."[37] It posits that national governments act rationally on behalf of their preferences, but Moravcsik downplays the significance of the EU's supranational institutions, whether the Commission, the European Parliament, or the European Court of Justice; indeed, he virtually ignores the EP and the ECJ, while rational choice institutionalism focuses on these bodies, although not exclusively. He is not even very explicit about the institutional characteristics of the intergovernmental bodies, the Council of Ministers and the European Council. These are arenas in which national players contest for advantage and reach compromise solutions. Simon Hix and other exponents of rational-choice institutionalism,[38] argue that national and supranational "actors" have preferences which they promote in the bargaining that goes on under the rules of the EU institutional framework. Some may have economic preferences, some more strictly political ones, and others various combinations of both. The contests between actors' priorities are more highly regulated by institutional rules and norms than Moravcsik suggests, as he concentrates on the more informal bargaining that goes on between heads of state and government over the larger architectural decisions, which, in fact, often determine what the institutional rules will be that guide decision making in other bodies (see Chapters 3–5).

Challenging Moravcsik's liberal intergovernmentalism is another theoretical perspective that puts more emphasis on the supranational decision-making processes of the EU. This is the theoretical framework known as "historical institutionalism."[39] It too is better at explaining the past than at predicting the future, but it may be better than the earlier theories at predicting what *will not* happen.

Historical institutionalism as advanced by Paul Pierson[40] does not offer a superior explanation for the historical bargains, but it insists that such bargains are only part of the story of European integration—indeed only the tip of the iceberg. The bargains have to be implemented, and the supranational institutions play an important role in their implementation, as do the member governments themselves. But once the bargains have been made and structures and processes have been developed or redirected to implement them, they take on a life of their own. Although the architectural decisions by the leaders have fashioned them in the first place, the institutions of implementation (which include national as well as EU institutions) cannot easily be redirected or dismantled, because this would require that new bargains be struck. This may be more difficult to achieve than was the original bargain that set up and empowered the implementive institutional framework in the first place. At the core of historical institutionalism is the premise that institutions are "path-dependent," which means that what happened at time 0 (the original authorization) will have a substantial influence upon what happens at time 1 (the up-and-running implementive structure), and what exists at time 1 will have a substantial effect on what we will discover at time 2. By the later stages, whatever persists from time 0 can be undone by the original decision makers only with great difficulty and in the face of considerable bureaucratic resistance.

Pierson gives an example of this logic in the case of the Maastricht Treaty negotiations, when British Prime Minister John Major negotiated an "opt-out" from the social-policy innovations that the other 11 members had agreed to. Major calculated that he could not get the treaty ratified by the British House of Commons if he committed to the social policy. The others went ahead with a Social Protocol that was placed in the treaty's appendix, which they pledged to implement by further action. According to Pierson, the catch for Major was that, once the social policy was in place in the form of institutions for implementing it in the 11 countries, there would be nothing to stop a future British government from "opting in" to it, which indeed is what the Labour government of Tony Blair did, shortly after the Labour Party won the May 1997 British general election. The Social Protocol then became a full-fledged part of what can be considered the European Union's constitutionally sanctioned agenda. But it had already been accepted by 11 members, and any effort to reverse what had been done would have been futile. Opt-outs by individual countries may be tolerated, but retrospective opt-outs by all the member governments—unanimous agreement to undo what had been done—had become flatly impossible.[41]

Pierson presents historical institutionalism as a successor to neofunctionalism in its emphasis on supranational institutions as key promoters of further European integration. But historical institutionalism does not provide much guidance as to how new departures, such as the Social Protocol, are initiated. It seems evident that intergovernmentalist approaches, as demonstrated by Moravcsik in his major study (1999), are better at accounting for the broad treaty revision agreements, such as the Single European Act and the Maastricht Treaty. They have involved trade-off bargains made between heads of state and government, but it does not appear that a strictly economic interpretation of the motivations behind the bargain, such as Moravcsik offers, is justified. Accordingly, in recounting the major decisions that created and modified the institutions and policy commitments of the European Union (Chapters 3–5), we will emphasize the roles played by heads, as well as key supranational actors, most notably the president of the Commission. But the motivations behind the agreements will be shown to have varied from instance to instance depending on the substance of the issues. Each government has certain long-standing national interests to defend and promote, but the nature of these vary from state to state, and over time, with changes of governments and the appearance of new problems to be faced.

When we turn from the broad agreements reached between governments to the process of implementing them, the focus on supranational institutions and processes becomes more appropriate. Rational-choice institutionalism will be used in Chapter 6 in addition to straight institutional description to analyze the ways in which decisions are made by the "Rome Treaty institutions" of the EU: the Council of Ministers, the Commission, the European Parliament, and the European Court of Justice. Historical institutionalism will come into play in tracing the evolution of policies over time, and in showing why some choices prevailed over others because of the need to build on existing commitments that could not be reversed.

Historical institutionalism is a theoretical framework whose major applications have been in the field of comparative politics. This is likewise true of rational-choice institutionalism. Borrowing from Hinich and Munger, Hix presents the following equation to summarize a wide variety of complex processes that can be interpreted via rational-choice institutionalism:

$$\text{Preferences} \times \text{Institutions} = \text{Outcomes}$$

According to Hix, "if *preferences change*, outcomes will change, even if *institutions remain constant*, and if *institutions change*, outcomes will change, even if *preferences remain constant*."[42] Thus, both preferences and institutions are important for analysis of what happens in any decision-making process. The example of the unanimity rule suggests that outcomes would change if the preferences of the last holdout changed to become more compatible with those of the rest of the members. But if the institutional rule were to change so that a qualified majority on the issue would suffice to adopt a proposed action, then the holdout can be ignored and concessions would not have to be made. Examples of this have occurred in the history of European integration. The ratification of the Single European Act (1987), which replaced the unanimity requirement for the adoption of single-market legislation, allowed a large shopping list of legislative measures to make their way through the EC legislative process before the target date of December 31, 1992. Fewer of these measures would have passed before the target date if, as was often the rule before that time, a single member had been able to veto their adoption.

Rational-choice institutionalism has contributed "middle-range" propositions to the study of European integration. To the extent that scholarly attention has been routed in this direction it has been at the expense of broader historical explanations. Some would argue that the latter have usually failed to *predict* actual developments that have occurred in the immediate aftermath of their publication. They have been much better at *explaining* what has already occurred. Thus, neofunctionalists could explain much of the process of integration that occurred before the mid-1960s. But Moravcsik's extensive revision of this history[43] demonstrates that a different system of explanation can interpret the same set of events quite differently, leaving one to imagine that the truth lies somewhere in between. Rational-choice institutionalism claims to be able to make more sense of what has happened in specific instances than can the broad explanatory theories.

The study of the European Union has become a highly specialized activity since the days when Jean Monnet helped to shape its original form and Ernst Haas theorized about the process of "community formation" that appeared to be following Monnet's blueprint. Today there are many middle-range theories of European integration, each focusing on a range of activity which the theory explores and explains. The broad terms—neofunctionalism, supranationalism, liberal intergovernmentalism—superceded idealism and realism decades ago. But each term highlights a different part of the EU's institutional arrangements. In Chapter 6 we will discuss how these and more recently developed theoretical perspectives have been applied to particular parts of the institutional framework: neofunctionalism to the Commission and the European Court of Justice, intergovernmentalism to the European Council and the Council of Ministers, and *democratic theory* to the European Parliament. But first we will show in the next three chapters how these institutions evolved from the relative simplicity of 50 years ago to the complexity we find today.

ENDNOTES

1. Hans J. Morgenthau, *Politics Among Nations: The Struggle for Power and Peace*, 3d ed. (New York: Knopf, 1962), pp. 507–509.
2. Robert O. Keohane, *After Hegemony: Cooperation and Discord in the World Political Economy* (Princeton, N.J.: Princeton University Press, 1984), pp. 136–141.
3. Charles W. Kegley, Jr., and Eugene R. Wittkopf, *World Politics: Trend and Transformation*, 3d ed. (New York: St. Martin's Press, 1989), pp. 12–15.
4. Charles Pentland, *International Theory and European Integration* (London: Faber and Faber, 1973), chap. 5.
5. F. Roy Willis, *France, Germany and the New Europe 1945–1967*, rev. ed. (London: Oxford University Press, 1968), chaps. 6 and 7.
6. Stephen George, *An Awkward Partner: Britain in the European Community* (Oxford: Oxford University Press, 1990), pp. 16–22.
7. David Mitrany, *A Working Peace System* (Chicago: Quadrangle Books, 1966).
8. Ibid., pp. 64–65. In a sense, Mitrany foreshadowed the insistence of British Prime Minister John Major in 1991–1992 on his country's right to "opt out" of some functions to be performed by the emerging European Union, such as a common defense and a common monetary policy.
9. See the essays on Monnet in Douglas Brinkley and Clifford Hackett, eds., *Jean Monnet: The Path to European Unity* (New York: St. Martin's Press, 1991).
10. Leon N. Lindberg and Stuart A. Scheingold, *Europe's Would-Be Polity: Patterns of Change in the European Community* (Englewood Cliffs, N.J.: Prentice-Hall, 1970), pp. 33–34.
11. Pentland, *International Theory*, p. 109. Although the boundary between high politics and low politics fluctuates depending upon who is using the terms and in what context, foreign and defense policy mat-

ters are commonly considered high politics and policies limited to particular economic sectors are considered low politics. The gray area in between is occupied by macroeconomic policy, especially monetary policy, which, given its widespread implications for countries' international standing, probably ought to be considered with the realm of high politics today. In other words, it is an area, along with foreign and defense policy, over which nation-states are least willing to give up control.

12. George, *An Awkward Partner*, p. 21.
13. George W. Ball, "Introduction," in Brinkley and Hackett, eds., *Jean Monnet*, p. xix; Derek W. Urwin, *The Community of Europe: A History of European Integration since 1945* (London and New York: Longman, 1991), p. 61.
14. A customs union is a regime established between states in which all tariffs and quotas restricting trade between the participating countries have been removed, while common tariffs and quotas are established vis-à-vis other countries. A common market goes further in removing all obstacles to trade between the countries, including such impediments as border controls and government regulations, state purchasing policies, and taxes that discriminate against the producers of one member country against those of another. The Single European Act of 1987, which provided for the removal of all such obstacles to trade among EC members by the end of 1992, popularly labeled "Project 1992," represents an effort to approximate the conditions of a true common market among the EC members.
15. Ernst B. Haas, *The Uniting of Europe: Political, Social, and Economic Forces, 1950–1957* (Stanford, Calif.: Stanford University Press, 1958); and Haas, *Beyond the Nation-State* (Stanford, Calif.: Stanford University Press, 1964).
16. Haas, *The Uniting of Europe*, chap. 1.
17. Ibid., chaps. 8 and 13.
18. Robert O. Keohane and Stanley Hoffmann, "Institutional Change in Europe in the 1980s," in Keohane and Hoffmann, eds., *The New European Community: Decision Making and Institutional Change* (Boulder, Colo.: Westview Press, 1991), p. 15.
19. Haas, *The Uniting of Europe*, p. 523.
20. Lindberg and Scheingold, *Europe's Would-Be Polity*, pp. 96–97.
21. Haas, *Beyond the Nation-State*.
22. Leon N. Lindberg, "Political Integration as a Multidimensional Phenomenon Requiring Multivariate Measurement," in Lindberg and Stuart A. Scheingold, eds., *Regional Integration: Theory and Research* (Cambridge, Mass.: Harvard University Press, 1971), pp. 94–95.
23. See John Newhouse, *Collision in Brussels: The Common Market Crisis of 30 June 1965* (New York: Norton, 1967).
24. Lindberg and Scheingold, *Europe's Would-Be Polity*, pp. 70–75.
25. Dale L. Smith and James Lee Ray, "European Integration: Gloomy Theory versus Rosy Reality," in Smith and Ray, eds., *The 1992 Project and the Future of Integration in Europe* (Armonk, N.Y., and London: Sharpe, 1993), pp. 32–33; Ernst B. Haas, *The Obsolescence of Regional Integration Theory*, Research Series no. 25 (Berkeley, Calif.: Institute for International Studies, 1975).
26. Paul Taylor, *The Limits of European Integration* (New York: Columbia University Press, 1983).
27. Wayne Sandholtz and John Zysman, "1992: Recasting the European Bargain," *World Politics* 42 (October 1989): 95–128.
28. Ibid., 111–113; Keohane and Hoffmann, "Institutional Change," pp. 23–24.
29. Andrew Moravcsik, "Negotiating the Single European Act," in Keohane and Hoffmann, eds., *The New European Community*, pp. 41–84.
30. The distinction between setting the agenda and choosing between alternatives is that of John W. Kingdom, *Agendas, Alternatives, and Public Policies* (Glenview, Ill., and London: Scott, Foresman, 1984), pp. 3–4.
31. Simon Hix, *The Political System of the European Union* (New York: St. Martin's Press, 1999), chap. 1.
32. Keohane, *After Hegemony*; Robert O. Keohane and Joseph S. Nye, *Power and Interdependence*, 2nd ed. (Glenview, Illinois: Scott, Foresman, 1989).
33. Dale L. Smith and James Lee Ray, "The 1992 Project," in Smith and Ray, eds., *The 1992 Project*, pp. 6–10; John Peterson and Elizabeth Bomberg, "The EU after the 1990s: Explaining Continuity and Change," in Maria Green Cowles and Michael Smith, eds., *The State of the European Union: Risks,*

Reform, Resistance, and Revival, vol. 5 of European Community Studies Association series (Oxford and New York: Oxford University Press, 2000), pp. 19–41.

34. Andrew Moravcsik, "Preferences and Power in the European Community: A Liberal Intergovernmentalist Approach," *Journal of Common Market Studies* 31 (December 1993): 473–524; Andrew Moravcsik, *The Choice for Europe: Social Purpose and State Power from Messina to Maastricht* (Ithaca, N.Y.: Cornell University Press, 1998).
35. Moravcsik, *Choice for Europe*, p. 481.
36. Ibid., p. 491.
37. See the debate between Moravcsik and Jeffrey Checkel, a "rationalist" versus a "constructivist," an up-dated version of intergovernmentalism versus supranationalism, in Jeffrey T. Checkel and Andrew Moravcsik, "A Constructivist Research Program in EU Studies?" *European Union Politics* 2 (June 2001): 219–249.
38. Simon Hix, "The Study of the European Community: The Challenge to Comparative Politics," *West European Politics* 17 (January 1994): 1–30; George Tsebelis, "The Power of the European Parliament as a Conditional Agenda-Setter," *American Political Science Review* 88 (1994): 128–142; Mark A. Pollack, "Delegation, Agency and Agenda Setting in the European Community," *International Organization* 51 (1997): 99–134.
39. Sven Steinmo, Kathleen Thelen, and Frank Longstreth, eds., *Structuring Politics: Historical Institutionalism in Comparative Analysis* (Cambridge: Cambridge University Press, 1992).
40. Paul Pierson, "The Path to European Integration: A Historical Institutionalist Analysis," *Comparative Political Studies* 29 (1996): 123–163; later version (same title) by Pierson in Wayne Sandholtz and Alec Stone Sweet, eds., *European Integration and Supranational Governance* (Oxford and New York: Oxford University Press, 1998), 27–58.
41. Ibid., 154–155; Laura Cram, *Policy-Making in the EU: Conceptual Lenses and the Integration Process* (London: Routledge, 1997).
42. Hix, *Political System*, p. 13 (Hix's emphasis); H. J. Hinich and M. C. Munger, *Analytical Politics* (Cambridge: Cambridge University Press, 1997), p. 17.
43. Moravcsik, *Choice for Europe*, chaps. 2–3.

3

The Rome Treaty and Its Original Agenda: 1957-1975

In this chapter, and in the two that follow, we will be reviewing the history of the European Union (EU) from the adoption of the Treaty of Rome to the present. The current chapter takes the story up to the mid-1970s, Chapter 4 carries it to the end of the 1980s, and Chapter 5 brings it through 2002. Box 3.1 lists governments in France, Germany, and Britain from the beginning of the EEC until the end of 2002. French governments are listed by presidents of the Republic (although there was more than one premier for each president), and German and British governments by chancellor and by prime minister, respectively. In all three chapters we relate political developments within the major member states and the European institutions to policy decisions made in implementing the original agenda of the EC and in bringing new items onto the agenda. Relevant changes in the larger world are taken into account as well. We begin in the mid-1950s with the decision by the European six to create a customs union. Pre-1957 developments that led up to the formation of the EEC were discussed in Chapter 2.

When the original six member states of the European Community (EC) agreed in 1957 to the Treaty of Rome, establishing the European Economic Community (EEC), they set an agenda for themselves and the new EEC institutions that was expected to preoccupy them for at least a decade. The principal items on this agenda were the first steps toward economic integration, involving the freeing of trade among the six economies and the establishment of a common trading policy with respect to the rest of the world. The principal areas of trade that they had in mind were manufactured goods and agricultural products, although eventually there were to be, among other things, free movement of persons and capital, a common transportation policy, a common monetary regime, and a common social policy.[1] Ultimately, the six

Box 3.1 Successive Governments in France, Germany, and Britain, 1958–2002

French Presidents and Supportive Parties and Coalitions

Charles de Gaulle, 1958–1969: Gaullists, assorted center and right support

Georges Pompidou, 1969–1974: Gaullists, assorted center and right support

Valéry Giscard d'Estaing, 1974–1981: Giscardist center-right, Gaullist RPR

François Mitterrand, 1981–1986: Socialists, Communists until 1984

François Mitterrand, 1986–1988: Cohabitation with Jacques Chirac's RPR-UDF coalition

François Mitterrand, 1988–1993: Socialists, center-left

François Mitterrand, 1993–1995: Cohabitation with Edouard Balladur's RPR-UDF coalition

Jacques Chirac, 1995–1997: Gaullists, assorted center and right support

Jacques Chirac, 1997–2002: Cohabitation with Lionel Jospin's Socialist-Green-Communist coalition

Jacques Chirac, 2002–present: Gaullists, assorted center and right support

German Chancellors and Supportive Parties and Coalitions (Chancellor's Party Listed First)

Konrad Adenauer, 1949–1963: CDU/CSU, FDP

Ludwig Erhard, 1963–1966: CDU/CSU, FDP

Kurt-Georg Kiesinger, 1966–1969: CDU/CSU, SPD

Willy Brandt, 1969–1974: SPD, FDP

Helmut Schmidt, 1974–1982: SPD, FDP

Helmut Kohl, 1982–1998: CDU/CSU, FDP

Gerhard Schröder, 1998–present: SPD, Greens

British Prime Ministers and Their Parties

Harold Macmillan, 1957–1963: Conservative

Sir Alec Douglas-Home, 1963–1964: Conservative

Harold Wilson, 1964–1970: Labour

Edward Heath, 1970–1974: Conservative

Harold Wilson, 1974–1976: Labour

James Callaghan, 1976–1979: Labour

Margaret Thatcher, 1979–1990: Conservative

John Major, 1990–1997: Conservative

Tony Blair, 1997–present: Labour

countries envisaged an evolution from an economic community to a political union. But, while these goals above and beyond the new trade and commercial regime were mentioned in the Treaty of Rome or, in the case of political goals, hinted at in the treaty's preamble, they were not considered priority items by the drafters of the treaty. The *ordinary agenda* was the new trading bloc, which was to be created by 1970, before most other steps were to be taken.[2]

When we refer to the *agenda* of the European Union, we have in mind the issues that are being actively addressed by its decision-making organs. Under the Treaty of Rome, the timing of proposed legislative measures envisaged by the treaty is within the job definition of the Commission. In the early years the steps taken to create the customs union and the common agricultural policy (see Chapter 8) were developed by the Commission as proposals and sent to the Council of Ministers for action, that is, placed on the Council's agenda. These were what we call the "ordinary agenda," because in putting them on the Council's agenda, the Commission was simply fulfilling its responsibilities under the Rome Treaty. However, during the first decade there were occasions when items that had not been authorized by the treaty, or over which member governments disputed the right of the Commission to make proposals, were placed on the "extraordinary agenda." An example that will be given prominent attention in this chapter was the 1965 set of proposals by Commission President Walter Hallstein, which touched off the famous empty-chair crisis.

A BRIEF PERIOD OF CONSENSUS

The Six in 1957

In 1957, the commitment to the original agenda was shared by political leaders and ruling political parties in all six of the original EEC countries. For the most part the leaders were centrists in the party politics of their countries: Christian Democrats of the center-right, Social Democrats of the center-left, or Liberals variously located between center-left and center-right. In France and Italy these political parties of the broad center coexisted between strong communist parties of the extreme left and nationalist parties on the far right that did not share the centrists' agenda. In West Germany and the three Benelux countries, any existing extreme parties were weak; in the case of West Germany, communist and "neo-Nazi" parties were outlawed.

The pro-European centrists in the six countries shared an acceptance of the Europe of the 1950s as it was and sought to make the best of it. What they had accepted in particular was the existence of the Cold War and the dominant role played by a "hegemon" on either side of the politically divided continent: the USSR to the east, and the United States to the west.[3] They were motivated to organize their part of Europe in such a way as to make their economic, and ultimately their political, development less dependent upon "their" hegemon, the United States. For the time being at least, little could be done about the Soviet hegemony by the six acting apart from Washington. The creation of the EEC and the priority it gave to reorganizing trade

TABLE 3.1 Positions of Parties in Four Countries on EEC Issues, 1950s

Country	Left/Anti	Left/Pro	Center/Pro	Right/Pro	Right/Anti
France	Communists	Socialists	MRP, Radicals	Independents	Gaullists
FRG		Social Democrats	FDP	CDU/CSU	
Italy	Communists		Chr. Dems.	Liberals	Neo-fascists
		Socialists	Soc. Dems., Repubs.		
Britain	Labour		Liberals		Conservatives

"Pro" and "anti" refer to position on EEC. FRG = Federal Republic of Germany, MRP = Popular Republican Movement (French Christian Democrats), FDP = Free Democratic Party (German Liberals), CDU/CSU = Christian Democratic Union (national)/Christian Social Union (Bavaria only).

relationships was a realistic way of putting Europe in a more self-sufficient position, economically, if not politically.[4]

Table 3.1 shows support for and opposition to the EEC among parties ranged from left to right for four countries: France, West Germany (FRG), Italy, and Britain. Among the six member countries, support for the new Community and its agenda was weakest in France in 1957. The extreme parties of both left and right in France were more strident in their opposition to European integration than were their counterparts in Italy. Communists in all West European countries accepted the leadership of the Soviet Communist Party in officially opposing integration as a means by which the United States maintained its hold on its allies and capitalists enriched themselves at the expense of the working class.[5] For the French Communist Party (PCF), European integration had special significance as an American-backed means by which German capitalists would gain control over the French economy. Throughout the 1950s, the PCF was unalterably opposed to each new initiative in the process of European integration.[6]

On the French right, the principal opposition to French membership in these various communities was provided by General Charles de Gaulle and the movement that supported him. The Gaullists were weaker at the time of the Rome Treaty than they had been during the debates over Europe earlier in the decade. De Gaulle himself was in semiretirement. Nevertheless, his views concerning France's role in Europe were well known and echoed by political figures and writers both inside and outside the Gaullist movement. De Gaulle had his own agenda for Europe, which he was to put into play after he returned to power in mid-1958.[7] He rejected the notion that the division of Europe between East and West was necessarily frozen, especially if this meant that France must subordinate its own interests to the wishes of the United States. De Gaulle saw the EEC as potentially destructive of the France that he knew and loved, and especially of the leading role in Europe that France could claim as U.S. influence declined.[8]

In West Germany by 1957, the political party system, at least as represented in the Bundestag, consisted almost exclusively of parties of the center-left and center-right, all officially committed to the EEC and its agenda, although the Social Democrats (SPD) on the center-left had only recently endorsed the new Community. Earlier in the 1950s the SPD had opposed the European Coal and Steel Community (ECSC) and the European Defense Community (EDC) as helping to solidify the division between East and West Germany, making reunification impossible in the foreseeable future. By contrast, Christian Democratic Chancellor Konrad Adenauer had pursued a policy of acceptance of the division of Europe and the consequent division of Germany as unalterable for the time being. Through membership in the Western European and Atlantic organizations, Adenauer sought to strengthen West Germany's economy, political structure, and national security while options in the East were closed off by Soviet power and policy. During the middle 1950s, the opposition SPD came around to a positive position on European integration.[9]

The British Problem

While the established centrists of the six gave solid support to the EEC and its original agenda, there was no clear "Euro-center" in the British political party system in the 1950s. The British had not joined the ECSC in the early 1950s, but they were invited in 1955 to the Messina conference, where plans were laid for the Rome Treaty. They arrived as skeptical observers, assuming that little would come out of the talks in view of the EDC debacle. When it became clear that the six were indeed going to create a customs union, Britain sought to entice them over to a broader plan for a European free-trade area that would be looser and without the pretensions to political integration that the six had in mind. The British were set against anything that resembled European federalism, even in the distant future. But, while there was sympathy among some of the six for the British plan, the desire to move ahead with a stronger form of market integration prevailed in each country, and the Treaty of Rome was duly signed and ratified. Britain then took the free-trade idea to smaller countries outside the six—Denmark, Sweden, Norway, Austria, Switzerland, and Portugal—and the European Free Trade Association (EFTA) was formed in 1960.[10]

A *free-trade area* differs from a *customs union*. The former allows each member state to choose its own level of tariffs to impose upon goods from nonmember countries, whereas states in a customs union have the same tariff levels imposed by all members on goods from outside the union. Without a common barrier to goods from outside, the markets of countries wanting to restrict such trade would be open to goods entering first through their low-tariff partners.[11] Opposition to the proposed customs union was shared by leaders of both major British political parties, Conservative and Labour. The weak center Liberal Party was the only one taking a positive position. The prevailing British view in 1957–1960 was that membership in the EEC would interfere with economic and political links Britain enjoyed with the United States and Commonwealth countries. Britain had a world role; membership in the EEC would narrow its focus to one region, albeit an important one. Leaders of both British parties believed that Britain had a "special relationship" with the United States, meaning that U.S. policymakers listened to British advice; it was therefore not necessary, they felt, for the British to join with other medium-sized powers to enhance their influence with the hegemon. There was also a deeply ingrained suspicion of French motives, as well as a belief that the British system of parliamentary sovereignty was unique and superior to institutional frameworks found on the continent of Europe.[12]

These attitudes on the part of the British government meant that the EEC and its agenda had a "British problem." The six could move ahead with their agenda, but if they were to go much beyond the initial priorities—that is, if they began to develop a new (extraordinary) agenda—it would become even more difficult to reach an accommodation that could bring Britain into the Community. If the six indeed saw the EEC as a step in the direction of a stronger, more independent Europe, able to operate on a plane of equality with the major world players, then it was reasonable that they would want Britain, which was still regarded as a major power in the world, to join them. This was the dilemma facing the Eurocentrists.

THE STRUGGLE TO CONTROL THE EXTRAORDINARY AGENDA

For Charles de Gaulle the British problem was quite different. In May 1958, the French Fourth Republic was embroiled militarily in a colonial war against the Algerian independence movement. Weak centrist governments in Paris vacillated in their policies toward the war, as they had done earlier in the 1950s in the process of losing French control over Indochina. On May 13, a revolt broke out in Algiers and other cities led by civilians, but taken over by French Army generals, in what was essentially a military coup directed against the government in Paris. After a few days of uncertainty, the leaders of the revolt called upon the politicians in Paris to hand power over to General de Gaulle.[13] When President René Coty called upon de Gaulle to become premier, de Gaulle expressed his willingness to do so, but on the condition that he would oversee the writing of a new constitution, which would be presented to the French voters for their approval. On September 16, 1958, the constitutional referendum was overwhelmingly supported by the voters, and the Fifth Republic came into being. In December, de Gaulle was elected the first president of the Fifth Republic.

From 1958 to 1962, when he brought the war to a conclusion by granting Algeria its independence, de Gaulle was a dominant leader willing to take extraordinary measures in order to defeat threats to his government and to his policy of gradually yielding independence to Algeria. But although Algeria was a continuing concern during this period, de Gaulle also began his efforts to change the agenda of the EEC to suit his purposes.

The Clash of Grand Designs

In the summer of 1961 two events occurred that were to reveal what de Gaulle's agenda for the EEC would be.[14] The first was his success in getting his fellow EEC government leaders, meeting in Bonn in July, to put on their own agenda a proposal for greater political cooperation that he had been advancing in one form or another since 1959. The heads of state and government agreed at Bonn to ask an ad hoc commission chaired by a close associate of de Gaulle, Christian Fouchet, to draft proposals for a treaty to establish a "union of states." The proposals were presented to the six governments in November 1961. By then, the second event had occurred, the August 1961 application of the Conservative British government headed by Prime Minister Harold Macmillan for membership in the EEC, which was followed by similar applications by two of Britain's EFTA associates, Denmark and Norway, and by the Republic of Ireland.

The French proposals considered by the Fouchet commission envisaged that major political decisions on foreign and defense policy matters, as well as on cultural and scientific matters, were to be taken *unanimously* by the heads of state and government meeting at the summit. In essence, the proposals anticipated amendment of the Treaty of Rome to create a "political union," with a new agenda and agenda-setting mechanism. There would be a separate "European Political Commission," comprising officials of the six foreign ministries who would reside in Paris and coordinate agendas for meetings of foreign ministers and heads, leaving the EEC Commission in Brussels with the ordinary economic agenda-setting role assigned it by the Treaty of Rome.[15]

There was a potential link between these proposals and British entry in that this more forthrightly intergovernmental mode of decision making was much more congenial to the British government than the mode that had been envisaged in the Rome Treaty. Already some decisions of the EEC Council of Ministers were officially being taken by qualified majority vote (QMV; see Chapter 1), rather than unanimously, and the treaty indicated that this would be true of many more Council decisions by 1966. If Britain and the others were to enter the EEC, they would have to accept majority decisions taken on the ordinary agenda. But the Fouchet plan for political union would ensure that any extraordinary agenda items, especially those involving matters of political significance that would threaten British autonomy, could be vetoed by Britain, even if supported by all of the other members. At least on this narrow basis, de Gaulle and the British shared an intergovernmentalist view of the Community's future. But the Fouchet proposals were too intergovernmentalist to suit the Eurocentrists in other EEC countries, especially the Netherlands and Belgium, and negotiations were broken off in 1962.[16]

In January 1963 de Gaulle vetoed British entry, which cancelled the entry bids of the other three as well. The standard interpretation of the French veto of British entry is that de Gaulle's vision for Europe differed from the British in a fundamental sense. The Macmillan government did not want to be drawn into political obligations in Europe that would interfere with Britain's ties with the United States and the Commonwealth. Britain was showing slower economic growth than the European six, which is what moved the Macmillan government to reverse direction and seek EEC membership. The British recognized that the customs union had produced more dynamic economic results in the first years of the EEC than had their own free-trade area; but they were throwing in only half a towel. They certainly did not want economic integration to spill over into political integration. As F.S. Northedge has observed:

For continental Europeans who had looked forward to the opportunity to build a united Europe during the long years of Nazi occupation, bodies like the Council of Europe, the Coal and Steel Community, the Economic Community, were the fulfillment of a dream. For Britain, joining organizations such as these represented the disappointment of expectations, of hopes of better things. In their inmost thoughts the British were never really convinced about the merits of European unity: unity was all right as a slogan, . . . but it was not a programme for practical action.[17]

De Gaulle wanted his proposed system of political cooperation to extend far enough to bind member countries to commonly agreed projects, so long as these were projects of French inspiration, following de Gaulle's own vision of Europe's political future. He believed that he had brought Chancellor Adenauer with him in this objective through the personal relationship they had established in 1959, which was to lead to a Treaty of Friendship and Reconciliation between the two countries in January 1963. With France and Germany coordinating their foreign policies in line with de Gaulle's vision, it would be a simple matter to bring the smaller and weaker members of the six along with them. If Britain, and perhaps three others likely to follow the British lead, were to join the EEC, there would be another grand design competing with de Gaulle's, a design he believed to be of American inspiration.[18] Before the year was out there was a new chancellor in Bonn, Ludwig Erhard, an "Atlanticist" who did not wish to play games in world politics according to French rules.[19]

A very different interpretation of de Gaulle's motives in vetoing British entry has been presented by political scientist Andrew Moravcsik.[20] Based on economic rather than political motivation, it suggests that the very economic benefits Britain wished to achieve through EEC membership were threatening to those de Gaulle anticipated for France. Moravcsik identifies the basis of de Gaulle's veto as follows:

> The preponderance of evidence, including most of de Gaulle's own statements, supports instead an economic interpretation. De Gaulle decided against British membership early on, despite common geopolitical interests on many issues—not least shared opposition to supranational institutions and concern about Germany—because Britain was certain to block generous financing for the CAP [the EEC's Common Agricultural Policy]. This would have negated the principal advantage for France from a customs union.[21]

To the British, an EEC trading regime that benefited French farmers and small, vulnerable French industries would be too costly for British consumers and taxpayers. In 1963, this regime was still being negotiated. The entry of Britain into the organization before the deal was solidified would clearly reduce the gains de Gaulle expected to achieve from the agreement for French farmers and taxpayers. Moravcsik's point is a solid one and needs to be taken into account in explaining the French veto. But it cannot substitute for the geopolitical motivation. De Gaulle's strength lay in the fact that his political design coincided with what he saw as the way to protect and strengthen the French economy.

The Empty-Chair Crisis

The refusal by France to allow Britain to enter the EEC left France in a smaller organization. Most of the other members continued to harbor preferences for an EEC that would eventually move beyond the Rome Treaty in a supranational direction. For the first 7 years of the EEC's life most important decisions were taken either by unanimous consent or by qualified majority voting, the latter according to a formula that was designed to protect smaller countries from being swamped by an alliance of bigger countries. Commission President Walter Hallstein had followed a pattern of encouraging the Council to continue its deliberations without voting until it was possible to register unanimous consent. A useful method was to combine measures into package deals so that on different issues countries would make concessions to each other. The package would then be accepted in its entirety, sometimes after days of negotiation among the ministers. Even after QMV came to be applicable in formal terms across a wider array of decisions, this same style of consensus building ensured that there would be no big winners or big losers.[22]

Much of the bargaining activity in the first half of the 1960s had involved a three-way struggle between France, West Germany, and Italy over the establishment of the customs union and the Common Agricultural Policy (CAP). The crisis that began on June 30, 1965, revolved around France's desire for an agricultural policy that would benefit farmers, to the detriment of consumers and taxpayers in all six countries, through higher farm prices and subsidies. As a strong exporter of manufactured goods, West Germany needed to establish a customs union for manufactured goods, one that would give German industries assured markets for their products, and protection from imports from non-EEC countries. Italy, which was experiencing a rapid shift from farming to manufacturing, expected to have to pay for the CAP out of the uncertain proceeds from the sale of its manufactures and wanted "side payments" in the form of regional assistance and a lessened share of budget contributions. A package that involved putting both the customs union and the CAP into place, while providing side payments to Italy, seemed to the Commission to be an obvious way of moving the EC ahead toward economic integration. The French government, which rested on the farmers' electoral support, appeared to have a high stake in achieving just that. Therefore, Commission president Hallstein believed he could up the ante with proposals that would enhance political, as well as economic, integration. In this he reckoned without de Gaulle's commitment to his own plans and his seemingly invulnerable domestic political position.[23]

According to regulations mandated by the Rome Treaty, the system for financing the CAP had to be in place by June 30, 1965; otherwise the EEC farm program could not operate.[24] Hallstein presented his proposals to the Council of Ministers in March 1965. Those relating to CAP financing involved the collection of levies on imports of farm goods from non-EEC countries and their disbursement to farmers in the member countries to compensate for the lower prices they were getting world-wide for their products. The other two features of the proposals were in effect an assertion of the Commission's right to control not only the ordinary but also the extraordinary agenda of the EEC. The CAP was to take full effect by July 1, 1967, but the customs union for manufactured goods was not to reach its completion until 1970. In an effort to gain the support of West Germany and other members, Hallstein proposed accelerating the customs union so that its completion would coincide with that of the CAP. This was linked to a proposal to route the proceeds of agricultural levies and customs duties to the Commission for it to administer as the EEC's "own resources." The Commission would remit to the six governments a portion of this amount, but it would keep a part for itself to be spent according to the provisions of the annual budget adopted by the Council of Ministers.[25]

But the third Hallstein proposal departed substantially from the Rome Treaty, requiring amendments to two treaty articles.[26] Because the six governments could join forces against the Commission and interfere with its planned uses of its new-found largesse, it was proposed that the European Parliament (EP) could make amendments to the Commission's annual draft budget by simple majority vote.[27] If the Commission approved such an amendment, the Council of Ministers could turn it down only if five of the six members voted to do so. Although this appeared to increase the Parliament's budgetary powers, it would also enhance the ability of the Commission to control the whole process, because it was also proposed that the Commission could propose amendments to the Parliament's amendments, which could be accepted by a two-thirds majority of the Council.[28] If accepted, the proposed procedures would mean that France and West Germany could be outvoted in the Council by the less powerful member states, and the will of the supranational bodies would then prevail over that of the two strongest states.

The proposals received an angry reaction from the French government.[29] For de Gaulle, the assertion by the Commission president of the authority to impose extraordinary agenda items upon the Council of Ministers was unacceptable. His earlier proposals for regular political cooperation among the governments of the six member countries had rested on the assumption that the Rome Treaty was *a restrictive document that authorized only those powers and functions explicitly stated in it*, and that any extension of EEC powers beyond those authorized by the treaty could only be made if all six governments decided to amend the treaty or reach a new contract. The problem for de Gaulle was that, with the imminent arrival of majority voting, the Commission could make proposals that would go beyond the French interpretation of the treaty and France could be outvoted. President Hallstein obviously considered the Rome Treaty *permissive of extensions of the competence of EEC institutions* in directions that were by a broad interpretation compatible with the intent of the treaty's drafters. The five member states other than France ranged along a continuum between the French position and that of the Commission.[30]

Just before the June 30 deadline the French foreign minister called an end to the Council of Ministers meeting that was deliberating over the Hallstein package.[31] This signified a French veto of the package. Six months still remained until the installation of more generalized majority voting, a rules change that was mandated by the treaty and would presumably be placed automatically on the Council's agenda. It soon became clear that by refusing to send his ministers to Council meetings, de Gaulle was forcing at least a postponement in the ordinary agenda of the Rome Treaty, attempting to force the others to accept a continuation of the unanimity rule in defiance of the intent of the framers of the Rome Treaty.[32]

In January 1966, the French ministers returned to their seat on the Council of Ministers. De Gaulle had been unexpectedly taken to a second ballot in the French presidential election of December 1965, failing to gain a majority on the first ballot as a result of unexpectedly strong showings by François Mitterrand, the candidate of the left, and a relatively unknown centrist candidate, Jean Lecanuet. The latter benefited from the votes of many farmers, who punished de Gaulle on the first ballot for producing the EEC crisis, thus jeopardizing the CAP and its expected benefits to French agriculture. While de Gaulle won the second ballot runoff against Mitterrand, a dent had been made in his image of invulnerability.[33]

For their part, the five other member governments were more willing to compromise by early 1966. While the question of who won and who lost in the crisis has long been disputed, it seems clear that on the most fundamental point at issue—whether the EEC would remain basically an intergovernmental organization or take a significant step toward supranationalism—the "Luxembourg compromise" sustained intergovernmentalism. First, the original Rome Treaty budget procedure remained intact, with the European Parliament having no more than an advisory role. EC budgets would continue to be controlled by the Council of Ministers, which would make the final determination about the distribution of the EEC's "own resources." Second, the ability of the Commission to put items on the agenda of the Council of Ministers was restricted by the requirement that they must first be shown to the representatives of the six governments permanently residing in Brussels (see the next section "Completing the Original Agenda"). Third, regarding voting in the Council of Ministers, a vague formula was mutually accepted that permitted the change from unanimity to majority voting to take place as scheduled in the treaty, but which stated that where "issues very important to one or more member countries are at stake," ministers will seek to reach solutions with which all can be comfortable.[34] From de Gaulle's standpoint, it legitimized the continued right of a state to veto unacceptable EEC initiatives. In any case, the compromise ruled out a reading of the Rome Treaty that would allow extraordinary agenda decisions to be taken with only majority, and not unanimous, support.[35]

ACCOMPLISHMENTS IN THE MIDST OF DIMINISHING EXPECTATIONS

Completing the Original Agenda

It is significant that, after 1966, further efforts on the part of the Commission to initiate agenda items had to be accepted by all member governments. Although this was not stated explicitly in January 1966, in fact, out of the Luxembourg compromise there arose a procedure whereby the Committee of Permanent Representatives

(COREPER) work closely with the Commission in examining and modifying Commission proposals to be sent to the Council. (COREPER members are ambassadors of the member governments residing in Brussels.) This has had two effects: By removing obstacles of lesser importance it smoothed the way for proposals once they would reach the Council. It also kept items off the Council's agenda that were likely to be rejected at the Council level by one or more governments. COREPER thus became the gatekeeper for the EC's ordinary agenda, playing a key role, along with the Commission, both in agenda setting and in defining alternatives to be addressed by their political superiors in the Council of Ministers.[36]

During the remainder of the 1960s the EEC completed a number of the tasks on its ordinary agenda with relatively little controversy.[37] In 1967, the executives of the ECSC, Euratom, and the EEC were merged into one, establishing a single Commission.[38] The customs union for manufactured products was completed in 1968, 18 months early and with all six members, including France, having lowered their tariffs according to the accelerated schedule. The previous year the Commission assumed responsibility for negotiating on behalf of all six members in the Kennedy Round of the General Agreement Tariffs and Trade (GATT) negotiations. Between 1967 and 1973, all six countries adopted a common value-added tax (VAT), a step that was designed to reduce disparities between the six markets in the prices ultimately charged consumers for the same goods.

After de Gaulle

In May 1968 the presidency of Charles de Gaulle was dealt a severe blow by the outbreak of a student revolt, which started in Paris, spread to other French cities, and was followed by a general strike of French workers. With the considerable help of his premier, Georges Pompidou, de Gaulle managed to weather the storm and order was restored in June. But de Gaulle's personal authority had been seriously weakened, as was confirmed in April 1969, when a referendum he presented to the voters was defeated, partly because a segment of his majority, led by former finance minister Valéry Giscard d'Estaing, opposed it. In response, De Gaulle resigned as president and returned to his country home to write his memoirs, until his death the following year. A new presidential election was held in June 1969, which Georges Pompidou won handily over a severely divided opposition. He appointed a fellow Gaullist as premier. Giscard d'Estaing, who led his own smaller and moderately pro-EC party, returned to his previous post as finance minister.

As a Gaullist, Pompidou had no sympathy for a supranationalist EC, but he was willing to take steps to remove the animosities between France and its EC partners that had accumulated during the de Gaulle years.[39] He made it clear that he would not automatically turn his back on a renewal of the British application for membership in the European Community.[40] Pompidou called for an EC summit meeting at the Hague in December 1969. This was the first such summit to be held since the early de Gaulle years, and it was to be the first of four meetings that can now be seen as forerunners to the regularly scheduled European Council meetings that have taken place since they were instituted in 1975.[41]

The Hague summit set in motion the first concrete actions that successfully went beyond the Rome Treaty. Pompidou decided to take these steps in part because of the growing significance of West Germany in the affairs of Europe. Between 1966 and 1969 the Christian Democratic (CDU) monopoly of power in the FRG had given way to a "Grand Coalition" of the CDU/CSU and the opposition SPD, now led by Willy Brandt.[42] On EC matters the SPD under Brandt had become Eurocentrist, verbally in favor of steps toward European integration, but usually preferring to wait for France to take the initiative. As foreign minister in the Grand Coalition government, Brandt had begun to fashion a new *Ostpolitik*, designed to reopen contact with Eastern Bloc countries, especially with the German Democratic Republic (GDR).[43]

In the parliamentary elections of September 1969 an emerging center-left coalition of the SPD and the smaller Free Democratic Party (FDP) defeated the CDU/CSU, and Willy Brandt became the new chancellor. From the point of view of his EC partners, this change augured a change in the direction of West Germany's principal foreign policy preoccupations. At a time when West Germany was emerging as one of the strongest and most dynamic world economies, Pompidou feared that it would turn its back on the EC and fashion a separate foreign policy toward the east. Bonn might be tempted to use its considerable economic power to lessen the opposition of the Soviet Union to closer relations between East and West Germany. This could be a step in the direction of German reunification. It was still too close to World War II for Pompidou to look favorably on such a prospect, which was a consideration that influenced him to promote the Hague summit. In fact, Brandt preceded Pompidou in calling for an opening of the EC's doors to Britain.[44]

The Hague summit produced a declaration of support for negotiations with Britain over the terms of entry. Conditions soon ripened in Britain for a new effort. In June 1970 the Conservatives returned to power, unexpectedly defeating Harold Wilson's Labour Party. The new prime minister was Edward Heath, who was unambiguously Eurocentrist.[45] Heath, in fact, had been the chief British negotiator during the first bid to enter the EC in 1961–1963. His Conservative Party had come a long way from the Macmillan days; there was now only a small fringe on the party right wing that opposed entry in 1970, whereas the Labour Party was sharply divided on the issue.[46] Negotiations for the British entry went fairly smoothly. The main issues involved Britain's budget contribution, a problem exacerbated by the fact that the benefits going to Britain's small but efficient farm sector would be outweighed by the cost to the British consumer of higher-priced food. But the issues involving CAP and the British contribution to the EC budget were fudged in the formula established for gradually phasing in the new member's obligations.[47] Heath was able to get the Treaty of Accession through the House of Commons, and Britain joined the EC in 1973, along with Ireland and Denmark, both of which ratified the treaty after comfortable yes votes in popular referenda. The fourth applicant, Norway, failed to ratify the treaty after a negative referendum vote, with farmers and fishing communities voting heavily against accession.[48]

In addition to paving the way for enlargement of the EC, the Hague summit approved the financial provisions for CAP through establishment of the EC's own resources by national contributions out of collection of agricultural levies and industrial customs duties.[49] The European Parliament obtained a say in the use of these funds. France had opposed such an arrangement since the empty-chair crisis, but now Pompidou stepped back from de Gaulle's negative position. At the summit it was also agreed that economic and monetary union would be achieved by 1980.[50] In 1970, the Council of Ministers appointed a committee headed by Luxembourg prime minister Pierre Werner to sort out the competing proposals for EMU. The Werner plan presented to the Council later in the year included proposals for coordination of economic and monetary policies and for an eventual common currency. But when the global monetary crisis began in 1971, the plan was shelved indefinitely.

So long as France's partners were willing to take an intergovernmental approach to achieving cooperation in the foreign policy realm, the French were all for it, as were the British. Following the Hague meeting the six foreign ministers commissioned a report by a committee headed by Belgian diplomat Etienne Davignon. The Davignon report on European "political cooperation," which came to be known as EPC, recommended regular meetings of the six foreign ministers wearing their hats as guardians of national interests rather than as EC Council of Ministers deliberating on general EC policy matters. The idea was to develop habits of regular contact and collaboration between the member countries to allow "Europe" to speak with a single voice in diplomatic questions. In fact, although confined to the member states, EPC would not be an integral part of the EC or its institutions. The early steps to EPC paved the way for more significant moves toward political cooperation taken in the mid-1970s after the European Community was enlarged to nine members.[51]

In general, the Hague summit represented the opening of a new extraordinary agenda for the EC. But it was an agenda that bore little evidence of the sort of Commission initiative taking and power aggrandizement that had been attempted under President Hallstein. Heads of government, foreign ministers, and career diplomats were in the forefront of the new steps being taken. In two cases the consequent steps were essentially intergovernmental. The entry of Britain into the EC strengthened the hand of intergovernmentalist France in the Council meetings. And the new procedures for EPC were decidedly intergovernmentalist, with the Commission having no more than the right to express its views on agenda items initiated by the governments.[52] However, the completion of CAP and the new budget provisions strengthened the supranational elements of the European Community.

The Rise of the European Council

The Hague summit of 1969 can be regarded as a prototype of the agenda-setting summit meetings that began to be held in the 1970s. The next major package deal was reached at the Paris summit of December 1974, at which the practice was established of holding thrice-yearly summit meetings of the heads of state and government. This was the inauguration of the European Council, whose presidency rotates among the member countries every 6 months, following the existing practice in the Council of Ministers.[53] It was at the initiative of the new French president, Valéry Giscard d'Estaing, who was not a Gaullist but was a center-right Gaullist ally. Giscard d'Estaing was elected president in May 1974, succeeding Georges Pompidou, who had died the previous month. The proposed European Council had the support of the new German chancellor, Helmut Schmidt, who had replaced his fellow SPD leader, Willy Brandt, in March 1974.

Giscard d'Estaing and Schmidt had already established a good working relationship in prior years. Both had served as finance ministers under their predecessors at a time when intense efforts were being made to cope with the monetary chaos of the 1971–1973 period (see Chapters 4 and 7). Both were of a practical bent, with little sympathy for the European visionaries found in the Commission, the European Parliament, or some of the governments of the other member countries.[54] Both recognized that France and West Germany working together held the key to a growing influence of the EC in Europe and in the larger world, and neither was looking for an edge over the other.[55]

Shortly before Schmidt and Giscard d'Estaing took the controls of their governments, in the general election of February 1974 power shifted back in Britain from the Conservatives under Edward Heath to the Labour Party headed by Harold Wilson. Whereas Heath had fit the pragmatic Europe-first mode of the new French and German leaders, Wilson, with an uncertain majority in Parliament and an economy in shambles, was necessarily more preoccupied with Britain than with Europe, and he tended to view European issues in the light of their significance for British domestic politics and economics.[56]

Wilson's strategy in domestic politics was to use the EC as a means of strengthening the moderate, or "social democratic," wing of the Labour Party against the party's left wing. The Labour left, led by industry minister Tony Benn, was calling for Britain to leave the EC and threatening to use the issue to siphon off some of Wilson's support base elsewhere in the party. To counter this danger, Wilson promised in the election campaign of February 1974 to renegotiate the Treaty of Accession under which Britain had entered the EC. After winning the election Wilson signaled to the other EC members that he wished to renegotiate the terms of British membership; failing this, Britain would leave the EC. The partners reluctantly agreed in principle, but while Wilson managed to gain some minor advantages for Britain out of the negotiations, he claimed for purposes of home consumption that he had gained more for Britain than the facts justified. Although Chancellor Schmidt lent the British considerable assistance in the negotiations, he had little patience with Wilson's tactics.[57]

The renegotiation was Wilson's highest priority at the December 1974 Paris summit. He accepted other elements of the package deal Giscard d'Estaing and Schmidt were putting together, including direct elections of the European Parliament, which had been promoted by the smaller member countries. At the first regularly scheduled European Council meeting, held in Dublin in March 1975, he further irritated his fellow heads of state and government by filling the agenda to overflowing with the British renegotiation. In the end, Wilson declared the modest Dublin concessions to be a victory and went on to win a strong yes vote in the referendum held in Britain to give advisory approval to the agreements reached.[58]

The heads of state and government agreed at the Paris summit to pursue an EC regional policy of giving economic assistance to the poorer regions of the member countries. This agreement represented side payments that France and West Germany made to Italy and Ireland in particular, although it was also a policy that the British Labour government supported in the hope that British regions would benefit as well. It represented a step beyond the Rome Treaty, as did the decision to create regular European Council meetings. Simon Bulmer and Wolfgang Wessels point out that "a key difference from earlier summits was that the commitments were not just pious hopes but had been based on the details of policy as well. . . . The EC's position had been stabilized; its relevance to the 1970s was confirmed."[59]

The decision at the Paris summit to put direct elections of the European Parliament on the agenda of the Council of Ministers was not so much a departure from the original Rome Treaty agenda as it was a long-delayed removal of French resistance to direct elections, which had stood in the way of fulfillment of the treaty for the 15 years of Gaullist rule. Beginning in 1978, there would be regular elections for all seats in the European Parliament every 5 years. Giscard was able to put together an ad hoc Eurocentrist majority in the French National Assembly against the combined opposition of the Communists and Gaullists to enable direct elections to be held in France. With French resistance to direct elections removed, the British became the foot-draggers. The British Parliament was slow to adopt the electoral law because of left-wing Labour and right-wing Conservative opposition; as a result the first Euro-elections were delayed in all nine countries until June 1979.[60]

The European Community in the Mid-1970s

The principal innovations in the European Community during the first half of the 1970s were set in motion in one fashion or another by the Hague summit of December 1969 and were rounded off by the Paris and Dublin summits 5 years later. They confirmed the significance of the empty-chair crisis and the Luxembourg compromise of the mid-1960s. It was now clear that additions to and alterations of the original Rome Treaty agenda could be undertaken only on the initiative of the heads of state and government. With the establishment of the European Council a regular procedure became available for agenda items to be introduced by the heads.[61]

The domestic preoccupations of the British government made it possible for Schmidt and Giscard d'Estaing to chart new courses in European political cooperation. In the mid-1970s, EPC was becoming a vehicle by which the EC nine could take foreign policy positions that were at least gently at odds with the priorities of the United States. Through EPC the heads of state and government probed alternatives to the American pro-Israel position in Middle East questions. More concretely, EPC followed along the lines of reducing tensions between Eastern and Western Europe that de Gaulle had pioneered in the second half of the 1960s with his policy of *détente*, and Brandt had dramatically achieved in the 1970s with his *Ostpolitik*. In 1975 the Conference on Security and Cooperation in Europe (CSCE) was held at Helsinki, which brought together the states of Western and Eastern Europe, including the Soviet Union, and the United States and Canada. A declaration was produced that outlined steps for reducing tensions and accelerating human contacts between East and West. The nine EPC states acted essentially as one under the leadership of the government currently holding the presidency of the Council. The process was strictly intergovernmental because EPC existed outside the Rome Treaty framework. Major initiatives to be taken in CSCE negotiations were decided upon in meetings of the nine foreign ministers under general guidelines given at summit meetings.[62]

With respect to the ordinary agenda, beyond finalizing the customs union and the common agricultural policy, the Rome Treaty provided only very general guidelines as to what should happen next. The budget was often the object of intense conflict between the Commission and the Council, between the EP and the Council, and between individual member states within the Council, but somehow budgets were produced, and the ability of the European Parliament to influence parts of them increased. In 1975 a treaty amending the Rome Treaty was adopted. For the first time it gave the Parliament the ability to reject the budget outright, and it created a Court of Auditors to monitor the EC's use of its revenues. Furthermore, appointment of members of the Court of Justice was now subject to review and endorsement by the EP.[63]

But the EC in this period was better known for its abortive ordinary agenda items, many of which were proposals by the Commission for harmonizing the separate technical standards that acted as barriers to inter-EC trade, preventing the customs union from having its full economic effect. Although some of these, including some with environmental significance, were adopted by the Council of Ministers in the 1970s, many were buried by COREPER or delayed in the Council of Ministers as a result of individual governments implicitly exercising a veto under pressure by economic interest groups that might be adversely affected by harmonization.[64] Movement on these blocked agenda items would await the achievement of the package deal in the mid-1980s that brought about the Single European Act with its Project 1992 measures for liberalization of trade and harmonization of regulatory regimes affecting trade between the member economies.[65]

On the other hand, below the surface of public attention, a process was going on in the 1960s and 1970s by which the interpretation of the Rome Treaty's ordinary agenda was being expanded. The European Court of Justice (ECJ) was in the process of establishing a body of EC constitutional law in a case-by-case fashion, much as the U.S. Supreme Court did in the early nineteenth century under John Marshall. Without challenging the member governments directly, in the 1960s the ECJ asserted the principle that the Rome Treaty has the status of a constitution and therefore that its provisions are superior to the laws of the member states. It also granted to "individuals" (usually companies registered in the member states) the right to challenge actions of the member states by bringing cases to the ECJ for interpretation; this might result in a finding that the member state was in violation of the Treaty of Rome. This led in the 1970s to the declaration that, when actions of the member states are in conflict with law-making actions of the EC taken in pursuit of the Rome Treaty, EC law would prevail.[66] These assertions would have had little effect if the courts of the member states had refused to accept them, simply regarding the treaty as an international agreement among sovereign states that were competent individually to interpret its meaning for themselves. But gradually in the 1960s and 1970s national courts did cite decisions of the ECJ as authority for upholding EC law in the face of resistance by national governments and parliaments.[67]

The opinions of the ECJ did not, in and of themselves, have the effect of expanding the ordinary agenda, unless the more politically oriented EC bodies were willing to use them for that purpose. The ECJ could not by itself force new EC legislation. The 1970s were years of Commission caution and serious disagreement among the member governments on many policy issues. Nevertheless, the eventual reopening of both the ordinary and the extraordinary agendas in the 1980s was to benefit from the less restrictive interpretation of the treaty that had emerged in the previous decade. The ECJ's work had helped to create the new atmosphere.[68]

CONCLUSION

By the end of 1975 much of the primary work which the six original EEC members had agreed upon in the Treaty of Rome had been accomplished. The customs union and the CAP were in place. Differences in conception of how the institutions were to function, which had come to a head in the mid-1960s crisis, had been smoothed over in practice. At least for the time being intergovernmentalism had come to prevail over supranationalism, not least of all because of the entry of intergovernmentalist Britain, the major holdout of the 1950s, along with Denmark and Ireland. To be sure, direct elections to the European Parliament had been agreed upon and the EP had gained a greater role in the budgetary process; but these supranational (and democratic) advances were counterbalanced by intergovernmentalist gains in the institutionalization of summit meetings and the forms established for European political cooperation. Meanwhile, the arrival of economic and monetary union, heralded in 1969, had been delayed indefinitely.

What supranationalists regarded as logical extensions of the customs union—monetary union and a true common market with all barriers to trade removed—seemed further away from realization than ever in the mid-1970s. Dissatisfaction was growing in particular with what CAP had become, a highly expensive program that was costly to consumers and, given the waning importance of agriculture in advanced industrial economies, constituted much too large a share of the EC budget. For Britain, a net food importer, agricultural exporters like France and the Netherlands were getting too large a share of the British consumers' and taxpayers' money. Three major issues of economic management were thus holdover items on the EC agenda for the period covered by the next chapter (1976 to 1989): monetary union, the internal market, and the intertwined issues of CAP and the British share of the EC budget.

ENDNOTES

1. "Preamble and Selected Articles of the Treaty Establishing the European Economic Community, March 25, 1957," in Howard Bliss, ed., *The Political Development of the European Community: A Documentary Collection* (Waltham, Mass.: Blaisdell, 1970), pp. 47–66.

2. Lindberg and Scheingold ranked decision-making functions of the EEC as of 1968 according to the mix of EC-level and national-level decisions involved. The highest rank received was for functions wherein there was policymaking at both levels, but where "Community activity predominates." The two functions in this category were "agricultural protection" and "movement of goods, services, and other factors of production within the customs union." For the 20 other functions listed, decision making was either exclusively or predominantly at the national level. Leon N. Lindberg and Stuart A. Scheingold, *Europe's Would-Be Polity: Patterns of Change in the European Community* (Englewood Cliffs, N.J.: Prentice-Hall, 1970), p. 71.

3. Robert O. Keohane defines "hegemony" as leadership in political, economic, and security matters which a state is able and willing to exercise over other states. See *After Hegemony: Cooperation and Discord in the World Political Economy* (Princeton, N.J.: Princeton University Press, 1984), p. 39. Benefits of this leadership are mutual, although not necessarily evenly balanced, for both leaders and followers (ibid., p. 128).

4. Derek W. Urwin, *Western Europe since 1945: A Political History*, 4th ed. (London and New York: Longman, 1989), pp. 131–134.

5. Roy Godson and Stephen Haseler, *'Eurocommunism': Implications for East and West* (New York: St. Martin's Press, 1978), pp. 97–99.

6. F. Roy Willis, *France, Germany and the New Europe, 1945–1967*, rev. ed. (London: Oxford University Press, 1968), pp. 98–99, 140–141, 262–264.

7. Extensive analyses of de Gaulle's strategy in Europe within the context of his general worldview are found in Philip G. Cerny, *The Politics of Grandeur: Ideological Aspects of de Gaulle's Foreign Policy* (Cambridge: Cambridge University Press, 1980); Alfred Grosser, *The Western Alliance: European-American Relations since 1945* (New York: Vintage Books, 1982); Stanley Hoffmann, *Decline or Renewal? France since the 1930s* (New York: Viking Press, 1974); and Edward Kolodziej, *French International Policy under de Gaulle and Pompidou: The Politics of Grandeur* (Ithaca, N.Y.: Cornell University Press, 1974).

8. Hoffmann, *Decline or Renewal?* pp. 301–302; Charles de Gaulle, *Memoirs of Hope: Renewal and Endeavor*, trans. Terence Kilmartin (New York: Simon and Schuster, 1971), pp. 163–170.

9. William E. Paterson, *The SPD and European Integration* (Lexington, Mass.: Lexington Books, 1974), chaps. 3–5.

10. Stephen George, *An Awkward Partner: Britain in the European Community* (Oxford: Oxford University Press, 1990), pp. 26–28.

11. John Pinder, *European Community: The Building of Union* (Oxford and New York: Oxford University Press, 1991), pp. 45–46; Dennis Swann, *The Economics of the Common Market*, 5th ed. (Hammondsworth: Penguin Books, 1984), p. 22.

12. F. S. Northedge, "Britain and the EEC Past and Present," in Roy Jenkins, ed., *Britain and the EEC* (London and Basingstoke: Macmillan, 1983), pp. 15–37.

13. For accounts of the Algerian War and the transformation of the Fourth Republic into the Fifth Republic, see Edgar S. Furniss, Jr., *France, Troubled Ally: De Gaulle's Heritage and Prospects* (New York: Praeger, 1960); and Roy C. Macridis and Bernard Brown, *The De Gaulle Republic: Quest for Unity* (Homewood, Ill.: Dorsey Press, 1960).

14. Derek W. Urwin, *The Community of Europe: A History of European Integration since 1945* (London and New York: Longman, 1991), pp. 103–107.

15. Suzanne J. Bodenheimer, *Political Union: A Microcosm of European Politics, 1960–1966* (Leiden, Netherlands: A. W. Sijthoff, 1967), pp. 59–60.

16. Ibid., pp. 92–99. The West German government sought unsuccessfully to reach a compromise between the French position and that of the others. Jan Werts, *The European Council* (Amsterdam: North Holland, 1992), pp. 23–25.

17. Northedge, "Britain and the EEC," p. 26.

18. This is the idea of Britain as a "Trojan horse" supporting U.S. interests within the EEC. Miriam Camps, *European Unification in the Sixties: From the Veto to the Crisis* (New York: McGraw-Hill, 1966), p. 3.

19. Werner J. Feld, *West Germany and the European Community: Changing Interests and Competing Policy Objectives* (New York: Praeger, 1981), pp. 50–51.

20. Andrew Moravcsik, *The Choice for Europe: Social Purpose and State Power from Messina to Maastricht* (London: UCL Press, 1999), pp. 176–193.

21. Ibid., p. 189.

22. Urwin, *The Community of Europe*, pp. 110–111.

23. John Newhouse, *Collision in Brussels: The Common Market Crisis of 30 June 1965* (New York: Norton, 1967), pp. 67–71.

24. Ibid., pp. 56–57.

25. Camps, *European Unification in the Sixties*, pp. 38–43.

26. Ibid., p. 43.

27. According to the Treaty of Rome, what we are consistently calling the European Parliament was officially named the "Assembly." The members of the Assembly themselves called it a Parliament from an early stage, although its powers were very weak under the treaty. It could propose budget amendments to the Council of Ministers, but the Council was "under no obligation to accept any amendments" and could adopt its original version of the budget by qualified majority. Ibid., p. 44.

28. Ibid., pp. 43–45.

29. Newhouse, *Collision in Brussels*, p. 77.

30. Camps, *European Unification in the Sixties*, pp. 81–85.

31. Urwin, *The Community of Europe*, p. 111.

32. Werts, *The European Council*, p. 28.

33. Camps, *European Unification in the Sixties*, pp. 95–101.

34. Ibid., p. 112.

35. Ibid., p. 113.

36. John W. Kingdon, *Agendas, Alternatives and Public Policies* (Glenview, Ill., and London: Scott, Foresman, 1984), p. 4; Newhouse, *Collision in Brussels*, pp. 161–165.

37. Urwin, *The Community of Europe*, pp. 130–132.

38. Willis, *France, Germany and the New Europe*, p. 361.

39. F. Roy Willis, *The French Paradox: Understanding Contemporary France* (Stanford, Calif.: Hoover Institution, 1982), pp. 10, 105.

40. In 1967 the government of Prime Minister Harold Wilson made a second effort to bring Britain into the community. For a second time, the bid was turned down by de Gaulle. George, *An Awkward Partner*, pp. 37–38.

41. Simon Bulmer and Wolfgang Wessels, *The European Council: Decision-Making in European Politics* (Basingstoke and London: Macmillan, 1987), p. 1.

42. Urwin, *The Community of Europe*, pp. 137–138.

43. Wolfram Hanrieder, *Germany, America, Europe: Forty Years of German Foreign Policy* (New Haven, Conn., and London: Yale University Press, 1989), pp. 196–198.

44. Ibid., pp. 285–296.

45. George, *An Awkward Partner*, p. 49.

46. David Butler and Uwe Kitzinger, *The 1975 Referendum* (New York: St. Martin's, 1976), pp. 17–20.

47. George, *An Awkward Partner*, p. 56.

48. Urwin, *The Community of Europe*, pp. 140–145.

49. For discussions of the Hague summit, see Bulmer and Wessels, *The European Council*, pp. 28–30; Urwin, *The Community of Europe*, chaps. 9 and 10.

50. Rainer Hellman, *Gold, the Dollar, and the European Currency Systems: The Seven-Year Monetary War* (New York: Praeger, 1979), pp. 20–22.

51. *European Political Cooperation (EPC)*, 5th ed. (Bonn: Press and Information Office of the Federal Government, 1988); Wolfgang Wessels, "New Forms of Foreign Policy Formulation in Western Europe," in Werner J. Feld, ed., *Western Europe's Global Reach: Regional Cooperation and Worldwide Aspirations* (New York: Pergamon, 1980), pp. 12–29.

52. *European Political Cooperation* (EPC), p. 28.

53. Bulmer and Wessels, *The European Council*, pp. 11–13.

54. Urwin, *The Community of Europe*, p. 173.

55. Bulmer and Wessels, *The European Council*, pp. 41–42.

56. George, *An Awkward Partner*, pp. 74–78.

57. Ibid., pp. 82–87.

58. Ibid., pp. 87–95; Butler and Kitzinger, *The 1975 Referendum*, pp. 39–47.

59. Bulmer and Wessels, *The European Council*, p. 46.

60. Urwin, *The Community of Europe*, pp. 167–168; Dominique Remy with Karl-Hermann Buck, "France: The Impossible Compromise or the End of Majority Parliamentarism?" pp. 99–125; Mark Hagger, "The United Kingdom: The Reluctant Europeans," in Valentine Herman and Mark Hagger, eds. *The Legislation of Direct Elections to the European Parliament* (Westmead: Gower, 1980), pp. 204–238; David M. Wood, "Comparing Parliamentary Voting on European Issues in France and Britain," *Legislative Studies Quarterly* 7 (February 1982): 101–117.

61. Bulmer and Wessels, *The European Council*, p. 46.

62. *European Political Cooperation (EPC)*, pp. 95–97; William Wallace, "Political Cooperation: Integration through Intergovernmentalism," in Helen Wallace et al., eds., *Policymaking in the European Community*, 3d ed. (Chichester, N.Y.: Wiley, 1983), pp. 378–380. See Chapter 12 for the evolution from EPC to the CFSP of today's EU.

63. Helen Wallace, *Budgetary Politics: The Finances of the European Communities* (London: Allen & Unwin, 1980), pp. 77–91, 102.

64. Alan Dashwood, "Hastening Slowly: The Community's Path Towards Harmonization," in Wallace et al., eds., *Policymaking in the European Community*, pp. 184–187; Bulmer and Wessels, *The European Council*, p. 5.

65. Alberta M. Sbragia, "Asymmetrical Integration in the European Community: The Single European Act and Institutional Developments," in Dale L. Smith and James Lee Ray, eds., *The 1992 Project and the Future of Integration in Europe* (Armonk, N.Y., and London: Sharpe, 1993), pp. 101–104; Helen Wallace, "The Council and the Commission after the Single European Act," in Leon Hurwitz and Christian Lequesne, eds., *The State of the European Community: Policies, Institutions and Debates in the Transition Years* (Boulder, Colo.: Lynne Reinner, 1991), pp. 24–25.

66. Anne-Marie Burley and Walter Mattli, "Europe Before the Court: A Political Theory of Legal Integration," *International Organization* 47 (Winter 1993): 41–76; Karen J. Alter, "The European Union's Legal System and Domestic Policy: Spillover or Backlash?" *International Organization* 54 (Summer 2000): 489–518.

67. Martin Shapiro, "The European Court of Justice," in Alberta M. Sbragia, ed., *Euro-Politics: Institutions and Policymaking in the New European Community* (Washington, D.C.: Brookings Institution, 1992), p. 127.

68. David R. Cameron, "The 1992 Initiative: Causes and Consequences," in Sbragia, ed., *Euro-Politics*, pp. 52–53.

4

■

From Euro-Pessimism to Renewed Euro-Optimism (1975–1989)

$\mathbf{B}$y the middle 1970s, optimism about the future of the European Community was in short supply. Governments of the EC member countries were exhausting their political capital in attempting to grapple with the problems of energy shortages, monetary instability, and stagflation, all of which were visited on them by a turbulent global economy over which they had little control, and about which they lacked a common understanding.[1]

Within the EC, the leadership potential of the European Commission and its president had seriously eroded in the years since the confrontation between President Hallstein and de Gaulle. Yet there was a strong sense that the member countries could cope with their economic problems more effectively by working together rather than pulling in different directions. In the late 1970s and early 1980s, leadership was found that energized both the supranational and the intergovernmental institutions of the EC sufficiently that new advances were made on the extraordinary agenda. By the mid-1980s Euro-pessimism was giving way to renewed Euro-optimism, which was to prevail for the rest of the decade. It emerged first in the business sector; then, as economies recovered, it affected political elites as well.

In the 1980s, advances were made toward both political and economic integration, and two further expansions of the EC occurred, in 1981 (entry of Greece) and 1986 (entry of Portugal and Spain). Inclusion of three less developed Mediterranean countries spurred on the completion of the common market via the adoption of the Single European Act (SEA). These and other developments enable us to see how the extraordinary agenda was processed, converting the problems of exchange rate instability, internal market blockage, and budgetary distortions from extraordinary into ordinary agenda items. A review of the early steps toward economic integration, from the Rome Treaty to the mid-1970s, will clarify the motivations behind later developments.

THE ROME TREATY AND ITS IMPLEMENTATION

The Rome Treaty, which set up the European Economic Community (EEC), came into effect on January 1, 1958. It is a long document containing 248 articles. Article 3(a) called for the elimination of internal trade barriers in the form of tariffs and quotas on manufactured products, creating a *free trade zone* covering the six countries. Article 3(b) provided for the creation of a common external tariff schedule for the member states, which would establish a *customs union* (CU). And Article 3(c) required the members to abolish all other restrictions and obstacles to freedom of movement of peoples, goods, and services, creating a *common market.*[2] For this purpose, Article 3(h) called for the harmonization of member state laws in order to facilitate realization of the common market, which was to be achieved over a period of 12 years (by 1969). Article 3(d) called for the establishment of a *common agricultural policy* (CAP) among the member countries that would remove barriers to trade in agricultural goods between the members and regulate trade in farm products with the rest of the world. From 1958 to 1969 the six member states proceeded to construct the basic elements of economic integration projected by the treaty. Although they did not achieve a common market, they did create a customs union and a common agricultural policy. The customs union was completed in 1968, with the removal of tariffs and quotas on manufactured goods between the member states and the consolidation of a common external tariff for manufactured goods produced in non-EEC countries.

Although agricultural production was a declining component of the national product of the member countries, and a smaller portion of gross national product in each country than the manufactured product, the political support of farmers was often crucial to the parliamentary support of governments in power. The economic status of less efficient farmers in Europe was vulnerable in the face of lower-priced farm products that could invade the markets of the six unless farmers were protected. In all six countries governments protected their farmers with subsidies and price-support systems, which guaranteed that they could compete with imported farm products, including products of the other member countries' farmers. Such state support ran counter to the idea of a common market, but farmers in all six countries, even highly industrialized West Germany, were too strong politically to allow governments to give up agricultural protectionism.

According to Article 39 of the Rome Treaty, the objectives of the CAP were to increase productivity, ensure a fair standard of living for the agrarian population, stabilize markets, and guarantee a steady supply of food and other agricultural goods at reasonable prices to the consumers. The CAP was to reflect and increase economic interdependence among the six. For example, while France needed markets for its agricultural products, West Germany needed food imports, including northern grains, meat and dairy products from the Benelux countries and northern France, and vegetables, fruits, and other Mediterranean products from Italy and southern France. In turn, West Germany wanted access to the markets of the other countries, especially France, for its manufactured goods. While the CAP was an expensive plan, particularly for the Germans, EEC leaders felt it was important to guarantee self-sufficiency in this area in view of the total wars that Europe had experienced twice in the century. Also, besides being an agricultural price-support system, CAP was designed to help restructure Western European agriculture by encouraging fewer, larger, and more efficient farms.[3]

As we have seen in the case of the empty-chair crisis, securing agreement among the six countries in support of CAP was not easy. Particularly vexing was the issue of how to finance CAP, as it was recognized that it would take up the lion's share of the EEC budget, at least in the early years. It still constitutes nearly 50 percent of the budget in 2003. The formulas used to determine how CAP monies are raised and distributed are not neutral in their effects. In general, the greater the proportion of a member country's economy that is taken up by agricultural production for export, the more its net receipts from the CAP; the smaller the share, the more its net contribution to the EC budget. Germany has always been a net budgetary contributor because of both its strong economic status and net CAP contributions, as has Britain, with a weaker economic base but relatively large CAP-related contributions. Even France has become a net contributor as its farm sector has diminished. Ireland, Greece, Portugal, and Spain—all newer, less industrialized members—gain from the system.[4]

As the barriers to trade between the member countries in manufactured and agricultural goods came down, the six economies became more vulnerable to fluctuations in one another's economic fortunes. A recession in Germany would reduce demand for the products of the other member countries. Devaluation of a member country's currency could reverberate throughout the EC. For example, when the French franc was devalued vis-à-vis the U.S. dollar, it was also devalued vis-à-vis the currencies of other member countries, which remained at a fixed rate of exchange with respect to the dollar. French consumers could not buy as much with their francs from other EC members as before the devaluation, and French demand for products of the other countries declined. Under the Bretton Woods system, discussed in the next section, such maladjustments could eventually work themselves out because demand for the now cheaper French imports would rise in the other countries, increasing the demand of holders of these harder currencies for francs, and thus returning the franc to its original value. But the point to remember is that interdependence in trade brought with it monetary interdependence.

FROM BRETTON WOODS TO EMS

The collapse of the Bretton Woods monetary regime in the early 1970s represented the first of a series of external economic shocks to the EC and tested the member countries' seriousness in achieving economic integration. Under Bretton Woods, the United States was required to buy and sell unlimited amounts of gold at the official price of $35 per ounce. In the latter half of the 1960s the United States began running balance-of-payments deficits (e.g., a net flow of dollars to Europe) due to overspending on the war in Vietnam and President Lyndon Johnson's war on poverty at home. In order to finance these efforts, the U.S. Treasury was rapidly creating money, European holdings of which equaled and then exceeded the value of gold the United States government held in reserve. Confidence in the dollar dropped, and holders of dollars sought to exchange them for more reliable currencies, thus further-ing the balance-of-payments deficit. The final blow to the Bretton Woods system came when the United States ran an alarming balance-of-payments deficit in 1971 that accompanied the first U.S. trade deficit of the twentieth century. Rather than waiting for its trade partners to knock on the door to exchange dollars for gold, the Nixon administration took the initiative and abrogated the U.S. obligation to the Bretton Woods system.[5]

Because the value of every EC currency was denominated in dollars, the loss of stable exchange rates vis-à-vis the dollar threatened the stability of the EC countries' exchange rates with one another. Their values had to be adjusted and readjusted by trial and error, affecting the stability of trade relations among the members as well. Inflationary pressures on some of the currencies, such as the French franc, the Italian lire, and the imminent newcomer, the British pound, were particularly high. By 1972 these currencies were floating in value against the dollar and, more importantly, against the major stable European currency, the German deutsche mark (DM). By trial and error the EC nine developed a joint float against the dollar, called the "snake." Each member pledged to keep its currency floating within a fairly narrow range against the floating dollar; this meant that the other EC currencies could re-main within a band against the DM as well (see Chapter 7). Stronger EC currencies were able to do this; others could not and moved in and out of the snake in the strug-gle to avoid the severe economic consequences of having currencies that were seri-ously overvalued, provoking trade and balance-of-payments deficits.[6] These problems were less severe for a large and relatively self-sufficient country like the United States in the early 1970s; but for the smaller, interdependent economies of Europe, getting their monetary policies right was absolutely crucial for their economic well-being. This was becoming apparent to national leaders, who began to perceive that the idea of an economic and monetary union, which had been initially put forth in the Werner plan, then set aside with the onslaught of the monetary crisis, might have had some merit after all. The extended crisis had both necessitated and made possible a learning experience for governments and even their highly qualified economic advis-ers. By 1977, some of the leading actors were rapidly moving up the learning curve.[7]

The first leader to speak out was Roy Jenkins, a former British finance minister. Jenkins became president of the European Commission in 1977. Speaking in Flo-rence in October 1977, Jenkins proposed the creation of an economic and monetary union (EMU). The reasons he gave for such a venture reflected the disillusionment of many economists with the conventional assumption of a tradeoff between inflation and unemployment—the belief that policies designed to get rid of one would only bring on the other. Jenkins took the monetarist position that monetary stability (low inflation) was necessary in order to stimulate more efficient and competitive industry across the EC, in turn reversing the reduced employment not only in the aggregate but in the countries and regions of the EC where industry had been less efficient.[8]

Then, in February 1978, Chancellor Helmut Schmidt told Jenkins that he fa-vored a major step toward EMU involving an EC-wide monetary bloc with a common currency pool. Schmidt was preoccupied at the time with what he considered to be irresponsible economic management by the Carter administration in the United States, which was allowing the dollar to float downward in value in order to reduce its trade deficits with other countries by pushing up the value of their currencies vis-à-vis the dollar. In order to protect the DM against a gain in value that could be damaging to German exporters, Schmidt wanted to tie the EC currencies closer together to keep the DM from rising in value relative to those of Germany's principal trade partners, whatever might happen to the DM–dollar exchange rate.[9] This could be accomplished by a plan that would more reliably link EC currencies to one another than the snake, still subject to dollar fluctuations. On the political side, Schmidt was concerned that upcoming state-level elections in Germany could result in a two-thirds majority for the opposition Christian Democrats in the Bundesrat (upper house of parliament) and thus seriously hamper with its veto power his government's legislation. He needed a way of showing the electorate that his government was able to take initiatives in their economic interest.

Schmidt was also signaling, in essence, that Germany would prefer sharing economic leadership in Europe with other European countries, especially with France. The French president, Giscard d'Estaing, was a supporter of EMU, but he faced legislative elections in March 1978 and was trying to pick up votes from both left and right. Overt support for EMU, or for a less ambitious project such as Schmidt was advancing, would bring criticism from both the socialist left, on economic policy grounds, and the Gaullist right, on grounds of loss of French sovereignty. But following the election success of his coalition, these inhibitions were removed, and Giscard d'Estaing sought to show France to be as committed as Germany was to monetary discipline.[10] In both countries, monetary values are symbolic of national prestige, and the state's willingness to protect the currency is an indication of self-assurance and political strength.[11] In April 1978, at the Copenhagen meeting of the European Council, the two closely allied leaders agreed to propose a joint project that would lead to more stability of exchange rates in Europe. Three months later, at the Bremen summit, experts were given the mandate to work out a stronger version of the joint float against the dollar, creating a new European unit of value (later called the European currency unit, or ecu) that would help the EC currencies themselves replace the dollar in interventions to adjust currency values. The final European Monetary System (EMS) plan emerged from the Brussels summit held in December 1978. It came into being in March 1979. Italy and Ireland, which were originally reticent about joining, were enticed into the system with side payments by the richer members. Britain was loosely a member of the EMS, remaining outside the exchange rate mechanism (ERM), which was the effective operating device for keeping the other currencies anchored to the DM. Weaker currencies moved in and out of the ERM in the following years as governments found it politically impossible to maintain the fiscal rigor necessary to support a tight monetary policy. In terms of effective EMS membership, then, it was never the same as the full membership of the EC. This constituted the first break in the principle that membership in the EC also implied membership in *all* of its functioning parts.

PRIME MINISTER THATCHER AND THE BUDGET ISSUE

British hesitancy in joining EMS was symptomatic of the same general reluctance to take new steps toward integration that had kept Britain out of the original Communities in the 1950s and moved de Gaulle to refuse British entry to the EEC in the 1960s.[12] Memories of past British glory, long-standing rivalry and, at times, enmity with France, and more recent brutal experiences with Germany were not easily erased in Britons' minds. Because of their special relationships with the United States and other areas of the world colonized by British subjects and still linked in the Commonwealth of Nations—Canada, New Zealand, and Australia—the British could not completely identify with their neighbors across the Channel. Although Washington endorsed EMS, the British Labour government under James Callaghan (who had replaced Wilson as prime minister in 1976) preferred to stay out of the line of fire in case of a future exchange rate war between the Carter administration and the EMS leaders. Besides, there was strong resistance to further British commitments to the EC from those within the Labour Party who had campaigned for a no vote in the 1975 referendum over continued British membership.[13]

The Callaghan government was at odds with its EC partners over another issue that reached down to the roots of the British "difference." From the British point of view the CAP was simply *unfair*. It was seen, first of all, as a mechanism by which taxpayers in EC countries like Britain that were net food importers were subsidizing not only the farmers of other EC countries but the governments of those countries, which were thus relieved by CAP of part of their responsibility for protecting farmers' incomes. Secondly, it was seen as a factor adding to both external dislocations (high oil prices) and internal strains (budgetary deficits, high labor costs) that had produced runaway British inflation in the mid-1970s.[14]

In order to alleviate British economic problems with a loan from the International Monetary Fund (IMF), the Callaghan government had been forced to cut back government spending in 1977 and impose limits on wage increases of their working-class supporters in 1977 and 1978. In addition to these economic hardships, British consumers were having to pay higher prices than they were used to for food, much of which came into their grocery stores in very visible form from France, Holland, and Denmark. In the winter of 1978–1979 large-scale strikes broke out in Britain as trade unions rebelled against "their own" government's wage-restraint policy. In the May 1979 general election Callaghan's Labour Party was defeated by the Conservatives, whose leader, Margaret Thatcher, then became the new prime minister.

The rise of Margaret Thatcher marked a new era in British politics. While Callaghan had ruffled feathers in EC circles from time to time, Thatcher adopted the politics of confrontation as a personal style. Like de Gaulle, she appeared intractible in negotiation; but she was not at all aloof and inscrutable. She jumped right into the middle of the fray, and her adversaries knew where she stood; but they were no happier with the positions she took than de Gaulle's opponents had been in the 1960s.[15] On the CAP budget issue she made it very clear that the existing arrangements were unfair and that Britain would not countenance further progress toward European union so long as the unfairness remained. Her stances and the persistence with which she argued them often angered her fellow government heads. By May 1982 the mutual antagonism got to the point that when Britain's minister of agriculture sought to invoke the 1966 Luxembourg compromise to block a Council of Ministers decision on CAP that would increase Britain's budgetary contribution, he was overruled by the Belgian presidency—a ruling that was strongly backed by France and upheld by the other members, leaving Britain in isolation. Thatcher decided not to insist on the veto by following de Gaulle's empty-chair precedent, even though she undoubtedly felt that an important British interest was at stake.

From the standpoint of the Commission in Brussels and the original six members, Britain had never accepted true "European" goals and norms. Britain resisted the goals of economic, monetary, and political union, and the others recognized that any moves they might make in this direction would elicit a British veto or refusal to take part, as in the EMS case. But Thatcher's claim of unfairness in the CAP budget discussions was seen by her fellow heads of state and government as a repudiation of norms of the European Community that had developed over the past 30 years. The term "community" reflected the belief of political elites in France, West Germany, Italy, and the Benelux countries that members had joined in the desire to engage in a cooperative effort to solve problems they could not solve on their own. Policies that the six had put in place prior to Britain's entry constituted what was called in French the *acquis communautaire*, that body of established laws and practices that made them a true *community*. This body had been accumulated through long and painful negotiations, involving the give-and-take of members who were ill-disposed to reexamine them at such a late date. When Britain joined the EC, it had accepted the *acquis communautaire* and its consequences, including its budgetary consequences. This did not mean Britain could not work to improve the CAP. None of the member countries would insist that the CAP was perfect and should not be reformed. But until agreement could be reached on CAP reform, the budgetary arrangements would have to continue.[16]

It was not lost on Thatcher that France, which was one of the members most resistant to an accommodation with Britain over the budget, had always fought for its own corner fiercely, even when the rest of the EC membership was aligned on the other side. But, while he was still Germany's chancellor, Helmut Schmidt sought to find ways to bring the British and the French together on the issue. According to Thatcher, he had pointed out to her that "the CAP was a price which had to be paid, however high, to persuade members like France and Italy to come into the Community from the beginning." In her memoirs Thatcher was to observe: "Although I had had serious disagreements with him, I always had the highest regard for Helmut Schmidt's wisdom, straightforwardness and grasp of international economics. Sadly, I never developed quite the same relationship with Chancellor Kohl."[17] In October 1982 a coalition of Helmut Kohl's CDU/CSU and the centrist FDP replaced the coalition of Schmidt's SPD and the FDP. The Free Democrats had changed sides, foreaking the center-left coalition for a new one of the center right.

Both Schmidt and Kohl had to deal with Margaret Thatcher's demand for a fairer mechanism involving the British budget contribution. On the one hand, they could sympathize with her argument that British taxpayers should not be subsidizing the French and other governments, because Germany was itself the largest net contributor to the EC budget. Thus, Kohl joined Thatcher in resisting a lifting of the budget ceiling within which the EC had to operate. But he was also cognizant that an important component of his electoral support as a Christian Democrat and that of his coalition partner, foreign minister Hans-Dietrich Genscher, came from West German farmers, who were more dependent on CAP than British farmers. So he resisted Thatcher's call for CAP reforms that would reduce payments to inefficient farmers, as well as her call for reform of the budget structure, because any substantial reduction in the British contribution would have to be picked up mainly by his own government.[18]

On the French side of the triangle, a major change in government occurred in May 1981, when François Mitterrand was elected president, defeating the incumbent Giscard d'Estaing. Although his socialist party won a majority in its own right in legislative elections held in June, Mitterrand's government included four Communist ministers, along with ministers drawn from the left wing of the Socialist Party. Traditional French left-wing hostility to European integration now had a voice in the French cabinet. In the first two years of his presidency, Mitterrand and his ministers were preoccupied with an ambitious and radical program of domestic socioeconomic reforms that included nationalization of leading multinational industrial firms and banks and a reflationary strategy to reduce unemployment. By 1983, it was clear that this program was too expensive and was threatening France's capacity to maintain its position in the EMS, with continual pressure being put on the franc that could only with great difficulty maintain its value vis-à-vis the strong DM. Left-wing members of Mitterrand's government were calling for France to pull out of the exchange rate mechanism of EMS, but in March 1983 Mitterrand decided to stay in, although the consequence would be a reversal of the socioeconomic reforms and a serious austerity program to defend the franc within the ERM.[19]

With his majority in disarray and his own popularity in decline, Mitterrand needed a success on the international scene to divert attention from the failure of his government's economic policies. Ready to foster progress on the European front, he found his target in a number of proposals for both economic and political integration that were being given attention by the Commission and in the European Parliament at the time, although they were by no means new. The main opportunity appeared in early 1984 when France assumed the EC Council presidency, affording Mitterrand a chance to play a leadership role.[20] To bring about a policy success at the European level, Mitterrand had to find a way to mollify the British prime minister. The obvious way was to make concessions to her regarding the British budget contribution.

In two summit meetings during the French presidency, at Brussels in March 1984 and at Fontainebleau three months later, an agreement was reached to reduce the British budgetary contribution in such a way as to reflect more accurately (and fairly, from the British viewpoint) the relative British economic position measured in terms of per capita income. This meant an approximately two-thirds reduction in the British CAP-mandated contribution. At Brussels confrontation prevailed over cooperation; Kohl refused to make up for the British reduction with a sizable increase in the German contribution, the Italians and French held up payment of a rebate to Britain that had been agreed on in 1983, and Britain threatened not to pay its 1984 contribution.[21] By the time of the Fontainebleau summit in June, Mitterrand's commitment to resolving the issue was manifested in his willingness to assume a major part of the financial burden that Germany was refusing, enabling Kohl to accept part of it as well.[22] Agreement on the British budgetary contribution received the headlines, while significant steps that were made at Fontainebleau toward what was to become the Single European Act (SEA) went largely unnoticed.

THE SINGLE EUROPEAN ACT

The Fontainebleau summit illustrates the value of regular summit meetings. They had become a means by which progress could be made in economic and political integration whenever favorable national and international circumstances coincided with the turn of the right member in the Council presidency. Such convergence has opened windows of opportunity,[23] such as those provided by the change in French economic policy shortly before it became France's turn to set the agenda for the European Council.[24] At Fontainebleau, the heads of government made the single market their first priority in the quest for economic union. This meant a commitment to removing barriers to the exchange of goods and services and to the movement of labor and capital among the member countries.

The three principal actors whose policy commitments converged initially in order to set the agenda for the SEA at Fontainebleau were Kohl, Mitterrand, and Thatcher. Once the budget issue was successfully managed, the heads of state and government gave the Commission the task of working out the details of the single market. The Commission had already prepared substantial parts of it for presentation to the Council of Ministers. The legislation had languished at the level of the Council, still under the pall of the Luxembourg compromise. But now, the inclusion of many items in one omnibus package of reforms appealed to the free-trade "neoliberalism" of Margaret Thatcher and her government and to important leaders of the German governing coalition.

The single market was more attractive to the heads of state and government because of increased Japanese and American competition in both international markets and in the EC market itself.[25] European business leaders became more focused on their disadvantageous position with respect to economies of scale. Cooperation among the business leaders began after a roundtable discussion of the European multinationals sponsored by Commission vice president Etienne Davignon.[26] It is also important to recognize that by the mid-1980s some degree of monetary stability had been achieved through the EMS, as member governments, including the French, acknowledged the value of monetary discipline imposed by their ties to the DM.[27] The strong push by the Commission to promote single-market legislation after French finance minister Jacques Delors became president in January 1985 was also crucial in the eventual achievement of the SEA.[28] As far as agenda setting is concerned,

Delors may have been important in influencing Mitterrand to take the initiative in the first place. But the Commission's subsequent role in selecting policy alternatives and in making sure that the single market took wings was of great importance, as was the support of Eurobusiness.

Delors assigned a British colleague, Lord Cockfield, the commissioner for the Internal Market, the task of preparing a white paper that included a list of 300 measures needed for achieving a true common market. He also laid out a timetable to be followed by the EC members to complete adoption of these measures by December 31, 1992—hence the name Project 1992. Most of the white paper measures were eventually agreed upon and mandated by the Single European Act. Scheduled to be removed were a wide array of laws and government practices of the member countries that served as barriers, often but not in all cases deliberate barriers, to intra-EC trade. These included, among others, bureaucratic procedures imposing delays in the movement of goods and persons at borders between member countries; differences in standards for manufacturing products that made illegal the sale in one member country of goods produced in another; government procurement policies discriminating against products from other member countries; conflicting taxes and levels of taxation making for differences in price of the same goods produced in different countries; and differences in the price of services involved in moving goods and persons from one country to another.[29]

Institutional reforms were a part of the SEA package as well. The European Parliament (EP) had continually urged that steps be taken toward political union, modest versions of which found their way into the SEA. Following the first direct elections to the EP in June 1979, Italian member of the European Parliament (MEP) Altiero Spinelli founded and led a cross-party group of MEPs, known as the "Crocodile Club."[30] This became the driving force behind EP demands for institutional reform to make the EC more democratic and politically accountable. The club's proposals were brought together as a draft European Union Treaty (EUT) to amend the Rome Treaty. The resolution supporting the EUT was adopted by the EP by an absolute majority of 237 to 31, with 43 abstentions, on February 14, 1984, four months before the Fontainebleau summit.[31] As support for the single-market idea began to build, Spinelli argued that institutional reform should be attached to it. Otherwise the single-market proposals might fail in the face of different governments vetoing different proposals. The most central provision of the EUT was therefore the abolition of the veto in the Council of Ministers. But another important proposal that saw the light of day in the SEA was that of a "cooperation" procedure between the EP and the Council of Ministers that would make it more difficult for the Council to ignore EP-proposed amendments (see Chapter 6).[32]

The EUT was one of two influential initiatives that preceded the SEA and contributed elements of institutional reform to it. The other was the Solemn Declaration on European Union, which was adopted by the European Council at the Stuttgart summit in June 1983. The EUT initiative included an effort to curtail the agenda-setting role of the European Council,[33] whereas the Solemn Declaration explicitly stated that the European Council "initiates cooperation in new areas of activity" and gives "general political guidelines for the European Communities and

European Political Co-operation."[34] It was an intergovernmental statement, down-playing the role of the Commission, especially in calling for greater intergovern-mental cooperation in foreign policymaking. Instead of the abolition of the veto ad-vocated by the EP, it suggested a voluntary discontinuation of its use in the Council of Ministers. This could be accomplished by governments abstaining instead of voting negatively, a practice which was already occurring in Council of Ministers meetings.[35]

At Fontainebleau, at the same time the single market reached the extraordinary agenda, the European Council added to it the institutional reforms that were to be-come part of the SEA at the urging of President Mitterrand. Earlier in the year Mit-terrand had held discussions with Altiero Spinelli, who evidently influenced the French president to add his weight to the increase in EP powers.[36] Mitterrand in-duced the heads of state and government at Fontainebleau to appoint a committee of governmental representatives to take both the EUT and the Solemn Declaration and work out a version of the EUT that would be acceptable to the 10 governments. This committee, headed by Senator James Dooge of Ireland, reported to the Milan sum-mit a year later recommending that an intergovernmental committee be formed to draft what the Dooge report called a Treaty on European Unity, but which became, after approval at the Luxembourg summit of December 1985 and subsequent signing (1986) and ratification (1987), the Single European Act.[37]

At Milan in June 1985, the Italian prime minister, Bettino Craxi, presiding over the European Council, proposed that an intergovernmental conference (IGC) be convened to propose a set of amendments to the Rome Treaty that would incorpo-rate changes in the institutions along some of the lines proposed in the EUT and the Solemn Declaration. Margaret Thatcher objected strenuously to this proposal, as she believed that the present rules would allow the single market to be legislated, given the substantial consensus she believed to be behind it. But Craxi, implicitly supported by the other eight heads of state and government, ruled that under the Rome Treaty the IGC could be called by simple majority vote in the Council of Ministers; this ran counter to the general understanding that European Council decisions would be taken only if there were no objections. Thatcher objected, but she was overruled. At this point she might have repeated de Gaulle's empty-chair ploy. She also had the op-tion of staying in the meeting but refusing to send a representative of the British gov-ernment to meetings of the IGC, implicitly vetoing any proposed amendments to the Rome Treaty that might emerge. She did neither of these, staying at the summit meeting and later sending her representative to the IGC meeting, which was held in Luxembourg during the second half of 1985. Unlike de Gaulle, her first priority was achieving her desired policy change: the trade-liberalizing features of the SEA. Ac-ceptance of more qualified majority voting could help achieve this end through legis-lation to achieve the single market.

Once agreed upon by the 10 heads of state and government at Luxembourg in December 1985 and fully ratified, the 1987 SEA "institutionalized" the European Council, with what was more a description of existing practice than a proposal for in-stitutional change. The cooperation procedure for internal market legislation gave the EP more leverage over measures adopted by the Council of Ministers. Elimination of the veto in the Council of Ministers applied under the SEA only to a restricted range of policy measures mainly involving the internal market. The SEA did not make the EP a coequal half of a bicameral parliament; but the opportunities the institutional reforms opened up for the EP have been used to the Parliament's advantage (see Chapter 5).[38] Prime Minister Thatcher later wrote that there was "no escape" from qualified majority voting, "because otherwise particular countries would succumb to domestic pressures and prevent the opening-up of their markets."[39]

An additional reason why 1984 and 1985 were years of opportunity for economic and political integration was that negotiations were going on between the EC 10 and Spain and Portugal regarding the terms of their entry into the Community. When they joined in 1986, this brought to 12 the number of member countries and added to the poorer countries and regions that were part of the Community. As in other enlargements, special provisions were made for the newcomers to ease them into the full system of obligations and benefits of membership. From the beginning, however, the new members would take their places in the EC institutions, giving them the opportunity to influence agenda setting and policymaking for the future. In the years immediately preceding the Iberian enlargement, the members already in place perceived the necessity before the new members entered to "deepen" the EC by completing the common market, and by making the institutions more efficient in the face of a larger membership through reduced opportunity to use the veto.

In response to the desires of the new members, the SEA specifically targeted regional issues, recognizing that redistribution of economic resources from richer to poorer areas of the EC was essential in order to achieve harmonious economic integration. In line with the SEA mandate, members reached an agreement in 1988 to double the size of the structural funds directed to the poorer regions before the completion of Project 1992. Moreover, they revised the mechanism and strengthened the specifications by which funds were to be distributed, giving the EC more control over the process, so that domestic political motives would have less effect in determining the allocation.[40]

The SEA also contained revisions of the sections of the Rome Treaty concerned with social policy, an area which had been given relatively little attention aside from ritualistic statements of aspirations by the Commission and the European Council. One of these had been the idea of a "social area" put forth in 1981 by the new Socialist government of France, and later adopted in the form of the Social Charter proposed by Jacques Delors. Basically, it argued that some degree of uniformity in Community-wide social standards was desirable because in an increasingly competitive environment, caused by the creation of the single market, countries with lower standards of social protection—minimum wages, social security, working conditions, status of trade unions—would undercut other members with higher standards, resulting in loss of market shares and company relocation. This is termed the "social-dumping" problem.[41] References to social policy harmonization in the SEA were brief, but they paved the way for the Social Charter, which became a protocol to the Maastricht Treaty of 1992.

THE DELORS INITIATIVES OF 1987–1989

By the beginning of 1988 Europe and the larger trading world were awakening to the potential significance of the single market. This was partly because of the early successes registered by the strategy adopted in the field of product-standards regulation, which allowed "mutual recognition" by each country of the regulatory standards prevailing in the others, so that borders were opened to goods previously excluded from countries with tougher standards but satisfying the standards of the country of origin.[42] It was also a result of the efforts by the Commission, supportive media, and business interests to publicize projections of rapid economic growth that would result from implementation of the single market as the world economy was on an upswing. Some assistance may have been given to the upward trend by increased business confidence influenced by the pro-single-market propaganda. Whatever the reasons, the late 1980s witnessed the zenith of the Commission's influence within EC policymaking circles, as the prestige of its president reached heights never achieved by his predecessors.[43]

In February 1987 Delors presented what became known as his "package," a combination of measures designed to reduce the complex of issues between member states over CAP and the budget. The Delors package included three components: (1) the creation of new budgetary resources by additions to member contributions from sources other than their CAP obligations, (2) reform of CAP to reduce spending obligations and the CAP share of the EC budget, and (3) enhancement of the system of redistribution favoring poorer states and regions.[44] This represented an effort by Delors to bring Margaret Thatcher into the consensual center of the EC, because it answered her call for greater control over CAP spending and a shifting of revenue obligations from those based on food imports to those reflecting the relative strength of members' economies. Although the package made little headway at summits held in 1987, when Germany took over the Council presidency in January 1988 the Kohl government was willing to lend its weight to support the Delors package, even though it would have an unfavorable effect on German farmers. The Delors package was adopted in February 1988 at an extraordinary Brussels summit called by Kohl to clear the ground for progress on single-market legislation and for initiating a new effort to achieve economic and monetary union.[45]

In the late 1980s, the surge of optimism that accompanied the early days of SEA was further sustained by the solid performance of the European Monetary System. By 1987 exchange rates within the ERM had become remarkably stable, and inflation rates had dropped from double digits in most EC countries in 1982 to less than 5 percent for all ERM members, while three of the four EC members not in the ERM were above that figure.[46] To the Delors Commission and the Mitterrand government the time seemed ripe to broach the issue of EMU again. EMU was put on the extraordinary agenda at the June 1988 meeting of the European Council at Hanover, with Chancellor Kohl presiding. The agenda-setting decision was to establish a committee headed by Delors to produce a document that could serve as a basis for revision of the Rome Treaty.[47]

The Delors report on EMU, officially presented to the member governments in April 1989, proposed a gradual process of economic and monetary unification.[48] The plan stated that stage 1 would begin on July 1, 1990, and include liberalization of capital markets, enlarged ERM membership, and coordination of monetary policies by the EC Committee of Central Bank Governors. Stage 2, which would require revision of the Treaty of Rome, would include creation of the European System of Central Banks (ESCB), similar to the U.S. Federal Reserve system. This institution would set monetary policy but would leave its execution to the national central banks. Furthermore, currency realignments would only be allowed under exceptional circumstances. Finally, in stage 3, exchange rates would irrevocably be fixed and national central banks would be replaced by the ESCB. The plan left open whether the process would culminate in the adoption of a single European currency[49] (see Chapter 8).

Of the major member states, France was the most enthusiastic about moving ahead to EMU. From the French standpoint, the dominant position of the Bundesbank in aligning ERM currencies around a strong DM meant that severe restrictions were placed upon French economic policymaking, especially limiting the ability of the French government to counteract recession and unemployment. EMU would make monetary policy subject to the collective decision making of the ESCB, thus reducing Bundesbank control and giving the Bank of France, and therefore the French government, more influence.[50] To Kohl, the idea of moving ahead to EMU was acceptable, although he had to set aside Bundesbank objections in giving the Delors report his government's approval.[51] To Margaret Thatcher, whose irritation with Delors had been stimulated the year before by statements he had made envisaging substantial transfers of sovereignty to the Community, EMU was far from acceptable. Delors's own enthusiasm for EMU was based on his expectation of precisely such a transfer of sovereignty to EC institutions. The Delors report effectively put EMU on the extraordinary agenda for the early 1990s.

CONCLUSION

There were three policy areas that were central to the EC's extraordinary agenda during much of the period under discussion in this chapter: the system of exchange rates between EC currencies, CAP and the budget, and the internal market. Considerable progress was made between 1975 and 1989 in finding more effective policy instruments for managing all three of these problem areas. The regularization of summit meetings, which began in 1975, was important for allowing agenda setting to occur in all three cases when the opportunities appeared, and the gradual movement away from the use and threat of the veto made progress easier on the third of these issues after adoption of the Single Europe Act.

The issue of how to achieve better monetary coordination in the face of the exchange rate crises of the 1970s was placed on the extraordinary agenda by the German chancellor, with the help of the French president and a verbal boost from the Commission president. The success of the ERM, especially the recognition by a

French Socialist president that France was better off staying in it, helped pave the way for the breakthrough of 1984–1985 that was spearheaded by President Mitterrand and resulted in the adoption of the Single European Act. The trade-liberalizing features of the SEA had the enthusiastic support of the British and German governments, but the British prime minister only allowed the SEA on the agenda when her budgetary concerns were dealt with, and she only reluctantly accepted the institutional changes in the SEA that made decision making in the Council of Ministers easier and enhanced the influence of the European Parliament. Once the issues that were dealt with in the SEA were placed on the agenda by the European Council at Fontainebleau, the Commission played an important role in working out the principal policy alternatives to best achieve the single market, while the institutional changes in the decision-making process were worked out by an intergovernmental body with inputs from the EP and the foreign ministers. Implementation of the SEA then followed the Rome Treaty pattern whereby the Commission sets the ordinary agenda by preparing legislative measures and the Council of Ministers determines whether they will be modified and adopted.

By the late 1980s the prestige and influence of the Commission president was at an all-time high. Delors played an important role in fostering agreement on a package of CAP budget reforms, largely resolving the principal British complaint about the way the EC worked. During the German presidency in the first half of 1988, Kohl helped to push the Delors package through the European Council and followed this up by sponsoring the return of EMU to the extraordinary agenda. Delors was given the assignment of heading the committee to work out the stages of EMU. With the Delors plan, reported in April 1989, the stage was set for another major revision of the Rome Treaty, which will be an important focus of Chapter 5.

ENDNOTES

1. Robert O. Keohane and Stanley Hoffmann, "Institutional Change in Europe in the 1980s," in Keohane and Hoffmann, eds., *The New European Community: Decisionmaking and Institutional Change* (Boulder, Colo.: Westview Press, 1991), pp. 5–8.
2. Dennis Swann, *The Economics of the Common Market* (London: Penguin Books, 1992), p. 12.
3. Stephen George, *Politics and Policy in the European Community*, 2d ed. (London: Oxford University Press, 1991), pp. 134–135
4. Michael Schackleton, "The Budget of the EC: Structure and Process," in Lodge, ed., *The European Community and the Challenge of the Future*, 2d ed. (New York: St. Martin's Press, 1993), p. 94.
5. Robert S. Walters and David H. Blake, *The Politics of Global Economic Relations*, 4th ed. (Englewood Cliffs, N.J.: Prentice-Hall, 1991), pp. 74–77.
6. Francesco Giavazzi and Alberto Giovannini, *Limiting Exchange Rate Flexibility: The European Monetary System* (Cambridge, Mass.: MIT Press, 1989), pp. 26–27.
7. David M. Wood and Birol A. Yesilada, "Learning to Cope with Global Turbulence: The Role of EMS in European Integration." Paper presented at the Annual Meeting of the Midwest Political Science Association, Chicago, April 18–20, 1991.
8. Robert A. Isaac, *International Political Economy: Managing World Economic Change* (Englewood Cliffs, N.J.: Prentice-Hall, 1991), p. 58.
9. Ibid., p. 125.
10. Jonathan Story, "The Launching of the EMS: An Analysis of Change in Foreign Economic Policy," *Political Studies* 36 (September 1988): 401.

11. Stanley Hoffman, "Europe's Identity Crisis Revisited," *Daedalus* 123 (Spring 1994): 5.
12. Recall Box 3.1 in Chapter 3, which lists the changes in government occurring in France, Germany, and Britain during the period covered in this chapter.
13. Pinder, *European Community*, p. 129.
14. Stephen George, *An Awkward Partner: Britain in the European Community* (Oxford: Oxford University Press, 1990), pp. 132–133
15. David M. Wood, "Old Thinking and the New Europe: The Persisting Influence of de Gaulle and Thatcher." Occasional paper no. 9211, Center for International Studies, University of Missouri, St. Louis, December 1992.
16. George, *An Awkward Partner*, p. 134.
17. Margaret Thatcher, *The Downing Street Years*, (New York: HarperCollins, 1993) p. 257.
18. Ibid., pp. 538–541.
19. Peter A. Hall, *Governing the Economy: The Politics of State Intervention in Britain and France* (Oxford: Oxford University Press, 1986), pp. 198–202.
20. Andrew Moravcsik, "Negotiating the Single European Act," in Keohane and Hoffmann, eds., *The New European Community*, pp. 51–52.
21. Ibid., pp. 55–56; George, *An Awkward Partner*, pp. 154–155.
22. Moravcsik, "Negotiating the Single European Act," pp. 56–57; George, *An Awkward Partner*, pp. 155–159.
23. See Wood, Yeşilada, and Robedeau, "Windows of Opportunity," where the application of Kingdon's concept to EC agenda setting is developed. John W. Kingdon, *Agendas, Alternatives, and Public Policies* (Glenview, Ill., and London: Scott, Foresman, 1984), chap. 8. For a thorough study of the Council presidency that frequently takes note of the opportunities provided by changes in the presidency, see Emil Joseph Kirchner, *Decision-making in the European Community: The Council Presidency and European Integration* (Manchester and New York: Manchester University Press, 1992).
24. This illustrates that the timing of changes in domestic politics of the member countries can affect the willingness of a government taking over the presidency to put new items on the extraordinary agenda. Moravcsik, "Negotiating the Single European Act."
25. There has been a considerable amount of work devoted to the process by which the single market came into being. See especially Paul Taylor, "The New Dynamics of EC Integration in the 1980s," in Juliet Lodge, ed., *The European Community and the Challenge of the Future*, 1st ed. (New York: St. Martin's Press, 1989), pp. 3–25; Moravcsik, "Negotiating the Single European Act;" David Cameron, "The 1992 Initiative: Causes and Consequences," in Alberta M. Sbragia, ed., *Euro-politics: Institutions and Policymaking in the "New" European Community* (Washington: The Brookings Institution, 1992), pp. 23–74.
26. Cameron, "The 1992 Initiative," pp. 54–55.
27. John T. Woolley, "Policy Credibility and the European Monetary System," in Sbragia, ed., *Euro-politics*, pp. 157–190.
28. The later arrival of both international business leaders and Jacques Delors has been pointed out by both Moravcsik, "Negotiating the Single European Act," p. 65; and Cameron, "The 1992 Initiative," pp. 49, 51.
29. Paolo Cecchini, *The European Challenge 1992: The Benefits of a Single Market* (Aldershot, U.K.: Wildwood House, for the Commission of the European Communities, 1989), pp. 1–7.
30. Juliet Lodge, "Ten Years of an Elected European Parliament," in Lodge, ed., *The 1989 Election of the European Parliament* (New York: St. Martin's Press, 1990), pp. 7, 14.
31. Juliet Lodge, "European Union and the First Elected European Parliament: The Spinelli Initiative," *Journal of Common Market Studies* 22 (June 1984): 378.
32. Ibid., pp. 381–394.
33. Ibid., p. 391.
34. Quoted in Simon Bulmer and Wolfgang Wessels, *The European Council: Decision-Making in European Politics* (Basingstoke and London: Macmillan, 1987), p. 77.
35. Cameron, "The 1992 Initiative," pp. 54–55.
36. Lodge, "Ten Years of an Elected European Parliament," p. 15.
37. Cameron, "The 1992 Initiative," pp. 23–24.

38. Lodge, "Ten Years of an Elected European Parliament," pp. 17–21.

39. Thatcher, *The Downing Street Years*, p. 553.

40. Judith Tomkins and Jim Twomey, "Regional Policy," in Frank McDonald and Stephen Dearden, eds., *European Economic Integration* (London: Longman, 1992), pp. 107–109.

41. Beverly Springer, *The Social Dimension of 1992* (New York: Praeger, 1992), chap. 4.

42. John Pinder, "The Single Market: A Step Towards European Union," in Lodge, ed., *The European Community and the Challenge of the Future*, 1st ed., p. 98.

43. Peter Ludlow "The European Commission," in Keohane and Hoffmann, eds., *The New European Commmunity*, pp. 116–121.

44. Loukas Tsoukalis, *The New European Economy: The Politics and Economics of Integration* (Oxford: Oxford University Press, 1991), p. 62.

45. Kirchner, *Decision-making in the European Community*, p. 99.

46. Cameron, "The 1992 Initiative," p. 48.

47. Kirchner, *Decision-making in the European Community*, p. 102.

48. Peter Ludlow, "Introduction: The Politics and Policies of the EC in 1989," in Centre for European Policy Studies, *The Annual Review of European Community Affairs 1990* (London: Brassey's, 1991), p. xli.

49. "How to Hatch an EMU," *The Economist*, April 22, 1989, p. 45.

50. David R. Cameron, "British Exit, German Voice, French Loyalty: Defection, Domination and Cooperation in the 1992–93 ERM Crisis." Paper presented at the Third International Conference of the European Community Studies Association, Washington, D.C., May 27–29, 1993, p. 13.

51. Ludlow, "Introduction," p. xlii.

5

■

The Emergence of the European Union, 1989-2002

The new European Union (EU) that came into being in late 1993 resulted from two main strands of activity by its principal architects. Between 1989 and 1992 they produced the blueprints for both Economic and Monetary Union (EMU) and Political Union. Plans for EMU were agreed upon in general terms at the Madrid summit of June 1989; then, with the overturn of Communist regimes in Eastern Europe and the unification of Germany, it was agreed that important steps toward Political Union would be undertaken. Both EMU and Political Union were outlined and agreed upon in the Maastricht Treaty. In the succeeding decade, the European Union has pursued implementation of agreements regarding EMU and Political Union and made plans for further enlargement. Three new members—Austria, Finland, and Sweden—were brought into the EU, bringing the new total to 15 members. Adjustments of the institutions left over from Maastricht were made in the Amsterdam Treaty of 1997, and in 1999 the third stage of EMU began with the inauguration of a single currency, the euro. Also on the agenda in the new millennium is enlargement to include countries in southern, central, and eastern Europe. This has stimulated further adjustments of the EU institutional framework, which were made at the Nice summit of December 2000. More are being considered in a special constitutional convention, which will report a draft constitution in 2003. Work on this latest treaty revision, based on the convention's proposed constitution, is the task of another intergovernmental conference, to be concluded before the first new members are accepted, in 2004 at the earliest.

THE MAASTRICHT STRUGGLE

Economic and Monetary Union on the Agenda

The first steps on the road to Maastricht, in the years from 1988 to 1990, brought to the extraordinary agenda Economic and Monetary Union and the Community Charter of Fundamental Social Rights for Workers (the "Social Charter"), both of which were conceived to be extensions of European Community (EC) powers that would be necessitated by the opening of the single market (see Chapter 4). Both EMU and the Social Charter, which was designed to achieve uniformity in social provisions, conditions of employment, and industrial relations, were put on the extraordinary agenda on the initiative of Delors, Kohl, and Mitterrand at the Hanover summit of June 1988. Both of these proposals were opposed by Margaret Thatcher, but she had greater difficulty in holding up progress on EMU at the summits held in 1988 and 1989 than on the Social Charter. After his reelection victory in March 1988, President Mitterrand joined Delors in giving strong support to EMU, succeeding in bringing along Chancellor Kohl, who overrode the objections of the Bundesbank, much to Prime Minister Thatcher's disappointment.[1] At the June 1989 Madrid summit, pressed hard by her foreign secretary and finance minister not to leave Britain in an isolated position, Thatcher conceded the creation of an intergovernmental conference (IGC) to draft treaty amendments that would provide for an EMU.[2] At the Strasbourg summit in December 1989, it was agreed to convene the IGC at the end of 1990.[3]

Prime Minister Thatcher's opposition to EMU was based on an unwillingness to see an EC central bank and single currency that would take away Britain's capacity to conduct its own monetary policy. She was even opposed to the idea of Britain's pound sterling being brought within the exchange rate mechanism (ERM) of the European Monetary System (EMS), which her finance minister, Nigel Lawson, was advocating from the middle of the 1980s. The argument between Thatcher and Lawson, which eventuated in the latter's resignation in October 1989, was on the rather technical ground of how best to control inflation. Prime Minister Thatcher's governments since 1979 had followed the monetarist premise that inflation is caused by an increase in the national money supply, and that it can therefore be controlled by controlling the money supply. Lawson had come to the conclusion that money supply could not be effectively controlled and that a more effective means of achieving monetary stability would be to anchor sterling to the strong deutsche mark (DM) through membership in the ERM. Since the Bundesbank pursued an effective counterinflationary policy by controlling interest rate levels, Britain could do likewise by following the German lead, as France, the Netherlands, and even Ireland were doing. Given her strong aversion to a loss of British sovereignty, Thatcher inevitably resisted this step, as well as the proposed EMU, the latter because it meant that a "Euroversion" of the Bundesbank would be controlling British macroeconomic policy. In October 1990, a year after Lawson's resignation, Thatcher finally allowed his successor, John Major, to take the pound into the ERM, but she did so with great reluctance.[4]

Thatcher's inability to forestall the French-led drive toward EMU, as well as her capitulation to the Treasury's desire to join the ERM, reflected the weakness of her position within the Conservative Party by 1989. Growing inflation and unemployment since the 1987 election had led to a loss of public support for the Conservatives, and especially for Thatcher. There was a growing number of Conservative MPs who felt she was being too intransigent on the EMU issue.[5] When she made it clear in a speech to the House of Commons that Britain would hold out alone against the version of EMU that was emerging from intergovernmental deliberations, her deputy prime minister, former foreign minister Geoffrey Howe, resigned from the Cabinet and gave a speech of his own that undoubtedly swung some Conservative backbenchers against her. These defectors combined with others wishing to find a more electable prime minister to deny her a majority in a vote of the parliamentary party of November 22, 1990. She resigned six days later, and John Major, with her support, became prime minister following a second vote of the Conservative MPs.[6] While it was generally expected that Major would follow the broad outlines of Thatcher's policies, it was also clear that an important obstacle to the achievement of a treaty on European Union had been removed.

Political Union on the Agenda

The other institutional innovations of the three pillars of the eventual Maastricht Treaty were of a more political nature, if the term is taken to include internal and external security concerns as well as institutional changes. They did not reach the extraordinary agenda until after the upheavals in central and eastern Europe and the October 1990 unification of Germany. The desire of the Federal Republic of Germany and of its EC partners to anchor the new Germany solidly into the EC framework propelled the EC 12 to join monetary and political union into a single project that reached its fruition in the agreements at the Maastricht summit of December 1991.

When the Berlin Wall came down in November 1989, there was general rejoicing throughout the EC, because it represented a victory for Western democracy and market economies. But when Chancellor Kohl began in late November to openly advocate early unification of the two Germanies, doubts began to be raised privately and hinted at publicly, by both Prime Minister Thatcher and President Mitterrand. In meetings with Mitterrand in December 1989 and January 1990, Prime Minister Thatcher expressed her opposition to unification on the grounds that a larger, more powerful Germany would upset the balance within Europe by gaining excessive influence over the newly emerging east European states. Britain and France should join forces, and attempt to prevent or at least slow the pace of German unification. While agreeing with Thatcher in principle, Mitterrand was pessimistic about the chances of preventing unification, and thought it best to exercise damage control by strengthening the EC, thus locking the new Germany into a cooperative mode. Thatcher opposed this view, believing that it was precisely within the EC that Germany's "hegemony" would assert itself, and that it was important for Britain and France to develop links with the eastern post-Communist European countries, looking toward a "widening" of the EC before attempting to "deepen" it through further political integration.[7]

This position of the British prime minister was, in fact, the opposite of the view Jacques Delors was then taking, which was that the EC should strengthen itself internally, especially by achieving EMU, before expanding either to include the Alpine and Scandinavian countries of the European Free Trade Association (EFTA) or Poland, Hungary, and Czechoslovakia, which were being widely mentioned as potential candidates for EC membership.[8] Mitterrand decided that, to keep the Franco-German coalition together and to keep Germany from going off in adventuresome directions to the east, it was best to continue supporting Delors's strategy. Chancellor Kohl enthusiastically endorsed it as well, and Thatcher found herself again facing a bloc of the other three principal EC actors solidly arrayed against her. During the course of the early months of 1990, she lost her arguments regarding both German unification and the direction the EC should take.[9]

Political Union was placed on the EC agenda in the first half of 1990. The most important initiative was taken in March by Mitterrand and Kohl, who jointly sent a letter to the Irish prime minister, Charles Haughey, asking him to convene a special meeting of the European Council in April to consider ways to strengthen political cooperation among EC members. After the meeting was called, Belgium weighed in with a set of proposals designed to strengthen the powers of the European Parliament, improve decision-making efficiency throughout the EC, give greater recognition to the principle of subsidiarity,[10] and move toward a common foreign policy. Jacques Delors, after initially calling for more far-reaching reforms, endorsed these incremental approaches to political union prior to the April summit meeting.[11] Before the April summit, Mitterrand and Kohl sent a letter to the other heads of state and government calling for the European Council to set up a second IGC to examine Political Union. At the summit meeting the EC foreign ministers were asked to study this proposal and report back to the regular June 1990 summit.[12]

At the second Dublin summit the decision was reached to commission an IGC for political union, which would begin its work in December in parallel with the IGC for economic and monetary union. Britain, still under Margaret Thatcher's leadership, again resigned itself to working within the IGC framework to try to minimize the federalizing features of the treaty that would emerge.[13]

Negotiation of the treaty in the two IGCs went on during 1991, under the Council presidencies of Luxembourg and the Netherlands, whose governments sought to find compromises regarding the most troublesome issues. Central issues that were eventually hedged in the treaty were:

1. Whether to fulfill the European Parliament's (EP) maximalist objective of achieving coequal status with the Council of Ministers as one the two "chambers" of a bicameral legislative body
2. Whether the EC institutions would acquire competence in the defense policy sphere, rivaling the North Atlantic Treaty Organization, to which all of the EC members at the time, except neutral Ireland, belonged

3. Whether all member states should be committed to reaching the third stage of EMU
4. Whether all member states should be committed to the Social Charter that Delors had broached in 1988

On all of these issues Britain took a negative stance. It was joined on the defense issue by smaller countries, Ireland, Denmark, and Greece; on the powers of the EP by France; and on the third stage of EMU by Denmark, the Bundesbank, and a growing percentage of the German public, though not by the Kohl government. On the Social Charter Britain was isolated even from its usual ally, Denmark, as upward harmonization of EC social policy was a strong Danish commitment.

At the Maastricht summit in December 1991, the treaty was agreed upon by all 12 heads of state and government. Thatcher's successor as Prime Minister, John Major, successfully held out for weak language regarding an EC defense policy, for Britain's right to opt out of a single currency, and for the Social Charter to be separated from the main body of the treaty, applicable to the other 11 countries but not to Britain. On the issue of legislative powers, Italy and Germany were able to get more for the EP than Britain and France wanted, but less than "maximalists" in the EP itself were seeking.[14] (For a review of the changes, see the section of this chapter titled "The Institutional Framework Established by the TEU.")

Ratification

The Maastricht Treaty was signed by the 12 foreign ministers on February 7, 1992.[15] It was expected that ratification could be completed by the end of the year, so the European Union would come into being at the same time as the conclusion of Project 1992. However, for this to occur, it would be necessary for all 12 member states to ratify the treaty, a process that turned out to be a great deal more difficult than was originally anticipated. Although putting together the treaty had been a difficult process, it was made possible by the skills of the negotiators, many of whom were national-level civil servants with years of experience working together on a wide variety of EC issues. The governments that approved the treaties had all made concessions to one another. But the general public had little idea of what was emerging and certainly lacked an understanding of the intricacies.

Eight parliaments succeeded in ratifying the treaty by large majorities before the end of 1992: the parliaments of Belgium, Greece, Italy, Luxembourg, the Netherlands, Portugal, Spain, and Germany. In Ireland a referendum was held in June, and the treaty was ratified with a 69 percent yes vote. But the treaty received a severe referendum setback in Denmark earlier the same month when 50.7 percent of those voting judged the treaty unacceptable. This put the later ratifications under a cloud of uncertainty, although the 12 foreign ministers met a few days later and agreed that the process should go on, assuming that the Danes would reconsider. Meanwhile, in order to demonstrate strong support for the treaty, François Mitterrand declared that ratification in France, which would normally have been accomplished simply by a parliamentary vote, would likewise be subject to a referendum.

Mitterrand's decision proved to be a miscalculation. Left-wing and right-wing opponents of the treaty, weak in the French National Assembly, were able to stir up hostility to the treaty among the public. The issue of loss of sovereignty was played up by the Communists on the left and by the National Front on the right, which also played to fears of an opening of French borders to additional immigrants with the creation of an EC citizenship superseding French citizenship. Mitterrand could not claim that the barely positive outcome—a 51 percent yes vote—represented a re-sounding endorsement of the treaty. But in any event, France had ratified the treaty.

With the referendum surprises in Denmark and France, Euro-skepticism came out of retirement. The optimism of the late 1980s and early 1990s now seemed to have been misplaced. Important sectors of opinion in all three of the major countries were expressing disagreement with the treaty. Polls in Germany were revealing that 70 percent opposed giving up the DM in favor of a single EC currency.[16] In the British House of Commons, which had provided a 336 to 92 majority for the treaty in its preliminary reading in May, Conservative Party backbenchers were expressing growing opposition, while from the House of Lords Margaret Thatcher, now Baroness Thatcher, was lobbying for an antiratification vote in an attempt to force the Major government to reverse its position in support of the treaty.

Coincidentally, on July 1, 1992, Britain assumed the presidency of the Council for the latter half of the year. Britain's term of office had not passed its halfway point before the European monetary system experienced a crisis in September 1992. This had been brought on by the Bundesbank's effort to keep the DM strong by raising in-terest rates. Other central banks and governments were forced to follow suit in order not to have to devalue their currencies. Speculation that Britain would devalue the pound drove its value downward vis-à-vis the DM. Reluctant to slow British eco-nomic growth by raising interest rates, the Major government was forced to take the pound out of the exchange rate mechanism. Opposition to the treaty was given fur-ther stimulus by this evidence of the inability of the member states to coordinate their macroeconomic policies, a capacity that would have to be developed anew if EMU were to succeed (see Chapter 8).

By October it was clear that the treaty could not be ratified before the end of 1992. A special summit, called by Major to deal with the monetary crisis, was held in Birmingham, England, in mid-October. Addressing the problem of ratifying the treaty, the heads of state and government issued a statement designed to assure Britain and Denmark that the treaty would be interpreted in practice so as not to trample on the sovereign rights of the member states. Major took this assurance to the House of Commons and on November 4 gained a majority of three on a vote sup-porting Maastricht, although not formally ratifying the treaty.[17] Major promised that British ratification would await the outcome of the Danish process. In December, the regular summit under the British presidency was held in Edinburgh, and there a se-ries of assurances were made to help the Danish government get a successful result from a second ratification referendum. Among the concessions made were commit-ments (1) to increase the transparency of decision making, especially in the Council of

Ministers; (2) to give real meaning to the principle of "subsidiarity," that is, to make sure that the EC would not take on new policymaking functions in areas that are best left to the national, or even subnational, governments; and (3) immediately after ratification, to begin the process of negotiation leading to the membership in the EU of Denmark's Nordic neighbors, Sweden, Finland, and Norway. These concessions to Denmark were likely to make Prime Minister Major's task easier as well.

During the same month of December 1992, both houses of the German Parliament voted overwhelmingly to ratify the treaty, but a challenge to the treaty's constitutionality was lodged in the Federal Constitutional Court, which did not rule favorably until late October the next year. This made Germany the last member to ratify the treaty. Denmark held a second referendum in May 1993, with a favorable vote of 56.8 percent resulting in part from the fact that the Social Democrats, in opposition the previous June, were now in power and strongly supporting a yes vote, thus turning around many of their voters. This cleared the way for John Major to steer the treaty through the House of Commons, which he did with some shaky moments. In July, when Major made ratification of the treaty as approved in Maastricht a vote of confidence, the anti-Maastricht Conservatives voted with him rather than bring the government down. Their votes barely offset those of the Labour Party, where supporters of the treaty voted against it in an effort to win a vote of no confidence, making it clear that they were not voting against the treaty as such.[18]

THE INSTITUTIONAL FRAMEWORK ESTABLISHED BY THE TEU

The Maastricht Treaty, formally the Treaty on European Union (TEU), rewrote the Rome Treaty (as amended by the Single European Act [SEA]) in order to create the new European *Union*. It indicates what the 12 member states agreed to abide by in the future, including former commitments, going back to those that the original six had agreed to at Rome. The 12 members expected any new entrants to the European Union to commit themselves to these old and new undertakings as well. The name was changed to "European Union" because the first "pillar"—the EC—was joined to two others: the Common Foreign and Security Policy (CFSP) pillar, which brought the former European political cooperation (EPC) into the Rome Treaty framework; and the Justice and Home Affairs (JHA) pillar, which added new functions in the realm of internal security to the functions specified in the Rome Treaty and the SEA. Compared to the EC pillar, the CFSP and JHA pillars have a more intergovernmental structure of decision making and implementation, wherein the Commission and the European Parliament play very limited roles. The treaty summarizes the institutional characteristics of the EU to indicate continuity with the three "communities" that were established in the 1950s:

Article C

The Union shall be served by a single institutional framework which shall ensure the consistency and the continuity of the activities carried out in order to attain the objectives while reflecting and building upon the *acquis communautaire* [the legal powers the EC had already acquired]. The Union shall in particular ensure the consistency of its external activities as a whole in the context of its external relations, security, economic, and development policies. The Council and the Commission shall be responsible for ensuring such consistency. They shall ensure the implementation of these policies, each in accordance with its respective powers.[19]

The next article significantly refers to the heads of state and government and their agenda-setting role:

Article D

The European Council shall provide the Union with the necessary impetus for development and shall define the general political guidelines thereof.[20]

Although this is worded very generally, Article D established that the European Council is the body, meeting "at least twice per year,"[21] that would take new initiatives, setting what we have called the extraordinary agenda for the new EU just as it had been doing for the now imbedded EC.

Citizens of the member countries now became, in a limited sense at least, citizens of the EU. The most important right of EU citizens is to live and work in any of the 12 countries without restrictions that do not apply to citizens of those countries. They also have certain political rights. In any of the member countries where an EU citizen of another member country resides, he or she may vote in local elections or become a candidate for and serve in local elective office and may be a candidate for the European Parliament.[22] Regarding the EC pillar, the principle of "subsidiarity" was stated, and reinforced by the declaration emerging from the December 1992 Edinburgh summit in a new article inserted into the Rome Treaty:

Article 3b

In areas which do not fall within its exclusive competence, the Community shall take action, in accordance with the principle of subsidiarity, only if and in so far as the objectives of the proposed action cannot be sufficiently achieved by the Member States and can therefore, by reason of the scale or effects of the proposed action, be better achieved by the Community. Any action by the Community shall not go beyond what is necessary to achieve the objectives of this Treaty.[23]

The European parliament gained power in certain policy areas by virtue of a new procedure called "codecision." Under this procedure, if a legislative act adopted by the Council of Ministers is amended by the EP, the Council may adopt any such amendments by qualified majority vote (QMV), except in the case of amendments on which the Commission has rendered a negative opinion, in which case the Council may pass them only if unanimity is obtained. If the Council should fail to adopt an

EP amendment, or if the EP should reject the Council's "common position," a "conciliation committee" would be established consisting of members of both the Council and the EP. This committee would then attempt to arrive at a version of the bill that is acceptable to both the EP and the Council. If so, the EP could adopt it by a simple majority (majority of the votes cast) and the Council by QMV. If either body failed to do so, the bill would fail.[24] If no joint text emerged from the conciliation committee, the Council could pass its own version (common position) by qualified majority vote, so long as the EP did not reject the common position by absolute majority. Note that the Commission is left out of the process, at least formally, once the Council has forced the establishment of a conciliation committee.

Thus, the EP was given the power to reject legislation the Council has adopted, while an opportunity exists for the EP and the Council to work out a mutually acceptable legislative measure. But the kinds of legislation to which the codecision procedure applies are restricted. Included are "measures on the single market, education, culture, health and consumer protection, as well as programmes for the environment, research and trans-European networks."[25] Also extended was the range of matters for which QMV applies in Council of Ministers votes, which was in all of the above policy areas except for culture and research, where unanimity still was to apply.[26] The EP's legislative powers remained restricted in politically sensitive domains such as agricultural and industrial policies. However, the parliamentary body gained further powers: the power to approve international agreements reached by the EU if they touch on budgetary matters or areas where the EP has a legislative veto; the power to approve the membership of the Commission, including its president, at the beginning of its new term; and the power to deny admission of new countries to EU membership.[27] (see Chapter 6 for further discussion).

The powers of the European Court of Justice (ECJ) to interpret EC legislation expanded as the legislative powers expanded. But the ECJ was not explicitly given a role to play concerning the third pillar, Justice and Home Affairs. Concerning first-pillar matters, in which the ECJ does have jurisdiction, if the Commission finds that a member state has failed to comply with a prior judgment of the Court, it can recommend that a fine be paid, and the ECJ may impose it if it so chooses. This represented an additional leverage over the process of implementing EU law, if the Commission and the ECJ act together.[28] Another new institutional development was the creation of a Committee of the Regions, consisting of members appointed by the Council on the proposal of member governments. The Committee's powers are advisory only, but its creation gave recognition to the growing voice of regions[29] (see Chapter 6).

The EC pillar[30] that is outlined in the treaty represented a considerable expansion of the domain of EU power beyond that found in the Rome Treaty and the Single European Act. They included education, research, culture, public health, consumer protection, trans-European infrastructure networks, labor market policy, and industrial policy. In three additional areas—regional development, social assistance, and environmental policies—EU functions that existed prior to the treaty's ratification were considerably expanded without a corresponding increase in EP powers. One of the policy areas which was left protected by individual member states' veto option was taxation, seen by some governments as a non-negotiable element of national sovereignty.

Social policy was an area in which EU powers were at least potentially expanded. As defined in EU parlance, it refers primarily to conditions of work, remuneration, and rights of employment, including equal entitlements for employees of both genders and processes of labor–management relations. The Social Protocol to the treaty registered the fact that 11 of the member states, with the exclusion of the United Kingdom, separately contracted to coordinate their social policies through legislation that would follow the original Rome Treaty procedures, with some measures subject to QMV in the Council of Ministers and others requiring unanimity. In actual practice, subsequent progress on the legislation of social policy measures was slow, while the other members awaited the results of the next British election.[31] When the Labour Party came back to power in the May 1997 election, after 18 years of Conservative rule, Britain opted in to the Social Protocol, and it became a part of the regular EU treaties (see Chapter 10).[32]

The most important policy development of the EC pillar was, of course, the inclusion of Economic and Monetary Union, which will be discussed at greater length in Chapter 8. The principal institutional developments involved in EMU were to be the creation of the European Central Bank (ECB) and a single currency. In another special protocol to the treaty, Britain was conceded the right to opt out of these developments if it so wished. The European Central Bank would be responsible to the economic and finance ministers of the member states, who meet as the Council of Ministers when they deal with these subjects. This body, known as the Council of Economic and Finance Ministers (ECOFIN), would also have the responsibility of monitoring members' fiscal policies and could recommend action to be taken to reduce excessive budget deficits. These would not be legislative powers, and the broadened supervisory powers of ECOFIN would represent an extension of intergovernmentalism. But the creation of the European Central Bank would represent a supranational step, as it was specified that the bank must be independent of political controls, just as must the members' central banks, whose governors sit on the council of the ECB.[33]

The second pillar, foreign and security policy coordination, would be the province of the foreign ministers meeting as the Council of Ministers between summit meetings where the heads of state and government make foreign policy decisions on their own. General foreign policy decisions, whether made by heads or by the foreign ministers, require unanimous approval; but more detailed implementative decisions by the foreign ministers can be taken by QMV. On defense matters, the Western European Union (WEU) may implement CFSP decisions. Linked to the North Atlantic Treaty Organization (NATO) as well as to the EU, the WEU contained 10 EU members; 2 EU members were not members of WEU: Denmark and Ireland. The unanimity rule would continue to apply to WEU decisions[34] (see Chapter 12).

Justice and Home Affairs—the third pillar—involves efforts of interior ministers (called the home secretary in Britain) to join forces in dealing with problems of asylum, immigration, and other cross-border law enforcement matters, such as those involving fugitive criminals, terrorism, and drugs. In all of these areas national laws are enforced within national borders, and it would be up to the interior ministers to reach agreement on conventions that define new rules and procedures. Such conventions may be adopted by two-thirds vote in the Council of Ministers, unless the conventions themselves provide otherwise. Functions may be shifted from JHA to the EC pillar if the Council votes unanimously to do so[35] (see Chapter 11).

THE AFTERMATH OF MAASTRICHT

In the months that followed ratification of the Maastricht Treaty in October 1993, the EU members were preoccupied with the enlargement of the EU to include four new member countries: Austria, Finland, Norway, and Sweden. The European Union's membership was scheduled to grow on January 1, 1995, from 12 to 16, with the addition of these four relatively small and relatively rich "northern" members, meaning a change in the Council voting balance between small and large members and between richer northern and poorer southern members. As both a larger and a poorer southern member, Spain was reluctant to see an enlargement that would take away the ability of two larger members and one smaller member (e.g., Britain, Spain, and Portugal) to block qualified majorities, because the enlargement would increase the number of votes necessary for blocking from 23 to 27. This would mean that if three members opposed, all three must be larger members to have enough votes to block action if faced by a solid majority of the other members. Spain sought to keep the blocking minority at 23, which would mean raising the necessary votes for a qualified majority from 71 percent to 75 percent of the total votes.[36] Prime Minister Major sided with Spain's demand for a freezing of the blocking minority at 23 votes so that Britain's chances of stopping further deepening with the help of two other members would remain.

While the specific issues outstanding between the EU and the four prospective entrants were settled by mid-March 1994, including the issue of fishing rights in Norwegian waters, the dispute over voting remained. Jacques Delors searched for a face-saving compromise. Spain eventually came around to the majority position, and Britain accepted a compromise proposed by Delors in late March, so that negotiations with the four prospective entrants were favorably completed.[37] The compromise, reached in a meeting on the Greek island of Ionnina, was as follows: although the number of votes needed to block a majority would rise from 23 to 26 with four new members, if 23 to 25 votes were cast in the Council against a measure requiring a qualified majority, there would be a cooling-off period of unspecified length for a compromise to be sought.

Ratification of the treaties of accession by voters in the potential new member countries began with the vote in Austria in June 1994, which was held the same Sunday as most of the EP election polls. Against predictions that the vote would be very close, the Austrians gave two-thirds of their votes to the yes side. This was interpreted as a good sign for success in the fall referenda of the three Nordic candidates, where the polls were running very close.[38] As it turned out, Finnish voters ratified the treaty on October 16, 1994, with 57 percent in favor, as did Swedish voters, by a narrower margin (52 percent) on November 13; but ratification failed in Norway on November 28, when 52 percent voted against it.

In all three Nordic countries, the governing parties supported ratification, but all three governments had difficulties convincing their own supporters to vote for it. In Finland, farmers were concerned about loss of subsidies, which are higher than they are under CAP for EU farmers. But a majority of Finnish voters saw membership in the EU as a security hedge against the uncertain political changes going on in neighboring Russia.[39] The farming population is a smaller component of the Swedish electorate, but to their opposition was added urban votes, concerned both with the lower environmental standards and less generous welfare systems prevailing in most EU countries. These concerns, plus workers' fear of job losses, made the vote quite close in Sweden.[40] In Norway, the more generalized belief that Norway's special advantages in oil and fishing would be interfered with by membership in the EU added to the concerns of farmers to defeat Norwegian accession. The size of the negative vote and the reasons for it were similar to what they were in 1972, when the Norwegian voters had previously rejected membership.[41]

With the failure of the referendum in Norway, membership of the EU rose to 15 members instead of the anticipated 16. This meant that the total number of votes in the Council of Ministers would rise from 76 to 87 and a blocking minority would be 25 instead of 27.[42] The Ionnina compromise would not, however, either rise or decline in significance, because a negative coalition of two larger and one smaller member would still not be quite enough to block a qualified majority. As the members headed into still another round of treaty revision, it was clear that the compromise could only be a temporary one. Not only were there three more members, but steps were being taken that would potentially bring in a much larger number of EU members.

THE AMSTERDAM TREATY AND FURTHER EU ENLARGEMENT

At the beginning of the twenty-first century, the EU has embarked on two major projects that transcend all of its other preoccupations. These are (1) the incorporation of states to its east and south and the revision of its institutional design to accommodate a potentially much larger membership, and (2) Economic and Monetary Union. Both of these projects were launched in the 1990s and have taken up the energies of EU political leaders and innumerable technical specialists. Both will be dealt with at greater length in subsequent chapters. Here the focus will be on the most important developments that occurred in these two realms during the period from 1995 to 2002.

At the December 1994 summit in Essen steps were taken that would lead to enlargement of the EU into central and eastern Europe. Six countries already had agreements with the EU: Poland, the Czech Republic, Slovakia, Hungary, Bulgaria, and Romania. The prospect of absorbing these poorer countries and others in the region into the EU was a daunting one. It was beginning to dominate discussions of the upcoming 1996 intergovernmental conference to reexamine the Maastricht Treaty. The issues that would face that conference included how to alter the institutional framework to give more expression to the values of democracy, subsidiarity, openness, and decisional efficiency. There would be serious debates over whether to extend further the powers of the EP (urged by Germany to reduce the democratic deficit); whether to transfer more power from the national to the supranational level by moving second- and third-pillar decisions to the first pillar or by extending qualified majority voting in the Council of Ministers to more first-pillar areas of legislation. And of course the vexing issue of the method of calculating a qualified majority would have to be dealt with once again. These were all likely to be contentious issues, dividing governments in different ways, but also raising the possibility of bargaining tradeoffs.

Added to the complexities was the uncertainty as to whether enough member countries would meet the standards listed in the Maastricht Treaty for membership in the Economic and Monetary Union. High public deficits in the Mediterranean countries—Italy, Spain, Portugal, and Greece—made their eligibility for EMU problematic. Public skepticism about a single currency was running high in Britain and Germany, given the conservatism of most people about what they carry in their wallets and pocketbooks.[43] The prospect of enlargement to newly democratized and newly capitalist eastern countries made an already complicated set of questions a virtual nightmare.[44] Eastward enlargement in its own right made many people in regions of the existing EU fearful that CAP subsidies or cohesion funding would have to be cut back in order to provide equal benefits to new members. Governments of the Mediterranean countries resisted the idea of enlargement to include countries that were even poorer and less industrialized.

In the late summer of 1994 Prime Minister Edouard Balladur of France tentatively broached the idea of varying degrees of EU membership: an inner core of countries that could meet the EMU criteria by the late 1990s, presumably Germany, France, and the smaller northern countries; a middle rank that would include Britain and the Mediterranean countries, which could not or would not fully join the EMU but would take part in most of the domestic and foreign policies of the EU; and an outer circle, made up of the east European countries. Similar ideas were put forward by the CDU, Chancellor Kohl's party. Because of the way they were advanced, the proposals got a hostile reception from the countries not included in the "inner core," especially the larger ones, Britain, Italy, and Spain. But, in fact, the idea was not so far-fetched, considering that EU programs like the exchange rate mechanism, the Social Charter, and the Western European Union already had varying memberships, with more variation anticipated when Austria and the Scandinavian countries joined.[45] Though France and Germany withdrew their suggestions in the face of criticism, they had managed to focus attention on some of the dilemmas facing the EU in the years ahead—dilemmas that would still be there in the new century.

But at the same time the EU was holding out the prospect of membership, it was also specifying the conditions that would have to be satisfied in order for new members to be admitted to the Western European "club." These had previously been outlined by the European Council in its June 1993 Copenhagen summit. In order for the newly emerging democracies to be eligible for membership they had to have:

1. Functioning market economies
2. Respect for the rule of law and human rights, including the rights of minorities within their populations
3. The capacity to take on the entire range of EU laws and policies, the *acquis communautaire* that the existing members had accepted over the preceding four decades, including the customs union, the Common Agricultural Policy, the single-market laws and regulations, competition policies, social and environmental policies
4. A realistic chance (as well as the objective) of joining the EMU

Clearly, if the EU insisted on all of this, the length of time before even the first new members could be admitted would be greater than they were initially anticipating, and, in point of fact, the 1995 intake of Austria, Finland, and Sweden was not to be followed quickly with new admissions.

One reason for the delay was the belief that the integration of the existing 15 members still involved some unfinished business held over from the Maastricht Treaty. The proposals emanating from France and Germany for a two-speed Europe represented one solution to the problem. If a handful of member countries, consisting primarily of the original six members, could be the first to get EMU underway, setting up a single currency and a single central bank, and perhaps moving more rapidly toward a common social policy and even a common foreign policy, the others could join in these endeavors at a later point. Meanwhile, new members whose economies were not yet ready for extensive economic liberalization or for a single currency could join the slower track along with poorer EU members and those members, like Britain or Denmark, that were reluctant on political grounds to join the fast track. The British government was no more pleased with the two-speeds idea than it was with the idea of a federal Europe developing out of the European Union with all member countries moving on the fast track. Instead, Britain circulated the idea of "flexibility," otherwise known as "variable geometry." This would allow different EU programs to be signed on to by different sets of EU members. Britain could pick and choose which programs it wanted to participate in, and so could everyone else. By the time the intergovernmental conference (IGC) convened in 1996, the two-speeds proposal was a dead issue, partly because it was no longer clear which, if any, of the EU members would satisfy the "convergence criteria" for member of EMU. Almost none of the members would have been eligible if the criteria were not relaxed.

The Amsterdam summit in June 1997 reviewed the recommendations of the intergovernmental conference, which had been working during the previous year but had reached many of its final recommendations only after the British government changed hands in the May general elections.[46] The Labour government of Tony Blair opted in to the Social Protocol, but it pledged to wait until after the next election (presumed to take place in 2001 or 2002) before making a decision on EMU membership. Apart from these issues, Blair did not appear any more enthusiastic about European "federalism" than his predecessor had been. True to British traditions, he was comfortable with the EU as an organization with primarily intergovernmental decision making for the most important issues, including foreign and security policy issues, where he wanted Britain to play a more positive role than it had previously.[47]

What emerged as the Amsterdam Treaty, amending the previous treaties (Rome, SEA, and TEU), involved a very modest tinkering with the supranational institutions and the "EC pillar" and a more innovative approach to the intergovernmental second and third pillars. With enlargement firmly in mind, the IGC attempted to work out institutional changes that would make decision making less unwieldy. Proposals were made to reduce the number of commissioners to one from each country. The five largest members were naturally opposed, as they would each lose the right to name one of the two commissioners to which they had been entitled. Germany sought a change in the voting weights in the Council of Ministers to reflect its larger population since unification, but other members were not yet ready for this change. Modifications in qualified majority voting rules along the lines of the informal Ionnina compromise were suggested by larger and richer members concerned with the possible influx of many smaller and poorer members. The outlines of a package deal were there, but the incentive to realize it was not, perhaps because many of the member governments were not yet ready to focus seriously on the addition of a large handful of new members. So the necessary institutional adjustments were postponed until another IGC could be commissioned to reach agreement on these issues. The likelihood of new entrants in the first two years of the next decade was starting to appear unrealistic.

Progress was made on other dimensions by the IGC and at the Amsterdam summit. The European Parliament's membership was capped at 700, not a huge increase from its 626 members following the 1995 enlargement. Clearly, if it were to be honored when the future enlargement occured, then some or all of the existing members' delegations would have to be reduced. The complicated procedural rules for the roles of the EP, the Commission, and the Council in the legislative process were simplified somewhat by the near elimination of the cooperation procedure (introduced by the SEA) and modification of the codecision procedure (introduced by the TEU) to make the EP more of a coequal of the Council. There are now essentially three procedures: consultation (the Rome Treaty procedure, which gives the EP only a very weak role); codecision, which puts the EP in a good position to bargain with the Council over changes in legislative proposals; and the assent procedure, which gives the EP an up-or-down veto (see Chapter 6).

Significant increments of EU capability were achieved under the Amsterdam Treaty in the areas of second- and third-pillar functions, Common Foreign and Security Policy and Justice and Home Affairs. In the case of CFSP, decision-making rules were changed to allow the Council of Ministers to vote by qualified majority in adopting common strategies that could be implemented by taking common EU positions or joint actions, so long as there were no military or defense implications in the proposed measures. Unanimity would continue to apply for decisions with military or defense implications. Where unanimity applies, the Council may act without expressed approval by some members, so long as they abstain from voting against the proposal. This has been labeled "constructive abstention." Its implication is that some members take actions with the tacit acceptance of other members that do not join in the action.[48]

A very serious concern of the negotiators of the Amsterdam Treaty was the absence of a single EU voice in foreign and security policy. This was especially evident in the failure of the EU to reach a common approach to the war in Bosnia in the mid-1990s. Achieving a reasonably effective cease-fire and negotiation of terms in this multisided crisis eventually required the intervention of NATO, led by the United States. Accordingly, one of the most significant Amsterdam Treaty steps was taken with the creation of a new role for the Council's Secretary General, that of High Representative for Common Foreign and Security Policy. This was intended to be a high-profile role that would be filled by a prominent European public figure who could serve as a spokesperson for CFSP and recommend initiatives to the Council as well as taking charge of their implementation if so directed. The first occupant of the role, former Spanish foreign minister and NATO secretary general Javier Solana, appointed in 1999, closely fit the job description[49] (see Chapter 12).

Finally, JHA was divided in two: some politically sensitive policy areas were transferred to the EC pillar, while the remainder continued to be subject to strictly intergovernmental decisions and actions. The first group included movement of persons over external borders into the EU for purposes of asylum or immigration; combating drug addiction; combating fraud on an international scale; and judicial cooperation on civil matters (e.g., white-collar crimes). Conversion of these areas of jurisdiction to the first pillar means that the Commission and the EP participate along with the Council in formulating and adopting EU laws, and the ECJ may rule on the validity of acts of the institutions and of member governments in these areas. The set of matters remaining within the third pillar were deemed by the governments to touch too closely on sovereignty to give up exclusive control. These include judicial cooperation on criminal matters, customs cooperation to combat crimes involving cross-border traffic, and police cooperation to prevent terrorism and other serious international crimes[50] (see Chapter 12).

During the remaining years of the decade, the principal preoccupation of the European Union and its members was the formation of Economic and Monetary Union, whose third stage was set to begin on January 1, 1999 (see Chapter 8). The Maastricht Treaty had set forth the time table and the criteria for conversion from a country's national currency to the single currency (subsequently called the "euro") and for the creation of the European Central Bank (ECB). Public attention during the two years between the Amsterdam summit and the mid-1998 decision regarding who was to be eligible focused on the criteria used to judge eligibility and the progress toward meeting them that the various would-be EMU members were making. Of the criteria the most important "acid test" for membership was the requirement that an EU member country's annual government deficit for the year 1997 not exceed 3 percent of its gross domestic product (GDP).

In fact, by the beginning of 1998, only one of the applicant countries, Greece, was clearly too far above the 3 percent mark to be considered a realistic candidate. Other applicants for EMU membership had brought their deficits down to the 3 percent level or below. Three countries—Denmark, Sweden, and the United Kingdom—had made it clear that they would not join in the single currency, whether or not they met the criteria. Eleven of the remaining countries were deemed eligible, even though most of them did not satisfy a second criterion, that the cumulative government debt should not exceed 60 percent of GDP. Greece became the twelfth member of EMU on January 1, 2001. At the beginning of 2002, bills and coins of these individual members were replaced with the new currency, the euro (see Chapter 8).

Another major set of uncertainties concerning the EU's future involved the 13 central, eastern, and southern European countries waiting to join. All of these applicants have been assessed according to economic and political criteria such as those applied (although less thoroughly) to Greece, Spain, and Portugal in the 1980s. As in the 1980s, candidates for entry are poor countries relative to existing members and are in most cases only recently democratized. The European Union has shown its capacity for helping such countries achieve economic growth and modernization. But unlike earlier enlargements, the magnitude of the anticipated enlargement is daunting. During the 1990s the projected dates for the first entrants moved to the next decade. (Chapter 7 will address the circumstances and issues of EU enlargement.)

An associated problem involves the movement of persons from east to west and from south to north in Europe. The applicant countries of eastern Europe are themselves experiencing an influx of immigrants from the former Soviet Union, many of whom continue westward into the current EU countries, joined by others from the poorer regions of the applicant countries, while additional flows come from countries on the Mediterranean and Adriatic shores to the south and east of the EU members. This has produced considerable strife within the member countries that are the first to receive the immigrant wave, especially Germany and Austria on the EU's eastern flank and France and Italy on its southern side. The domestic politics of these countries have been affected, with normal voting patterns altered and existing political coalitions threatened by rising parties of the extreme right.

The most striking case has been Austria, where, in September 1999, the far-right Freedom Party led by Jorg Haider, governor of the province of Carinthia in southern Austria, for the first time won enough seats to be seriously considered for membership in the governing coalition. When the Freedom Party was brought into the Austrian government in early 2000, even though Haider stayed out, it produced a strong reaction elsewhere in the EU, especially in France and Belgium, whose governments fear the rise of similar right-wing anti-immigrant parties. EU members responded by informally agreeing not to hold bilateral meetings with the new Austrian government, in effect demonstrating that they consider the government illegitimate by EU standards. This was not an official EU action, and it was met with protests from the Austrian government. Gradually, as it was demonstrated that the new government had not changed Austria's commitments to existing EU norms and policies, the situation has eased. But it shows that the political spillover of the EU's policies toward its eastern neighbors cannot be taken for granted while efforts are made to soften economic impacts.[51] The French legislative and presidential elections of 2002 provided another example of the potency of the immigration issue for upsetting normal electoral politics (see Chapter 1).

By the year 2000 divisions among the governments of the member states were becoming more evident as considerations of institutional change followed closely upon tensions over EMU eligibility and prospects for enlargement. A certain amount of solidarity could be discerned among the original six members, which constituted a sort of inner core of members intent on developing their own pattern of "closer cooperation," whatever exceptions might have to be made for later arrivals wishing to preserve what they considered vital sovereign rights.[52]

The Treaty of Nice

During the second week in December 2000 the EU heads of state and government met as the European Council in the city of Nice, France. Although the summit had several matters on its agenda, the largest amount of its time was taken up with the attempt to pick up where the Amsterdam Treaty had ended and make the EU institutions more "efficient," that is, to change the institutional decision-making process before the countries of central, eastern, and southern Europe joined the EU. The summit lasted more than four days, a record length, and produced a package of institutional changes that would require ratification by all 15 member states.[53]

The Nice Treaty changes come into effect on January 1, 2005, perhaps coinciding with the admission of the first applicant countries.[54] Among the most important institutional changes are those that concentrate on the decision-making powers of the Council of Ministers. The most obvious way of making the Council's decisions more efficient would be to do away with the unanimity rule for decisions where it applied and replace it with qualified majority voting, so that no single member, old or new, would be in a position to block decisions desired by all the other members. With the addition of new members the chances of such vetoes being wielded would increase. At the time approximately 80 percent of treaty articles involved Council decisions by QMV; but the remaining 20 percent, including some of the most important decisions, required unanimity. The summit managed to reduce this percentage to about 10 percent.[55] QMV now will apply to approval of trade negotiations on services and on some immigration and asylum issues, but France insisted on continuance of the veto for culture and education, and Britain wanted the veto for taxation and social security issues.[56] Outside of the legislative field, QMV replaced unanimity in the election by member governments of the Commission President and the Secretary General of the Council Secretariat, the latter of whom, since the ratification of the Amsterdam Treaty, had become the High Representative for foreign and security policy.

Voting weights in the Council of Ministers were altered to give the larger current members a greater voting weight relative to smaller members (see Table 7.3). For example, Luxembourg's increase is to be from 2 to 4 votes (a 100 percent increase), while Britain's is from 10 to 29 votes (an increase of 190 percent). However, because of French resistance, Germany's total will remain equal to that of the other three larger countries (after an identical 190 percent increase), even though its population is considerably larger since reunification than it was when the old weights were set.[57] The total voting weights of the Netherlands, Belgium, and Luxembourg, were arranged to equal that of each of the larger members. The Netherlands was given one more vote than Belgium, which was compensated by the decision that future official meetings of the European Council would be held in Brussels (see Chapter 6).

In order to compensate Germany it was agreed that any of the larger countries may question a decision made by QMV, which will not be adopted unless countries totaling 62 percent of the total EU population support it; so Germany plus two of the next three largest states could together block it. To compensate the small states for their lesser share in decision making, a decision must also have the support of a majority of countries, regardless of their populations. This means that the application of QMV should generally be more difficult than it had been, although not so much so as in cases where unanimity will still apply. As further compensation to the smaller members, the number of commissioners assigned to each of the five largest current members would be reduced from two to one with the beginning of a new Commission, January 1, 2005. Whenever the total membership reaches 27, the Commission size will be fixed at an unspecified figure, but at a figure lower than 27, necessitating a rotation system of some sort.[58] The capacity of the Commission President to coordinate Commission action was strengthened by a freer hand in appointing enough Commission vice presidents to allow effective coordination of a larger number of member states.[59]

The idea of "closer" or "enhanced" cooperation, which had come up in the Amsterdam Treaty negotiations, was accepted in order to give the enlarged EU more flexibility without setting up sharply separate tiers of members. It was agreed that any group of eight or more member countries could move ahead more rapidly with integration in certain policy areas—for example, environmental policy, justice and home affairs, or taxation. Such arrangements could be authorized by QMV, since a unanimity rule would make its adoption highly unlikely.[60] Whereas the Conservative British government of John Major had opposed the idea at the time of the Amsterdam negotiations, it was accepted in principle by Tony Blair, whose vision of EU foreign policy included a leading role for Britain, while more neutralist members might opt out of future foreign policy coordination. However, the concept of enhanced cooperation remains vague and ill-defined. Like other features of the Nice Treaty, it was adopted in anticipation of the coming accession to EU membership of countries that have been experiencing afresh the opportunities and pitfalls of the rule of law and of democratic political institutions and market economies. Would the second-class status of these new entrants last only for a brief interim period, or would it become fixed and permanent as longer-standing members set themselves up as participants in an enhanced and restrictive higher order of membership?[61]

On June 7, 2001, Irish voters rejected ratification of the Nice Treaty in a referendum vote for which only 35 percent of the electorate turned out (as opposed to 62 percent in the Irish ratification of the Amsterdam Treaty). In spite of the substantial economic benefits Ireland has received from the EU, of which Irish voters are fully aware, 54 percent of those voting voted no. This uncertainty about when the treaty would come into effect ended when 63 percent voted yes in a second Irish referendum on October 19, 2002.

Annexed to the Nice Treaty when it was signed by the 15 foreign ministers in February 2001 was a "Declaration on the Future of the European Union." The language of the Declaration was vague, but since 1999 the member governments had been committed to agreement on an EU Charter of Fundamental Rights, a document which might well accompany a "Constitution for the European Union." It was speculated that at least some of the heads at Nice had such a Constitution in mind. Opinion leaders of more advanced integrationist ideas took it as a strong signal in that direction, encouraged by statements made by German leaders, especially Foreign Minister Joschka Fischer.[62] A year later, at the Laeken summit of December 2001, it was decided that a convention would be set up to recommend a "Constitutional Treaty for Europe." It was agreed that former French president Valery Giscard d'Estaing would chair the convention. The convention would comprise representatives of the 15 member states and 13 applicants, for a total of 104 convention delegates. Its task would be to draft a treaty which would be closer to a definitive constitution of the EU, more federalist than the original Rome Treaty, plus its amending treaties. But Giscard's influence, backed by the member governments, could mean enhanced intergovernmental features as well.

Some have likened the convention to that held at Philadelphia in 1787 that formulated the U.S. Constitution. The largest category of delegates are members of legislative bodies, the European Parliament (16 delegates) and national parliaments (56 delegates), while the 28 member and candidate governments have 28. Two former prime ministers, Jean-Luc Dehaene of Belgium and Giuliano Amato of Italy, assist Giscard d'Estaing in chairing the convention. Most basically, it will decide whether the current treaties of the European Union should give way to a constitution, which might be federal in spirit if not in name.[63] Another intergovernmental conference, called by a European Council meeting, at earliest in June 2003, will follow the convention to work out a final draft for agreement by the European Council, the procedure employed in earlier treaty revisions. Ratification by the candidate countries will follow, and the candidate countries are expected to join in 2004.

An issue of considerable significance is whether the existing rotating presidency of the Council should be maintained or replaced, either (1) with a single president, who might be expected, however chosen, to transcend the influence of the individual governments; or (2) with a collective presidency of a mixture of large and small state members, changing every $2\frac{1}{2}$ years (a Swedish proposal). Either might make for greater continuity in Council, including European Council policies, than is true of the existing six-month rotation system, but it would leave coordination of an eventual 27 or more members just as difficult. The first proposal, supported by three of the larger current members' leaders—French President Jacques Chirac, British Prime Minister Tony Blair, and Spanish Prime Minister Jose Maria Aznar, all considered EU heavyweights—would bring about greater change, but whether it would be in the expected direction is hard to say. An elected president of the Council would very likely become a rival to the Commission president, further reducing the effectiveness of the Commission in the EU as a whole.[64] The convention has dealt with high stakes.

CONCLUSION

In this chapter we have related how the two main elements of the eventual Maastricht Treaty—EMU and Political Union—were placed on the extraordinary agenda, through the coordinated efforts of Commission president Jacques Delors, German chancellor Helmut Kohl, and French president Francois Mitterrand, with British prime minister Margaret Thatcher opposing most of the way until her political demise in November 1990. The treaty agreed on at Maastricht in December 1991 was delivered a setback in the Danish and French referenda of mid-1992, then, in December 1992, was adjusted in such a way as to reinforce the principles of subsidiarity and openness. This helped ratification succeed in Denmark and Britain, so the treaty could come into effect before the end of 1993.

A further enlargement of the EU occurred in 1995 with the inclusion of Austria, Finland, and Sweden, but not Norway, whose voters failed to ratify the accession treaty. By the end of 1994 EU leaders were turning their attention to the questions of whether and when to admit new members from central and eastern Europe and the Mediterranean area. The Amsterdam summit of 1997 was held with the purpose of revising EU institutions to make it easier to absorb what could be a dozen new members in the near future. The treaty fell short of the needed adjustments, and a further effort had to be made at Nice in 2000, with still another treaty revision projected for 2004, the year tentatively set for the first central and eastern European countries to enter. Meanwhile, Economic and Monetary Union was launched in 1998–1999 with what are today 12 members.

During the decade since the ratification of the Maastricht Treaty, the European Union took on a much heavier extraordinary agenda than it had in the 1980s, including much of the implementation of the Single European Act, Economic and Monetary Union, preparation for enlargement, and an enhanced role in world trade and in relations with countries to its east and south, many of which became candidates for membership. But the institutions for carrying out this heavier workload had not changed fundamentally from those that were in place at the beginning of the decade, and improvement of the institutions remained at the head of the extraordinary agenda.

ENDNOTES

1. Margaret Thatcher, *The Downing Street Years* (New York: HarperCollins, 1993), pp. 740–758.
2. Ibid., p. 752. Cf. Geoffrey Howe, "The Triumph and Tragedy of the Thatcher Years," *Financial Times*, October 23–24, 1993, Section 2, p. 7. Creating an IGC has become the principal means by which the European Council puts negotiation of a major treaty-revising package such as the SEA or the TEU on the extraordinary agenda. See Mary Troy Johnston, *The European Council: Gatekeeper of the European Community* (Boulder, Colo.: Westview Press, 1994), p. xiii.

3. Neill Nugent, "The Deepening and Widening of the European Community: Recent Evolution, Maastricht, and Beyond," *Journal of Common Market Studies* 30 (September 1992): 313.

4. Thatcher, *The Downing Street Years*, pp. 688–726.

5. Howe, "The Triumph and Tragedy," p. 7.

6. Philip Norton, "The Conservative Party from Thatcher to Major," in Anthony King, et al., *Britain at the Polls* (Chatham, N.J.: Chatham House, 1993), pp. 29–59.

7. Thatcher, *The Downing Street Years*, pp. 796–798.

8. Peter Ludlow, "The Politics and Policies of the European Community in 1989," in Ludlow, et al., eds., *The Annual Review of European Community Affairs 1990* (London: Brassey's for the Centre for European Policy Studies, 1991), p. xlvi.

9. Thatcher, *The Downing Street Years*, pp. 812–815.

10. Subsidiarity is the principle that only those powers should be exercised at the EU level that cannot be exercised as effectively at the national or subnational level.

11. Peter Ludlow, "Reshaping Europe: The Origins of the Intergovernmental Conferences and the Emergence of a New European Political Architecture," in Ludlow, Jorgen Mortensen, and Jacques Pelkmans, eds., *The Annual Review of European Community Affairs 1991*, pp. 400–406. A similar incrementalist approach was presented to the EP in March 1990 by rapporteur David Martin, British Labour Party MEP, but there was division within the EP between those following Martin's strategy and others, mainly Christian Democrats, seeking a more far-reaching leap to Euro-federalism (Ibid., pp. 401–402). However, Richard Corbett argues that the Martin report influenced the shape of the Belgian memorandum, and therefore the shape of the subsequent IGC discussions. Richard Corbett, "The Intergovernmental Conference on Political Union," *Journal of Common Market Studies* 30 (September 1992): 274.

12. Corbett, loc. cit.

13. Ludlow, "Reshaping Europe," pp. 414–415.

14. For a discussion of the issues and government positions in the making of the TEU, see Andrew Moravcsik, *The Choice for Europe: Social Purpose and State Power from Messina to Maastricht* (Ithaca, N.Y.: Cornell University Press, 1998), chap. 6.

15. A useful summary of the events covered in the remainder of this section is found in Richard Corbett, "Governance and Institutional Developments," *Journal of Common Market Studies* 31 (August 1993): 27–50.

16. Walter Goldstein, "Europe after Maastricht," *Foreign Affairs* 71 (Winter 1992/93): 117–132.

17. David Baker, Andrew Gamble, and Steve Ludlam, "Whips or Scorpions? The Maastricht Vote and the Conservative Party," *Parliamentary Affairs* 46 (April, 1993): 151–166.

18. *The Economist*, July 31, 1993, pp. 19–21; Philip Norton, "The Conservative Party: 'In Office but Not in Power,'" in Anthony King, ed., *New Labour Triumphs: Britain at the Polls* (Chatham, N.J.: Chatham House, 1998), pp. 75–112.

19. Council and Commission of the European Communities, *Treaty on European Union* (Luxembourg: Office for Official Publications of the European Communities, 1992), p. 8.

20. Ibid., p. 8.

21. Ibid.

22. Ibid., pp. 15–16.

23. Ibid., pp. 13–14.

24. Ibid., pp. 76–78.

25. *The Economist*, October 17, 1992, p. 60. "Trans-European networks" refers to "transport, telecommunications and energy infrastructures." *Treaty on European Union*, p. 51.

26. *Treaty on European Union*, pp. 49, 51.

27. Juliet Lodge, "EC Policymaking: Institutional Dynamics," in Lodge, ed., *The European Community and the Challenge of the Future* (New York: St. Martin's Press, 1993), p. 32.

28. *Treaty on European Union*, p. 69.

29. Ibid., p. 82.

30. Although the discussion in this paragraph refers to the provisions of the treaty applying to the EC pillar, the initials EU are used so that it will be clear we are referring to the *post-Maastricht* powers of the *European Union*.

31. Laura Cram, *Policy-Making in the EU: Conceptual Lenses and the Integration Process* (London: Routledge, 1997), pp. 54–55.
32. Desmond Dinan, *Ever Closer Union: An Introduction to European Integration*, 2d ed. (Boulder, Colo.: Lynne Rienner, 1999), pp. 175, 428.
33. *The Economist*, October 17, 1992, p. 61.
34. *Treaty on European Union*, pp. 123–129.
35. Ibid., pp. 131–135.
36. *The Economist*, March 12, 1994, pp. 53–54. Under the rules applying to 12 members, with varying numbers of votes at their disposal depending on the country's size, the total number of votes was 76, and the requisite number for a qualified majority was 54, which could not be attained if 23 or more votes were lined up on the negative side of a motion. With 16 members, the total would be 90, and the qualified majority 64, so 27 negative votes would be needed to prevent a qualified majority.
37. *The Economist*, June 18, 1994, pp. 55–57.
38. *Financial Times*, October 11, 1994, p. 16.
39. Ibid., November 8, 1994, p. 2; November 15, 1994, p. 17.
40. Ibid., November 30, 1994, p. 2.
41. Ibid., December 5, 1994, p. 2.
42. David Galloway, *The Treaty of Nice and Beyond: Realities and Illusions of Power in the EU* (Sheffield: Sheffield Academic Press, 2001), Box 4.2, p. 70.
43. *Financial Times*, September 27, 1994, p. 3.
44. Ibid., September 3, 1994, p. 3; September 5, 1994, p. 3.
45. Ibid., December 12, 1994, pp. 1–2.
46. Andrew Moravcsik and Kalypso Nicolaidis, "Explaining the Treaty of Amsterdam: Interests, Influence, Institutions," *Journal of Common Market Studies* 37 (March 1999): 59–85.
47. Ibid., 68.
48. Desmond Dinan, *Encyclopedia of the European Union*, updated edition (Boulder, Colo.: Lynne Rienner, 2000), pp. 84–85.
49. Anthony Forster and William Wallace, "Common Foreign and Security Policy: From Shadow to Substance?" in Helen Wallace and William Wallace, eds., *Policy-Making in the European Union*, 4th ed. (Oxford: Oxford University Press, 2000), p. 484.
50. Monica den Boer and William Wallace, "Justice and Home Affairs: Integration through Intergovernmentalism?" in Wallace and Wallace, eds., *Policy-Making in the European Union*, pp. 513–514.
51. *Financial Times*, December 7, 2000, special section on Austria.
52. Desmond Dinan and Sophie Vanhoonacker, "IGC 2000 Watch (Part 2): The Opening Round," *ECSA Review* 13 (Summer 2000): 8.
53. *The Economist*, December 16, 2000, pp. 25–28.
54. Galloway, *The Treaty of Nice*, p. 82.
55. *Financial Times*, December 12, 2000, p. 2.
56. *The Economist*, December 16, 2000, p. 2.
57. Desmond Dinan and Sophie Vanhoonacker, "IGC 2000 Watch (Part 3): Pre- and Post-Nice," *ECSA Review* 13 (Fall 2000): 1.
58. Galloway, *The Treaty of Nice*, pp. 80–81.
59. Ibid., p. 50.
60. Eric Philippart, "The New Provisions for 'Closer Cooperation'? A Call for Prudent Politics," *ECSA Review* 14 (Spring 2001): 6–7.
61. George A. Bermann, "Law in an Enlarged European Union," *EUSA* (formerly *ECSA*) *Review* 14 (Summer 2001): 1–6.
62. Bruno de Witte, "Apres Nice: Time for a European Constitution?" *ECSA Review* 14 (Spring 2001): 10–11.
63. *Financial Times*, February 25, 2002, p. 14; June 10, 2002, p. 13.
64. *Financial Times*, June 10, 2001, p. 2.

6

Institutional Dynamics in the European Union

This chapter will examine the institutions of the European Union (EU) in terms of how they are structured and the processes by which decisions are reached on the ordinary and extraordinary agendas. We have distinguished the two agendas from one another in terms of the plan of action that was set by the Rome Treaty and its modifications (the ordinary agenda) and the agenda for the modifications of the treaty themselves (the extraordinary agenda). Most of the formal treaty modifications have been brought together in the four packages of amendments: the Single European Act (SEA), the Maastricht Treaty on European Union (TEU), the Amsterdam Treaty, and the Nice Treaty. Other basic changes have been less formal and have been made on an ad hoc basis, such as the establishment in the 1970s of European Political Co-operation (Chapter 3) and of the European Monetary System (Chapter 4). We discussed agenda setting for the main amendment packages in Chapter 4 (SEA) and Chapter 5 (TEU, Amsterdam, and Nice treaties), where we placed emphasis on the role of the heads of state and government in the European Council and the president of the Commission as principal actors in the process of setting the extraordinary agenda. In this chapter we will look at the institutions themselves and the functions they perform. We will start with the distinction between "the governments," organized collectively as the European Council and the Council of Ministers, and the "first-pillar institutions," namely, the Commission, the European Court of Justice (ECJ), and the European Parliament (EP). Regarding the latter three, we will make the traditional distinction between executive, judicial, and legislative functions. The chapter concludes with evaluation of the institutions by democratic standards. Figure 6.1 distinguishes between extraordinary and ordinary agenda setting in European institutions and the respective roles the institutions play.

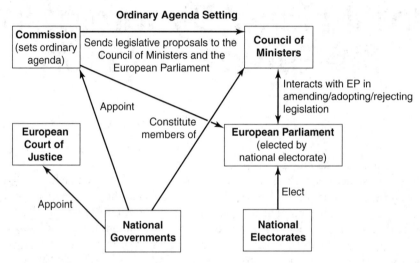

FIGURE 6.1   Agenda Setting in European Union Institutions

SOURCE: Adapted from BBC (http://news.bbc.co.uk/hi/english/static/in_depth/europe/2001/ inside_europe/eu_institutions/flow_chart.stm)

THE GOVERNMENTS

The European Council

The term "council" is often used to refer generally to any of the bodies in which members of the 15 EU governments meet to decide issues of common policy concern. By "members" we mean heads of state and government and cabinet ministers. There are many more bodies of national civil servants and technical advisers from the 15 governments that meet together for various EU advisory, supervisory, and administrative purposes, but the principal policy decisions that governments make collectively are made by the councils. The most important of these is the European Council—the summit meetings of heads of state and government. The principal focus of the European Council is the extraordinary agenda. Since the Maastricht Treaty, the other councils have collectively been called the Council of the European Union, but we will use the older, but still commonly used, Council of Ministers, in referring to them. Interpretation of the roles played by the governments and their councils will follow the theoretical perspective we have referred to as intergovernmentalism (see Chapter 2).

Because of its unique role and overriding importance, the European Council should be considered separately from the other councils, all the more so because it has become an institution in its own right and has been since the decision at the Paris summit of December 1974 determined that the heads of state and government would meet three times a year. Simon Bulmer and Wolfgang Wessels have discussed the reasons why institutionalized summit meetings came into being in the 1970s.[1] The "institutional inertia" of the European Community (EC) itself, especially the dead-locks occurring in the Council of Ministers, made it necessary for the heads to step in with the authority to achieve breakthroughs. Beginning with the Hague summit of December 1969, the heads had been meeting, though not on a regular basis, in part to take pressure off their foreign ministers who were doing double duty in the foreign policy realm and partly to try out new ideas for European integration, such as Economic and Monetary Union (EMU) and political cooperation.[2]

The European Council is more than simply the most comprehensive and power-ful of the councils established under the Rome Treaty. Initially, the responsibilities of the Council of Ministers were divided between the General Affairs Council comprising the foreign ministers of member states and the various functionally specialized councils (e.g., budget, agriculture, environment) that emerged after 1957. Most of these were already established when the European Council held its first meeting in 1975. By 1989, there were 89 council meetings, of which only three were meetings of the European Council. From 1975 on, the leadership role that the foreign ministers attempted to play vis-à-vis their ministerial counterparts has been subordinated to that of the heads of state and government in the European Council.[3]

The Single European Act was the first EC "constitutional" source to give any legal recognition to the European Council, which it did in a two-sentence reference to its composition.[4] By that time the European Council had assumed a leadership role for the EC that exceeded that of the Commission and transcended that of the General Affairs Council. According to Peter Ludlow:

> The conclusions of European Council meetings are, together with the Treaties, the most authoritative guide to the EC's evolving agenda. They usually include a list of tasks to be carried out by the Commission and/or the Council, as well as a definition of principles in the policy areas discussed at the Council in question.[5]

As a body of such transcendent importance, it should properly be treated separately from the Council of Ministers wearing their various hats.

When originally established, the European Council was to meet three times per year. Usually two of the three meetings were located in cities of the countries holding the presidency of the Council of Ministers, which rotated every 6 months in alphabetical order based on the official names of the states in their own languages. The third meeting was usually held in Brussels. The Single European Act reduced the number of prescribed annual meetings from three to two, one held at the end of each of the year's two 6-month presidencies in a city of the country having that status. However, the press of business has been such that in some years a third and even a fourth European Council meeting has been held. In fact, it became common for the presidency during the first 6 months of the year to schedule a mini-summit to discuss common problems halfway through its term, and an end-of-term summit to deal with the most important issues requiring more formal commitments by the heads of state and government. Thus, in the latter half of 2001, the Belgian presidency hosted a mini-summit in Ghent in October to discuss common positions on "post-September 11" terrorism and how to deal with the troubling economic conditions.[6] Then, in December, in Laeken, a suburb of Brussels, the European Council agreed to the holding of a constitutional convention, which would produce a draft European Union constitution for the EU, to be presented to the heads at a meeting of the European Council in late 2003, before being presented, with instructions by the heads, to a 2003–2004 intergovernmental conference (IGC). The IGC would then work on a draft treaty revision, possibly an EU constitution, for approval by the European Council and ultimate ratification by the member states.[7]

Formal sessions of the European Council are restricted to two representatives from each member state: in most cases the head of state or government and the foreign minister (see Chapter 1). Also attending are the president of the Commission and one other Commissioner. Interpreters are, of course, present, as well as a very restricted number of national and European civil servants, the latter from the Council and Commission secretariats.[8] But, overall, the summits have become well-attended events, considering the pervasive presence of the media.

Neill Nugent has listed the main sources of items on the European Council's agenda.[9] At all summit meetings the heads of state and government discuss the state of the EU economy. This may result in a very general statement of purpose on the part of the member states to work harder to improve economic conditions, and in that sense it may add some urgency to actions on the separate agendas of the member governments. There may be ordinary agenda matters over which the Council of Ministers is deadlocked, resolution of which requires an appeal to the summit. Nugent gives the examples of budgetary and Common Agricultural Policy (CAP) deadlocks that cropped up frequently in the 1980s and could only be resolved by the heads. In the 1980s the observation was commonly made that resolving deadlocks produced at the lower level was the primary function the heads of state and government performed.[10] This was even true in cases where qualified majority voting had applied in the Council of Ministers. If the minister of a particular country objects strongly enough on a matter of urgency, rather than voting on the matter, the ministers might well refer it to the summit. Of course, the fact that a particular matter comes within the purview of the European Council does not necessarily mean that the heads will be able to reach agreement.

A more severe instance of disagreement helped to produce deadlock at the March 2003 meeting of the European Council in Brussels, at which the heads were scheduled to renew their commitment to economic reform. Prior to the summit the EU had split into two blocs opposing and supporting the American intention to initiate war with Iraq. The leaders of France, Germany and Belgium were at odds with those of the United Kingdom and Spain. The summit witnessed a "filibuster" by Italian Prime Minister Silvio Berlusconi, which barely masked the fact that the heads on both sides were not ready for a serious discussion of economics. Less divisive international crises can become extraordinary agenda items for the summit because they are major preoccupations of the heads of state and government individually, or because they defy the boundary line between the Maastricht first-pillar responsibilities of the EC and the second pillar of foreign and security policies (see Chapter 6). The heads are likely, in such situations, to instruct their foreign ministers in the General Affairs Council to agree upon measures to be taken. In fact, in a newly developing crisis, the foreign ministers may meet one or more times before the heads can get together. They may also delegate responsibility or signal their general intent to the Commission that will enable the latter to take steps on its own, as when responsibility for aid to post–Cold War central European countries was given to the Commission in December 1989. At the following summit meeting the heads will then review the action taken and mandate further action by the other bodies as it deems necessary.

There are three institutional sources of summit agenda items. The most frequent initiator is the Commission, which is represented by its president in European Council meetings and can make recommendations to the heads of state and government regarding matters that it considers to be within its sphere of responsibility. Among the most important examples of extraordinary agenda items initiated by the Commission are EMU and the Social Charter proposed by Jacques Delors and accepted onto the larger EC agenda by the heads at summits in 1988 and 1989, respectively. Others have had important Commission input at the initiating stage. As seen in Chapter 4, Commission president Roy Jenkins played an important role alongside Chancellor Schmidt in getting the European Monetary System to the agenda in 1978.

Other extraordinary agenda-setting initiatives have come from the country holding the Council presidency; for example, in early 1984 France pushed for the European Council to take concrete steps to advance the goal of European Union, which resulted in the decision at the June 1984 Fontainebleau summit to commission an intergovernmental committee (the Dooge committee) to study proposals for political union and make recommendations. And finally, the European Council itself sets its own extraordinary agenda by creating special intergovernmental bodies to examine issues and report back its recommendations, like the intergovernmental conference which the December 2000 Nice summit scheduled to follow the 2002–2003 constitutional convention.

The centrality of the European Council concerning the EU's extraordinary agenda does not rule out the capacity of the normal Rome Treaty institutions to take on new responsibilities in the wake of fast-moving events such as those that occurred in Europe beginning in 1989. These have especially involved the Commission and the Council of Ministers, both having to take action during the time when the European Council is not in session, dealing especially with the economic problems of the central and eastern European states.[11] The role of the Commission has been to conduct trade and assistance negotiations with these states and to propose action to be taken by either the foreign ministers or the heads of state and government, depending on who is meeting next. This suggests that the *existence* of the European Council as a body that will meet later to approve or modify the actions taken by the other bodies in between its meetings has lessened the danger of inaction on the part of those bodies in the face of unanticipated situations that demand immediate responses.

From the standpoint of intergovernmentalist theory, the role of the European Council has been to guard elements of national sovereignty, while delegating responsibility to the Council of Ministers and the Commission. This does not preclude the Commission and the other supranational bodies from interpreting the authority granted them in ways that will increase their own powers and responsibilities. To the extent that European Council decisions give direction to the Council of Ministers, the latter stands in between ultimate intergovernmental authority and the supranational opportunity that is emphasized by neofunctionalist theory. Discussion of the remaining institutions in this chapter will focus primarily, although not exclusively, on how they process the ordinary agenda.

The Council of Ministers

The Council of Ministers is a body with variable membership and responsibilities. Prior to the application of decisions made at the Seville summit in June 2002, depending upon the area of EU policy and administration being discussed, the Council of Ministers has met as any of more than 20 different councils. Each one grouped a set of cabinet or noncabinet ministers from the 15 member countries.[12] The three most important of these, as is clearly measured by the fact that they meet the most often, are the General Affairs Council, the Agricultural Council, and the Economic and Finance Council (Ecofin). These have met 10 to 15 times per year. Two of them bring together the ministers who, next to their heads of state and government, are typically the most important members of their governments: the General Affairs Council (foreign ministers) and Ecofin (finance ministers). The third, the Agricultural Council, groups the ministers concerned with the Common Agricultural Policy, which accounts for the largest part of the EU budget. Less important are, for example, the environment ministers and the internal market ministers, who meet three or four times per year, and the education ministers and tourism ministers, who meet once or twice per year. The descending frequency of meetings suggests the descending importance of these ministerial posts in national government terms, but also of the policy areas in EU terms.[13]

As discussed previously, the European Council and the Council of Ministers are presided over at any given time by the appropriate executive official from the country which holds the EU presidency for that 6-month period. This responsibility is passed from country to country every 6 months. The most significant of the various functions of the presidency is the ability of the government that holds it to control the agenda of the Council of Ministers. Insofar as legislative measures are concerned, it is the Commission that puts items on the Council's agenda; but having the presidency of the Council gives a government that opposes a particular Commission proposal the ability to keep it off the agenda for 6 months.[14] Until fairly recently, the presidency rotated among the member countries in alphabetical order according to the spelling of the country's name in its own language. The order was altered in 1998 to make it possible for older and newer, as well as larger and smaller, member states to alternate with one another. A "troika" arrangement adds to the effectiveness of the alternation by assuring that the current president will be assisted by those immediately preceding and following. So, for example, when Spain held the presidency from January to June 2002, it was assisted by the other members of the troika, Belgium, its immediate predecessor, and Denmark, its successor.

For most matters that the Council of Ministers deals with, and certainly for all legislative matters, the ministers are dependent upon the Commission to initiate proposals—in other words, to draft the bills. Legislation proposed to the Council of Ministers falls into two categories: (1) regulations and decisions, and (2) directives. Regulations and decisions are applicable directly to member states and/or to individuals within them, and take effect immediately within member states, obliging governments to enforce them but without requiring further legislation on their part. Regulations are of general application in all member states, while decisions are more specific in terms of the member to which they are addressed. Directives are binding upon member states in the sense of obliging them to bring about the necessary legal instruments (laws or executive acts) to give them force within their boundaries.[15]

Despite the Luxembourg compromise discussed in Chapter 3, the ability of the EC decision-making bodies to set and process the ordinary agenda did not disappear in the late 1960s. The big news items of the 1970s involved actions on the extraordinary agenda: European political cooperation, British entry, and creation of the European Council and the European Monetary System. But more quietly, as a study by Thomas Smoot and Piet Verschuren reveals, in 1975 the Council of Ministers considered 329 proposals from the Commission and adopted 75 percent within two years, averaging 150 days from the time they were sent to the Council by the Commission.[16] Arguably, the Commission would have proposed more if it had expected a higher success rate, and many of the measures adopted were of relatively minor significance, but both the success rate and the average length of time in processing were surprising in light of the conventional wisdom about the inefficiency and ineffectiveness of EC policymaking during the period.[17]

Although the Single European Act, which extended the range of voting by qualified majority, did not go into effect until 1987, in the previous year 617 proposals were made by the Commission with a success rate of 87.4 percent.[18] The rising number of proposals reflects the growing range of detailed policy areas to which EC competence was extending, but it also shows greater confidence on the part of the Commission that proposals it had previously withheld would now be adopted. Today it is not likely that a legislative measure will be defeated by a vote in the Council of Ministers. To be sure, many legislative proposals are set aside or returned to the drawing board at early stages, but by the time a measure comes to a vote, the bargaining deals have been firmed up, so that, whether the vote is by qualified majority or unanimity, the requisite number of positive votes will usually be there.[19] Still, the number of positive votes required is of great significance if a bill is to get to the voting stage at all.

When QMV applies in the Council of Ministers, France, Germany, Italy, and Britain have 10 votes apiece; Spain has 8; Belgium, Greece, the Netherlands, and Portugal, 5; Austria and Sweden, 4; Denmark, Finland, and Ireland, 3; and Luxembourg, 2. This totals 87 votes, of which 62, or 71.3 percent, constitutes a qualified majority and 25 votes will suffice to block the measure on which the Council is voting[20] (see Chapter 5). In 1986, according to Neill Nugent, over 100 decisions were taken by QMV, mostly in settled Rome Treaty areas, such as the budget, agriculture, and trade. The Single European Act of 1987 added new subjects to the ordinary agenda in order to complete the single market. Most of these were made subject to QMV under the SEA, and the number of such votes per year in the Council then rose further.[21] According to Fiona Hayes-Renshaw and Helen Wallace,[22] from December 1993 to December 1994, 64 contested votes were taken in the Council of Ministers out of 261 decisions altogether; that is, 24.5 percent of all decisions were contested. In only five of the contested cases did as many as three or four member states vote negatively. Compromises will normally be reached before a vote is ever taken, failing which the issue will be set aside until such time as a decision by QMV becomes likely. This is all the more true when unanimity must be reached for a measure to pass the Council of Ministers.[23]

One reason for the extension of QMV was the concern, with the enlargement of the Community to 12 members, that achieving unanimity in the Council was likely to become an ever more unwieldy process. On the grounds of sheer decision-making efficiency, QMV seemed necessary. But Nugent observes that unanimity is still sought in controversial matters and votes are delayed or not held in order not to isolate a member in disagreement.[24] Paradoxically, the unanimity principle sometimes makes it *easier* for certain decisions to be reached, because when majority voting applies, abstentions count as negative votes. When unanimity is required, abstentions are simply not counted. Ministers may use abstentions when unanimity is required if they wish to permit a positive result while not having to tell critics at home that they voted for it.[25] But if there is likelihood of a veto when unanimity applies, it may mean the issue will be set aside for further bargaining, or perhaps sent to the European Council in the hope that a bargain can be struck that is satisfactory to the government withholding its agreement.

Voting in the Council has been an important focus of rational choice institutionalism (see Chapter 2). Underlying conflict between, say, Euro-skeptics Britain and Denmark on the one hand, and Italy and the Benelux countries, on the other, with France, Germany, and others found somewhere in between, can be overcome if the Commission as agenda setter can fashion a proposal that captures the agreement of the pivotal voter whose weighted votes are needed to achieve the necessary 62 positive votes. Where the unanimity rule applies, coalitions of like-minded members (e.g., Germany and Benelux, poorer countries, Scandinavian countries) are taken as stable building blocks for achieving unanimity behind carefully crafted package deals.

Such formulations are useful for making our assumptions clearer, but they may not be very close to reality, which must certainly be that policymaking in the EU aligns 15 members in a wide variety of ways depending on the substance of issues and the preferences of parties and leaders in charge of governments.[26] So the composition of winning or blocking coalitions will differ from one issue to another, as studies of bargaining in the intergovernmental conferences preceding the Maastricht and Amsterdam treaties have shown.[27] The assumption of a single ordering or of stable coalitions like the Benelux three may have been less heroic when the EC had only 6 members, but it allows us to make only the most abstract of speculations with 15 members, let alone with eventual enlargements to 27 or more members.

A very different approach to the Council of Ministers has been taken by scholars who emphasize the processes by which consensus is fashioned among the individuals who represent their governments in the intergovernmental bodies. In fact, there is a considerable infrastructure of Council civil servants and national civil servants meeting in a variety of committees and working groups. One of the two most important of these bodies is the Council's General Secretariat, with a staff of approximately 2,000, which prepares meetings of the Council of Ministers and whose Secretary General, hitherto a relatively obscure but powerful official, was given by the Amsterdam Treaty an important leadership role in the formulation and execution of Common Foreign and Security Policy (CFSP).[28] The other is the Committee of Permanent Representatives (COREPER), consisting of ambassadorial level officials and a substantial supporting infrastructure, which examines proposals for legislation prior to Council of Ministers deliberations on them and, together with specialized groups of national civil servants who report to it, actually makes decisions on matters that are the easiest to resolve, about 85 percent of the total Council decisions.[29]

The more difficult decisions are made by the ministers on the advice of their permanent officials who have gone over them and identified the points at issue and the positions their fellow ministers are likely to take on them. COREPER and the specialized committees that deal with EMU, EU commercial policy, CFSP, and Justice and Home Affairs play a very important role in shaping the alternatives between which the ministers will decide.[30] COREPER in particular consists of permanent residents in Brussels who are in constant contact with one another and who have developed a common way of looking at EU issues which undoubtedly influences the decisions made, and often (but certainly not always) enables agreement to be reached in the Council of Ministers itself.

Unlike more restrictive intergovernmental perspectives, including that of rational-choice institutionalism, this is a perspective on EU decision making that stresses consensus-building processes that go on not only under assumptions of confidentiality but away from the investigative light of the media. It is more compatible with the neofunctional assumption that pragmatic decisions will be reached leading to greater integration because of an appreciation by experts of what else must be done in order to make already agreed-upon tasks more workable. This is a "pragmatic culture" that exists below the surface of what may at times appear to be a "veto culture" at higher levels. Member states continue to act on a perception of their best interests and negative outcomes do occur. But intergovernmentalist accounts of the work of the Councils explain more than vetoes. They explain bargains that are struck and the willingness of member states to delegate authority to supranational bodies.[31]

The Treaty of Nice (see Chapter 5) has been analyzed from a rational choice perspective by George Tsebelis and Xenephon Yataganas, with very pessimistic conclusions.[32] They point to the complications introduced into the qualified majority vote requirement by the additional necessity of gaining support of a majority of member states and, if one member requests, 62 percent of the total EU population. The first addition strengthens the position of smaller states, while the second advantages larger states, especially Germany, the most populous. Tsebelis and Yataganas stress the members' veto capacities. But this will not often be expressed in actual votes. It may mean a lengthening of the process of consensus building, but this will be inevitable anyway, given enlargement of the EU from 15 to 27 members.

It might be argued that the addition of a population majority as a requirement for adoption of legislation is a democratic feature. But, in fact, it gives the largest member, Germany, a heavy bloc vote, which, if added to that of two other larger members, could stymie the passage of legislation. Therefore, in what may become an even longer bargaining that precedes a Council of Ministers vote, the greater would be the influence of the larger members.[33] If Tsebelis and Yataganas are correct in judging that adopting legislation will become more difficult under the Nice treaty, the balance between intergovernmental and supranational elements in EU ordinary agenda processing will shift in an intergovernmental direction. If anything, this tendency will be reinforced with enlargement bringing into the EU about a dozen additional members in the foreseeable future.

THE FIRST-PILLAR INSTITUTIONS

In this part of the chapter we review the supranational EU institutions: the Commission, the European Court of Justice, and the European Parliament. Study of the first two is still usefully informed by neofunctionalist theory, as well as by a newer offshoot, historical institutionalism (see Chapter 2). These perspectives can also be applied to the European Parliament; but, because it is a directly elected body, unlike the other EU institutions, democratic theory is useful in explaining how it operates.

The Commission

When we examine the decision-making process for legislation authorized by the Rome Treaty, the SEA, and the Maastricht Treaty (first pillar), the strong role of the Commission becomes quite apparent.[34] It is the Commission that sets the legislative (ordinary) agenda for the Council of Ministers. The Commission generates its own proposals as a result of its interpretation of what has been mandated by the treaties; or it may respond to pressures from interest groups, from the European Parliament, or from member governments individually or member governments speaking collectively in the Council. In preparing a draft legislative measure, the appropriate Direc-torate General (DG) of the Commission consults with other units of the Commission.[35] In consultation with COREPER, it takes in the views of governmental and nongovernmental experts, including interest-group representatives, relevant to the policy area in which the legislation would take effect. Then the DG drafts the proposal. The decision to go ahead is taken by the college of 20 commissioners, usually without dissent, although if a vote is needed, a majority of those present is required for adoption.[36] If approved by the commissioners, the proposal is sent to the European Parliament. This gives the Commission an important role as exclusive legislative agenda setter. Thereafter, the Commission is kept apprised of proposed changes in the legislative measures and, under some procedural circumstances, may reject proposed amendments, suggest alternatives to them, or even withdraw a proposal, so long as the Council has not yet approved it.[37] The legislative process will be examined in greater depth subsequently. The literature on this process has emphasized the interaction between the European Parliament and the Council of Ministers, but it should not be forgotten that the process is not set in motion until the Commission sends a draft proposal to the European Parliament. Moreover, the Commission is in close touch with the other bodies throughout the process.

Most EU legislation is implemented by actions taken at the national level. The Commission oversees this implementation and calls it to the attention of the offending government when it discovers a failure to act or action that is contrary to EU legislative intent. Continued failure of a state to comply with the Commission's wishes may lead the latter to refer the case to the European Court of Justice (ECJ). Several member states show higher rates of noncompliance than do others, Italy being the most notorious foot-dragger.[38] However, if the ECJ finds that a state has failed to comply with EC law, the failure will usually be rectified. The ECJ has the power, given it by the Maastricht Treaty on the initiative of the Commission, to levy substantial fines against states that continue to violate its interpretations of their obligations under the treaties.[39]

The Commission also has administrative responsibilities of its own, as in the case of efforts to detect monopolistic and market-sharing violations of EC competition legislation or in the case of agricultural, regional, and social funds, the allocation of which it administers. These supervisory and direct administrative functions of the Commission mostly involve technically complex policy areas, and the phenomena to be dealt with far exceed the capacity of the relatively small Commission bureaucracy. Decisions as to which cases to pursue or which needs to satisfy within the industrialized member countries, each with its own vast bureaucracy, must inevitably be highly selective.[40] This may contribute to a certain negative image of the Commission, which is often accused of bureaucratic interference with national economies, even when it is taking action designed to open the market against state or private-sector interference.

Increasing scholarly attention has focused on the Commission's role in the implementation of EU policy. The Commission is in a position to determine in what ways and to what extent EU laws will be enforced. In doing so, according to the analysts,[41] it acts as the "agent" of a "principal," that is, of the governments. The latter have acted collectively in adopting the legislation, and the Commission acts to see that the governments individually will comply with the policies they have collectively chosen.

According to a public-choice perspective, the Commission will interpret the Council's wishes in such a way as to extend the overall *competence* of the EU as far as possible into policy domains that have previously been under the exclusive individual control of the national governments. In principal/agency theory, as applied to the EU, after the principal (Council of Ministers) has delegated authority to the agent (Commission), it finds that the agent is not easy to control and will be likely to interpret the responsibility placed upon it more expansively than the principal intended. Given that the Council is a collective decision-making body, it will be easy for the Commission to satisfy enough of the member governments to make it unlikely that a majority will be found to withdraw the powers that were originally delegated. An example given by Jonas Tallberg[42] is the liberal use of competition policy enforcement powers against multinational corporations, sometimes to the consternation of national governments in the countries where the corporations are based.

The legislative role of the European Parliament is outlined subsequently. But the EP has another role that has been growing through successive treaty revisions as well. In fact, the EP shares with the Council of Ministers the job of overseeing the work of the executive. The Parliament has powers vis-à-vis the Commission akin in some respects to those of national parliaments involved in keeping the executive in check. In Europe's parliamentary and semiparliamentary democracies, parliaments have the power to censure or vote no confidence in the government, which, under a variety of controlled circumstances, can mean the end of the repudiated government's tenure in office. In recent years the EP has gained a portion of powers to hold the Commission accountable. Since the Rome Treaty it has had the power to censure and thus force the dismissal of the entire Commission by a two-thirds majority. Until 1999 this had never seemed a very realistic possibility, not because two-thirds was an impossibly high bar to clear, but because the EP and the Commission were seen as natural allies against the governments and thus unlikely to be seriously at odds with one another on important issues of European integration. But criticism of the Santer Commission's incompetence (which was seen to be undermining the progress of integration) was mounting in the EP during the late 1990s. The criticisms were focused on particular commissioners, but the power of censure that the EP holds is of the all-or-nothing type. If censured, the whole Commission would have to resign.

In January 1999 a censure vote was taken in the European Parliament against the whole Commission, but the necessary votes for a two-thirds majority were lacking. However, a report by a committee of independent experts confirmed complaints against Santer and other commissioners for avoiding responsibility and, in some cases, for favoritism in appointments to responsible positions under their authority. Rather than face another censure vote, the Santer College of Commissioners collectively resigned in March 1999.[43]

The European Parliament also has a role to play in the appointment of a new College of Commissioners, as in the case of the Romano Prodi Commission, which was approved later in 1999 after its members were individually examined very closely in hearings conducted by the Parliament. The EP does not have the power to refuse appointment of individual commissioners, but it can vote down the proposed College of Commissioners, including the member of that body whom the governments have designated as president. The Prodi College was accepted, but by its careful scrutiny, the EP had served notice that it would be monitoring the commissioners' activities very closely. This is an additional factor that must be taken into account when the Commission decides how energetically it should implement EU policy. But if the EP's role as "principal" bears some similarity to the Council's, the EP's standards for Commission performance are different. The EP may even be critical of the Commission for not going far enough in introducing legislation that might exceed the wishes of the member governments.

The Court of Justice

The European Court of Justice consists of 15 judges, one appointed by each of the member governments. The judges are expected to be appointed on the basis of their stature as jurists, their expertise in jurisprudence, and their independence of political influence. They are appointed for 6-year terms, with approximately half of the terms coming to an end every 3 years. Since the Commission became more active in introducing new legislation in the late 1970s, the ECJ has found itself deciding many important cases that sort out the respective powers of the member governments and the supranational institutions. Yet already in the 1960s it had enunciated two doctrines that paved the way for its judicial activism of more recent years. First, treaties have direct effect in the legal systems of the member countries and may be enforced in the courts of the member states. And second, EC law has supremacy over national law, even if the national laws are adopted after the EC laws.[44] The decisions did not attract a great deal of attention at the time but they have since formed the basis for extending the court's ability to rule that member governments are in violation of EU law in implementing national laws that violate EU law or in failing to implement laws that have been adopted by the EU institutions.

And the ECJ has gone further. Article 235 of the Treaty of Rome contains a provision reminiscent of the "necessary and proper" clause of the U.S. Constitution:

> If any action by the Community appears necessary to achieve, in the functioning of the Common Market, one of the aims of the Community in cases where this Treaty has not provided for the requisite powers of action, the Council, acting by means of an unanimous vote on a proposal of the Commission and after the Assembly has been consulted, shall enact the appropriate provision.[45]

This has enabled the Council of Ministers, on the Commission's initiative and when the Council can attain unanimity, to enter into fields of activity not strictly outlined in the Rome Treaty—in other words, to pursue an extraordinary agenda. Principal examples have been in the domain of environmental policy, for example, a 1980 directive "on the protection of ground water against pollution caused by certain dangerous substances" justified under Article 235 as necessary to improve the "quality of life." This was based on references at the beginning of the treaty to the objective of raising living standards in the member countries.[46] The ECJ has permitted such extensions of the treaty as long as the Council has voted unanimously in favor of them.

Although it operates quietly in the small duchy of Luxembourg, the role of the Court of Justice in facilitating a looser interpretation of the Rome Treaty should not be underestimated. Anne-Marie Burley and Walter Mattli have persuasively argued that neofunctionalism is alive and well, although it is to be found operating in purer form in Luxembourg than at Commission headquarters in Brussels.[47] In Luxembourg "technical-economic" logic is couched in legalistic terms, but the effect is similar to what Ernst Haas had predicted: Community powers would expand through a gradual process of treaty interpretation by EU institutions under the pressure of economic interests seeking to gain advantages at the EU level that are denied them at the national level. Business and farmers' organizations, as well as national and multinational companies, put pressure on the Commission and the national governments, but they also employ lawyers specializing in Community law. These legal specialists present briefs to the ECJ, offering legal arguments for expanding EU authority.[48]

The judges in Luxembourg have responded by finding authority in the Rome Treaty, as in Article 235, for expanded powers. They have also declared actions—and inaction—by member governments as treaty violations in that they encroach on or detract from the authority of the original EC institutions as granted by or implied in the Rome Treaty. The ability of the ECJ to interpret the EU treaties and laws in ways that enhance the freedom of the Commission to make decisions is considered by supranational theorists to be the trump card that the Commission holds, enabling it to impose its own interpretations of its powers upon the governments.[49] Threats by member states to rein in the Court are not credible in the absence of "a high degree of consensus," and "the perception, by the Court, of the credibility of the threat that it might be curbed or its decisions reversed, by the member-states."[50]

Since the adoption of the Single European Act, there have been calls for the ECJ to assume a more juridical, less political stance.[51] Indeed, the Maastricht Treaty clipped the ECJ's wings by excluding its jurisdiction from reaching into new policy domains that the European Union enters, most significantly the area of "justice and home affairs."[52] The more overtly political organs of the EU have taken greater control of the extraordinary agenda since the mid-1980s, making it less necessary for the ECJ to prod them in the direction of new initiatives. Further, national courts have been emboldened to assert a greater role in examining the validity of national legislation, even in member states where there is not a tradition of judicial review. On the other hand, there is evidence, at least in the case of the federal constitutional court of Germany (the Bundesverfassungsgericht), that national courts that *do* exercise judicial review may combat the ECJ's interpretations of the EU treaties with their own interpretations of national constitutional law. The German court has asserted the right to determine whether EU treaties (e.g., the Maastricht Treaty) are in accord with the

German constitution, an assertion that may have given the ECJ pause. But the ECJ still has "the power to pursue its own agenda."[53] If, in the future, leadership elsewhere in the EU is dormant, it may again provide the format for new ECJ initiatives.

The European Parliament

Today the European Parliament is a body of 626 members, elected every five years by the voters of the 15 countries. The members divide into eight parliamentary groups distinguishable in ideological terms as Christian Democrats, Socialists, Liberals, Greens, and so on, each grouping together members of similar ideological persuasion across the country delegations. The EP also divides into approximately 20 substantively specialized committees, which examine and report their recommendations regarding legislation and conduct fact-finding inquiries. The committees roughly correspond in subject matter to the directorates general of the Commission. The leaders of the parliamentary groups and committees play important roles in organizing and motivating the Members of the European Parliament (MEPs) in their week-to-week activities.[54]

The role of the EP in the legislative process remained quite limited until the Single European Act extended its legislative powers. Despite the direct elections of MEPs from 1979, before the SEA the EP was consulted by the Council of Ministers and the Commission during the legislative process, but neither of the latter had to adhere to the Parliament's opinions.[55]

In the formulation of the EC annual budget, however, the EP gained in power at an early date. A treaty amendment of 1970 gave it the power to propose changes in EC spending of a "noncompulsory" nature. This included the various forms of social and regional assistance that were of considerable interest to MEPs but did not include the majority of the budget, agricultural spending, which even the Commission and the Council of Ministers could not bring under effective control. Following a treaty amendment of 1975, the EP also gained the power to reject the annual budget outright, in which case the three principal Rome Treaty bodies would have to negotiate an agreed budget, with the EP being in a good position to get the Council to approve expenditure increases, at least when the Commission supported the Parliament. The Council votes by qualified majority on budget issues, which were not made subject to the Luxembourg compromise, and it is faced with a timetable of rigid deadlines. These features give the Parliament an opportunity to seek allies among the member states in order to gain concessions from those, such as France and Britain, which are inclined to oppose extensions of EP powers at the expense of the member states.

Once the SEA went into effect in July 1987, there existed three different types of procedure for EC legislation, the *assent* procedure; the *consultation* procedure, which is a continuation of the procedure existing before the SEA; and the *cooperation* procedure, which added to the capacity of the EP to influence the outcome of legislation. The assent procedure involves an up or down vote without amendments, and applies today to citizenship, structural funds, and the Cohesion Fund. More importantly, it gives the EP a role in the "ratification" of EU-negotiated treaties with third countries, particularly enlargement and association treaties. But it can neither delay nor amend agreements that have already been reached with non-EU states, so its ability to vote such treaties up or down is not the sharpest of weapons.[56]

Under the Rome Treaty's consultation procedure, the EP's role is to give a legislative proposal (henceforth called a "bill") a *single reading* after it has been received from the Commission. The EP may suggest amendments. If the Commission accepts them, the Council of Ministers must consider them as part of the bill. A Commission-supported measure can be finally adopted by the Council, either by unanimity or by qualified majority, depending on treaty specifications. According to a 1980 ruling of the ECJ, the Council must wait until the EP has expressed its opinion before acting on the legislation.[57]

The cooperation procedure introduced by the SEA applied to much of the legislation designed to create the single market by the end of 1992. It is more complicated than the consultation procedure, but in essence it gives the EP a *second reading* of a bill after the Council has given it a first reading and adopted a common position (which is the point at which the legislation is adopted in the consultation procedure). The Commission plays a crucial role in being able to accept or reject EP amendments at the second as well as at the first reading. The EP may reject the bill outright on second reading, if a majority of all its members vote to do so, in which case the measure can only become EC law if the Council votes unanimously to override the EP veto. The cooperation procedure applied mainly to single-market legislation under the SEA. Today it applies only to aspects of Economic and Monetary Union.[58]

The Maastricht Treaty provided for a third procedure, *codecision*. This replaced consultation for some but not all types of legislation where consultation applied, and it applied in some but not all the new areas of EU competence under the treaty. Unlike the cooperation procedure, failure of the EP and the Council to reach agreement at the second reading touched off a new step, the formation of a "conciliation committee," including representatives of the Council and the EP, who would attempt to work out an agreed position. If the committee could not reach agreement on a common version, the proposal was shelved unless the Council passed its first version (its common position) by qualified majority. But it was the Commission's job to try to find common ground between the Council and the EP. If a commonly agreed version was produced, it still could be defeated when returned to the Council, which needed a QMV to pass it, or to the EP, which could defeat the final version if a simple majority were not found for it. In the first 4½ years that the procedure was in effect, of 130 completed codecision procedures, "agreement between the Council and the EP was reached in 127 cases, . . . in only three cases did the two institutions fail to agree on a joint text."[59] In essence, with codecision, the EP became a coequal legislative body, but only in those domains of policymaking where the procedure applied.

Political scientists George Tsebelis and Geoffrey Garrett have questioned whether the codecision procedure of the Maastricht Treaty actually served to increase the powers of the European Parliament vis-à-vis those of the Council of Ministers, although they agree with others that the powers of the Commission were weakened relative to those of both the EP and the Council.[60] They argue first that the cooperation procedure established by the Single European Act had put the EP in the position, along with the Commission, of being a "conditional agenda setter." By this they mean that the Council of Ministers, after the EP's second reading and the Commission's approval of EP amendments, was faced with the alternatives of voting for the amended measure under the qualified majority rule or rejecting the EP's amendments, which it could only do by a unanimous vote. Basically, though the Council had the final decision, its realistic options were to vote for a bill that contained the EP's amendments or vote against the bill as amended. This is because there would be at least a minority of states willing to accept the EP's amendments. The rest of the states might be in a position to refuse QMV, but they could not reset the agenda. The measure they voted up or down would contain propositions of European Parliament origin, and the Council might actually have seen some of its original amendments rejected by the EP on second reading.

When it comes to the codecision procedure, they argue, the Maastricht Treaty changed the conditional agenda setter from the EP (working together with the Commission) to the Council of Ministers. By opposing EP amendments to the proposed legislation, the Council was in a position, in the conciliation committee deliberations, to hold on to its own version of the proposal essentially as it had been prior to the convening of the conciliation committee, after which the EP was no longer able to change it and had to vote it either up or down. Tsebelis and Garrett argue that the bill would represent enough of a change in the status quo in the direction the EP wanted that they would prefer adoption of a flawed version to none at all. Moreover, the Council might stick to its original version and adopt it by QMV, so the EP had a motivation to accede to the Council's wishes in the conciliation committee.

It is noteworthy that the Amsterdam Treaty, which was signed in 1997 and went into effect in 1999, gave some support for the Tsebelis-Garrett interpretation by changing the "end game" of the codecision process so that the Council lost its ability to adopt the treaty without the amendments proposed by the Parliament.[61] This put the Parliament in a strong position to move a bill's contents closer to what rational choice theorists call its median preference, which is further to the supranational side than is the Council's median preference. However, although the Tsebelis-Garrett argument may be persuasive if one accepts the influence they attribute to conditional agenda setting, other observers have called attention to an informal process of negotiation in the original codecision procedure that the Commission was involved in with the other two bodies before the conciliation committee convened. The Commission attempted to broker agreements between the EP and the Council during the first reading. According to Michael Shackleton, this made it possible for the Parliament to "win" in the ultimate bargaining more often than the Council of Ministers.[62] At any rate, the Amsterdam Treaty removed cooperation as a process for ordinary legislation, replacing it with the new version of codecision.

It may well be that to assign "success scores" to the Parliament and the Council is to make these two bodies, and the potential coalitions within both, too concrete to enable us to capture their complex alignments and working procedures. The true coalitions cut across the memberships of the two bodies such that neither one consistently wins or loses; nor does the Commission, which is itself neither a monolith nor a passive bystander.

Amie Kreppel finds the growth of formal EP powers in the 1990s to have been accompanied by a considerable concentration of power in the two main Europarties that together constitute a majority of the Parliament's membership, the cross-national Party of European Socialists (center-left) and European People's Party (center-right). Together they have developed a predominance in the EP that rivals that of the two parties in the United States, although in the case of the EP party system they are not the only two parties to hold seats. According to Kreppel, the dominance of these two groups has "led to a highly centralized and largely bipartisan European Parliament that much more closely resembles the U.S. Congress than it does the [British] House of Commons."[63] Like the Congress and unlike the House of Commons, power in the EU is not concentrated in an executive that can threaten its majority in parliament with resignation and/or new elections. There is a separation of powers, and the Parliament is now in a position vis-à-vis the Commission and the Council of Ministers to give as well as it gets.

OTHER INSTITUTIONS

The Economic and Social Committee (ESC)

The ESC was created under the Rome Treaty and now consists of 222 members appointed by the Council of Ministers on the proposal of the national governments. Members are individuals considered representative of important economic interests, especially employers, workers, farmers, and various professional categories. In fact, many are leaders of important interest groups at the national level, and as such, their influence on EU legislation comes in at various points in the legislative process, making the collective views of the ESC somewhat redundant. However, when it speaks with one voice on issues, such as social legislation, in which interests might be expected to diverge, it can be influential. Whether or not the Commission and the Council must solicit its views depends on classifications of legislative measures set forth in the Rome Treaty and the SEA. The ESC may also issue its opinions on policy matters not involving immediate legislation, such as trade relations with various regions of the world.[64]

Committee of the Regions (COR)

The COR bears some resemblance to the ESC, outlined previously. It was created by the Maastricht Treaty to give an advisory role to subnational autonomous regions such as Scotland and Wales in the United Kingdom, Catalonia in Spain, and the Länder of the German Federal Republic. However, member countries are represented in it with the same weights as in the ESC, whether or not there are autonomous regions within a country. The European Parliament and the ESC see it as a redundant body that could only compete with their own representative functions, but the COR was established in response to a growing demand for greater regional autonomy and a corresponding belief that, as regions grow in self-governing capacity, they too should have a voice in the EU.[65]

According to Liesbet Hooghe and Gary Marks, the COR is handicapped in its effort to give representation to regions because it must give representation to whatever passes for a region in every country, some of which do not have regions with distinctive traditions and contemporary interests.[66] Regions that are newly empowered in their own countries, such as Scotland and Wales in the United Kingdom, did not benefit from direct COR help so much as they did from their own ability to find leverage within their own national political party system, and from the symbolic support that creation of the COR had given member states' regions that were seeking greater autonomy. The growth of regionally based interest group activity in Brussels played an important role as well.[67]

THE EU AND DEMOCRATIC GOVERNANCE

In the 1990s it became apparent that the European Union was no longer the exclusive property of political elites to shape as they wish whenever there is consensus among them. In the past the public was consulted from time to time in referenda, usually on the question of whether to join the EC after governmental leaders had worked out the terms. Elite calculations that the public would support their initiatives proved correct—until the referenda on the Maastricht Treaty.[68] When the treaty was rejected by Danish voters the first time around, and almost rejected by French voters, it became apparent that voter approval could neither be taken for granted nor easily manipulated.

There is, of course, a directly elected body that is part of the institutional arrangements of the EU, the European Parliament, which has played a minor role at best in setting EU agendas. Its involvement in processing the ordinary agenda is growing, and it has used its growing capacities effectively while seeking to gain respect from the Commission and the Council. In fact, the growing concern that the EP, *as the only democratic EU body*, is weaker than the other bodies has come to overshadow the sense of solidarity between the EP and the Commission that rested on their common identification as *supranational* bodies, sharing a perspective that challenged the hegemony of the national governments. The fact that the EP is still the least powerful of these three bodies is a source of disappointment for those who are critical of the alleged elitism and technocratic aloofness of the Commission and the frequent cases of timidity on the part of the Council. It is also at the heart of criticisms about a democratic deficit.[69]

The "democratic deficit" refers to the absence of direct links between the Commission and the Council of Ministers, and the voters in the 15 member countries. Voters vote for national political leaders in parliamentary elections and (in five of the countries) in presidential elections. But for the most part, the issues they vote on and the images of the candidates are displayed in terms that bear little direct relationship to Europe. A common European agenda is not put before the voters at national elections to be voted up or down by the public. Instead, voters vote on the basis of *national* issues and the performance of national governing and opposition parties and their leaders. Accordingly, if the set of leaders who get together in the European Council and the Council of Ministers represents a clear stand on issues before the EU, it is a coincidental result of 15 separate political processes that have not been coordinated from Brussels or anywhere else. Also coincidental is the set of persons appointed to the Commission as the choices of government leaders in 15 different countries, although the Commissioners may be able to develop a certain *esprit de corps* and consensus on EU policy issues through their interaction with one another. But if so, it is more likely to be influenced by elites in the public and private sectors with whom they interact on a frequent basis than it is by public opinion in the member countries, which may provide mixed signals to the Commissioners.

The EP Election of June 1999[70]

The European Parliament is the only directly elected EU body, and it is one that potentially speaks with a consensual voice on EU issues. The question that is relevant to the democratic deficit problem is whether elections to the EP are conducted in such a way that voters in the member countries can communicate their wishes to the EU power holders through their representatives in the European Parliament.

At the time of the first direct elections to the European Parliament in June 1979, public indifference to the EC was a source of concern for those hoping that direct elections would make Community governance more democratic. In June 1979 the turnout across the nine countries was 62 percent, not unrespectable by U.S. standards but well below the 75 to 90 percent levels usually recorded back then in Europe's national elections. Twenty years later, at the time of the June 1999 European Parliament elections, the image of the European Union had suffered from the lack of a publicly relevant role in the Kosovo war that had recently ended. Economic and Monetary Union had gotten underway at the beginning of the year, and the euro was off to a good start in exchange markets; but there were public squabbles over what degree of independence the European Central Bank should have vis-à-vis the member governments. A new Commission president, Romano Prodi, had been named and his colleagues chosen, all of whom would come under the scrutiny of the newly elected European Parliament. But as usual, the elections to that Parliament were not the subject of close public attention. Also as usual, the issues of the election were national in scope in every country; public attention was being drawn to the battles between national parties, with the elections seen as indicators of how the parties stood in the public eye and what the parties' prospects were for the next national elections.

The previous EP, elected in June 1994, numbered 567 MEPs. The two leading party groupings were the Party of European Socialists (PES), with 214 MEPs, and the Christian Democrats and allies in the European People's Party (EPP), which grouped 201 MEPs. The British Labour Party MEPs within the PES held 62 seats, the single largest national party bloc. Next in size were the European Liberal Democrats and Republicans (ELDR), which grouped 42. Other groups included the European United Left (34), the Union for Europe (34), the Greens (27), the European Radical Alliance (21), and the Europe of Nations Group (16). Each of these contained MEPs from more than one country, belonging to parties that were more or less in the same region of the left–right spectrum in different countries. The large numbers of parties that succeeded in getting MEPs elected reflected the use of proportional representation in all countries but the UK in 1994. By the 1999 EP elections, the British too had opted for a version of proportional representation for these elections.

By its left–right orientation the party system in the European Parliament reflects the traditional dynamics of party conflict found in national parliaments. The predominance of the EPP and the PES reflect the mainstream center-right Christian Democrats or Conservatives found in all of the countries and the center-left Social Democratic parties also found in all of them. But the two Euro-parties are not far apart in their attitudes toward European integration. Most MEPs in both are strong supporters of further European integration. To find Euro-skeptics in the EP one would have to turn to smaller fringe parties and independent MEPs.

Turnout has gone down with each election since 1979. In 1994 it was 57 percent and in 1999 it dropped to 49.9 percent, its lowest percentage ever. In all three of the newest member countries it was below 50 percent: 49 percent in Austria, 39 percent in Sweden, and 30 percent in Finland. But the lowest percentage was in the United Kingdom, where it fell from 36 percent in the two previous elections to 24 percent in 1999. In two of the "charter" members, Belgium and Luxembourg, it held at 91 percent and 86 percent, respectively, yet in France it was down from 53 percent to 47 percent, in Germany from 60 percent to 45 percent, in Italy from 75 percent to 71 percent, and in the Netherlands from 36 percent to 30 percent. Although these should not necessarily be interpreted as measures of negative feelings toward the EU, it could easily be argued that indifference, at least, has risen.

There is also evidence that parties in power at the national level, especially the parties of the center-left PES Eurogroup, which were in power in most governments, suffered a substantial withdrawal of voter support. This may have reflected voter disagreement with these parties more on national-level issues than on EU-related ones, but it suggests a growing disenchantment of European voters with those in power generally at the end of the decade.

It should be clear from the foregoing that, even in countries where many voters have strong views about EU issues, the opportunities to express them in EP elections are few. In most member countries most of the parties support the EU as it is today. Wherever a party has taken a stance against a treaty or certain parts of it, many of the voters who agree with the party may be supporters of other parties on domestic issues. Many voters are pleased with the new powers that have transferred to the EU by the Maastricht and Amsterdam treaties. But many others who were basically indifferent to the old EC have become alarmed about where the new EU is headed. Uncertainty about the political, as well as the social and economic effects of a massive enlargement of the current EU toward the east and south is registered in the slow pace and postponements that have characterized the preparatory stages. Rejection by the Danish voters of EMU and the euro in 2000 and by the Irish voters of the Nice Treaty in 2001 are further evidence. From the standpoint of removing the EU's "democratic deficit," this heightened public concern may not be such a bad sign. Whatever size and shape the EU takes in the future, it cannot even dimly resemble a single democratic polity unless the issues that divide the member governments when they meet in Council are issues which also divide (or unite) the voters as well as the political parties in each of the member countries.

Levels of Public Support for the EU

Ordinary voters in the member countries of the European Union have only intermittently been energized by battles over treaty ratification or Euro-elections, and primarily in a handful of countries where EU issues are featured in election and referendum campaigns, as they have sometimes been in the United Kingdom, France, Denmark, Austria, Sweden, and Ireland. Surveys of public attitudes in the 15 member countries, undertaken by Eurobarometer, an agency of the EU Commission, have shown that support for the EU and its institutions declined during the 1990s; but polls have also shown that support for member governments and their institutions has been in decline during the same period. The one institution at either level that has retained positive support is the European Parliament, perhaps because it has been openly critical of the governments and of the Commission and because its own powers are not yet sufficiently great to make it an object of public dissatisfaction.[71]

Surveys have shown that across the 15 member countries support for the EU is higher for citizens with higher levels of education, higher income, and employment in the professions and larger business enterprises. Support is also higher among younger adults, although this may be as much a function of level of education as of age. If we follow the argument of Ronald Inglehart, persons with higher levels of education are more intellectually mobile and less tied to immediate material concerns. Inglehart has linked support for the EU with what he calls "post-materialist" attitudes.[72] Younger, well-educated Europeans have enjoyed greater prosperity than had their parents and grandparents in earlier decades, and they can appreciate the role that European integration has played, by opening up markets and helping to lift the income and purchasing power of millions of Europeans. But given that they are comfortably situated themselves, they can turn their attention to collective objectives that lack the obvious ability to gratify immediate material needs, objectives such as environmental protection, civil rights, and European integration—all of which, according to Inglehart, are on the postmaterialist agenda.

A study by Matthew J. Gabel rejects Inglehart's postmaterialism argument.[73] Gabel's surveys have asked representative samples of EU citizens whether they were "for or against" each of four EU goals of the 1990s: a common defense policy, a single currency, a common foreign policy and European parliamentary government. He finds that the positions of respondents on the scale formed by these items, labeled "support for integration," is best predicted by objective social status indicators. Items that represented Inglehart's postmaterialist explanation lacked significance in Gabel's regression analyses. Respondents with higher status exhibited higher evaluations of EU goals, irrespective of their preferences on a scale of material versus post-material values. Seemingly at odds with this finding, however, was Gabel's additional finding, when aggregating his data at the national level: a negative relationship between objective indicators of national economic health and support for integration. Technically, this is not a contradiction, because individual-level inferences cannot be drawn from aggregate level findings. A similar aggregate level finding has been reported by Ignacio Sanchez-Cuenca, who interprets it as reflecting a transfer of support from the national level to the EU by those who are critical of their own governments' economic performances.[74] It remains for further studies to show whether this will be a stable finding.

The percentage of ordinary citizens who express positive views vary from nation to nation and from class to class within nations, but it is the supportive elites who provide its drive and are responsible for interpreting its successes and failures to the broader population. But it is doubtful that anything like a sense of European nationhood has taken root within the larger population. In medieval Europe, most people felt closer attachment to their immediate locale and often to a local landholder than to a larger entity such as nation-state.[75] Loyalties to European nation states developed in the growing and urbanizing populations of the nineteenth and twentieth centuries. Today, the loyalty to the nation-state rivals more particularistic loyalties in Western Europe; but attachment to the European Union is conditional and is potentially revocable if the economic promise is not realized.

CONCLUSION

We have discussed in this chapter the structures, powers, and rules of the EU in terms of their bearing on the ways in which the ordinary and extraordinary EU agendas are set and processed. Ordinary agenda setting is primarily the job of the Commission, while processing the agenda involves an interaction between the Council of Ministers and the European Parliament, with the Commission playing a mediating role that often is used in practice to augment the influence of the EP. Three different procedures are used, as specified by the Treaty of Rome, the Single European Act, the Maastricht Treaty on European Union, and the Amsterdam Treaty. In order of the ascending importance of the EP, the procedures have been (1) consultation, which gives the EP a voice; (2) cooperation, which gives it a conditional blocking power; and (3) codecision (Amsterdam Treaty version), which gives it an ultimate veto. The capacity of one member government to block a legislative measure in the Council of Ministers has been diminished further by each treaty, including the recent Nice Treaty.

The treaties are essentially silent on the question of how democratic the EU institutions ought to be. The burden of making them responsive to voters is in the hands of the directly elected European Parliament, and it depends heavily upon the EP elections held every 5 years in the member countries. But the issues are often so complicated that only elites can debate them with other elites. The lack of attention to European issues in most of the countries in the 1999 EP election campaign suggests that the EU remains a largely elite-driven set of political institutions.

ENDNOTES

1. Simon Bulmer and Wolfgang Wessels, *The European Council: Decision-Making in European Politics* (Basingstoke and London: Macmillan, 1987), pp. 17–27.
2. Ibid., p. 20.
3. Peter Ludlow, ed., "Introduction: The Politics and Policies of the EC in 1989," *The Annual Review of European Community Affairs: 1990* (London: Brassey's for the Center for European Studies, 1991), pp. xvi–xviii.
4. Neill Nugent, *The Government and Politics of the European Community*, 2d ed., (Durham, N.C.: Duke University Press, 1991), p. 195.
5. Ludlow, "Introduction," p. xvi.
6. *Financial Times*, October 19, 2001.
7. *The Economist*, December 22, 2001, pp. 57–58.
8. Nugent, *The Government and Politics of the European Community*, 2d ed., p. 195.
9. Ibid., p. 197.
10. Bulmer and Wessels, *The European Council*, p. 101.
11. Anna Murphy and Peter Ludlow, "The Community's External Relations," in Ludlow, ed., *The Annual Review of European Community Affairs: 1990*, pp. 205–217.
12. The Heads at the Seville summit agreed to reduce the number of councils to nine, combining most of the existing councils. Presumably, these will meet more often than did the average council previously. "Measures Concerning the Structure and Functioning of the Council," Annex II of European Council, Seville, Conclusions of the Presidency, June 21 and 22, 2002, Bulletin 24.06, 2002, p. 31.
13. Neill Nugent, *The Government and Politics of the European Union*, 2d ed., Table 7.1, p. 147.
14. Simon Hix, *The Political System of the European Union* (New York: St. Martin's Press, 1999), p. 66.
15. Neill Nugent, *The European Commission* (Basingstoke and New York: Palgrave, 2001), p. 235.
16. Thomas Smoot and Piet Verschuren, "Decision-Making Speed in the European Community," *Journal of Common Market Studies* 29 (September 1990): 77.
17. Also see Helen Wallace, "The Council and the Commission after the Single European Act," in Leon Hurwitz and Christian Lequesne, eds., *The State of the European Community: Policies, Institutions and Debates in the Transition Years* (Boulder, Colo.: Lynne Rienner Publishers, 1991), p. 25; Jonathan Golub, "In the Shadow of the Vote? Decision Making in the European Community," *International Organization* 53 (Autumn 1999): 753.
18. Smoot and Verschuren, "Decision-Making Speed," 77–83.
19. Axel Moberg, "The Nice Treaty and Voting Rules in the Council," *Journal of Common Market Studies* 40 (2002): 259–282.
20. These numbers are subject to change once the Treaty of Nice comes into effect.
21. Nugent, *The Government and Politics of the European Community*, 2d ed., p. 123.
22. Fiona Hayes-Renshaw and Helen Wallace, *The Council of Ministers* (Basingstoke and London: Macmillan, 1977), Table 2.3, p. 55.
23. One study found that the percentage of Council of Ministers votes that received unanimous support, with no abstentions, per year, from 1994 to 1998, ranged from 75 percent to 86 percent and the percentage of decisions in which at least one negative vote was cast ranged from 12 percent to 19 percent. Mikko Mattila and Jan-Erik Lane, "Why Unanimity in the Council? A Roll Call Analysis of Council Voting," *European Union Politics* 2 (2001): 40.

24. Nugent, *The Government and Politics of the European Community*, 2d ed., p. 124.
25. Hayes-Renshaw and Wallace, *The Council of Ministers*, p. 148.
26. Richard Corbett, "Academic Modelling of the Codecision Procedure: A Practitioner's Puzzled Reaction," in Christophe Crombez, Bernard Steunenberg and Richard Corbett, "Forum: Understanding the EU Legislative Process: Political Scientists' and Practitioners' Perspectives," *European Union Politics* 1 (2000), 363–381.
27. For example, Andrew Moravcsik, *The Choice for Europe: Social Purpose and State Power from Messina to Maastricht* (Ithaca, N.Y.: Cornell University Press, 1998), chap. 6; Andrew Moravcsik and Kalypso Nicolaidis, "Explaining the Treaty of Amsterdam: Interests, Influence, Institutions," *Journal of Common Market Studies* 37 (March 1999): 59–85.
28. For the work of the Secretariat, see Hayes-Renshaw and Wallace, *The Council of Ministers*, ch. 4.
29. Hayes-Renshaw and Wallace, *The Council of Ministers*, p. 78.
30. Jeffrey Lewis, "Administrative Rivalry in the Council's Infrastructure: Diagnosing the Methods of Community and EU Decision-Making." Paper presented at the Sixth Bicentennial European Community Studies Association conference, Pittsburgh, June 2–5, 1999.
31. Peterson and Bomberg argue that several theoretical perspectives are useful, given the complexity of EU decision making. John Peterson and Elizabeth Bomberg, *Decision-making in the European Union* (New York: St. Martin's Press, 1999).
32. George Tsebelis and Xenephon Yataganas, "Veto Players and Decision-making in the EU after Nice," *Journal of Common Market Studies* 40 (2002): 283–307.
33. Moberg, "The Nice Treaty and Voting Rules," 277–278.
34. Leon N. Lindberg and Stuart A. Scheingold, *Europe's Would-Be Polity: Patterns of Change in the European Community* (Englewood Cliffs, N.J.: Prentice-Hall, Inc., 1970), pp. 87–95.
35. The Commission is organized into 23 Directorates General (like the departments of a national government's executive-administrative structure). These are headed by 20 commissioners, some of whom have responsibility for more than one DG or for parts of DGs.
36. Nugent, *The European Commission*, pp. 99–100.
37. Ibid., p. 255.
38. Heather D. Mbaye, "Why National States Comply with Supranational Law: Explaining Implementation Infringements in the European Union, 1972–1993," *European Union Politics* 2 (2001): Table 2, p. 269.
39. Anne-Marie Burley and Walter Mattli, "Europe before the Court: A Political Theory of Legal Integration," *International Organization* 47 (Winter 1993): 67–68.
40. Nugent, *The Government and Politics of the European Community*, 2d ed., pp. 77–93.
41. Mark A. Pollack, "Delegation, Agency, and Agenda Setting in the European Community," *International Organization* 51 (Winter 1997): 99–134.
42. Jonas Tallberg, "Delegation to Supranational Institutions: Why, How, and with What Consequences?" *West European Politics* 25 (January 2002): 23–46.
43. Neill Nugent, *The Government and Politics of the European Union*, 4th ed. (Durham, N.C.: Duke University Press, 1999), pp. 216–217.
44. Alec Stone Sweet and James A. Caporaso, "From Free Trade to Supranational Polity: The European Court and Supranational Governance," in Wayne Sandholtz and Alec Stone Sweet, eds., *European Integration and Supranational Governance* (Oxford and New York: Oxford University Press, 1998), pp. 102–103.
45. "Preamble and Selected Articles of the Treaty Establishing the European Economic Commmunty (March 25, 1957)," in Howard Bliss, ed., *The Political Development of the European Community: A Documentary Collection* (Waltham, Mass.: Blaisdell, 1970), p. 65.
46. J. A. Usher, "The Scope of Community Competence: Its Recognition and Enforcement," *Journal of Common Market Studies* 24 (December 1985): 121.
47. Burley and Mattli, "Europe before the Court," 41–76.
48. Ibid., 58–59.
49. Tallberg, "Delegation to Supranational Institutions," 33–36; Stone Sweet and Caporaso, "From Free Trade to Supranational Policy," pp. 101–105.
50. Stone Sweet and Caporaso, "From Free Trade to Supranational Polity," p. 98.
51. Ibid., 71.

52. Ibid., 73–74.
53. Hix, *The Political System of the European Union*, p. 121; Burley and Mattli, "Europe before the Court," p. 74; Jonas Tallberg, "The Anatomy of Autonomy: An Institutional Account of Variation in Supranational Influence," *Journal of Common Market Studies* 38 (December 2000): 843–864. Tallberg applies the principal/agent analysis to the ECJ as well as to the Commission, finding the ECJ to be less vulnerable than the Commission to efforts by the governments to rein it in.
54. Nugent, *The Government and Politics of the European Union*, 4th ed., pp. 223–240.
55. Amie Kreppel, *The European Parliament and Supranational Party System: A Study in Institutional Development* (Cambridge: Cambridge University Press, 2002), p. 70.
56. Dinan, *Ever Closer Union: An Introduction to European Integration*, 2d ed. (Boulder, Colo.: Lynne Rienner Publishers, 1999), pp. 287–288; Hix, *The Political System of the European Union*, Figure 3.5, p. 86.
57. Ibid., pp. 281–282.
58. Nugent, *The European Commission*, p. 256.
59. Nugent, *The Government and Politics of the European Union*, 4th ed., p. 211.
60. Tsebelis, "The Power of the European Parliament as Conditional Agenda-Setter," *American Political Science Review* 88 (1994): 128–142; Geoffrey Garrett, "From the Luxembourg Compromise to Codecision: Decision-Making in the European Union," *Electoral Studies* 14 (1955): 289–308.
61. Nugent, *The Government and Politics of the European Union*, 4th ed., p. 208.
62. Michael Shackleton, "The Politics of Codecision," *Journal of Common Market Studies* 38 (June 2000): 325–342; Richard Corbett, "Academic Modelling of the Codecision Procedure: A Practitioner's Puzzled Reaction," *European Union Politics* 1 (October 2000): 373–379. Moreover, the EP signaled in the post-Maastricht period that it would vote down the original Council version if the Council held to it. Hix, *The Political System of the European Union*, pp. 93–94.
63. Kreppel, *The European Parliament and the Supranational Party System*, p. 10.
64. Nugent, *The Government and Politics of the European Community*, pp. 210–217.
65. Dinan, *Ever Closer Union*, pp. 70–71.
66. Liesbet Hooghe and Gary Marks, *Multi-Level Governance and European Integration* (Lanham, Md.: Rowman and Littlefield Publishers, Inc., 2001), p. 82.
67. Kelly Shaw, "The Scottish Lobby in Contemporary Britain: Devolution and European Integration," Ph.D. dissertation, University of Missouri—Columbia, August 2002.
68. The exception before 1992 was the 1972 rejection of EC membership by Norwegian voters.
69. See Shirley Williams, "Sovereignty and Accountability in the European Community," in Keohane and Hoffmann, eds., *The New European Community*, pp. 155–176; Juliet Lodge, "The European Parliament," in Sven S. Andersen and Kjell A. Eliassen, eds., *The European Union: How Democratic Is It?* (London: Sage Publications, 1996), pp. 187–214.
70. Alain Guyomarch, "The June 1999 European Parliament Elections," *West European Politics* 23 (January 2000): 101–124.
71. Hix, *The Political System of the European Union*, pp. 134–137.
72. Ronald Inglehart, *The Silent Revolution: Changing Values and Political Styles among Western Publics* (Princeton: Princeton University Press, 1977).
73. Matthew J. Gabel, *Interests and Integration: Market Liberalization, Public Opinion, and European Union* (Ann Arbor, Mich.: University of Michigan Press, 1998), pp. 97–99.
74. Ignacio Sanchez-Cuenca, "The Political Basis of Support for European Integration," *European Union Politics* 1 (2000), 147–161.
75. Kees van Kersbergen, "Political Allegiances and European Integration," *European Journal of Political Research* 37 (2000): 1–17.

7

Enlargement

The decision of the European Union to expand its membership to the Central and East European Countries (CEECs) represents the largest expansion plan in the Union's history. This enlargement is taking place against a background of complex political and economic changes in Europe and the international system. The implications of this enlargement are significant for both the EU and CEEC's respective political, economic, and security interests, and for future stability of Europe.

REASONS BEHIND ENLARGEMENT

Progress made in the single market did not go unnoticed by the other countries around the European Union. Particularly noteworthy were the EFTA countries that applied to the EC for membership in the late 1980s and early 1990s: Austria (1988), Finland (1992), Norway (1992), and Sweden (1991). With the exception of Norway, citizens of these countries voted to join the EU as of January 1, 1995. Furthermore, many of the eastern European and the Mediterranean countries applied for full membership in the EU soon after they obtained their freedoms following the collapse of the Eastern Bloc.

The EU members were interested in enlargement because this would enhance their influence in Europe and in the world. Periphery countries wanted to join because of the expected economic benefits of integration. EU officials expressed their view of enlargement in the joint declaration of the heads of state and government at the Edinburgh summit in December 1992. They stated that the EU intended to extend membership to the central and eastern European countries sometime in the future. At the Copenhagen summit in June 1993, it was announced that the next enlargement would include the EFTA countries and that the EU intended to improve economic and political relations with the other European countries that would apply for membership.

The EU strategic view of enlargement was also reflected in an opinion paper prepared by the Economic and Social Council on January 25, 1989. This report argued that the EC found itself in a global competition with the United States and Japan:

> Even once it is reinforced by establishment of a barrier-free internal market, the [EC] will not be able to withstand competition from the two main strategic areas of America and Asia unless it expands its economic area and market. To create this strategic European area, the [EC] will have to turn to its neighbors: European Free Trade Association (EFTA), central and east Europe, and the Mediterranean. In this latter region, the Community must rapidly make up for lost time: the Mediterranean is now a focus of United States and Japanese trade, investment, economic aid, and above all, technological "colonization."[1]

The efforts of the EU in providing economic assistance and leadership to the new democracies of the central and eastern European countries through the establishment of the European Bank for Reconstruction and Development (EBRD), revisions of the EU's Global Mediterranean Policy (GMP), and participation in peace negotiations in the former Yugoslavia in partnership with the United Nations were all made with views such as those expressed by the Economic and Social Council in mind. While improvement of economic and political relations between the EU and its periphery were in the interest of both sides, the eventual membership in the EU for any candidate state depended on two factors: how well the candidate fares with regard to the conditions for membership and whether there exists a consensus among the EU members to grant membership to the applicant.

Membership criteria as outlined in various EU documents are summarized as the Copenhagen Criteria:

1. *Europeanness:* The applicant country has to be a member of the European family of states
2. *Political criteria:* The political system must be characterized by democracy and the rule of law, respect of human rights, and protection of minorities
3. *Economic criteria:* The country must have a strong market economy that encompasses the free movement of goods, capital, services, and people
4. *Other obligations*
   a. The aims of political, economic, and monetary union
   b. Adoption of the *acquis communautaire*, the rights and obligations derived from EU treaties, laws, and regulations over the years

The *acquis communautaire* is one of the main requirements for membership in the EU. The requirements are quite specific about what conditions candidate countries must meet prior to accession. Furthermore, the EU leaders are clearly committed to preparing these countries for membership.

In its relations with periphery countries, the EU also tries to improve ties by establishing association agreements. These agreements provide for greater economic and political cooperation between the EU and recipient countries. There are two types of association agreements extended to nonmember countries. The first type provides for economic and technical assistance and for improvement of trade relations in specified commodity categories. Countries in this category, the African, Caribbean and Pacific (ACP) countries and most of the Mediterranean Basin countries, are not targeted for eventual accession to full membership. The second type of association prepares nonmembers for eventual membership in the EU or calls for the creation of a customs union between the nonmember state and the EU. Agreements with EFTA countries; with Cyprus, Malta, and Turkey; and with the CEEC states all fall into this second category.[2]

Prelude to Eastern Enlargement: Post-Cold War Relations with Central and Eastern European Countries

Democratization in central and eastern Europe served as a catalyst to refashion EU policies toward this region. Soon after the collapse of the Communist regimes, the EU initiated an economic reconstruction program for the newly emerging democratic states. This initiative resulted, in part, from a call in July 1989 by the G7 countries to the Commission to coordinate the western countries' support for political and economic reforms in the CEEC.[3] The initial program, known as PHARE, called for assistance to Hungary and Poland. Later, the program expanded to include other CEEC states as they abandoned communism. The scope of the program also expanded from development credit to cooperation and reconstruction. Finally, the EU went a step further and proposed a "global policy," similar in nature to the Global Mediterranean Policy, which emphasizes the importance of establishing mutual association relationships with the CEEC. The prerequisites for establishing such relationships, on the part of the former Communist states, were political democratization and economic reforms toward a market system. According to Françoise de la Serre, "more than anything else, the experience the [EU] has accumulated in terms of trade and cooperation policy with third countries or in the field of operations (e.g., food aid) has allowed it to become the privileged interlocutor for eastern Europe."[4] The program developed by the EU Commission to help the CEEC had four major points:

1. Trade liberalization to establish a free trade area with eastern Europe
2. Industrial, technical, and scientific cooperation
3. A program of financial assistance
4. The creation of a system of political dialogue[5]

One year after negotiations started with the new democracies, the EU initiated "Europe agreements" with Czechoslovakia, Hungary, and Poland; these were known as the "Visegrad countries" because on February 15, 1991, a Hungarian–Polish–Czechoslovak summit was held in Visegrad, a small town at the Danube bend in northern Hungary. At this summit, the Hungarian prime minister, Jozsef Antall, President Lech Walesa of Poland, and the Czech president, Václav Havel, signed a comprehensive agreement to cooperate in their efforts to attain EU membership for their countries by the end of this century. While these agreements were similar in scope to the association agreements that helped Greece, Portugal, and Spain to join the EU, they had one important difference in that there was no timetable set for membership in the EU. After Czechoslovakia split, the EU renegotiated the Europe agreements with the Czech Republic and Slovakia. The EU then signed two more Europe agreements, with Bulgaria (1992) and Romania (1992).

These agreements were similar in structure but varied in content according to the specific needs of each country. For example, the agreements with Hungary and Poland stressed that these countries were more dependent on agricultural exports and, consequently, were more vulnerable to the EU's CAP restrictions than were the Czech Republic and Slovakia.

In addition to the Europe agreements, there were interim agreements signed between the EC and the Visegrad and other CEEC states covering the trade and related questions of the association agreements. These did not require ratification by the EC's 12 national parliaments, and they became effective on March 1, 1992.[6] They were for a period of 10 years, except for Poland, which was for 5 years. They aimed at the development and diversification of trade, the promotion of commercial relations, and economic cooperation between these countries and the EU. In essence, these interim and association agreements aimed to normalize commercial and economic relations between the EU and the CEECs. However, there were certain problems in the way they are interpreted and applied by the EU. In a survey of the EU, *The Economist* explained:

> The essence of the Europe agreements is that they will "gradually" establish a free trade area between the [EU] and [Visegrad countries] over a transition period . . . and that this mutual opening will be asymmetric—the [EU] will do more in the first five years, the trio in the second. . . . The commitment does not hold for farm products, which, in Hungary's case, currently account for one-quarter of its exports to the [EU]. Hungary will be permitted to sell just 5,000 tonnes of beef to the [Union]. This annual allowance will rise to 6,600 tonnes over five years. In the mid-1970s Hungary was selling a smaller [EU] some 100,000 tonnes of beef a year, paying whatever levies the [EU] was charging to bring imported beef up to the CAP price.[7]

There were similar restrictions for nonfarm products—such as steel, textiles, and clothing—that fall into the "sensitive industry" categories of the EU. These restrictions affected all the Visegrad countries.

The scale of the economic and financial aid package for CEEC has been very large. On December 18, 1989, the EU allocated 300 million ecus, through Regulation 3906/89, for financing projects aimed at the economic restructuring of Poland and Hungary, and on September 17, 1990, the Council of Ministers passed Regulation 2698/90, amending Regulation 3906/89, to extend assistance to other states in the CEEC.[8] Part of the aid package was nonreimbursable and the remaining was in the form of loans. For 1990, the nonreimbursable part was 500 million ecus; for 1991 850 million ecus; and for 1992, the allocation was around 1 billion ecus.[9] Loans, on the other hand, came in different forms and from a variety of sources. Initially, the EU granted Hungary a medium-term loan to a maximum amount of 870 million ecus and 375 million ecus to Czechoslovakia contingent upon credit approval by the International Monetary Fund (IMF). The European Investment Bank (EIB) was given permission to grant loans to countries belonging to the PHARE program. Furthermore, the European Bank for Reconstruction and Development, modeled after the International Bank for Reconstruction and Development (the World Bank), became operational on April 15, 1991, with a capital stock of 10 billion ecus designed for development projects in these countries.

With CEEC countries attaining candidacy status, the EU began concentrating on the two key priorities involved in the adoption of the Community *acquis* and the financing of investment projects. These account for 30 and 70 percent, respectively, of its budget for the applicant countries, with the exception of the investments funded by the pre-accession structural and agricultural instruments. PHARE resources totaled 1,560 million euros annually as of year 2000.[10] In addition to PHARE, the EU provides two other forms of assistance for pre-accession purposes: agricultural aid (SAPARD) and structural assistance (ISPA) outlined in the Berlin agreement.

The Eastern Enlargement

At the Essen meeting of the European Council during December 9–10, 1994, the EU leaders agreed to prepare six CEEC countries (Poland, Hungary, the Czech Republic, Slovakia, Bulgaria, and Romania) for accession to full membership.[11] While the EU made this commitment, it also stated that accession negotiations with these countries would not start until after the 1996 Intergovernmental Conference to review the state of the Maastricht Treaty. Since then, the EU has been proceeding ahead with a complex set of assistance policies aimed at preparing first 11, and now 13, CEEC states for membership.

The first 12 countries are the ones identified at the Luxembourg 1998 summit of the European Council in a two-phase enlargement plan. The first phase would include Cyprus, the Czech Republic, Estonia, Hungary, Malta, Poland, and Slovenia. The second phase would include Bulgaria, Latvia, Lithuania, Romania, and Slovakia. After briefly withdrawing its candidacy, Malta reentered the picture in February 1999, and at the Helsinki summit in December 1999, the European Council invited Turkey to be a candidate but without committing to accession talks until the Turks meet the Copenhagen criteria for membership. At the EU summit in Nice (December 4–6, 2000), the member states reaffirmed their commitment to enlargement and outlined institutional changes that will take place after enlargement such as changing voting weights in the Council and seats in the EP (see Table 7.3).[12] The Nice Treaty initially ran into a problem in Ireland when the Irish voters rejected it in a national referendum in 2001. After a yearlong intense campaign by the Irish government, the voters revisited the Nice Treaty in a new referendum on October 19, 2000 and gave it a 63 percent thumbs up.[13] Finally, at the Copenhagen summit on December 12, 2002, the EU invited 10 candidates to become members on May 1, 2004.[14]

ASSESSING THE REASONS. As stated earlier, when we assess the reasons behind this ambitious enlargement plan, it becomes clear that, with the end of the Cold War, the EU and the CEECs had no real alternative but to reach out to each other. The CEECs needed to achieve market reforms, integrate their economies with global financial markets, and build democratic institutions. EU membership provides the easiest possible way to achieve these objectives. On the other hand, the CEECs represent new market opportunities that would increase the EU's collective power in the new international economic order by making it the largest economic bloc. Agenda 2000 further elaborates on these issues by identifying three challenges facing the EU at the end of the century:

1. How to strengthen and reform the EU's policies so that they can deal with enlargement and deliver sustainable growth, higher employment, and improved living conditions for Europe's citizens
2. How to negotiate enlargement while at the same time vigorously preparing all applicant countries for the moment of accession
3. How to finance enlargement, the advance preparations, and the development of the EU's internal policies[15]

The EU citizens generally support these plans. According to the *Eurobarometer* survey number 56, 51 percent of EU citizens support enlargement. The highest level of support was in Greece with 74 percent, followed by Denmark and Sweden with 69 percent respectively. In five countries, the level of support for enlargement was below the EU average: Belgium—49 percent; Germany—47 percent; Austria—46 percent; Britain—41 percent; and France—39 percent.[16] Moreover, 68 percent believed that enlargement will make the EU a more important actor in world affairs and 64 percent viewed enlargement as contributing to the cultural richness of the EU and more peace and security in Europe.[17] However, their views of candidate countries varied greatly (Table 7.1).

Support is highest for Malta and ranges from 72 percent in Greece to 36 percent in France. The next highest support is for four other first-wave countries (Cyprus, the Czech Republic, Hungary, and Poland, but not for Slovenia). Support for Hungary ranges from 65 percent in Denmark and Sweden to 36 percent in France, while for Poland support ranges from 70 percent in Denmark to 23 percent in Austria. The support for Cyprus is highest in Greece, as expected—88 percent. France and Germany present the lowest support for Cyprus at 32 percent. Support for Turkey is the lowest among all of the candidate countries. Only 34 percent of EU citizens are in favor of Turkey's membership, and the support ranges from 44 percent in Ireland to 20 percent in Germany.[18]

Finally, it is important to note EU citizens' views on the conditions for membership for candidate countries. The surveyors presented the respondents with a list of statements pertaining to the Copenhagen criteria. Table 7.2 presents these results.

ASSESSING THE CANDIDATES. The two most recent Commission Reports (2001 and 2002) on enlargement show satisfactory progress in the area of democratization

TABLE 7.1 EU 15 Public Support for Membership of Candidate Countries

Candidate Country	In Favor (%)	Against (%)	No Opinion (%)
Bulgaria	38	40	22
Cyprus	46	33	21
Czech Republic	45	34	21
Estonia	40	38	22
Hungary	50	30	20
Latvia	39	38	23
Lithuania	39	38	23
Malta	51	28	21
Poland	47	34	19
Romania	36	42	24
Slovakia	37	43	20
Slovenia	37	40	23
Turkey	34	46	20

SOURCE: *Eurobarometer 56* Fig. 6.6a, p. 78.

TABLE 7.2 Importance of Copenhagen Criteria for Accession of Candidate Countries

Statement on Enlargement Criteria	Important (%)	Not Important (%)	No Opinion (%)
1. The country has to respect human rights and the principles of democracy	95	2	3
2. It has to fight organized crime and drug trafficking	92	3	5
3. It has to protect the environment	92	4	4
4. It has to be able to pay its share of the EU budget	85	8	7
5. Its joining should not be costly for existing member countries	81	11	8
6. It has to accept the *acquis*: whatever has already been decided and put into place throughout the process of building Europe	82	9	9
7. Its level of economic development should be close to that of other member states	77	15	8
8. It has to be prepared to put the interests of the EU above its own	72	16	12

SOURCE: *Eurobarometer 56*, Fig. 6.6, p. 77.

among the first-wave CEEC candidates (Cyprus, the Czech Republic, Estonia, Hungary, Poland, and Slovenia), though there are lingering problems concerning the slowness of the legal system (the Czech Republic, Estonia, Poland, and Slovenia). There are some problems with the independence of the judiciary in Slovakia, and with minorities in Latvia (Russians), Hungary (Romanians), the Czech Republic (Gypsies), Bulgaria (Turks), Romania (Hungarians and Gypsies), Cyprus (Turks), and Turkey (Kurds). The second-tier countries still had problems with democratic reforms. Among this group the Turkish case is by far the most serious as its candidacy agreement does not open the door for accession talks until Turkey meets certain conditions outlined by the EU.

In terms of their economic readiness for EU membership, all of the candidates, except Bulgaria and Romania, have met most of the necessary economic structural reforms for membership. Among these first wave countries, Cyprus and Malta have small and highly developed market economies that would not be costly to integrate with the EU. However, the present political division of Cyprus, the existence of constitutional issues that require both Greek and Turkish Cypriot communities' willingness to join any international body, and the veto power Turkey claims over Cyprus's EU membership (due to the Treaty of Guarantee) present serious obstacles for this country's accession to EU membership.[19] Delicate diplomatic efforts are currently under way to find a fair and just resolution of this problem. (See below, this chapter)

THE TURKISH PROBLEM. The case of Turkish application for membership is a complex one and deserves special attention because of its significance to the EU's other interests—the Cyprus problem for one, and the future of the European Security and Defense Identity (ESDI, discussed in Chapter 12). Turkey applied for EU membership in 1987, and on May 18, 1989, the European Commission concluded that the EU was not ready to enter into accession talks with Turkey because the Turkish economy was not as developed as the EU's, the Turkish democracy lacked extensive individual civil and political rights, and unemployment in Turkey posed a serious threat to the EU markets.[20] An additional and very serious problem in Turkey's case was the ongoing Greek–Turkish conflicts over Cyprus, territorial waters, the Aegean airspace, the continental shelf, and the rights of the Greek and Turkish minorities in their respective countries. Given the extent of this conflict, Greece would veto Turkey's membership in the EU even if the latter were to meet all the conditions for membership.

However, all was not lost after this initial European response. Recognizing Turkey's economic and political significance for the EU following the end of the Cold War, European leaders began a series of talks with their Turkish counterparts that eventually resulted in a compromise solution that neither shut the door on future membership nor granted the Turks immediate accession. The outcome was the customs union agreement of 1995 that went into effect on December 31, 1995.[21] This agreement gave the Turks closer economic ties with the EU than any other nonmember country at the time, with the exception of Iceland, Norway, and Switzerland, and opened the Turkish market of 65 million consumers to EU companies. For the Turks, the customs union symbolized their membership in Europe and thus put Turkey on track for membership in the EU. For the EU members, however, the customs union was the most Turkey could expect from the EU for the foreseeable future.

The next crucial event in EU–Turkey relations came at the Luxembourg summit of December 1997. At this summit, the EU leaders decided on the list of candidate countries for membership in line with the recommendations of the European Commission outlined earlier in Agenda 2000. The announcement excluded Turkey as a candidate country. The Turkish government reacted harshly on several fronts. First, it announced that it no longer viewed the EU as a third-party mediator in Greek–Turkish affairs and the Cyprus problem. Second, as explained in Chapter 12, the Turkish government vetoed the European allies' ESDI plans on agenda setting in the North Atlantic Treaty Organization (NATO). And finally, on the economic front Turkey decided not to purchase military hardware from EU states.

Relations between the two sides were extremely tense, and it was clear that something had to be done to improve this situation. Not only was Turkey moving away from the EU; several important foreign policy and security matters on NATO's agenda were deadlocked: lack of progress on Cyprus, the Aegean, and the future reformulation of NATO–ESDI relations. Greek–Turkish relations also reached a low point in early 1999 after the capture of the separatist Kurdish leader Abdullah Ocalan by Turkish special forces in Kenya as he was leaving the Greek ambassador's residence.

The initiative for a possible solution to the EU–Turkish problem came from the Clinton administration. These efforts gained added momentum after the devastating earthquakes in Turkey in August 1999 and also occurring to a lesser degree in Greece, when the peoples of the two countries began a series of bilateral goodwill initiatives. The governments of Greece and Turkey, led by their respective foreign ministers, seized this opportunity and started building cooperation in many technical areas such as tourism and drug trafficking. The first sign of improvement came when the Commission recommended to the Council that Turkey be included as a formal candidate but without any definite time set for the start of accession talks. The European Council meeting at Helsinki in December 1999 followed these recommendations and invited Turkey to join the CEEC candidates. After intense diplomatic pressure the EU and Turkey came to an agreement, with the understanding that both sides will work in an atmosphere of goodwill to settle disputes between them. The lifting of the Greek veto was the most significant issue in this compromise. In return, Turkey agreed to the EU's statement that it will adapt to the *acquis* and work with Greece to resolve disputes between the two countries and Cyprus; and the EU agreed to review progress on these fronts by the end of 2004. The EU stated that if Greek–Turkish problems were not resolved by the set date, the Commission would consider recommending taking the problems to the Hague Court for resolution, though this is not a binding statement.

Despite these developments, EU–Turkish relations once again took a turn for the worse with the most recent recommendation of the Commission on enlargement, which gives Turkey no definitive timetable for starting accession talks.[22] The recommendation provides the basis for the 2002 accession assessment of the candidates and served as a guideline for the European Council summit in Copenhagen in December 2002. According to the Commission, the other 12 countries had made substantial progress in their reform efforts, enough to warrant membership in the Union. Ten countries will become members in 2004, and two others, Bulgaria and Romania, will join them in 2007. This conclusion of the Commission drew criticism from Turkish officials for two reasons. First, the Turkish parliament had passed substantial reforms of the constitution to satisfy the EU's political *acquis* standards in September 2002. And second, the Commission's position on Cyprus's membership is seen as a pro-Greek policy that ignores Turkey's and Turkish Cypriots' treaty rights over Cyprus's membership in international organizations/institutions (see the next section).

THE CYPRUS CASE. The Cyprus case does not present economic obstacles for its accession; rather, the issue is the unresolved political tension between the island's Greek and Turkish populations. This problem has troubled the Western alliance since 1963. The agreement between the EU, Turkey, and Greece included an intent to set a date for accession talks with Cyprus. The Cyprus government, which is dominated by Greek Cypriots, believes that both communities of the island will benefit from EU accession. However, the Turkish Cypriots and Turkey strongly disagree. Since July 1974, when Turkey intervened to protect the Turkish Cypriot minority and prevent the union of Cyprus and Greece, the island has been divided into a Turkish Republic of Northern Cyprus (TRNC) and the internationally recognized Cyprus Republic in the south. The TRNC is only recognized by Turkey. In addition, the island is one of the most militarized pieces of real estate in the world. Unless the international community resolves the Cyprus problem and forges a political partnership between the two communities, it would be highly risky for the EU to admit the Greek part of Cyprus into the EU because of a possible reaction of Turkey that could involve annexation of the TRNC. This would complicate EU–Turkey relations and contribute to regional instability.

At the December 1997 Luxembourg summit, the European Council took the decisions necessary to set the enlargement process in motion. It decided to convene bilateral intergovernmental conferences in the spring of 1998 to begin negotiations with Cyprus, Hungary, Poland, Estonia, the Czech Republic, and Slovenia on the conditions for their entry into the Union and the ensuing Treaty adjustments. In addition, the Luxembourg European Council stated that the accession of Cyprus should benefit all communities and help to bring about civil peace and reconciliation. The accession negotiations should contribute positively to the search for a political solution to the Cyprus problem through the talks under the aegis of the United Nations that must continue with a view to creating a bicommunal, bizonal federation. In this context, the European Council requested that the willingness of the Government of Cyprus to include representatives of the Turkish Cypriot community in the accession negotiating delegation be acted upon.

Unfortunately, accession talks between Cyprus and the Union have not progressed as hoped. On March 12, 1998, President Glafkos Clerides attended the European Conference in London and presented a timetable to the EU outlining the Cypriot strategy for accession talks. The proposal included an invitation to the Turkish Cypriots to take part in the Cyprus negotiating team. The Turkish Cypriots rejected this invitation on grounds that the Greek Cypriot government did not represent all of Cyprus and that the Turkish Cypriot side had been excluded in prior EU–Cyprus relations. Additional objections raised by the Turkish Cypriots include controversies surrounding the Republic's constitution. The first problem is over the legality of the Cypriot application for membership. The Constitution of Cyprus requires that both communities support the decision to apply for membership in the EU. The Turkish Cypriots were clearly excluded in this process. The second complicating legal factor pertains to the Turks' objection to Greek Cypriot application on the basis of international treaties signed in 1960. The Turkish side maintains that Greek Cypriots' application for EU membership on behalf of the whole island is simply illegal based on Articles I and II of the 1960 Treaty of Guarantee, Annex F of the Treaty of Establishment, and Article 50 Par. 1(a) and Article 185 No. 2 of the 1960 Constitution of Cyprus. The 1959 Zurich and London Agreements stipulate that Cyprus cannot join international organizations or pacts of alliance of which both Turkey and Greece are not members, and the 1960 Treaty of Guarantee contains the provision that Cyprus cannot participate, in whole or in part, in any political or economic union with any state whatsoever.[23]

There is a lot of speculation about whether the EU is an intergovernmental organization (IGO) or a state. It is an IGO that has state-like aspirations. Nevertheless, this is not the key problem with "union with another state." The EU is a union—an economic and monetary union and, to a lesser extent, a political union. To verify this point, one must start with the Maastricht Treaty and end with the Nice Treaty of the EU. When a country joins the EU, it gives up part of its national sovereignty, whether it be monetary policy or EU regulations and guidelines. Moreover, the new member enters into a full economic and monetary union and a partial political union with the current members of the EU.

The Greek Cypriot government, Greece, and the EU reject these legal issues as a real problem. They maintain that in the current state of affairs in Cyprus where Turkey is viewed as an occupying power and where the Turkish Cypriots have established their own "illegal" state in the north, the Turks are in no position to argue the legitimacy of the very treaties they have violated. Art. II par. 2. of the Cyprus constitution clearly prohibits any action that could result in partitioning of Cyprus. Furthermore, Turkey's military presence in northern Cyprus and its recognition of TRNC independence contradict the guarantor powers' commitment to Cyprus's unity under this treaty. Faced with such problems, the Bush administration pursued a shuttle diplomacy between the parties concerned to find a compromise solution before the Copenhagen summit in December 2002. The United Nations joined this effort and pushed for a settlement under a new comprehensive plan, known as the Annan Plan, that envisioned a new United Cyprus constructed as a cross between a federal and confederal state made up of two politically equal entities (a Greek Cypriot and a Turkish Cypriot state). The plan also called for a limited migration between the two states for settlement and addressed the future of peace building on the island. The new state would then join the EU as a single country. Despite serious efforts of the international community, the Turkish Cypriot leadership rejected the Annan

Plan. With this rejection, the talks failed and the Greek Cypriots and future enlargement of the EU seem to be poised to include only the southern part of Cyprus. At the time of writing, some diplomatic efforts are underway to try to find a solution to the Cyprus stalemate. However, these efforts were hampered by the War in Iraq that diverted attention of the world community away from Cyprus.[24]

In light of these complications, coupled with the Commission's proposal not to give Turkey a timetable for starting accession talks, the Copenhagen summit in December 2002 was poised to be critical for the future EU–Turkish relations, as will be its aftermath. It is feared that if the EU proceeds with admitting the Greek part of Cyprus and places Turkey in an uncertain waiting game, the Turks might react negatively and move to annex the TRNC.

Implications of Enlargement

Enlargement presents several internal complications for the EU. As the Union prepares to receive 10 new members in 2004, followed by at least 2 in 2007, the institutions and policies of the EU face necessary reforms to reflect the enlargement process. These issues cover such items as the number of parliamentarians from the new members, the number of commissioners, judges, and auditors, and revision of the QMV system in the Council of Ministers. At the same time, CAP, cohesion policies, and the budget of the EU require reforms to make it possible for the new countries to be integrated into the Union. While these challenges are not impossible to overcome, they nevertheless present serious policy dilemmas for the current and candidate members alike.

INSTITUTIONS. The prospect of a dozen new members entering the EU within a few years was the motivating factor behind the Nice Treaty, which required an exhausting process of negotiation in order to bring about agreement on major changes in the EU institutional arrangements (see Chapter 6 and Table 7.3). The Treaty proved unacceptable to Irish voters the first time around. By the time Irish voters approved it in October 2002, the ratification process had been delayed 22 months. Meanwhile, dissatisfaction with the EU institutions, even in their revised version, took a variety of forms. The institutions were criticized for being at once insufficiently democratic, excessively complex and unwieldy, too intergovernmental, too supranational, too small-country protective, and too big-country dominated. Depending upon the aspect of the institutions in question, all of these criticisms have a degree of validity. Hence, the voices calling for a comprehensive review and overhaul of the Treaties have grown in volume, to the point where the member governments agreed to the creation of the "constitutional convention," which began its deliberations in 2002 and is scheduled to report its recommendations by 2003. Unofficial reports of progress on these recommendations suggest that all of the previously mentioned complaints, and more, are gaining a hearing. But, whatever emerges from the convention will have to gain the acceptance of the heads of state and government in the European Council, probably with revisions protecting member state prerogatives.

TABLE 7.3   Institutional Implications of Enlargement

	Votes		% EU Population		Population	MEPS	
	Current	Post-Nice	Current	EU-27	(millions)	Current	Post-Nice
Germany	10	29	21.90	17.05	82.04	99	99
France	10	29	15.74	12.25	58.97	87	72
Britain	10	29	15.81	12.31	59.25	87	72
Italy	10	29	15.38	11.97	57.61	87	72
Spain	8	27	10.51	8.18	39.39	64	50
Poland	0	27	0.00	8.03	38.67	0	50
Romania	0	14	0.00	4.67	22.49	0	33
Netherlands	5	13	4.20	3.27	15.76	31	25
Greece	5	12	2.81	2.18	10.53	25	22
Czech Rep.	0	12	0.00	2.13	10.29	0	20
Belgium	5	12	2.72	2.12	10.21	25	22
Hungary	0	12	0.00	2.09	10.09	0	20
Portugal	5	12	2.66	2.07	9.98	25	22
Sweden	4	10	2.36	1.83	8.85	22	18
Bulgaria	0	10	0.00	1.71	8.23	0	17
Austria	4	10	2.15	1.67	8.08	21	17
Slovakia	0	7	0.00	1.12	5.39	0	13
Denmark	3	7	1.41	1.10	5.31	16	13
Finland	3	7	1.37	1.07	5.16	16	13
Ireland	3	7	0.99	0.77	3.74	15	12
Lithuania	0	7	0.00	0.76	3.70	0	12
Latvia	0	4	0.00	0.50	2.44	0	8
Slovenia	0	4	0.00	0.41	1.98	0	7
Estonia	0	4	0.00	0.30	1.45	0	6
Cyprus	0	4	0.00	0.15	0.75	0	6
Luxembourg	2	4	0.11	0.08	0.43	6	6
Malta	0	3	0.00	0.07	0.38	0	5
		EU-15	EU-27				
TOTALS	87	237	345 million		481.2	626	732
QMV	62	169	255 million				
		(71.3%)	(73.9%)				
Blocking Minority	26	69	91				

SOURCE: http://www.eurunion.org/infores/euguide/Chapter2.htm#chartvoting

So the impending enlargement of the EU is both the primary motivation for institutional reform and the source of dilemmas that will make a coherent package as unlikely to be produced from the constitution writing process as it was from the Nice treaty-writing process. The Nice Treaty set forth voting weights of current and future members in the Council of Ministers and reduced the number of Commissioners supplied by the larger countries from two to one. The effects of enlargement are mitigated by a further reduction in the number of legislation categories where unanimity applies. But, where the veto still applies, the number of possible veto wielders rises from 15 to somewhere in the mid-20s with the enlargement, eventually rising close to 30, or double what it was in 2002. Most of the new members will have voting weights in the small-country category, while larger members are compensated with the two-pronged requirement for a positive QMV. This will increase the difficulty of adopting legislation and may lengthen the time to adopt legislative measures once they come out of the Commission. Treaty revisions in the 1990s had been in the direction of a more efficient process. Supporters of a stronger European Parliament may find further arguments for reducing the veto opportunities of member governments. While the new member governments may themselves be more enthusiastic about the integrative process, at least so long as it promises greater benefits for poorer countries, the more cumbersome voting procedures may also slow down the integrative process rather than accelerate it. The wealthier countries may become more coalition-prone, encouraging a common interest in blocking proposals they deem too costly. Much will depend on whether political priorities can overcome perceived adverse economic consequences, at a time when economic problems may continue to be a preoccupation across the different parts of Europe.

The British weekly *Economist* exemplifies the growing criticism of the treaty revision process:

> What else is new? In Europe, you might say, turmoil like this is business as usual. Europe's model of change has long been based on lurch then muddle. And it works. The EU's boldest initiatives—the single currency, for instance—have been shaped by a grand vision and an insatiable appetite for innovation among the Union's leaders (rarely among its citizens) together with an equally impressive tolerance of loose ends. . . . When you look at what the EU has achieved, as a self-propagating organism if in no other way, who is to say this rough-and-ready method has failed? But perhaps the drawbacks of muddling through are growing. . . . Enlargement from a Union of 15 members to one of 25 or more will pose an even bigger challenge to the lurch-and-muddle approach than the single currency. No question, this influx of mainly poor economies is welcome in itself; indeed is is scandalously overdue. But it is going to expose very cruelly these and other loose ends in the EU's institutional design.[25]

Greater understanding of the problems facing the process of refashioning EU institutions is shown in the following observation by political scientists John Peterson and Elizabeth Bomberg:

> The project has always been a *risky* enterprise, involving unprecedented and experimental acts of cooperation between sovereign nation-states. Risk-averse behavior is certainly a prime characteristic of EU decision-making and helps explain the EU's tendency towards lowest common denominator

outcomes. Yet, the risk of inertia, inaction (especially in external policy), and policy stagnation have perceptibly increased for the EU in the 1990s.[26]

For the EU institutions, "muddling through" is another way of saying that the EU makes its important decisions through difficult and often prolonged processes of negotiation among member governments. This method and the way the institutions really work are being tested by the current maxi-enlargement.

BUDGET. Reform of the CAP budget is one of the major policy issues facing EU members before enlargement. EU foreign ministers discussed the funding of enlargement at a meeting in Luxembourg on October 22–23, 2002, amid continued disagreement between France and Germany over the future of the costly CAP (see Chapter 9). Denmark, which held the EU presidency, warned that financial and other thorny issues must be wrapped up at the October 24–25 summit of the 15 heads of member states and governments, or else final enlargement talks set for December could be delayed. France rejected a German call to scale down EU farm aid from 2004 to help fund expansion, finding it too early to discuss such reform. The CAP eats up nearly half of the EU's €95 billion annual budget. Germany, a net contributor to the EU budget, is worried about the long-term costs of extending generous farm subsidies to often inefficient producers in Poland, Hungary, and other candidate countries.

COHESION. Enlargement presents three major challenges for cohesion policy. First, regional disparities in economic development in the Union will become more apparent (Table 7.4). Whereas enlargement will increase the EU's population by one-

TABLE 7.4 Key Statistics: EU15 and Applicant Countries

	Population million	Area 000 km	GDP € billion	GDP € per head	GDP Change %	Inflation %
Bulgaria	8.2	111	44.3	5,400	5.8	10.3
Cyprus	0.8	9	12.4	18,500	4.8	4.9
Czech Republic	10.3	79	135.1	13,500	2.9	3.9
Estonia	1.4	45	12.1	8,500	6.9	3.9
Hungary	10.0	93	117.0	11,700	5.2	10.0
Latvia	2.4	65	15.6	6,600	6.6	2.6
Lithuania	3.7	65	24.3	6,600	3.3	0.9
Malta	0.4	0.3	4.6	11,900	5.0	2.4
Poland	38.6	313	337.9	8,700	4.0	10.1
Romania	22.4	238	135.4	6,000	1.6	45.7
Slovak Republic	5.4	49	58.3	10,800	2.2	12.1
Slovenia	2.0	20	32.0	16,100	4.6	8.9
Turkey	65.3	775	433.3	6,400	7.2	54.9
EU15	378.3	3,191	8,499	22,500	3.4	2.1

SOURCE: *Eurostat, from national sources Year: 2000.* http://europa.eu.int/comm/enlargement/faq/faq2.htm#statistics

third, it will add only 5 percent to the overall GDP. Second, the focus of cohesion policy will mostly shift to eastern Europe where 98 million live in regions whose current GDP is below 75 percent of the average of the enlarged EU. And third, the existing inequalities among the EU15 regions will remain, adding to the complicated picture. In order to address these problems, the Commission proposed a strengthening of the existing pre-accession assistance programs with an action plan for the Union's regions bordering candidate countries,[27] which complements the Second Report on Economic and Social Commission, adopted in January 2001. Under the program the Instrument for Structural Policies for Pre-accession (ISPA) provides assistance to candidate countries with environment and transport projects and has a budget of €1,040 million per year during 2000–2006. Also, under the INTERREG III program, cooperation projects are possible between regions in the EU15 and the candidate countries.

EASTERN BORDERS. With Poland and the Baltic states joining the EU, the tiny Russian enclave of Kaliningrad (population 900,000) presents a serious problem for EU–Russian relations. Kaliningrad is bordered on two sides by the members-to-be and by the Baltic Sea on the other. When Lithuania and Poland join the EU, visa-free travel for Russians crossing their territories will come to an end. This will certainly complicate travel for Russians between Kaliningrad and Russia. The Brussels Commission states that the EU will not relax its policy of requiring visas for Russians traveling to and from Kaliningrad through Lithuania or Poland. The Russian government, on the other hand, warned that such a policy would damage EU–Russia relations. President Vladimir Putin went as far as calling this dilemma a matter of national principle and vowed to defend the right of the Russians for free travel between Kaliningrad and Russia.[28] Russia favors establishment of a special 160-mile rail and freight corridor through Lithuania to link this enclave to Russia. The EU, on the other hand, rejects this proposal as unworkable.

CONCLUSION AND PROSPECTS

The EU has set a course of action for itself that is both ambitious and necessary. Regional developments and global systemic changes have pushed the expansion plans of the EU. The desire of the candidates to join the Union helps push completion of the necessary structural (economic and political) reforms in each respective country. However, there will be a substantial impact of eastern expansion on the EU's internal institutional structure, and the cost associated with enlargement is a major problem as the EU takes up reform of its budget to meet targets identified in *Agenda 2000*. Furthermore, most of the newcomers fall into the category of the "poor members" of the EU, thus further straining the already tight structural and regional funds.

ENDNOTES

1. EC Economic and Social Council, "Opinion on the Mediterranean Policy of the European Community," *Official Journal of the European Communities*, No. C221/16 (January 25, 1989).

2. Birol A. Yeşilada, "Further Enlargement of the European Community: The Cases of the European Periphery States," *National Forum* (Spring, 1992): 21–25.

3. Marc Maresceau, "The European Community, Eastern Europe and the USSR," in John Redmond, ed., *The External Relations of the European Community: The Internal Response to 1992* (New York: St. Martin's Press, 1992), pp. 97–98.

4. Françoise de la Serre, "The EC and Central and Eastern Europe," in Leon Hurwitz and Christian Lequesne, eds., *The State of the European Community: Policies, Institutions, and Debates in the Transition Years* (Boulder, Colo.: Lynne Reinner, 1991), p. 310.

5. Frank McDonald and Keith Penketh, "The European Community and the Rest of Europe," in Frank McDonald and Stephen Dearden, eds., *European Economic Integration* (London: Longman, 1992), p. 193.

6. Commission of the European Communities. Directorate General, *EC-East Europe: Relations with Central and Eastern Europe and the Commonwealth of Independent States* (Brussels: Office of EC Publications, 1992).

7. "Survey: The European Community," *The Economist*, July 11, 1992, p. 26.

8. Maresceau, "The European Community, Eastern Europe and the USSR," p. 97.

9. Ibid., p. 98.

10. European Commission, *Enlargement: Financial Instruments* (http://europa.eu.int/scadplus/leg/en/lvb/e50003.htm).

11. "Essen Summit Endorses Eastern European Strategy," *Eurecom* 6 (December 1994): 1.

12. "Leaders Agree on Institutional Changes at Nice," *Financial Times*, December 12, 2000, p. 2.

13. Alan Cowell, "Irish Vote for a Wider Union, and Europe Celebrates," *New York Times* (October 21, 2002). http://www.nytimes.com/ads/amexpopup_ftp.html.

14. The European Commission, http://europa.eu.int/comm/enlargement/enlargement.htm. The ten countries are: Cyprus, the Czech Republic, Estonia, Hungary, Latvia, Lithuania, Malta, Poland, the Slovak Republic, and Slovenia.

15. European Commission, *Agenda 2000* (Brussels: European Commission, 1997), p. 2.

16. European Commission, *Eurobarometer 56* (Brussels: European Commission, April 2002), p. 71.

17. Ibid., p. 76.

18. Ibid.

19. Birol Yeşilada, "The Worsening EU–Turkey Relations," *SAIS Review* (Winter–Spring 1999): 148–153.

20. European Commission, *Commission Opinion on Turkey's Request for Accession to the Community*, Sec. (89) 2290 final (Brussels: Official Publications of the European Communities, December 18, 1989).

21. Yeşilada, "The Worsening EU–Turkey Relations," pp. 144–161.

22. Associated Press, "EU Says Turkey Not Ready for Accession Talks," October 7, 2002.

23. Republic of Cyprus, *The Treaty of Guarantee* 16 August 1960 http://www.cypnet.com/ncyprus/cyproblem/ganati.html and http://www.kypros.org/Cyprus_Problem/treaty.html

24. "The Annan Plan" Kibris (Turkish Cypriot Daily) November 11, 2002.

25. *The Economist*, October 25, 2002, p. 11.

26. John Peterson and Elizabeth Bomberg, "The EU after the 1990s: Explaining Continuity and Change," in Maria Green Cowles and Michael Smith, eds., *The State of the European Union: Risks, Reforms, and Revival*, vol. 5 of series sponsored by the European Community Studies Association (Oxford and New York: Oxford University Press, 2000), p. 39.

27. European Commission, "Challenges of Enlargement," http://europa.eu.int/comm/enlargement/docs/index.htm#sec2002-102.

28. Ian Traynor, "EU and Russia Clash over Baltic Enclave," *The Guardian* (Thursday May 30, 2002), p. 4.

8

∎

Economic and
Monetary Union

Eleven members of the European Union (EU) launched the Economic and Monetary Union (EMU) on January 1, 1999. The history of the EMU represents a very big adventure that carries with it political and economic risks. With a single monetary authority and a single European currency (€) replacing the national banknotes and coins of 12 member states, EMU represents the climax of European economic integration. In this chapter, we will provide an overview of the regional and systemic developments that gave rise to the coordination of exchange rate policy in the EU countries, followed by the analysis of "snake in a tunnel" and the failure of the members to achieve a zone of monetary stability in Europe. We will then examine the European Monetary System (EMS) and EMU. Finally, we will analyze the economic and political implications of EMU for member states and the global monetary system.

After the creation of the customs union and until the adoption of the EMS in 1978, members of the European Community (EC) experienced serious economic difficulties that threatened the future of economic integration. Whereas many scholars argue that this was a period of disintegration, we believe that this conclusion is misplaced (see Chapter 4). If disintegration was the order of this period, then how can one account for the creation of the EMS that highlighted a process of trial and learning in exchange rate policy? Moreover, the European Regional Development Fund came into effect in 1975. As we will explain in Chapter 9, this fund is crucial for the development of the underprivileged regions of the EC. Finally, the Community expanded to nine countries when Britain, Denmark, and Ireland became members in 1973.

The economic difficulties experienced by the EC resulted from important changes in the international economic order. The collapse of the Bretton Woods monetary system represented the first serious shock to the EC and tested its seriousness in achieving economic integration. During the 1960s, there were important developments that weakened this monetary system. The weakening of the U.S. dollar strained the stability of European currencies: the West German government revalued the deutsche mark (DM) in 1961 and 1969, and the French government devalued the franc in 1969. These measures were intended to stabilize the U.S. dollar in international markets. However, they failed to eliminate exchange rate instability in the system and persuaded EC leaders that alternative policy options had to be considered for the Community. The policy recommendation came at the Hague summit of 1969, where the EC heads of state and governments accepted Willy Brandt's call for EMU. Subsequently, the Werner plan of 1970 laid down the basic idea for this monetary union.[1] Unfortunately, its introduction coincided with the collapse of Bretton Woods and the rise of the everyone-for-oneself period of the floating exchange rates.

According to Miltiades Chacholiades, "two or more countries form an *economic union* when they form a common market and, in addition, proceed to unify their fiscal, monetary, and socioeconomic policies. An economic union is the most complete form of economic integration."[2] A common market involves establishing a customs union between two or more countries and free movement of all factors of production among the member states. The United States represents the most successful economic and monetary union.

Europeans' interest in EMU stemmed from their fear that continued revaluation of their national currencies vis-à-vis the dollar would threaten the stability of exchange rates, and thus of intra-EC trade, that had existed in the Community since 1957. The customs union and the maintenance of the Common Agricultural Policy required stability; unstable exchange rates threatened the survival of the Community. Therefore, a drastic policy initiative was needed to achieve a zone of monetary stability among the EU member states.

TRIAL AND ERROR IN EXCHANGE RATE POLICIES: THE ROAD TO EMS, 1971–1979

When the Bretton Woods system collapsed, the United States wanted the DM and the Japanese yen to be revalued against the dollar. This would have had the same effect on the U.S. trade deficit as an approximately 10 percent devaluation of the dollar; the difference would be that its impact would have been on those economies that contributed the most to the American trade deficit. The subsequent Smithsonian Agreement of 1971, where the industrialized democracies' leaders attempted to coordinate their monetary policies, failed to bring stability to this situation. More crucial from the European point of view, this agreement and the subsequent reaction of the EC members to the collapse of Bretton Woods demonstrated how uncoordinated the European response was to the apparent crisis.

In accord with the Smithsonian Agreement, the U.S. government devalued the dollar by 10 percent. Intra-EC trade faced immense obstacles from unstable prices due to exchange rate fluctuation. The EC responded to this pressure by establishing the snake in the tunnel and reduced the excursion allowed by the Smithsonian Agreement by half. The limit for fluctuations between EU currencies was to be only 4.5 percent. Before accession to EC membership, Britain, Ireland, and Denmark agreed to join the snake. The par value of each EC currency vis-à-vis the dollar represented the center of the tunnel. According to the agreed formulation, a variation of plus or minus 2.25 percent on either side of the dollar exchange rate determined the walls of the tunnel. Effectively, this arrangement established a joint float (snake) of the EC currencies that stayed within the walls of the tunnel formed by the maximum fluctuations around the dollar.

Despite initial enthusiasm about the snake, this arrangement lasted for only a short period, from April 1972 to March 1973. In June 1972, the British pound left the snake and began to free-float. Ireland and Denmark followed soon after, though Denmark later rejoined the snake. In February 1973, the Italian government took the lira out of the tunnel. Finally, in March 1973, the EC central banks ended their support of the margins vis-à-vis the dollar, and the snake left the tunnel to free-float. To make matters worse, the United States devalued the dollar by another 10 percent in 1973. The subsequent "floating snake" of the EU lasted until 1979, but it only included West Germany and four other members—Belgium, the Netherlands, Luxembourg, and Denmark—which kept their currencies close to the DM.

Problems faced by the Europeans worsened as the U.S. administration continued to pressure its trade partners to undertake enormous economic responsibilities. For example, President Carter's "locomotive theory" called for West Germany and Japan to assume major responsibilities in reviving the world economy.[3] According to this theory, countries with balance-of-payments surpluses (Japan and West Germany) were to follow expansionary policies that would serve as engines of growth for the rest of the world. Chancellor Helmut Schmidt, who was already at odds with the American president over Western defense policy, opposed this theory and began to search for alternative policies for West Germany and its EC partners. Schmidt worried about the implications of U.S. policies for the future of economic stability in Europe. First, the worsening of the U.S. balance-of-payments deficit could cause the value of the dollar to fall against the DM and thus allow more funds to flow to the DM zone. This would result in the overvaluation of the DM and put pressure on West Germany's exports. Second, the depreciation of the dollar resulted in the DM becoming a de facto international reserve currency as investors looked for alternative reserves to the dollar. The result would then be increased upward pressure on German interest rates, probably beyond the limits set by the Bundesbank. Furthermore, as the United States continued to experience large balance-of-payments deficits, the dollar crisis of 1978 emerged: the dollar fell by 10 percent between October 1977 and February 1978, and by another 10 percent by the fall of 1978.[4] These were background conditions that influenced the decision to create a European monetary system.

Another dimension of this monetary problem was that the traditional Keynesian macroeconomic policies did not seem to work following the 1973 oil crisis. The countries with the worst inflation, France and Italy, also experienced the highest unemployment rates. In addition, they also had the poorest economic growth rates. According to Stephen George, "the tradeoff between inflation and growth did not appear to be working, and accelerating inflation threatened economic collapse."[5] Under these circumstances, it became clear to the EC leaders that they had to protect EC currencies against fluctuations in the value of the U.S. dollar. Furthermore, there was a general dissatisfaction with the floating exchange rates among EC officials because exchange rates had been highly volatile during the mid-1970s due to overspeculation in the currency markets. Lastly, the European leaders believed that fixed rates had a beneficial effect upon intra-EC trade.[6]

The answer to these problems seemed to lie in the formulation of a new exchange rate system for the EC currencies. However, the EC leaders had to make sure the mistakes of the snake in the tunnel would not be repeated. They had learned that the previous system failed because of the asymmetry of the exchange rate mechanism and the failure of the exchange market intervention rules to provide the necessary credibility to the margins allowed for currency fluctuations.[7] Under the snake, the central banks had agreed to provide each other unlimited financing for intervention in currency markets. This new facility was the Very Short Term Financing Facility, administered by the European Monetary Cooperation Fund. Furthermore, the claims and liabilities between the central banks had to be settled within a period of one month. Not only was this period very short, but also there were insufficient funds available under the Very Short Term Financing Facility for intervention by several central banks. As a result, the system did not operate efficiently, and it contributed to the breakup of the snake.[8]

The system that emerged in 1979 was a compromise around a Belgian proposal that combined the German plan with the French, Italian, and British alternative. The West Germans wanted to continue the arrangement of bilateral parities found under the snake, where each currency would be tied to every other currency in the system. Furthermore, in order to ease the pressure on currencies, the Germans called for wider margins than the old plus or minus 2.25 percent of the snake for exchange rate fluctuations and argued that the central banks should intervene to restore the agreed parities. In the alternative parity grid plan, the French, the British, and the Italians asked that instead of bilateral parities, all currency values be determined in relation to an alternative basket currency system based on the weighted averages of all EC currencies known as the European currency unit (ecu). They argued that the German proposal was an unfair system because it placed an unnecessary burden on countries with weaker currencies. Finally, a compromise was reached around a Belgian proposal that combined the two systems. It was a substantial improvement over the old snake system. It included four main components: (1) a basket currency, the ecu; (2) the exchange rate mechanism (ERM); (3) credit provisions among the participating central banks; and (4) the pooling of reserve assets among the members.[9]

The ecu was the renamed and restructured European unit of account (EUA, introduced in 1975). It was a basket currency that served four functions: (1) the denominator for the ERM, (2) the basis for a divergence indicator, (3) the denominator for operations in both the intervention and credit mechanism, and (4) a reserve instrument and a means of settlement between monetary authorities in the Community.[10] Basket currencies, like the ecu and the International Monetary Fund's special drawing rights (SDR), are stable reserve currencies that counteract exchange rate volatility.

The ERM called for participating countries to maintain their exchange rates within bilateral limits of plus or minus 2.25 percent. More precisely, the upper part of the band was 2.275 percent above the central parity, while the lower part of the band was 2.225 percent of the central parity. Italy negotiated a wider margin of plus or minus 6 percent due to its weak national currency. As Michael Artis and Mark Taylor explain, "According to these provisions, when a currency triggered its divergence indicator threshold (calculated as the ecu value of a 75 percent departure of its bilateral rates against all the other countries), a presumption was created that the country concerned should take corrective action."[11]

To enable member countries to meet this obligation, the EC created a large credit fund, known as the European Monetary Cooperation Fund, and the member states contributed 20 percent of their gold and dollar holdings to this fund in exchange for ecus. The facilities involved in the intervention mechanisms were the Very Short Term Financing Facility, the Short-Term Monetary Support, and the Medium-Term Financing Assistance. The latter two indicated significant improvements over the system that existed under the snake.

The EMS seemed to work rather well throughout the 1980s, and it looked as though the EC had finally managed to create a zone of monetary stability. During these years, the EC currencies became less variable against one another as well as against the U.S. dollar and the Japanese yen (Table 8.1). At the same time, the ERM countries experienced a steady decline in inflation.[12] Thus, the European leaders believed that they had found the answer to the currency problems of the EC in the new EMS. With this apparent success, they again moved to consider monetary union among the EC states.

TABLE 8.1   Bilateral Nominal Exchange Rates against ERM Currencies, 1974–1990*

Currency/ Country	Pre-EMS 1974–1978	Recession of 1979–1983	SEA Period 1984–1986	Post-SEA 1987–1990	Post-EMS Average 1979–1990
Belgium/Luxembourg franc	1.2	1.3	0.6	0.4	0.9
Danish crown	1.4	1.0	0.5	0.5	0.8
German DM	1.5	1.0	0.5	0.5	0.8
Greek drachma	1.8	2.3	2.5	0.7	2.1
Portuguese escudo	3.0	2.1	0.8	1.1	1.8
French franc	1.9	1.1	0.7	0.5	0.7
Irish punt	2.0	0.7	1.2	0.5	1.0
Italian lira	2.2	1.0	0.9	0.6	0.8
Dutch guilder	1.0	0.8	0.6	0.3	0.5
Spanish peseta	2.8	2.0	1.1	0.5	1.7
UK pound	2.2	2.6	2.4	1.9	2.4
EC mean	1.7	0.7	0.5	0.4	0.4
US dollar	2.2	2.5	2.9	2.7	2.7
Japanese yen	2.3	2.7	2.0	1.9	2.5

SOURCE: Data obtained from *International Financial Statistics* (Washington, D.C.: IMF, quarterly publications).
*Variability is the weighted sum of standard deviations of monthly percent changes.

THE EMU AGAIN

The concept of economic and monetary union was not new. The Werner plan of 1970 had promoted this idea. Furthermore, while the Single European Act (SEA) did not call for an EMU, it did recall in one of its preambles that in 1972 the European Council "approved the objective of progressively creating an EMU."[13] With the relative success of the EMS in bringing about a zone of monetary stability in Europe during the mid-1980s, the EC moved to reexamine the feasibility of an EMU at the Hanover summit in 1988. At this meeting, the European Council agreed to set up a committee of central bankers and technical experts under the leadership of the European Commission president, Jacques Delors, to prepare a report by the June 1989 Madrid summit on the steps to be taken to achieve EMU. The resulting report, known as the Delors plan, proposed a three-stage plan toward the EMU[14]:

Stage 1

Economic:	Completion of the internal market (Project 1992); strengthened competition policy; full implementation of the reform of the structural funds; enhanced coordination and surveillance of economic policies; budgetary adjustments in high debt/deficit countries
Monetary:	Capital market liberalization; enhanced monetary and exchange rate policy coordination; realignments possible but infrequent; all EC currencies in the narrow bands of the ERM; extended use of the ecu

Stage 2

Economic:	Evaluation and adaptation of stage 1 policies; review of national macroeconomic adjustments
Monetary:	Establishment of the European System of Central Banks (ESCB), (called a Eurofed in the report); a possible narrowing of the EMS exchange rate bands

Stage 3

Economic:	Definitive budgetary coordination among the member states; a possible strengthening of the structural and regional policies
Monetary:	ESCB or a similar institution in charge of monetary policy; irrevocably fixed exchange rates that would pave the way to replace national currencies with a single currency, the ecu, administered by the European Monetary Cooperation Fund

The Delors plan was much more explicit about the EMU, its institutions, and the necessary deadlines than any previous plan on the subject. Stage 1 was to commence in July 1990 and was linked to the completion of the single market. Stage 2 was to start on January 1, 1994, and stage 3 would be completed by the end of the century.

The European Council accepted the plan at the Madrid summit in June 1989, but the decision was not unanimous. A major objection to the plan came from the British government. Prime Minister Margaret Thatcher made it very clear that she was not pleased with the plan's objective and methods even though she accepted the general goal of establishing a single market (stage 1). At the following Milan summit, Thatcher outlined the conditions for putting the pound sterling into the ERM: the British inflation rate must be on a falling trend toward convergence with the other member states' rates; there must be tangible progress toward the achievement of the single market; and other members must have dismantled their controls on the movement of capital.[15] Following this move, the British government announced that it would propose its alternative plan to the Delors report. The plan, which the new chancellor of the Exchequer, John Major, revealed to other members in November 1989, called for a parallel currency to the national currencies. The parallel currency would be used for trade, bank deposits, and the issuance of Eurobonds (which were in substantial use). Against this background, the European Council decided at its Strasbourg summit in December 1989 to set up an intergovernmental conference (IGC) to consider the EMU in Rome in December 1990. The only objection to this conference came from Margaret Thatcher. Her objection to the EMU was based on the view that it would undermine British monetary sovereignty. The idea of a parallel currency received little support from the other member countries.

The final agreement on EMU came during the Maastricht summit in December 1991. The resulting Maastricht Treaty, based on a revised Treaty of Rome, established the European Union, which consisted of the old community (EC), EMU, and two additions: the Common Foreign and Security Policy (CFSP) and cooperation between the member states' governments in justice and police matters (see Chapter 5). The Maastricht Treaty included several provisions and deadlines that committed the members to implementation of EMU.

First, the treaty specified a timetable that called for stage 2 to start in January 1994. The European Monetary Institute (EMI) would then be in charge of preparing the ground for stage 3. It would coordinate monetary policies, oversee preparations for the transfer to the ecu, and create the right conditions for stage 3. Frankfurt was chosen to be the site for the EMI in 1993. National governments still retained monetary sovereignty, but their central banks were to be independent by the end of stage 2. The EMI was to become the European Central Bank (ECB) shortly before the final stage of EMU began.

Second, stage 3 was to begin in 1997 by a decision of the European Council, through a qualified majority vote, if the majority of EU members met the EMU criteria. Otherwise, EMU would start in 1999 with as many members as could make the grade.[16]

Third, the treaty specified convergence criteria for qualifying for EMU: an average inflation rate within 1.5 percent and interest rates within 2 percent of the three best performing states; a budget deficit of less than 3 percent of gross domestic product (GDP); a ratio of public debt to GDP not to exceed 60 percent; and no devaluation within the exchange rate mechanism for the past two years.

Fourth, the treaty specified how monetary policy and coordination would operate under EMU. The ECB would have a policymaking council composed of national central bank governors and an executive board. This council would be an independent body similar to the U.S. Federal Reserve Board. The president of the ECB Council would report to the EU finance ministers and the European Parliament. The meeting of the ECB Council president and the Council of Economic and Finance

Ministers is referred to as Ecofin. Ecofin's functions include determining ecu exchange rates in consultation with the ECB and issuing broad guidelines for the EU's economic policy. Moreover, Ecofin would have the authority to recommend changes to any member states' economic policies if these policies were considered to be inconsistent with the broad goals of EMU.

As a concession to the United Kingdom (UK), the other members agreed to allow it the right to opt out of EMU. Moreover, any member that stays outside the currency union will not be allowed to vote on EU monetary policy. Those inside the EMU would lock their exchange rates irrevocably and later replace their respective national currencies with the ecu. The ECB would determine interest rates in accordance with its commitment to price stability. In determining interest rates, the ECB is also required to support the EU's economic policies and objectives, such as sustainable economic growth, social welfare, and high employment.

INTERESTS AND MOTIVES FOR AND AGAINST THE EMU

The acceptance of the EMU as part of the Maastricht Treaty by the EC member states owes much to French persistence at the time. The French wanted to have a greater say in monetary policymaking than they had under the EMS. This was a calculated move to weaken the Bundesbank's dominant position over monetary policy and to strengthen the EC institutions as a constraint upon German power.[17] However, the Germans did not oppose EMU. On the contrary, the German government was one of the greatest supporters of this idea. So why were the French so eager to push for EMU at the IGC? One explanation could be that Mitterrand wanted to lock the Germans into the EU before German reunification gave them any idea of opting out of Europe. More generally, as Wayne Sandholtz explains, "many leaders, including key Germans, desired to bind Germany irrevocably to the EU, and monetary union was a crucial means of doing so. In short, foreign policy ideas seem to provide the best explanation for German support for EMU."[18]

Sandholtz also provides other political reasons for the enthusiasm for EMU. The first is the spillover effect from the single market. The success of the EC in achieving the necessary requirements of Project 1992 persuaded the Commission that there was a functional linkage between the single market and EMU. The single market was a major step toward a complete economic union where greater economic benefits could be realized.[19] The other explanation relates to the idea of an independent monetary authority, the Eurofed, or European Central Bank. This independent institution would provide credibility to monetary policy, guarantee member states low inflation, and assure price stability. As Sandholtz states, "For governments that found it difficult domestically to achieve monetary discipline, EMU offered the chance to have it implemented from without."[20]

The EMU plan also received considerable support from the business sector. In 1992, corporate leaders created an Association for the Monetary Union of Europe. The president of this institution was the president of Philips Corporation and its vice president was the chairman of Fiat of Italy. The main reason for this private-sector support was that big business in Europe had become thoroughly transnationalized. Therefore, complete economic integration with full monetary union promised increased benefits to big business. Even under the single market, the multiplicity of currencies imposes transaction costs and information costs. The transaction costs were estimated to be around 15 billion ecus.

There were other foreseen benefits of EMU. It would provide macroeconomic stability by sound, coordinated fiscal policies, price stability, and the disappearance of noncooperative exchange rate policies.[21] In terms of its external effects, EMU, with a common currency, would strengthen the EU's position in the international economic system. It would provide an alternative hard currency to the U.S. dollar, especially in the portfolios market with increases in ecu-denominated assets. Moreover, as the EU's international power increases, it would be able to alter the present balance of power in the international monetary system against the dollar and the yen. The EU would be more likely to absorb rather than set international monetary conditions. Though it is doubtful that the dollar would lose much of its dominance, the EMU could give the EU more influence in the international monetary system.[22]

Critics of EMU, led by the British government, argued that the costs of monetary union would outweigh its potential benefits. One influential critic, Nobel Prize–winning economist Martin Feldstein, argued that the creation of a single market would not require a single currency and that a single currency would result in the unnecessary loss of monetary autonomy.[23]

It is quite correct that sometimes the effects of exchange rates on trade are exaggerated. Yet, events in Europe, especially since the collapse of the ERM in September 1992, suggest that companies and states had sustained considerable costs from volatile exchange rates. This was particularly the case of intra-EU trade-dependent economies. Since all the EU states trade with each other more than they do with non-EU countries, exchange rate stability is an important issue for them.

With regard to the loss of monetary autonomy, the critics are quite correct. EMU specifically calls for greater monetary union (loss of monetary policy autonomy for the individual states) with exchange rate stability in a highly integrated financial market. The fear was that the weaker economies would lose out when they are tied so closely to the German economy because they would end up following the strict monetary policies of the Bundesbank. Ironically, the Germans, particularly the former president of the Bundesbank, Helmut Schlesinger, worried that Germany would import inflation from its partners. Finally, Margaret Thatcher seemed least willing, among the member state leaders, to share monetary sovereignty with the EU. However, in the present information age, with the internationalization of the financial and money markets and the technological revolution in telecommunications, economic agents are increasingly holding diverse currency portfolios. This means that even when countries control their money supply, as the UK tried to do in the 1980s, they could not control the domestic inflation rate in the long run because only international monetary policies could ensure any meaningful control of inflation.[24] Thus, monetary autonomy of member states in the EU was already limited.

Although the supporters and critics of EMU argued over the feasibility of such a union, they were stunned by the collapse of the ERM in September 1992. As speculators continued to test the willingness of the British government to defend the parity of the pound in the ERM, the pound sterling dropped out of its target zone on Black Wednesday, September 16, 1992, and began to free-float. Speculators then began to test one EC currency after another. In the end, the Italian lira also dropped out of the ERM, the other weak currencies (the escudo, peseta, and punt) faced major devaluations, and finally in August 1993, the EC finance ministers revised the target zone of the ERM to plus or minus 15 percent. The causes and effects of the ERM crisis raised serious concerns about the future of EMU.

What Went Wrong in the Exchange Rate Mechanism?

During the ERM crisis of September 1992, early explanations of its causes focused too much on German interest rates. However, with 20/20 hindsight, we now realize that there were several factors behind the currency crisis. As David Cameron points out, many factors contributed to the ERM crisis of September 1992:

1. The EMS became a quasi-fixed system that failed to carry out a currency realignment needed since 1987; that is, although the mechanism was supposed to adjust in response to changing pressures from the international currency markets, the EC failed to bring about the necessary realignment of the ERM currencies with the mechanism behaving as if it were a fixed system.
2. The rapid expansion of the currency markets caused instability.
3. The economic and monetary policies of the German government and the Bundesbank were at fault as they tried to fight inflationary pressures in Germany caused by unification.
4. Political uncertainties resulted from the Danish rejection of the Maastricht Treaty and the possible similar outcome in the French referendum of September 1992.[25]

Two additional factors contributed to the ERM crisis. The first was the British government's failure to control public spending at a time of economic recession in Britain; this increasingly exposed the pound to speculative attacks. The second was the role of the U.S. dollar in international markets. During 1991–1992, the dollar fell and continued to fall. In an attempt to stimulate the U.S. economy, the Federal Reserve cut interest rates no fewer than eight times after 1990. In response to these cuts, the dollar lost value against other major currencies. By September 1992, the dollar was 48 percent lower than its peak in February 1985, and 8 percent lower than in September 1991. In the early 1980s, the dollar had reached as high as 3.47 DM. In September 1992, it was 1.39 DM—a total decline of 60 percent. The net result for the United States was increased competitiveness of American products in international markets. This weakness of the dollar placed the ERM under great pressure as investors and currency speculators switched from dollars to DMs. At the same time, investors and speculators were abandoning the pound sterling in favor of DMs. In view of these developments we can ascertain whether the EMS was a success in creating a zone of monetary stability.

To appraise the actual performance and soundness of any international monetary system, economists use three tests: adjustment, liquidity, and confidence. *Adjustment* mechanisms involve monetary costs. *Liquidity* means the availability of an adequate supply of reserves in order to make the financing of adjustments possible. And *confidence* means absence of panicky shifts by the monetary authorities from one reserve asset to another. Another element of confidence is the reputation of the monetary system among economic agents.

The founders of the EMS thought that they eliminated the inherent problems of the snake (insufficient availability of funds for intervention, weak adjustment mechanism, and lack of confidence) from lessons learned during the 1970s. The economic agents in the financial markets of the late 1980s and early 1990s, on the other hand, discovered that they had the power to crack the system by speculative attacks. At the end, one of the ERM's most important elements, the credibility of the central banks in honoring exchange rate commitments, suffered serious damage. This means that there was very little confidence in the system even though the monetary authorities had announced their willingness to defend any future exchange rate parities.

The fault really lay with the monetary authorities in the EC during the late 1980s and early 1990s. As speculative pressures on the ERM gradually increased, officials refused to acknowledge the seriousness of the problem and realign ERM currencies. One could say that the ERM had become too rigid because the member governments treated the ERM like a fixed exchange rate system. According to *The Economist*, a revaluation of the DM against other ERM currencies was necessary after German reunification in order to offset the inflationary pressures of German budget deficits. Yet the French dismissed this idea, and the Bundesbank was left with no option but to push German interest rates upward.[26] In a similar fashion, the British and French officials publicly asked for a lowering of German interest rates during the spring and summer of 1992, when they knew quite well that the idea was not acceptable to the Germans. They could have instead privately asked for revaluation of the DM against all other ERM currencies, which may have been more acceptable to the Germans.

The failure of EC monetary officials to recognize the urgency of currency realignments was further underscored in a special report of the *Financial Times*. In its review of the events and actions of finance ministers during the two weeks prior to Black Wednesday, *Financial Times* experts found that when pressures on currencies mounted and the finance ministers met in Bath on September 4–5, the leaders failed to address the issue of currency realignments largely for political reasons.[27] According to the Dutch prime minister, Ruud Lubbers, "realignment was not possible because England had its pride and France said that it couldn't be done because it was facing a difficult referendum and they couldn't discuss it; and the English said then that the Bundesbank should do something first, and so the discussion went."[28] Basically, the French finance minister, Michel Sapin, and his British counterpart, Chancellor Norman Lamont, succeeded in keeping realignment off the agenda. Lamont repeatedly pressured Helmut Schlesinger to cut German interest rates, which Schlesinger, as "mere *primus inter pares* on the Bundesbank's decision-making council,"[29] could not do on his own even if he wanted to. At the end of the meeting, the ministers decided to defend ERM rates, and the Germans only agreed not to increase interest rates further.[30]

In the days following the Bath meeting, the ERM continued to suffer under speculative attacks that led to its collapse. On September 12, 1992, the Italian government devalued the lira by 7 percent; on September 16, the pound sterling left the ERM and the lira left the next day; on November 22, 1992, the Portuguese escudo and Spanish peseta were devalued 6 percent each; on January 30, 1993, the Irish punt was devalued 10 percent; and on May 13, 1993, the escudo and peseta faced devaluation once again, by 6.5 percent and 8 percent, respectively. Finally, the French franc, which had been shored up in September 1992, came under speculative attack in July 1993. Economic recession, high unemployment, and interest rates that remained high to maintain the DM-franc ERM parity convinced the speculators to test France's ability to match the Bundesbank's tight monetary policy.[31] Similar attacks on the Danish crown, the Belgian franc, the peseta, and the escudo followed. The central banks tried to intervene to stabilize the ERM parities, but their efforts failed, and on July 30, 1993, the EC Monetary Committee called an emergency meeting of the finance ministers and central bank governors. At this meeting, following the Bundesbank's decision not to cut its discount rate, EC finance ministers and central bank governors agreed to widen the fluctuation bands between ERM currencies to plus or minus 15 percent of their rates effective August 2, 1993.[32] The only exception to this rule was a voluntary agreement between Germany and the Netherlands to retain the previous plus or minus 2.25 percent between the DM and guilder.

Many factors led to the ERM crisis: Germany's problems in absorbing the East German economy prevented the Bundesbank from lowering its interest rates to help its EC partners; the overvalued DM put immense pressure on other currencies to maintain their par values vis-à-vis the DM within the ERM bands; the budget deficit continued in the UK; speculations arose about the future of the Maastricht Treaty; and the decline of the U.S. dollar had a destabilizing effect on currency markets. What were the lessons learned from this experience and its implications for the future of EMU?

THE COSTS OF EXCHANGE RATE INSTABILITY: A CRUCIAL REASON FOR EMU

There is no doubt that the collapse of the ERM inflicted political and credibility damage on the EU. But there were some very serious economic costs as well. It is estimated that the Bank of England and other central banks spent £15 to 20 billion to defend the British currency during the days leading to Black Wednesday.[33] When the lira came under attack, the Bundesbank spent DM 90 billion in support of currencies against their ERM margins, and this was on top of some DM 200 billion that were previously expended on currency support.[34] The bulk of these sums went into the hands of the speculators.

The move to more flexible rates also did not ease economic recession in the EU. In fact, the 1992–1993 recession in Europe was the deepest since the recession of 1974–1975. Several factors contributed to this problem. During the 15 months following September 1992, the EC currencies fell against the U.S. dollar: DM, 22 percent; franc, 23 percent; guilder, 21 percent; lira, 58 percent; and the pound, 34 percent. However, this did not translate into increased overall exports by Germany because the DM also rose sharply against other EU currencies. Because intra-EC trade far outweighs extra-EC trade for the Community members, it was the ERM shifts that had greater consequence for export competitiveness. Unpublished figures from the Organization for Economic Cooperation and Development (OECD) showed that the volume of exports of manufactured goods from Germany fell by 11 percent during the first half of 1993, compared to a 1.9 percent increase during the same period a year before.[35] The French exports also showed a similar trend to Germany's. During the same period in 1993, "exports from France declined by 11.3 percent. By contrast, exports of Italy increased by 19 percent and the British trade deficit declined to 7.6 billion pounds from 13.4 billion pounds in the previous year particularly in trade with non-EU countries."[36] By this time the pound and the lira were both outside the ERM. Exports of EC countries, except Germany and France, showed marked improvement owing to improved exchange rates vis-à-vis the dollar, DM, and franc, but the EC-wide economic recession worsened nevertheless.

The answer was found in the economic problems of Germany and, to a lesser extent, France. Benefits of devalued British, Spanish, and other EC currencies were canceled by the negative economic impact of currency appreciation (with regard to EC currencies) in Germany. In addition, the costs of German unification contributed to roughly a 1.5 percent contraction of the German economy. Since an average 20 percent of total non-German exports in the EU are destined to Germany's market, this economic contraction contributed to the overall export problems of other member states.

ALL AHEAD WITH EMU

Despite these economic difficulties, the EU leaders seemed determined to push ahead with EMU in order to overcome problems associated with currency alignment. In accordance with a provision in the Maastricht Treaty, Article 109G, the composition of the ecu basket was frozen on November 1, 1993.[37] According to this decision, the ecu basket remained as defined on September 21, 1989, which is the last time it was adjusted. In January 1994, stage 2 started with the establishment of the EMI in Frankfurt. This institution assisted member states in coordination of monetary policies and paved the way for the start of stage 3 on January 1, 1999, when the ECB and the euro entered into effect. At that time 11 member countries joined the new euro zone (Austria, Belgium, Finland, France, Germany, Italy, Ireland, Luxembourg, the

Netherlands, Portugal, and Spain). With this final stage of EMU, the participants committed themselves to the following timetable for the realization of monetary union:

		Responsible Parties
Jan. 1, 1999 to Jan. 1, 2002	Change over to the € by the banking and finance industries	Commission and the member states
Jan. 1, 2002	Start circulation of € banknotes and coins; complete changeover to the € in public administration	ESCB and the member states
July 1, 2002	Cancel the legal tender status of national banknotes and coins of countries in the euro zone	ESCB and the member states

SOURCE: "Profile of the EU: Common Policies," outlined by the European Commission Delegation in Washington, D.C.

On the day stage 3 entered into force, the EMS was replaced by a new exchange rate mechanism (ERM II) that allowed non–euro-zone states of the EU (Denmark, Greece, Sweden, and the UK) to link their currencies to the euro. As in the old ERM, there are two bands, a narrow band of plus or minus 2.25 percent and a wider band of plus or minus 15 percent. Moreover, the Very Short Term Financing Facility provides funds for assisting the central banks during interventions. Denmark joined ERM II in the narrow band, while Greece, prior to joining the euro on January 1, 2001, had opted for the wider band. The central rate for the Danish crown against 1 € is 7.46038, with the upper rate of 7.62824 and the lower rate of 7.29252. The Danish government stayed out of the euro zone by choice, and there are no clear indications from the government about joining in the future. This view is further reinforced by the Danish referendum on September 28, 2000, in which the voters rejected the single European currency by a vote of 53 to 47 percent.[38] The significance of the Danish referendum is that it could force into effect a "two-speed Europe," allowing some members to go ahead with finalizing EMU while leaving others behind. The situation is rather complicated because while Denmark is currently outside the euro zone, it is in the ERM II. With this Danish currency in the ERM II, only Sweden and the UK are left outside of both the euro zone and ERM II. The British position was discussed earlier under the Maastricht Treaty, but there are indications that there may be changes on this front as the Blair government plans to hold a referendum on the euro in 2003. Sweden, however, cited technical grounds for its decision to stay out of the euro zone. Furthermore, the Euro-barometer shows rising support for the euro among Swedish citizens.[39] In summing up the current picture, we see three groups of EU member states: those which are in the euro, now including Greece, one which is not in the euro but is in ERM II, and those which are not in either. While the current system is more stable than the earlier ERM I, possible currency instability is still a threat as long as the euro is not adopted by all member states.

THE EUROPEAN SYSTEM OF CENTRAL BANKS

The ESCB defines and implements monetary policy in the euro zone. It comprises the central banks of the EU states and the ECB (Figure 8.1). It is important to note that the national central banks (NCBs) are not restricted to those states which have joined EMU at present time. The inclusion of the entire membership highlights the end goal of having everyone in the euro zone.

The two major bodies of the ECB are the executive board and a governing council. The executive board has a president, a vice president, and four members, each appointed to 8-year nonrenewable terms. At this writing, the president is Willem Duisenberg, who served as president of the EMI in 1997–1998. His term as president of ECB ends on July 1, 2003. The Governing Council includes the executive board and the governors of the central banks of the euro zone states. Decisions of the ECB are by simple majority. Once all the member states join the euro zone, the third institution, the General Council, will cease to exist. These are the main responsibilities of the Governing Council:

1. To adopt the guidelines and make the decisions necessary to ensure the performance of the tasks entrusted to the Eurosystem

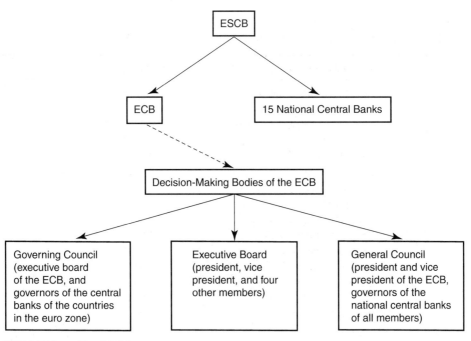

FIGURE 8.1   The ESCB

SOURCE: http://www.ecb.int "Organization of the ECB."

2. To formulate the monetary policy of the Community, including, as appropriate, decisions relating to intermediate monetary objectives, key interest rates, and the supply of reserves in the Eurosystem
3. To establish the necessary guidelines for their implementation[40]

The set capital account of the ECB is 5€ billion. The national central banks of the EU countries are solely responsible for this subscription and are holders of this capital. The respective contribution of each national central bank is based on a key established on the basis of the member's respective share in the GDP and population of the EU (Table 8.2). At present, the 12 euro zone members have paid their subscriptions in full. The remaining three have paid about 5 percent of their respective share. Thus, the current capital account of the ECB is slightly under 4€ billion. In addition to the capital account, the ECB has a foreign reserve asset of 40€ billion contributed by the 12: 15 percent in gold and 85 percent in U.S. dollars and Japanese yen.

The ECB is similar to the German Bundesbank and the U.S. Federal Reserve in its structure, but it is more decentralized. The Bundesbank's council of 17 members includes 9 Landesbank presidents, who have less autonomy than ECB's central bank governors. The Federal Reserve, on the other hand, has a 12-member open-market committee made up of 7 governors from the center and 5 from among the 12 district branches of the Fed.[41]

It is incorrect to assume that the ECB escapes any political oversight. The Ecofin and the Monetary Committee of the EP carefully observe the decisions of the ECB.[42]

TABLE 8.2   Central Banks' Shares in the ECB (December 1, 1999)

National Central Bank	Share in the ECB (%)
National Bank of Belgium	2.8658
National Bank of Denmark	1.6709
Bundesbank Deutsche	24.4935
Bank of Greece	2.0564
Bank of Spain	8.8935
Bank of France	16.8337
Central Bank of Ireland	0.8496
Bank of Italy	14.8950
Central Bank of Luxembourg	0.1492
Bank of the Netherlands	4.2780
National Bank of Austria	2.3594
Bank of Portugal	1.9232
Central Bank of Finland	1.3970
Central Bank of Sweden	2.6537
Bank of England	14.6811
Total	100.0000

The president of the ECB presents an annual report to Ecofin outlining the overall monetary policies and their outcomes, including projections, for the EU. The EP, on the other hand, uses the Monetary Committee to request hearings on the activities of the ECB. This committee's operating procedures resemble those of the U.S. Senate committee hearings.[43] Finally, while individual member governments cannot influence ECB policies, they can affect future policy orientation of the bank through the appointment of the bank officials.

THE €

The euro came into existence on January 1, 1999, as the accounting currency of the EU. It replaced the former ecu on a one-to-one basis. From then on, the value of the euro against the U.S. dollar and all other currencies started to fluctuate according to market conditions. This new currency became the legal tender in all participating member states on January 1, 2002, by replacing their respective national currencies. The conversion rates for member states' currencies against the euro were as follows:

Austrian shilling	13.7603
Belgian franc	40.3399
Dutch guilder	2.2037
Finnish markka	5.94572
French franc	6.5595
German DM	1.9558
Greek drachma	340.750
Irish punt	0.78756
Italian lira	1936.27
Luxembourg franc	40.3399
Portuguese escudo	200.482
Spanish peseta	166.386

As the new single currency of the EU, the euro has important domestic and international implications. In addition to the domestic implications of a single currency the new euro zone accounts for 15 percent of the world's GDP. This is much larger than the 4 percent share held by the biggest single EU member state, Germany. While the combined share of the 12 is less than that of the United States, which is about 20.5 percent of world GDP, it is roughly twice as large as the Japanese share. Internationally, the euro has become one of the key investment currencies, despite the decline in the euro value against the dollar since 1999. When the euro was first introduced, its exchange rate value against the U.S. dollar was 1.32. By August 12, 1999, it had lost considerable ground against the dollar, with a par value of $.92. This decline continued through 2000 and reached an average parity of U.S. $0.85–0.87 in October 2000. Despite its initial fall against the dollar, the euro has become an important international reserve currency. Recently, the two currencies neared parity as the dollar began to lose value in currency markets as investors hedged against further declines due to concerns over the financial health of the U.S.[44] By September 2002, the average parity stood within two cents.

THE GROWTH AND STABILITY PACT: TOWARD CLOSER ECONOMIC POLICY COORDINATION

With EMU attained among euro zone countries, fiscal and monetary policy coordination became essential for stable economic growth in the Union. As the ESCB sets guidelines for monetary policy for the whole of the euro area through interest rates, fiscal policies need to be coordinated amongst the members states similar to the way these countries coordinated EMU target rates during the second and third stages of the Delors Plan. Otherwise, macroeconomic imbalances are likely to emerge between the member economies. This means that with monetary policy surrendered to the ECB, governments have only fiscal policy to rely on when they need to stimulate their economies. Thus, in order to ensure stable economic growth, EU member states signed the Stability and Growth Pact at the Amsterdam European Council in June 1997 as a future commitment to fiscal discipline previously accepted under the EMU convergence criteria.

The Stability and Growth Pact is an agreement between all the member states that requires adherence to specific fiscal and budgetary disciplines as a part of their medium-term economic objectives. The pact has two main rules: (1) a budget in balance or in surplus in the medium term (11 of 15 members have already achieved this), and (2) no budget deficit over 3 percent of GDP through 2004.[45] Failure to attain these targets could result in penalties imposed by the Commission equal to 0.5 percent of GDP and/or denied access to the EU's cohesion funds. The fine imposed is in the form of a required non–interest-bearing deposit. This deposit would become a fine after two years, and thus "lost" for that member state, only if the offending member state has not corrected its excessive deficit (a budget deficit of more than 3 percent of gross domestic product) within the two-year period. The architects of the pact, most of them German, argued that euro's credibility might be tarnished by fiscal negligence among its members. If member states' governments run fiscal deficits resulting in unsustainable borrowing, the national central banks of these countries will be forced to bail them out, thus further inflating the real value of their debts. Such bailouts are not permitted in the euro zone area, and the pact forces the member governments to adhere to strict fiscal discipline to complement the ECB's position on monetary policy discipline.

Thus far the Stability Pact has worked well for most of the members. However, there are signs of serious dangers of key countries failing to meet their targets. Portugal became the first country to break the rules by running a budget deficit in 2001 of 3.9–4.1 percent of GDP.[46] This is particularly critical for Portugal since it is one of the four poorer members of the EU that receives cohesion funds. If the Commission imposes the fines of the pact, Portugal stands to lose 6€ billion over six years, which may further deepen this country's budget deficit. However, the impact of Portugal's deficit on the euro, in the form of a run on currency, is very slim since this country is a small partner in the currency zone.

There are other signs of trouble ahead for the stability pact. Already, France, Germany, and Italy are good candidates to violate the target set for budget deficit (Figure 8.2). Given the fact that these countries together account for 70 percent the euro zone's GDP, the spillover effect on the euro of any conflict between the governments and the Commission over stability pact rules would be great. In an attempt to avert any potential crisis, the parties concerned are discussing a compromise at this writing. France initially asked for an extension of the deadline to 2007 but was turned down by the others. In response, the French government announced "it would not feel bound to respect its pledges, if its economic growth fell below 3% [the target needed to secure the necessary fiscal balance]."[47] Italians also made it clear that they view the pact to be too rigid and would like to see some revisions of the targets. So far the Commission seems unwilling to entertain these positions, and it is backed by the ECB. However, the problem is much deeper than a mere short-term challenge for member states. There are long-term rising costs (e.g., hefty pension liabilities), which

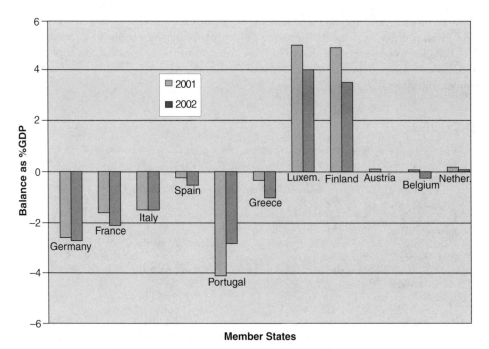

FIGURE 8.2   Fiscal Balances in the Euro Zone

SOURCE: Eurostat. *Data for Short-term Economic Analysis No. 8/9/2002*

will undoubtedly put strains on governments' fiscal discipline. Furthermore, the euro zone public debt reached 72 percent of GDP, higher than the 60 percent figure stipulated in the Maastricht Treaty.

CONCLUSION

EMU represents the final stage of economic integration between the member states of the EU. It is the final stretch in establishing a complete economic union that started with the European Economic Community almost five decades ago. While political union has not proceeded with the same speed, EMU holds the promise of providing economies of scale for its citizens and businesses. Under EMU, asymmetric economic shocks between the member economies can be addressed with a single monetary policy. With a single monetary authority, the EU can finally achieve labor mobility, capital mobility, fiscal transfers, and wage flexibility. Furthermore, with a single currency, the EU will eliminate transaction costs and have a fairly stable international reserve currency that will continue to attract the interest of international portfolio investors. Yet the real test of how well economic union has been realized comes during times of recession. With political union lagging far behind EMU, political will and commitment of member governments and citizens in abiding by the policies of the ECB become the key factors. Maintaining fiscal discipline, continuing with economic reforms, and agreeing to supranational fiscal transfers are sensitive and often politically risky decisions for governments during economic recessions. If the EMU is to be successful, member states cannot afford a repeat of the "politically safe" economic policies that hold domestic national interests of individual countries above collective EU interests.

ENDNOTES

1. For a detailed discussion of the Werner plan see John Pinder, *European Community: The Building of a Union* (Oxford: Oxford University Press, 1991), pp. 119–121.
2. Miltiades Chacholiades, *International Economics* (New York: McGraw-Hill, 1989), p. 225.
3. Stephen George, *Politics and Policy in the European Community* (London: Oxford University Press, 1991), p. 174; and Pinder, *European Community*, pp. 119–124.
4. Pinder, *European Community*, p. 176.
5. George, *Politics and Policy in the European Community*, p. 176.
6. Dennis Swann, *The Economics of the Common Market* (London: Penguin Books, 1992), pp. 202–203.
7. Neil Thygesen, "The Emerging European Monetary System: A View from Germany," in R. Triffen, ed., *EMS—The Emerging European Monetary System*. Offprint from the *Bulletin of the National Bank of Belgium*, 50 (1): 1979.
8. Francesco Giavazzi and Alberto Giovannini, *Limiting Exchange Rate Flexibility: The European Monetary System* (Cambridge: MIT Press, 1989), p. 26.
9. For a detailed description of the EMS see Michele Fratianni and Jürgen von Hagen, *The European Monetary System and European Monetary Union* (Boulder, Colo.: Westview Press, 1992); and Giavazzi and Giovannini, *Limiting Exchange Rate Flexibility*.
10. David M. Wood, Birol A. Yeşilada, and Beth Robedeau, "Windows of Opportunity: When EC Agendas Are Set and Why." Paper presented at the Third Biennial International Conference of the European Community Studies Association in Washington, D.C., May 27–29, 1993, p. 11. Following three

realignments of exchange rates inside the ERM in November 1992, the new ecu central rates (in units of national currencies per ecu) were: Belgian franc, 40.6304; Danish crown, 7.51410; DM 1.96992; Spanish peseta, 143.386; French franc, 6.60683; Irish punt, 0.735334; Luxembourg franc, 40.6304; Dutch guilder, 2.21958; Portuguese escudo, 182.194; Italian lira, 1,690.76; British pound, 0.805748; and Greek drachma, 254.254. These central rates establish a parity grid of bilateral exchange rates between the national currencies. See *Financial Times*, November 23, 1992, p. 2.

11. Michael J. Artis and Mark Taylor, "Exchange Rates, Interest Rates, Capital Controls and the European Monetary System: Assessing the Track Record," in Francesco Giavazzi, Stefano Micossi, and Marcus Miller, eds., *The European Monetary System* (Cambridge: Cambridge University Press, 1988), p. 187.

12. For a detailed analysis see Birol A. Yeşilada and David M. Wood, "Learning to Cope with Global Turbulence: The Role of EMS in European Integration." Paper presented at the Annual Meeting of the Midwest Political Science Association, Chicago, Illinois, April 18–20, 1991.

13. Dennis Swann, *The Economics of the Common Market* (London: Penguin Books, 1992), p. 216.

14. The Delors report as cited by the EC Commission, *Report on Economic and Monetary Union in the European Community* (Luxembourg: Office for Official Publications of the European Communities, 1988).

15. According to Stephen George, Sir Geoffrey Howe, then foreign secretary, said that the Madrid conditions were only adopted by the prime minister after both he and chancellor of the Exchequer, Nigel Lawson, threatened to resign unless they were adopted. See Stephen George, *Politics and Policy in the European Community*, 2d ed. (London: Oxford University Press, 1991), p. 183.

16. "Maastricht at a Glance," *The Economist*, October 17, 1992, pp. 60–61.

17. Pinder, *European Community*, p. 139.

18. Wayne Sandholtz, "Choosing Union: Monetary Politics and Maastricht," *International Organization*, 47 (Winter, 1993): 32–33.

19. Ibid., p. 20.

20. Ibid., p. 38.

21. European Communities, *European Economy: One Market, One Money* (Brussels: Official Publications of the European Communities, 1990), p. 50.

22. Pinder, *European Community*, p. 140.

23. Martin Feldstein, "The Case Against EMU," *The Economist*, June 13, 1992, pp. 19–22.

24. George Zis, "European Monetary Union: The Case for Complete Monetary Integration," in Frank McDonald and Stephen Dearden, eds., *European Economic Integration* (London and New York: Longman, 1992), p. 45.

25. David Cameron, "British Exit, German Voice, French Loyalty: Defection, Domination, and Cooperation in the 1992–93 ERM Crisis." Paper presented at the Third International Conference of the European Studies Association, in Washington, D.C., May 27–29, 1993, p. 5.

26. "Shooting the Messengers," *The Economist*, August 7, 1993, p. 23.

27. "The Monetary Tragedy of Errors That Led to Currency Chaos," *Financial Times*, December 11, 1993, p. 2.

28. Ibid.

29. Ibid.

30. David Smith, "Ministers Promise to Defend ERM Rates," *The Sunday Times*, London September 6, 1992, Section 3, p. 8.

31. "Currency Crisis Spurs EC to Widen EMS Bands of Fluctuation," *Eurecom*, 5.8 (September, 1993), p. 1.

32. Larry Neil, "An American Perspective on the Euro," in *The European Union*, Dean J. Kotlowski, ed. (Athens, Ohio: Ohio University Press, 2000), p. 165.

33. Samuel Brittan, "Black Wednesday's Cost," *Financial Times*, November 30, 1992, p. 18.

34. Ibid.

35. "Fluctuations in the Balance," *Financial Times*, December 15, 1993, p. 13.

36. Ibid.

37. "EMU Moves Forward," *Eurecom* 5 (November, 1993), p. 3.

38. "Denmark Rejects Euro, Holds on to Identity," *The Oregonian*, September 30, 2000, p. D2.

39. European Commission, *Eurobarometer* 52 (Brussels: European Commission, March 1999).

40. "About the ECB," ECB Web site, 2000, p. 1. http://www.ecb.int. Click on "About ECB"

41. "Survey: EMU—Nuts and Bolts," *The Economist*, April 11, 1998, pp. 10–14. See also http://www.economist.com/surveys/issue=19980411.
42. Simon Hix, *The Political System of the European Union* (New York: St. Martin's Press, 1999), p. 298.
43. Ibid.
44. "Dollar near parity with euro," *Financial Times*, June 25, 2002, p. 1.
45. George Parker, Peter Weis, and Haig Simonian, "Berlin and Paris May Put Stability Pact to Test," *Financial Times* July 27/28 2002, p. 4.
46. Ibid., and "Too Much Red Ink for the Euro-Zone," *The Economist*, July 6–12, 2002, p. 47.
47. "Rules Are Made to Be Bent, Aren't They?" *The Economist*, July 27–August 2, 2002, pp. 43–44.

9

The Common Agricultural Policy

This chapter will examine the Common Agricultural Policy's (CAP) structure, operations, position in the European Union (EU) budget, and importance to the EU's external trade policies. As we noted in Chapter 4, CAP highlighted increased eco nomic interdependence among the original European Economic Community (EEC) states. For example, while France needed markets for its agricultural products, West Germany was in need of food imports. Inclusion of Italy in this picture provided the otherwise unavailable Mediterranean goods in Europe's northern markets. West Germany, on the other hand, needed markets for its manufactured exports. Therefore, in a unique way, CAP ensured the steady supply of a variety of agricultural products for EEC citizens. It is also important to realize that while CAP is an agricultural price support system, it also led to the restructuring of EEC farming and the establishment of fewer, larger, and more efficient farms.[1] Despite its achievements over the years, CAP has also been one of the biggest public policy headaches in the developed world, due in part to its huge expenses for consumers and taxpayers.

THE EVOLUTION OF CAP

From the signing of the Rome Treaty until CAP came into effect in 1968, the EEC achieved three important objectives. First, it eliminated national agricultural support systems. Second, it replaced the national systems with a Community-wide agricultural support system. And third, agricultural protection between EEC countries was eliminated and common agricultural prices took effect.[2] The Council of Ministers, following the proposals of the Brussels Commission, set annual agricultural support prices.

The evolution of CAP was a difficult process. Every year the Council of Ministers held a series of marathon meetings, during which package deals were reached on

EEC regulations for different products. For example, in December 1961, a marathon meeting resulted in common policies in grains, eggs, poultry and pig products, fruit and vegetables, and wine. Also, the ministers agreed on general principles regarding the financing of these policies.[3] Other marathon sessions in December 1963 and December 1964 resulted in regulations on milk and dairy produce, beef and veal, rice, fats, and grain.[4]

It was hard to arrive at an agreement over the financing of the EEC budget. It was the Commission's view that France would be interested in the financing of the budget because of its strong agricultural production, which the CAP was designed to help finance. In 1965, the Commission proposed that expenditure on CAP be financed from the customs duties on industrial products entering the EEC countries and the variable levies on agricultural imports, which were to be effective as soon as the customs union became operational. The Commission also argued that it should receive these receipts directly, rather than waiting for the national parliaments' approval of the budget every year. Furthermore, the budget should also be approved by the European Parliament (EP). With the exception of France, all other member states supported this proposal. As a result, de Gaulle withdrew France from participation in all EEC business until further notice, thus precipitating the empty-chair crisis (see Chapter 3). Under the Luxembourg compromise, the EEC shelved the issue of parliamentary control of the EEC budget. When CAP was reintroduced in mid-1967, its main source of finance came from contributions by the member states. This arrangement continued until after de Gaulle resigned as president of France.

The CAP adopted by the EEC is a unique system known as the variable levy (*prélèvement*). The basic idea is quite simple. The Council of Ministers determines in advance the desired internal price of each agricultural product. This is the support price, known as the target price (*prix indicatif*). It also estimates expected domestic production and consumption of these products. Then, the EU imposes a variable levy on non-EU farm products equal to the difference between the lowest world market price and the EU target price. When there is a change in the world market price, the variable levy is adjusted accordingly. In effect, the variable levy shifts the burden of adjustment to variations in EU consumption and production onto third-country providers, and this discourages the other countries from subsidizing their exports. Other support policies in CAP include export subsidies, supplementary and fixed-rate aid, and structural aid to farmers. Export subsidies make up the difference between intra-EU prices and world market prices and enable the European farmers to compete in international markets. By the early 1980s, export subsidies accounted for about half of all CAP spending. The supplementary and fixed-rate aid, on the other hand, only apply to a handful of commodities where support prices remain low (e.g., durum wheat, olive oil, tobacco, and oilseeds). In these cases, the farmers receive direct payments in proportion to their output. Finally, structural aid refers to payments toward farm modernization and improved productivity.

It is important to note that the EEC introduced the CAP payments programs during the world of fixed exchange rates. Since the collapse of the fixed exchange rate system in 1972, the CAP financing has faced difficult problems, which forced the implementation of the use of "green money," a set of special exchange rates that the Commission uses to convert common farm prices into national currencies through a mechanism known as the mandatory compensatory accounts (MCA).

Following the adoption of CAP, the Commission introduced a memorandum titled Agriculture 1980, which became known as the Mansholt plan, named after Commissioner Sicco Mansholt in December 1968.[5] This plan called for restructuring agriculture by encouraging small farmers to leave the land and giving financial assistance for the amalgamation of holdings. The incentives included grants, pensions to farmers over the age of 55, and assistance to younger farmers in finding new careers. However, there was one other point of this plan that created problems with the French and West German farmers. This was the proposal to cut price levels so that inefficient farmers would be forced to leave agriculture.[6] The only supporter of this plan was Britain, which was in the process of applying for a membership in the Community at the time. However, the British government was not eager to make reform of CAP a condition for the United Kingdom's entry into the European Community (EC). The result of the growing opposition to this plan in France and West Germany was three years of discussion in the Council of Ministers. When the final decision came in April 1972, the EC revised the Mansholt plan: it only provided for a modest financing of loans to the farmers, early-retirement incentives, and assistance for information and training to increase efficiency. The budget for price support did increase every year, but its component for "guidance" remained rather small.

REFORMING CAP: A NEVER-ENDING STORY

During the 1980s, additional reforms of the CAP occurred. In 1984, the member countries agreed on a system of quotas for dairy products, supports for which had been very costly to the EC budget. During this time, CAP accounted for about 64 percent of the EC budget. The reforms also included phasing out of the MCA by 1988 and controlling future expenditure on agricultural subsidies and other support mechanisms.[7] The dairy sector reforms were followed by a more serious attack on other sectors. In 1985, the Council of Ministers agreed on a general price package that restricted agricultural price increases to a figure below the EU's inflation rate.

The reforms then moved into the beef sector when the EC decided to modify beef support arrangements in 1986. Previously, the EC's intervention price in this sector acted as the floor price. The reforms changed this practice by specifying when support buying would take place. Accordingly, the EU would engage in support buying when (1) the average market price in the EC was 90 percent of the intervention price, and (2) the price in the target country was 87 percent of the intervention price.[8] All in all, this meant a 17 percent decline in price. Yet, despite these measures, the cost of the CAP increased by an average of 18 percent per year between 1985 and 1987. One new problem area was cereals, which witnessed a substantial increase in production because of new technological advances, coupled with a decline in world market prices.

The problem proved to be a major cause for concern. In 1986, Jacques Delors announced that the EC was running out of funds and expected an estimated budgetary shortfall of 4 to 5 billion ecus in 1987. The expansion of the EC to include agricultural countries like Portugal and Spain further complicated this problem. Thus, additional sources of funding seemed to be in order, but not all members agreed to this. The Netherlands and the UK demanded strong limitations on agricultural production. The UK went so far as to indicate that it would not agree to more funds until this issue was seriously addressed. Following intense debates, the European Council accepted a series of measures, known as the Delors package, to reform the CAP:

1. Budgetary discipline was to be realized through an agreed-upon resources ceiling of 1.2 percent of EC gross national product (GNP) and an expenditure ceiling of 27.5 billion ecus for the European Agricultural Guidance and Guarantee Fund (EAGGF).[9]
2. The increase in agricultural expenditure was to be equal to or less than 74 percent of the EC's GNP growth rate.[10]
3. It was agreed that from 1988 to 1992 the threshold for cereals was to be 160 million tons. Any production beyond this limit would result in price cuts of 3 percent and continue until production fell within the allowed limit.[11]

During the early 1990s, the EU adopted other policies to reform the CAP. These included the MacSharry II plan, named after the proposals made by the agricultural commissioner in 1991, and provisions covered in *Agenda 2000*. The former called for a significant reduction in support for cereals and the establishment of much of a two-tier EC farm policy that would favor small and medium-size farms.[12]

The MacSharry II reforms represented a major step in achieving what the European leaders envisioned in 1968, namely, the development of a smaller and more productive agricultural sector where the EU could better sustain incomes and levels of production, thus eliminating a major budgetary burden. The reforms introduced in 1992, in the form of direct payments to farmers as compensation for cuts in price supports, made the subsidies more transparent. Furthermore, as we noted earlier, the single market reforms called for elimination of MCA by the end of 1992. Yet, with the rapid pace of changes taking place in the EU during the 1990s (the completion of the single market, the EMU, and more countries joining the EU), additional reform of CAP became essential. In 1994, CAP accounted for half of the EU budget and had a 36.5 billion ecu price tag.

A major push for additional reform of CAP came from Sir Leon Brittan, the EU trade commissioner, who called for a new debate on the future of CAP based on four academic reports from Britain, France, Germany, and Italy.[13] These reports examined CAP in light of the EU's decision to expand its membership to include Eastern European countries in the next decade.[14]

The reports indicated that adopting CAP in its present form would seriously hurt consumers in these countries, although the farmers would benefit. Higher farm prices also meant increased output in these countries, and therefore more surplus for the EU. These developments would also undermine the EU's commitment to abide by General Agreement on Tariffs and Trade (GATT) agreements on agricultural subsidies. Moreover, the long-term cost of this CAP expansion would be around 23 to 27 billion ecus, a 70 percent rise in the current farm subsidies. Given the urgency of this picture, in 1997 agriculture commissioner Franz Fischler, presented a comprehensive reform package for CAP as part of the EU's Agenda 2000.

When the Commission presented these proposals in March 1998, the idea was to transform CAP from a policy of price support to one of income support.[15] The main aspects of this package included competition without oversubsidizing agricultural products, commitment to a fair standard of living for the agricultural community, production methods that emphasized consumer demand while being sensitive to the environment, diversity in production methods, a simpler agricultural and rural development policy (know as the "second pillar" of CAP), and a balance between agricultural expenditures and society's expectations from farmers.[16] In order to achieve these aims, the reforms called for further price cuts in the cereals, beef, and dairy sectors; decentralization of management; rationalization of intervention; and increased indirect aid payments to farmers.[17]

Emphasis on the environment and rural development represents a significant shift in CAP orientation. From now on, member states must draft regional and national programs from a comprehensive list of measures in which ecological practices are compulsory. These measures include retraining of farmers in new practices and support in less developed areas of high ecological value, such as forests. In addition, there is support for funding changes in milk and beef production to make them more environmentally friendly. This last point is especially crucial, given the agreement to cut prices in these sectors. Planned reforms will have varying impact on member states because of their respective share in EU agriculture. Table 9.1 provides the 1998 figures on agricultural production in the EU.

In accordance with treaty requirements, the Commission carried out a mid-term review (MTR) of CAP in early 2002 and issued far-reaching recommendations for

TABLE 9.1   Individual States' Shares in Total Agricultural Production (1998)

Member State	Share (%)	Member State	Share (%)
Austria	1.6	Italy	16.1
Belgium	3.0	Luxembourg	0.1
Denmark	3.2	Netherlands	7.5
Finland	1.1	Portugal	2.0
France	21.6	Spain	12.3
Germany	15.1	Sweden	1.5
Greece	4.1	United Kingdom	8.7
Ireland	2.0	Total	99.9

SOURCE: European Commission, *2000 Eurostat* (Economic Accounts for Agriculture) p. 7, from

http://europa.eu.int/commun/agriculture/agrista/table_en/fulltab.pdf.

further reforms in light of pending enlargement of the EU.[18] The report states that public expenditure for the farm sector must be better justified and yield more in return in such policy areas as food quality, preservation of the environment and animal welfare, environmental landscape, cultural heritage of rural regions, and enhancement of social balance and equity. To achieve these goals, the review proposes:

1. Cutting the link between production and farm payments
2. Making those payments conditional on environmental, food safety, animal welfare, and occupational safety
3. Increasing EU support for rural development
4. Introducing a new farm audit system and
5. Introducing rural development measures to increase quality production, food safety, and animal welfare, and to cover the cost of farm audits[19]

In addition, the Commission proposed additional measures for specific agricultural commodities to strengthen market competitiveness. For example, it called for a final 5 percent cut in the intervention price for cereals, a compensated decrease in the rice intervention price, and further adjustments in the dried fodder, protein crop, and nuts sectors.

Reforms proposed by the Commission are quite modest. They do not eliminate subsidies altogether. Rather, the proposals are meant to decouple subsidies and production, and promote more CAP spending in areas that promote environmentally friendly and rural development projects. Under the new CAP, the rural sector will receive substantial funds to achieve social goals, people working in these areas would be able to stay in the countryside and afford a quality life, and farmers would become greener. Nevertheless, member states will certainly find reason to object to or support these proposals largely due to who gets what from the CAP budget.

REFORM OF THE BUDGET

The annual agriculture expenditures of the EU are financed by a single fund known as the European Agricultural Guidance and Guarantee Fund. In 1998, this fund amounted to 38.7 billion €, or about 50 percent of the total EU budget. The EAGGF has two parts, the Guarantee section and the Guidance section, accounting for 88 and 12 percent of total funds, respectively.[20] The Guarantee section covers market intervention, export refund, direct aid to farmers, and cofinancing of environmental measures, afforestation, and early-retirement plans. The Guidance section is part of the structural funds that finance structural adjustment programs and rural development (see Chapter 11). Table 9.2 provides figures on planned agricultural expenditure from 1999 to 2006.

The introduction of the euro also changed how the EU administers its monetary conversion system to make payments to member countries. With transition

TABLE 9.2 Financial Framework for 2000–2006 (billions of €)

	2000	2001	2002	2003	2004	2005	2006
Agriculture	40.920	42.800	43.900	43.770	42.760	41.930	41.660
Expenditure	36.620	38.480	39.570	39.430	38.410	37.570	37.290
rural development	4.300	4.320	4.330	4.340	4.350	4.360	4.370
Structural operations	32.045	31.455	30.865	30.285	29.595	29.595	29.170
Internal policies[1]	5.930	6.040	6.150	6.260	6.370	6.480	6.600
External action	4.550	4.560	4.570	4.580	4.590	4.600	4.610
Administration[2]	4.560	4.600	4.700	4.800	4.900	5.000	5.100
Reserves	.900	.900	.650	.400	.400	.400	.400
Pre-accession aid (total)	3.120	3.120	3.120	3.120	3.120	3.120	3.120
agriculture	.520	.520	.520	.520	.520	.520	.520
pre-accession structural adjustment	1.040	1.040	1.040	1.040	1.040	1.040	1.040
PI IARE	1.560	1.560	1.560	1.560	1.560	1.560	1.560
Ceiling of appropriations for commitments	92.025	93.475	93.955	93.215	91.735	91.125	90.660
Ceiling of appropriations for payments	89.600	91.110	98.360	101.590	100.800	101.600	103.840

SOURCE: European Commission, *Financial Framework, 2000–2006.* http://europa.eu.int/comm/budget/en/cadrefinancier/cadrefin2000–2006.htm.
[1] Under Article 2 of Decision No. 182/1999/EC of the Parliament and of the Council and Article 2 of Decision 1999/64 Euratom (OJ L 26, 1.2. 1999, p. 1 and p. 34) the share of expenditure available for research over the period 2000–2002 comes to € 11,510 million at current prices.
[2] Expenditure on pensions included within the ceiling for this heading is calculated net of staff contributions to the pension scheme, with a maximum of € 1,100 million at 1999 prices for the period 2000–2006.

from green money (green ecus) to the euro, the agricultural monetary regime, the MCA, came to an end in the euro zone. Among the 12 euro-zone countries, a separate currency conversion mechanism is no longer needed. The MCA now applies only to the remaining three states, with one major change. Emphasis is no longer on the green money. Rather, the EU uses market conversion rates to determine transfers. Figure 9.1 provides information on CAP spending and transfers for members in 2000. The information clearly shows that France is the biggest beneficiary of the EU's farm subsidy regime while Britain and Germany are net contributors despite past reforms of CAP. Thus, one can expect these countries to hold different positions on the Commission's MTR of CAP and its recommendations for further reform. Moreover, as will be discussed later, agricultural subsidies in the EU continue to present a major problem in EU–U.S. trade talks.

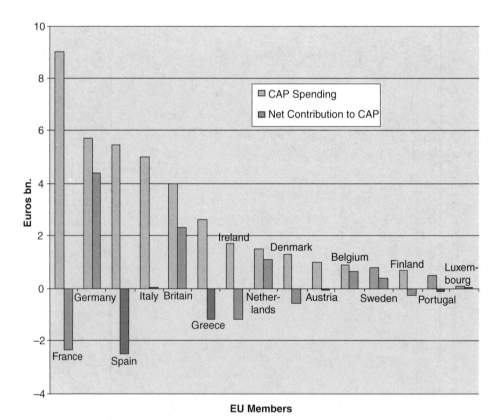

FIGURE 9.1   CAP Spending in 2000 (billions €)

SOURCE: European Commission, *2000 Eurostat* (Economic Accounts for Agriculture), p. 7, from http://europa.eu.int/commun/agriculture/agrista/table_en/fulltab.pdf.

WHO SUPPORTS CAP REFORMS?

France is probably the most isolated country in the EU in defending the old-style CAP, which emphasized high food prices and import barriers to benefit the farmers. The real reason, however, is that France makes more money from CAP than any other member of the EU. Roughly one-fourth of all CAP spending goes to France. Therefore, it is not surprising that the French government and French farmers desire higher prices to keep pace with rising farm costs and declining incomes. According to the Agricultural Directorate, the index of agricultural producer prices declined by 2.8 percent in nominal terms (EU average) in 1999. In the previous year, the average decline was 4 percent in real terms.[21] Until recently, France's major coalition partner in opposing serious CAP reforms was the Kohl government in Germany. However, Chancellor Gerhard Schröder is far less dependent on the farm vote, and therefore less keen on backing the French position.

The first test of the members' commitment to reforming CAP came during March 1999 at the Berlin summit of the European Council. The key agenda item was the reforms proposed by the Commission within the framework of *Agenda 2000*. Not only did the EU heads of state and government fail to substantially reduce the CAP budget; they also left subsidies for farm exports intact. These have been a constant target in international trade talks with the United States. One positive outcome of the summit was the agreement to carry out phased cuts in EU prices for cereals, beef, and milk. However, even with these cuts, planned CAP spending remains well above the ceiling set by Agenda 2000.

In view of member states' positions on CAP and reform, it is also crucial to consider what the EU citizens think of this expensive policy. Eurobarometer surveys in 2000 and 2001 show that a majority of EU citizens want to see a change in CAP support for farmers.[22] More than 60 percent of the respondents see a shift of subsidies from production to direct support for farmers as a good policy. They also supported respect for the environment, healthy and safe food policies, protection of medium- and small-size farms, making EU farm products competitive in world markets, emphasis on organic farming, and protection of the rural sector with adequate level of income and sustainable development. Special surveys of public opinion on these issues in April 2002 display similar views with stronger results (Figures 9.2 and 9.3).

EXTERNAL IMPACT OF CAP

While the reforms represent significant changes in the EU's agricultural policy, the CAP has had a negative effect on world market prices by subsidizing exports and by contributing to instability in the market. The CAP was viewed as one of the major hurdles in the Uruguay Round of the GATT, which lasted from September 1986 to December 1993. However, it is unfair to single out the EU as the only guilty party. According to Loukas Tsoukalis, agricultural support levels in 1991 were 35 percent of agricultural output in the United States, 46 percent in Canada, 75 percent in

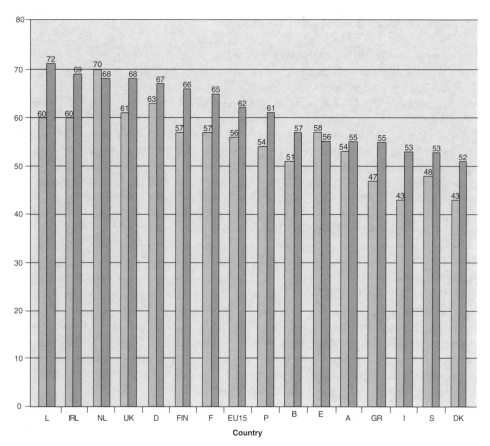

FIGURE 9.2   European Support for CAP

SOURCE: The Agriculture DG. *Eurobarometer 57.* Europeans and the Common Agricultural Policy (2002). Data obtained from section 3., p. 7.

Japan, and 49 percent in the EU.[23] Table 9.3 provides figures on agricultural supports in the EU and other selected countries at the peak of the Uruguay Round (see Chapter 11 for further discussion).

CONFLICT DURING AND BEYOND THE URUGUAY ROUND TALKS

External trade policy of the EU is significantly affected by the CAP, as demonstrated by developments in the GATT negotiations. The Uruguay Round trade talks, begun in September 1986 in Punta del Este, Uruguay, were by far the most complex and ambitious talks on free trade since the founding of GATT in 1947. This was the first time that members addressed trade rules for agriculture, textiles, services, intellectual

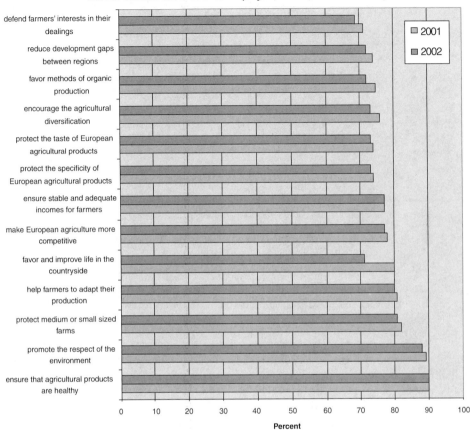

FIGURE 9.3 EU Citizens' Views on CAP Priorities

SOURCE: *Eurobarometer57*. Ibid.

property rights, and foreign investment. It is not our intention to discuss all aspects of the Uruguay negotiations, but we will examine the specifics of the agricultural talks, since disagreements in this area between the EU and the United States threatened to derail the entire effort. The negotiators did not have an easy time getting the parties to sign a trade agreement, and the continued existence of the GATT was thrown into question. The breakthrough came in November 1992 with the Blair House agreement between the United States and EU negotiators, which established the following conditions:

1. Subsidized farm exports to be cut by 21 percent in volume over six years. Value to be cut by 36 percent, with internal supports trimmed by 20 percent
2. EU land for oilseeds production limited to 5.128 million hectares
3. Oilseeds for industrial use limited to 1 million tons

TABLE 9.3   Transfers to Agriculture, 1991

Country	Total $ billion	Taxpayers ($ per head)	Consumers ($ per head)	Total ($ per head)
Austria	4.1	143	381	524
EU	142	168	241	409
Finland	5.9	460	677	1,137
Sweden	3.6	100	316	416
Norway	4.2	493	494	987
Switzerland	6.4	236	689	925
United States	81	200	118	318
Australia	1.2	41	29	70
Japan	63.2	16	494	510

SOURCE: "Survey of the European Community," *The Economist*, July 11, 1992, p. 22.

4. Ten percent of EU oilseeds land to be set aside permanently
5. Compensation allowed to farmers for taking land out of production
6. A 6-year "peace clause" agreed on outstanding disputes, preventing either the United States or EU from taking unilateral action against each other on trade
7. Extension to EU of the agreement to curb exports of subsidized beef to Asian countries[24]

The French government reacted angrily to the agreement and stated that the deal did not jibe with the EU's reform of the CAP, which France supported. It then called for reopening the agreement for more negotiations. The French position created a division within the EU and prompted John Major to threaten to block French initiatives on Europe. After long arguments between the different parties, the United States decided to make some concessions in order to secure French acceptance of the GATT accords:

1. Exempt the EU's existing 25-million-ton cereal stockpile from the Blair House agreement.
2. Switch the base year from which subsidized exports must be reined in from the 1986–1989 average to 1992. Since the EU's subsidized cereal exports rose from 17 million tons to over 20 million tons in 1992, the change significantly reduced the impact of the Blair House accord and, over the 6-year life of the implementation of the agreement, allows the EU (primarily France) to export an additional 8 million tons of cereal.
3. Extend from 6 to 8 years the "peace clause" under which the United States would not challenge the EU's export subsidy regime.[25]

In response to the U.S. concessions, the Europeans agreed to improve market access for American pork, grains, dairy products, and specialty goods (nuts, vegetables, almonds, and processed turkey). These allowances, however, did not mean much. They were not expected to significantly increase the sale of American goods in the EU markets because the demand is not expected to increase significantly. The EU also agreed to other concessions for the United States: tariffs on steel, wood, pulp, and paper would be cut to zero; semiconductor equipment would also see tariff reduction to zero, but the semiconductors themselves would retain protection averaging 3 percent; and tariffs on nonferrous metals would also be reduced.[26]

The signing of the Uruguay Round, however, did not mean that the EU–U.S. trade relations were without future problems. Soon after, more issues surfaced that required mediation by the newly established World Trade Organization (WTO). At the Doha Round (2001–2005) of international trade negotiations, agricultural subsidies and their impact on free trade continued to be issues of bilateral dispute between the EU and the U.S. Both sides maintain expensive policies. The cost per capita to U.S. citizens (total support estimate, TSE) of U.S. farm policy is $338/capita/year while the cost per capita of the EU farm policy is $276/capita/year. This translates to $20,000/farmer in the U.S. and $14,000/farmer in the EU.[27] The EU position on further cuts in agricultural subsidies is described by the Agriculture Commissioner Franz Fischler:

> We do not say "no" to further reductions in export subsidies. We say "yes" provided that equivalent disciplines are introduced for other export competition tools. What we cannot accept is that export subsidies should be the sole target for further discipline, while export credits are subject to no discipline at all, while state trading or other monopoly exporters can use one market to subsidise another and while food aid can be used not to relieve suffering (an objective we of course share) but to dispose of surpluses, open up markets or drive out competitors. All such measures must be tackled in the negotiations.[28]

Today, trade policies in agricultural products continue to present major disagreement between the EU and the United States. These issues covered trade in bananas, hormone-grown beef products, genetically modified organisms, and the U.S. Helms-Barton Act. We will return to current trade disputes between the EU and its trade partners in Chapter 11.

RECENT INTERNAL MARKET CRISES IN AGRICULTURE

Two very expensive crises—the foot-and-mouth disease and mad cow disease (BSE)—put severe strain on the EU's internal agricultural and trade policies. In each case, the country of origin (Britain) had to kill thousands of farm animals and was prohibited from exporting meat products to other EU countries. While the worst seems to be over, some areas of Britain are still under quarantine by the Commission to eradicate the problem.

BSE or Mad Cow Disease

Bovine spongiform encephalopathy (BSE) is a disease of the brain in cattle. It first appeared in the UK in 1986. The disease reached epidemic proportions because meat and bone meal produced from animal carcasses was included in cattle feed. By February 28, 2001, there had been 180,903 cases in the UK and 1,924 cases elsewhere in the EU. If transferred to humans the disease could be lethal. In response to the outbreak of the disease, the European Commission put in place a comprehensive set of measures to fight BSE:

- A ban on the feeding of mammalian meat and bone meal to cattle, sheep, and goats
- Higher processing standards for the treatment of animal waste to reduce infectivity to a minimum
- Surveillance measures for the detection, control, and eradication of BSE
- The requirement to remove specified risk materials (e.g., spinal cord, brain, eyes, tonsils, parts of the intestines) from cattle, sheep, and goats throughout the EU from October 1, 2000, from the human and animal food chains (also mandatory for imports of meat and meat products from third countries into the EU except Argentina, Australia, Botswana, Brazil, Chile, Namibia, Nicaragua, Norway, New Zealand, Paraguay, Singapore, Swaziland, and Uruguay)
- The introduction of targeted testing for BSE, with a focus on high risk animal categories
- The prohibition to use dead animals not fit for human consumption in feed production from March 1, 2001, onwards[29]

Moreover, in response to the crisis in consumer confidence that followed the crisis, the Commission introduced a series of additional measures to combat the mad cow disease:

- A ban on the use of ruminant meat and bone meal and certain other animal proteins in feedstuffs for all farm animals, to avoid risks of cross-contamination, at least until end of June 2001
- The testing of all cattle aged over 30 months destined for human consumption
- The extension of the list of specified risk materials to include the entire intestine of bovines and the vertebral column and
- A ban on the use of mechanically recovered meat derived from bones of cattle, sheep, and goats in feed and food[30]

To ensure transparency of the implementation of these measures, the Commission's Food and Veterinary Office carries out inspections to verify correct enforcement and controls of Community legislation by member states' relevant authorities, and publishes its findings on the Commission's Web site.[31]

Foot-and-Mouth Disease

Foot-and-mouth disease is economically the most significant infectious livestock disease. While it is usually a disease of low mortality in animals and has no public health relevance, it has important consequences for animal welfare and production. Clinically diseased animals normally suffer quite seriously, especially animals of highly productive breeds, and there are serious losses of growth and milk production.[32]

Foot-and-mouth disease hit Britain in February 2001 for the first time since 1967. The British government and the Commission immediately took steps to prevent the spread of the disease in the EU. Exports of milk, meat, and livestock products were banned; movement in the countryside was restricted; and farm animals across Europe were burnt. However, these measures had limited effect. As new cases were discovered in Britain in March 2001 and subsequent outbreaks occurred in Ireland, France, and the Netherlands, the Commission and the respective governments decided to widen the application of the measures. Other EU member states took sanitary measures at ports of entry to make sure those who had traveled to Britain had their shoes disinfected prior to entering the respective country. In all, the eradication program has been successful as well as costly. Over 4 million animals were killed and destroyed.[33]

As for financial assistance to farmers affected by this disease, the Commission provides compensation, up to 60 percent, toward the costs of animals destroyed, disinfection, and so on, under an Emergency Veterinary Fund. An advance of €400 million will be provided from the budget 2001, with €355 million foreseen for the UK, €39 million for the Netherlands, €2 million for Ireland and €3 million for France. A further €400 million are already earmarked for 2002.[34] The total amount paid depends upon the receipt and acknowledgement of all requests for compensation and may take years until final settlement.

CONCLUSION

Despite all the serious efforts aimed at reforming CAP to best serve the interests of the member states, and to a lesser extent the interests of the international free-trade regime, this policy remains the most controversial of all EU policies. While CAP spending has declined from 60 percent of the EU budget in the 1980s to 40 percent in the late 1990s, it continues to be the largest single budget item, with much room for additional reform. The significance of CAP for the EU is not surprising given the fact that the EU is currently the biggest importer and the second biggest exporter of agricultural products in the world. The other giant in this sector is the United States; its agricultural policies and commitments often conflict with those of the EU. As a result, the two transatlantic allies frequently find themselves at opposing ends of agricultural policy and trade issues, and this results in trade wars or threats of retaliatory action. This relationship is bound to get even more sensitive as the EU expands its membership to Eastern European countries. As the EU prepares for enlargement, further reform of the CAP will be necessary so that Europe's agricultural production can meet budgetary constraints of Agenda 2000 as well as WTO obligations. This is no easy task, as Agenda 2000 calls for reforms based on competitiveness through lower prices, food safety, rural development, and environmental protection while keeping expenditures within strict budgetary guidelines.

ENDNOTES

1. Stephen George, *Politics and Policy in the European Community*, 2d ed. (Oxford: Oxford University Press, 1991), pp. 134–135.
2. Dennis Swann, *The Economics of the Common Market* (London: Penguin Books, 1991), p. 229.
3. Ibid.
4. Ibid.
5. Commission of the European Communities, "Memorandum on the Reform of Agriculture in the European Economic Community," *Bulletin of the European Communities: Supplement 1/69 Z* (Brussels: European Communities, 1969).
6. John Pinder, *European Community: The Building of a Union* (London: Oxford University Press, 1991), pp. 84–85.
7. George, *Politics and Policy in the European Community*, p. 148.
8. Swann, *The Economics of the Common Market*, p. 247.
9. Fiona Butler, "The EC's Common Agricultural Policy (CAP)," in Juliet Lodge, ed., *The European Community and the Challenge of the Future*, 2d ed. (New York: St. Martin's Press, 1993), p. 116.
10. Ibid.
11. Swann, *The Economics of the Common Market*, p. 248.
12. John Gibbons, "The Common Agricultural Policy," in Frank McDonald and Stephen Dearden, eds., *European Economic Integration* (London: Longman, 1992), p. 139.
13. Caroline Southey, "Brittan Seeks CAP Debate after Critical Reports," *Financial Times*, January 16, 1995, pp. 1–2.
14. The reports are by Allan Buckwell of Wye College, University of London, UK; Stefan Tangermann, University of Göttinger, Germany; Secondo Tarditi, University of Siena, Italy; and Louis Mahe, University of Rennes, France.
15. Simon Hix, *The Political System of the European Union* (New York: St. Martin's Press, 1999), pp. 252–253.
16. European Commission, *Agenda 2000: Setting the Scene for Reform* (Brussels: European Commission Publications, 1998), p. 8.
17. Ibid., pp. 8–9.
18. EC Commission, *Communication from the Commission to the Council and the European Parliament: Mid-Term Review of Common Agricultural Policy* (Brussels: European Commission Publications, 10.7.2002. COM 2002), 394 final.
19. Ibid., pp. 18–26.
20. European Commission, *Agenda 2000*, p. 24.
21. European Commission Agriculture Directorate, *Agriculture in the European Union: Statistical and Economic Information 1999* (Brussels: Agricultural Directorate Publications, 2000).
22. http://www.europa.eu.int/comm/agriculture/survey/index_en.htm, accessed 07/08/2002.
23. Loukas Tsoukalis, *The New European Economy* (Oxford: Oxford University Press, 1991), p. 260.
24. David Gardner, "Hopes Rising that Deal Can Be Saved," *Financial Times*, September 20, 1993, p. 3.
25. David Dodwell, "Concessions by U.S. Sweeten GATT Pill," *Financial Times*, December 6, 1993, p. 3.
26. Ibid.
27. Presentation by Commissioner Franz Fischler at Commission Seminar on MTR, April 17, 2002. http://www.europa.eu.int/comm/agriculture/mtr/mtr_en.pdf, accessed 09/23/2002.
28. http://europa.eu.int/comm/agriculture/external/wto/index_en.htm, accessed 09/23/2002.
29. European Commission, Directorate General Health and Consumer Protection, *BSE Frequently Asked Questions* (Brussels: Agriculture Directorate Publication, April 9, 2001), pp. 2–4.
30. Ibid.
31. See http://europa.eu.int/comm/food/fs/inspections/vi/reports/index_en.html for current and past reports.
32. European Commission, Agriculture Directorate, *Questions and Answers on Foot-and-Mouth Disease* (Brussels: Agriculture Directorate Publication 12 December 2001, pp. 1–2.
33. Ibid., p. 1.
34. Ibid. p. 6.

10

■

Cohesion, Environmental, and Industrial Policies

In this chapter we will turn our attention to other important internal policies of the European Union (EU) that aim to promote economic and social cohesion by reducing disparities between different regions of the EU. This goal, known as the "cohesion policy", is an integral part of Europeans' belief in the social welfare state. Its main emphasis is to transfer resources from the more developed regions of the EU to those lagging behind. We will first discuss cohesion policy aimed at reducing economic and social disparities between richer and poorer regions in the EU. This is followed by an analysis of industrial and environmental policies, both of which have consequences for and are affected by cohesion policy.

COHESION POLICY

Cohesion policy comprises regional policy, some aspects of social policy, and part of Common Agricultural Policy (CAP). Regional policy seeks to reduce the gap between the developed and the less developed regions of the EU. The relevant parts of the social policy for cohesion pertain to combating long-term unemployment and to vocational education and training. The CAP portion relates to assistance for rural development. As the most crucial part of cohesion policy, regional policy relies upon structural funds to achieve its objectives. These are the European Regional Development Fund (ERDF), the European Social Fund (ESF), the European Agricultural Guidance and Guarantee Fund (EAGGF), and the Financial Instrument for Fisheries Guidance (FIFG). The ERDF was set up in 1975; it is managed by Directorate General XVI of the European Commission and represents the largest portion of the cohesion budget. The ESF was established in 1960 under DGV and is the second largest portion of the budget. The EAGGF is part of CAP and is under DGVI. Its share of the cohesion budget is 18 to 20 percent. Finally, the FIFG, the newest of the

173

four, established in 1994, is managed by DGXIV and accounts for roughly 3 percent of the cohesion budget.

The Structural Funds and Regional Objectives

One major accomplishment of the EU during the difficult times of the 1970s was the establishment of the ERDF in 1975. This fund originally provided compensation to the United Kingdom for the budgetary loss it suffered from participating in the CAP.[1] However, from the day the European Economic Community (EEC) was established, the Commission worked hard to develop a system by which it could tackle the challenges of the regional problems in the Community. The Action Program of 1962, the Memorandum on Regional Problems in 1965,[2] and the Memorandum on Regional Policy in 1969 addressed the problem in detail. These proposals recommended coordination of national policies and Community policies to overcome regional imbalances and the creation of the ERDF. Of the original members, only Italy, which had its own regional development problem, viewed these proposals favorably. The other two larger members of the EEC, France and West Germany, did not want to provide more funds for the European Community (EC) budget or surrender more national regional policies to the Commission. The sovereignty issue particularly disturbed the French, and the Germans were feeling the pressures of making large contributions to the CAP.[3] Nevertheless, the UK application for membership in the EU changed the views of these countries about the ERDF. A commitment to an attractive regional policy became linked with British entry into the Community. Two factors explain the change in the French and German positions.

First, it was clear that the UK's membership would provide additional export markets for German exports. If the British stayed out of the Community, then Germany would have likely faced greater competition from the United States in the UK market. The French also favored British membership, but for political reasons. According to Stephen George, "President Pompidou had made British entry one of the bases of his *rapprochement* with the center parties, and he had staked his personal prestige on the exercise."[4] Furthermore, Pompidou and Prime Minister Edward Heath had a working relationship. Thus, the shift in the French and German position on regional policy became clear at the Paris summit of the European Council in 1972. At this meeting the EC leaders announced that a high priority should be given to correcting regional imbalances in the EC, which could otherwise hinder the future development of Economic and Monetary Union (EMU). Therefore, they agreed to establish the ERDF by the end of 1973.

However, several developments prevented the realization of this deadline. First, the oil crisis of 1973 pushed regional funding to a lower priority on the Community agenda. The British government did not want the EC to interfere in any way in future production and distribution of North Sea oil. The Germans, on the other hand, wanted to link this issue with the regional development fund. When the British refused to link the two issues, the Germans changed their position on the ERDF and pulled out of the negotiations.[5] Second, the new Labour government in the UK, which was divided on EC membership, refused to accept "offset payments towards CAP with receipts from the ERDF."[6] And third, with the accession to power of Helmut Schmidt and Valéry Giscard d'Estaing, a Franco-German alliance dominated the EU for the rest of the 1970s. The Franco-German alliance would oppose the British position on the ERDF as long as it required additional funds from these two countries. Yet, despite the gloomy picture, the Community leaders reached an agreement to set up the ERDF at the Paris summit of December 1974. This development was a direct result of the Irish and Italian governments making it known that unless a compromise was reached on the ERDF, they would boycott the summit meeting.

The ERDF started with a small budget of 1,300 million European units of account (EUA), which was considerably lower than the Commission's proposal of 2,500 million EUAs (Table 10.1).

Since its establishment, the ERDF has operated under separate sets of rules: 1975–1979, 1980–1984, 1985–1988, rules that became effective after 1989 as a result of the Single European Act, and finally changes recommended by Agenda 2000. Initially, the allocation of funds was based on the quotas of the member states subject to approval by the Council of Ministers. In 1979, the Council amended the structure of the ERDF to allow for a proportion of the fund to be disbursed on a strictly regional basis, separate from the national allocations. This was an important development because it allowed the consideration of region-specific problems without having to deal with national politics.[7] It is important to note that the net impact of the ERDF was greatly hampered by other EC policies, notably CAP. CAP was not based on regional needs. Rather, it provided assistance based on productivity and type of product and

TABLE 10.1   ERDF Appropriations, 1975–1988 (millions of ecus)

Year	Total	Annual Increase (%)	Share of EC Budget (%)
1975	257.6*	—	4.8
1976	394.3*	53.1	5.6
1977	378.5*	(4.0)	4.9
1978	581.0	53.5	4.6
1979	945.0	62.7	6.1
1980	1,165.0	23.3	6.7
1981	1,540.0	32.2	7.3
1982	1,759.5	14.3	7.6
1983	2,010.0	14.2	7.6
1984	2,140.0	6.5	7.3
1985	2,289.9	7.0	7.5
1986	3,098.0	35.3	8.6
1987	3,311.0	6.9	9.1
1988	3,684.0	11.3	8.1

SOURCE: Dennis Swann, *The Economics of the Common Market* (Penguin Books 1970, Sixth, 1988) Copyright © Dennis Swann, 1970, 1972, 1975, 1978, 1981, 1984, 1988. Reprinted with permission.
*These figures are converted from EUA to ecu at January 1978 rates.

did not take into account the regional distribution. In this way, CAP, which had a much bigger budgetary allocation, often worked in the opposite direction of the ERDF, allocating funds to regions less in need of them than others. Nevertheless, two significant developments in the 1980s resulted in a much-improved ERDF. The first was the expansion of EC membership to include Greece (1981), and Portugal and Spain (1986). And the second was the adoption of the Single European Act (SEA) in 1986. Addition of the three Mediterranean countries increased the pool of the countries with large underdeveloped regions: Greece, Ireland, southern Italy, Portugal, Spain, and northern UK. More recent inclusion of East Germany also placed pressures on the EU to seriously address regional issues. Finally, it has become essential to review cohesion policy and recommend necessary reforms as the EU prepares for expansion eastward. Agenda 2000 outlines reforms that will be discussed in the next section. Each objective received its own respective fund.

The EU's structural funds initially had five objectives. Following the membership of Austria, Finland, and Sweden, objective 6 was added to the list. However, with the adoption of recommendations made in Agenda 2000, the EU reconfigured these objectives. At the Berlin summit of March 24–25, 2000, the heads of state and government adopted the second reform of the structural funds. The priority objectives were redefined and reduced to three, making the available funds better targeted to favor the most disadvantaged regions and social groups.[8]

The original objective 1 referred to the development of structurally backward regions and received funds through the ERDF, the ESF, and the EAGGF. In this category the allocation of funds to members, in billion ecus, between 1989 and 1993 was as follows: Spain, 9.78; Italy (southern provinces), 7.44; Portugal, 6.96; the UK (Northern Ireland), 0.88; Ireland, 3.67; and France (overseas departments), 0.88.[9] In these regions, per capita gross national product (GNP) in purchasing power standard was less than 75 percent of the EC average.

The second objective pertains to reconverting regions in industrial decline and funding through the ERDF and ESF. The distribution of funds during 1989–1991 in billions of ecus was Spain, 0.74; Italy, 0.26; UK, 1.51; France, 0.70; Germany, 0.36; Belgium, 0.20; the Netherlands, 0.10; Denmark, 0.03; and Luxembourg, 0.02.[10] The UK has been the chief beneficiary under this program. However, since it is largely excluded from objective 1, with the exception of Northern Ireland, the UK has not received the larger amounts available through the structural funds. Between 1994 and 1999, objective 2 funds increased to a total of 15.36 billion euros: Spain, 2.42; Italy, 1.46; Finland, 0.18; Germany, 1.56; Luxembourg, 0.015; France, 3.77; UK, 4.58; Belgium, 0.34; Austria, 0.10; the Netherlands, 0.65; Denmark, 0.12; and Sweden, 0.16.[11]

Objectives 3 and 4 received funding by the ESF and addressed the need to combat long-term unemployment and youth unemployment. Between 1990 and 1992 the allocations of funds for these purposes, in billions of ecus, was Spain, 0.56; Italy, 0.59; UK, 1.03; France, 0.87; Germany, 0.57; Belgium, 0.17; the Netherlands, 0.23; Denmark, 0.10; and Luxembourg, 0.01.[12] Regions do not restrict these objectives, but some newer priorities seem to show regional considerations. During the second phase of funding the EU provided 15.18 billion euros for these objectives: Spain, 1.84; Italy, 1.71; Finland, 0.33; Germany, 1.94; Luxembourg, 0.02; France, 3.20; UK,

3.37; Belgium, 0.46; Austria, 0.37; the Netherlands, 1.09; Denmark, 0.30; and Sweden, 0.51.[13]

Objective 5 had two parts. The first referred to adjustment of agricultural structures (related to reform of CAP) and was funded under the EAGGF Guidance. The second part addressed development of rural areas and was funded by the ERDF, the ESF, and the EAGGF Guidance. Between 1989 and 1993, a sum of 2.64 billion ecus reached member states under this objective.[14] During 1994–1999, the amount of funds in these categories increased to 13.7 billion euros combined: Spain, 1.10; Italy, 1.71; Finland, 0.53; Germany, 2.37; Luxembourg, 0.046; France, 4.16; UK, 1.26; Belgium, 0.26; Austria, 0.78; the Netherlands, 0.31; Denmark, 0.31; and Sweden, 0.33.[15]

In addition to these objectives, the EU also set up separate Community initiatives funded by the structural funds. Between 1994 and 1999, the EU set aside 14 billion euros to finance such programs as planning and cooperation between border regions; support to labor in job transition and employment opportunities for women; structural changes in regions that traditionally relied on steel, defense, and coal-mining industries; rural development; small and medium-sized enterprise development; urban renewal; integration of peripheral regions; and promoting peace in Northern Ireland.[16]

Finally, the Cohesion Fund was established in 1994 for purposes of implementing the Maastricht Treaty by assisting poorer members (Greece, Ireland, Portugal, and Spain) in meeting EMU criteria. In total, this fund had 15 billion euros available to support projects related to environmental protection and infrastructure.

With the Berlin decision of March 1999 on Agenda 2000, three new objectives replaced the previously mentioned programs under new headings and with an expanded budget. The structural funds have a budget of 213 billion euros for the period 2000–2006. They target financial assistance under three objectives (93 percent of the budget) and four Community initiatives (5.35 percent of the budget).[17]

Objective 1, with a budget of 135.9 € billion, focuses on the development and structural adjustment of regions whose development is lagging behind. These regions have 22 percent of the total population of the EU living where per capita gross domestic product (GDP) is below 75 percent of the EU average, Finnish and Swedish regions of the former objective 6, and the most remote areas like the French overseas departments, the Canary Islands, Azores, and Madeira. Under the new regulations, regions that were eligible for objective 1 during 1994–1999 but have lost this entitlement will receive transitional assistance. In addition, objective 1 supports two special programs: the Peace Program in Northern Ireland (2000–2004) and an assistance program for certain Swedish regions that meet the low population density defined in objective 6 and the Swedish Act of Accession (2000–2006).[18]

Under objective 2 the EU addresses regions that face structural difficulties in industries, rural areas, urban areas, and areas dependent on fisheries. The funds available in this objective total 22.5 billion euros for the period 2000–2006. Industrial areas have to meet three conditions: an unemployment rate above the EU average, a higher percentage of jobs in the industrial sector than the EU average, and a decline in industrial employment. Rural areas must have a population density of less than 100 individuals per square kilometer or have workers in the agricultural sector at a ratio

higher than twice the EU average. A decline in population or an overall unemployment rate higher than the EU average also makes rural regions eligible for objective 2
funds. For urban areas the EU emphasizes poverty, unemployment, damaged environment, high crime rate, and low education level.[19] The fisheries' dependence is
measured in the percentage of labor employed in this industry and the degree of reduction in its employment.

The main goal of objective 3 is the development of human resources. Its funds
total 24.05 billion euros for 2000–2006. Areas of support include policies to combat
unemployment, improve access to jobs by those facing social exclusion, education and
training programs to improve people's chances in getting jobs, and the promotion of
equal opportunities for men and women.[20]

Once again, these objectives are coupled with Community initiatives and Cohesion funding. The former have a budget of 10.44 billion euros and cover Interreg III
(cross-border, transnational, and interregional cooperation), urban initiatives (regen-
eration of urban areas in crisis), Leader 1 (rural development by local action groups),
and Equal (transnational cooperation to fight against discrimination and inequality in
access to work). The Cohesion Fund, on the other hand, has 18 billion euros that is
adjusted to inflation every year. As was the case in the 1994–1999 funding period,
only Greece (16–20 percent), Ireland (7–10 percent), Portugal (16–20 percent), and
Spain (52–58 percent) qualify for assistance through the Cohesion Fund.[21] Projects
must belong to one of two categories: (1) environment projects, that is, projects that
help to achieve the objectives of the Community's environmental policy;[22] and
(2) transport infrastructure projects, that is, projects to establish or develop transport
infrastructure within the Trans-European Network (TEN), or projects providing access to the TEN. An appropriate balance must be ensured between financing for
transport infrastructure projects and environment projects; the Commission has set
the target of a 50-50 share-out between the two categories. Table 10.2 provides information on structural funds for 2000–2006. When the different categories are combined, the funds available in the three objectives total 135.9 billion euros for objective
1, 22.5 billion euros for objective 2, and 24.05 billion for objective 3.

The Social Policy

Social policy in the EU evolved over two phases. The first phase began with the
Treaty of Paris and continued until the Single European Act. During this period, the
Treaty of Paris included provision for the Coal and Steel Community's High Authority (the forerunner of the Commission) to address occupational safety in the coal
and steel industries and to sponsor research that would achieve better safety standards
in these areas. The EEC treaty also addressed the need to achieve economic and social cohesion in the Community. The second phase began with the Single European
Act and continues through present, during which social policy has received more attention on the EU agenda.

During the first phase, there was general concern to improve "health and safety
at work, to facilitate free movement of labor, to improve the equality of men and

TABLE 10.2   Structural Funds (in billions of euros; 1999 prices)

Member State	Objective 1	Transitional Support for Objective 1	Objective 2	Transitional Support for Objectives 2 and 5b	Objective 3
Belgium	0	0.625	0.368	0.065	0.737
Denmark	0	0	0.156	0.027	0.365
Germany	19.29	0.729	2.984	0.526	4.581
Greece	20.961	0	0	0	0
Spain	37.744	0.352	2.553	0.098	2.140
France	3.254	0.551	5.437	0.613	4.540
Ireland*	1.315	1.773	0	0	0
Italy	21.935	0.187	2.145	0.377	3.744
Luxembourg	0	0	0.034	0.006	0.038
Netherlands	0	0.123	0.676	0.119	1.686
Austria	0.261	0	0.578	0.102	0.528
Portugal	16.124	0	0	0	0
Finland	0.913	0	0.459	0.030	0.403
Sweden†	0.722	0	0.354	0.052	0.720
UK*	5.085	1.166	3.989	0.706	4.568
EU15	127.543	8.411	19.733	2.721	24.050

SOURCE: European Communities. "Regional Policy-Available Funds,"
http://europa.eu.int/comm/regional_policy/activity/erdf/erdf3_en.htm.
*Including Peace 2000–2004.
†Including the special programs for Swedish coastal areas.

women in the work place, to harmonize social security provisions, and to promote a social dialogue between management and workers at the Community level."[23] Articles 117–122 of the Rome Treaty addressed these needs, and Articles 3 and 123–128 focused on the European Social Fund, which was essential to the retraining and resettlement of unemployed workers and maintenance of occupations while enterprises changed their activities due to economic difficulties. However, the role and functioning of the ESF underwent significant revision. The financing of the ESF changed from reliance on levies of member states to financing from the Community budget. In addition, two sets of broad objectives were identified: (1) to facilitate employment adjustment resulting from EU policies, and (2) to overcome structural problems experienced by regions or economic sectors.[24] These goals required reallocation of some 90 percent of the fund's resources to vocational training. During the 1970s, as unemployment became a serious problem for the Community, the fund's resources increased fourfold.

The Paris summit of 1972 was very crucial for the social image of the Community. At this meeting, the leaders called for a proposal from the Commission on social policy. The Commission produced a Social Action Program in 1973 that was accepted by the Council of Ministers in January 1974 for implementation from 1974 to

1976. The policy goals covered three areas: attainment of full and better employment; improvement and harmonization of living conditions; and involvement of management and labor in the economic and social decisions of the EC, and of workers in the operations of their companies.[25] However, due to the economic recession, little progress was made on these fronts until the mid-1980s, when the Single European Act was adopted.[26]

The second phase of the social policy began with the French idea of the "social area" in 1981 that the Commission president, Jacques Delors, endorsed in 1985. This idea argues for greater equality in Community-wide social standards because in an increasingly competitive environment, caused by the creation of the single market, countries with lower standards of social protection would undercut other members, a process known as "social dumping."

The Single European Act made revisions to the section of the Rome Treaty concerned with social policy. Article 118A requires member countries to encourage improvements in health and safety of workers by continuing the harmonization of policies. A second amendment, Article 118B, emphasized the need to promote a social dialogue at the Community level. Furthermore, the SEA also placed important proposals that have significant social policy implications (e.g., measures relating to free movement of labor and professionals) on the EC agenda. What eventually came out of these various efforts toward social policy was a document of wide-ranging social commitments known as the Proposal for a Community Charter for Fundamental Social Rights, or Social Charter. It did not receive the unanimous support of the EC members at the Strasbourg summit in December 1989. The strongest opposition came from the UK and was sustained at Maastricht in 1991. As a result of the British opposition, the other 11 members signed a separate social protocol as a move to renew their commitment to EC-wide social policy.[27] The Social Charter specifies the following commitments:

1. *The right to freedom of movement.* This right enables EC citizens to establish themselves and to exercise any occupation in any of the member countries on the same terms as those applied to the nationals of the host country.
2. *The right to employment and remuneration.* This principle recognizes that any citizen of the EC has the right to employment and to fair remuneration of that employment. It aims at the establishment of a decent basic wage, receipt of a fair wage and the guarantee of an equitable reference wage for workers who are not in full-time employment of indefinite duration, and the maintenance of adequate means of subsistence in the event of attachment of wages.
3. *The right to improved living and working conditions.* This is directed against the threat of social dumping, as discussed previously.
4. *The right to social protection.* This refers to minimum wage and social security.
5. *The right to freedom of association and collective bargaining.*
6. *The right to vocational training.* This right implies the organization of training leave that would enable EC citizens to be retrained or to obtain additional skills by taking advantage of the facilities for continuing and permanent train-

ing, which the public officials, companies, and the two sides of the industry are called on to set up.

7. *The right of men and women to equal treatment.*
8. *The right to worker information, consultation, and participation.* This principle concerns the right of workers to be informed and even consulted about major events affecting their companies and work conditions.
9. *The right to health and safety protection at the workplace.*
10. *The right to protection of children and adolescents.* This principle sets the minimum working age at 16 and gives young workers the right to a fair wage, to be covered by labor regulations which take into account their specific characteristics, and also to embark, after completion of statutory schooling, upon 2 years of vocational training.
11. *The rights of elderly people to receive an income that guarantees a decent standard of living.*
12. *The rights of disabled persons.* Every disabled person has the right to take advantage of specific measures, especially in the field of training and occupational and social integration and rehabilitation.[28]

Social Policy after Maastricht

The social policy of the EU continues to cause divisions within the EU because of labor–management relations in each member state. There is no question that the Maastricht Treaty significantly expands the scope of social policy. The allocation of the ESF now requires the consideration of the goal of "economic and social cohesion." Initially, the UK chose to opt out of the Social Charter that was agreed to by the other 11 states in the Maastricht Treaty. The compromise agreement between the UK and EC11 in 1992 was called the Social Protocol, to which Britain did not adhere. This Protocol kept unanimity voting in sensitive policy areas like social security. At the Amsterdam Treaty negotiations the UK agreed to incorporate the Protocol into the Social Charter and in 1997 the Blair government opted in.

The decision of the British government to opt out of the Social Charter created additional concern for other members of the EU; they felt that the UK might be trying to gain unfair advantage over its EU partners by becoming a very attractive site for European investors because businesses would not pay the full price for labor costs.[29] These concerns were all the more relevant to the EU leaders as they faced the task of reducing the unemployment rate from 20 million workers.[30]

The Amsterdam Treaty incorporated the social protocol into the Social Charter, with Britain going along with the other members (see Chapter 5).[31] This treaty added provisions for cooperation in fighting unemployment and outlined decision-making procedures for Council voting and the role of the European Parliament (EP) in different policy issues: the Council voting is based on qualified majority vote (QMV), with the EP having a codecision role in policy areas of health and safety at work; working conditions; information and consultation of workers; social inclusion; equal opportunities and treatment of the sexes; and equal pay for both sexes. Unanimity in the Council and a consultative role for the EP are specified for social security. No role is given to the EP in the area of contractual agreement between management and labor.[32]

Despite the recent developments, social policy is merely complementary to national policies of the member states. Much work is needed to establish EU-wide rules pertaining to working conditions, industrial relations, and labor market policies. One area of success is equalization of working conditions across the EU— harmonization of policies regarding maternity leave, working hours, temporary employment, and part-time employees.

Education and Training Policies

Education and training policies represent major challenges for the EU. Although both topics affect the lives of all EU citizens, Community-wide policies in these areas were introduced only recently, in conjunction with the single market, and have faced serious financing problems and political obstacles on the grounds of national sovereignty.[33] Prior to the SEA, the EU initiated a limited training program to tackle unemployment problems in the 1970s. The European Center for the Development of Vocational Training (CEDEFOP) administered this program and had only limited support from some of the EU countries. However, the challenges of the single market, and post-Maastricht Europe, required a more comprehensive policy package. The following sections discuss these new programs.

SOCRATES. This program focuses on educational cooperation aimed at a wide range of people and institutions at all levels of education. It has seven categories for cooperation: Comenius for school education, Erasmus for higher education, Grundtvig for adult education, Lingua for language teaching and learning, Minerva for information and communication technologies in education, Observation and Innovation in educational systems and policies, and Joint Actions with other Community programs.[34]

LEONARDO DA VINCI. This is a community vocational training and action program. It has two planned phases: 1995–1999 and 2000–2006. During the first phase, the program's key objective was to support the development of cross-Community projects. With a budget of 620 million euros, it provided coverage not only to member states but also to the three countries of European Free Trade Association (EFTA) and the European Economic Area, Iceland, Liechtenstein, and Norway, and the candidate countries of central and eastern Europe.[35]

YOUTH PROGRAMS. These programs address citizens of the EU and the previously mentioned countries (including Malta and Turkey as of 2001) that are in the 15–25-year-old age group. The programs include the old Youth for Europe and European Voluntary Service programs. The programs include youth exchange, launching initiatives at the local level, youth organizations, youth leadership, youth workers, project management and organization, and education. Action items provide additional avenues for youth education: Action 1 for Europe-wide exchanges; Action 2 for voluntary services; Action 3 for youth initiatives; Action 4 for joint actions with Socrates, Leonardo, and Youth programs; and Action 5 for support measures.

TEMPUS. This program is a trans-European cooperation scheme for higher education as adopted by the Council on May 7, 1990. It is currently in its Phase III (2000–2006) and is part of the EU's overall program for economic and social restructuring of the central and eastern European countries, including Technical Assistance for Central and Eastern Europe (PHARE program), and for economic recovery of the former Soviet Union countries and Mongolia Technical Assistance in Confederation of Independent States (TACIS program).

Industrial Policy and Research and Development

Unlike regional policy, industrial policy provides assistance to sectors of the economy, regardless of geographical location, at least in initial policy choices. The Treaty of Rome made no specific reference to a Community-wide industrial policy. This is not surprising since industrial policies of the member states vary greatly: in France and Germany the state intervenes to shape industrial policy, whereas in the UK there is a relatively hands-off approach. However, with the launching of Project 1992, the Commission argued that in order to have a viable EU-wide industrial base, with a strong competition policy, coordinated policies were essential.[36] According to John Kemp, the Commission supported the idea of subsidiarity where "the EC would only become involved when national policies of the member states were ineffective, or harmful to other member states."[37] The Commission argued that policy coordination was necessary between industrial policy and other policy areas: common external policy, social and environmental policies, research and development (R&D) policy, and greater coordination of the member states' national industrial policies.

The EC adopted two main programs to support R&D at the European level. The first set of programs, known as the framework programs, started in 1985 and are run by the Commission. The second set, known as EUREKA, are much less coordinated R&D programs between 18 European countries and the EU.[38]

The framework programs started in 1985 with the introduction of the European Strategic Program for Research and Development in Information Technologies (ESPRIT). The second framework program went into effect in 1987 and lasted through 1991; it was followed by the third phase (1990–1994). The other R&D framework programs that were introduced under the second and third phases include the following:

- RACE, Research in Advanced Communications in Europe
- BRITE, Basic Research in Industrial Technologies for Europe
- EURAM, European Research in Advanced Materials
- SCIENCE, Plan to Stimulate the International Cooperation and Interchange needed by European Research Scientists

- SPES, European Stimulation Plan for Economic Sciences
- STEP, Science and Technology for Environmental Protection
- DELTA, Development of European Learning through Technological Advance[39]

Following Maastricht, the EU accepted the Commission's proposal for the size and funding of the fourth phase of the framework programs to cover the period between 1994 and 1998. The Commission's proposal called for a budget of 13.1 billion ecus as compared to the 6.6 billion ecus for the third phase. Nevertheless, in real terms, the budget still remained at about 4 percent of the overall Community budget.[40]

The Commission's push for R&D was also a critical part of the Delors 1993 white paper. The paper stressed that one of the main reasons for Europe's decline in competitiveness was the slowdown in infrastructure investment during the 1980s. In order to meet the challenges of the twenty-first century, the white paper called for new investments in information highways, pan-European transport, energy, and environmental infrastructure.[41] The development of new information technologies and highways would be financed by private capital, and a mixture of public and private sources would cover transport and energy networks. The paper also argued that the new information highways and technologies could not reach their potential advances unless the current industries were decentralized. Decentralization represented a major problem for several EU countries where information and telecommunication industries were state monopolies. For the information industries, the Commission estimates a cost of 150 billion ecus over a period of 10 years.[42] In addition, a task force would be needed to start the drive with a mandate from the EU countries. The transport and energy infrastructure, on the other hand, would require an estimated funding of 250 billion ecus to establish better road, rail, airport, and gas pipeline infrastructures between the EU and its neighbors in eastern and southern Europe.[43] On March 25, 1996, the Council and the EP modified the budget to account for the new members of the EU. This decision added 800 million ecus to the programs and 100 million ecus to the Euratom program.

More recently, the EU revised the R&D policies and adopted the fifth framework program for 1998–2002.[44] This package identifies priorities for EU research, technology, and development strategies and differs from previous programs in that its subprograms are aimed at solving problems and socioeconomic challenges facing EU citizens. Its two main parts are the EC framework program covering research and technological development, and the Euratom program for research and development in nuclear industries. The budget for the EC part is 13.9 billion euros; for Euratom it is 979 million euros.[45] The main action programs of the EC part are as follows:

1. *Quality of life and management of living resources*, 2.4 billion euros: Covers research in the areas of food, nutrition and health, control of infectious diseases, the cell factory, environment and health, sustainable agriculture, fisheries, forestry, and the aging population and disabilities.

2. *User-friendly information society*, 3.6 billion euros: Covers systems and services for citizens, new methods of work and e-commerce, multimedia content and tools, and essential technologies and infrastructure.
3. *Competitive and sustainable growth*, 2.7 billion euros: Includes innovative products, processes and organization, sustainable mobility, land transport and marine technologies, and new perspectives for aeronautics.
4. *Energy, environment, and sustainable growth*, 2.1 billion euros: Covers controlled thermonuclear fusion and nuclear fission (975 million euros). Other programs include sustainable management and quality of water, global change, climate and biodiversity, sustainable marine ecosystems, the city of tomorrow and cultural heritage, cleaner energy systems that include renewable sources, and economic and efficient energy for a competitive Community.
5. *Confirming the international role of Community research*, 0.475 billion euros.
6. *Promotion of innovation and encouragement of participation of state monopolies*, 0.36 billion euros.
7. *Improving human research potential and the socioeconomic knowledge base*, 1.3 billion euros: Involves studies in improving the socioeconomic knowledge base.
8. *Joint Research Center (JRC)*, 1.0 billion euros:[46] The JRC is the only Community institution carrying out research and technological development work and is considered to be the "scientific arm" of the Community. It is a Commission department which functions as a scientific reference center that provides scientific and technological assistance independent of any national and commercial interest. The JRC conducts "direct action," which means that the Community conducts research of its own, with a staff of 1,500 scientists working in eight institutes at five sites—Brussels and Geel (Belgium), Ispra (Italy), Karlsruhe (Germany), Petten (Netherlands), and Seville (Spain)—and with its own technical and financial resources. The action taken by the JRC revolves around three topics: serving the citizens, enhancing sustainability, and underpinning European competitiveness.

ENVIRONMENTAL POLICY

The Rome Treaty made no reference to environmental policy, and the topic did not enter the EC agenda until 1971, when the Commission gave its first detailed report on the environment to the European Council. At the subsequent 1972 Paris summit, the Council agreed to adopt an EC environmental policy and establish the Environmental and Protection Service.[47] Since then, the environmental policy goals have been defined in four different environmental action programs (EAPs). Unfortunately, these programs did not represent a definitive commitment from the member states for implementation, because each country has maintained its own set of environmental regulations. Nevertheless, the EAPs represent a growing emphasis in the EU on better coordinating its industrial policy with protecting the environment. It has become clear that most environmental problems transcend national boundaries and cannot be dealt with at the national level alone. Furthermore, with the Maastricht Treaty, the Commission attained more influence over EU environmental policy. "Towards Sustainability," the fifth Community Action Program (renamed from EAP) on the environment, established a strategy for voluntary action in 1992–2000 and marked the beginning of a cross-Community approach to all causes of environmental pollution. The Amsterdam Treaty further emphasized sustainable growth as one of the main goals of the EU.

The first EAP (1973–1977) set the main principles of the EC's environmental policy: the "polluter pays" principle, emphasis on preventive measures, and the need to consider the environmental impact of the Community's socioeconomic decisions. These principles were endorsed in the second EAP (1977–1981). The third EAP (1982–1986) placed stronger emphasis on environmental protection. It stated that "an overall strategy has to be formulated in which prevention, rather than cure, should be the rule."[48] Later, the principle of prevention was included in the Single European Act and became a central issue in the fourth EAP.

The developments under the SEA are important for the future implementation of environmental policies. Even though Article 130 of the SEA, which deals with environmental policies, still required unanimity in the Council of Ministers, Article 100A permitted directives approved by a qualified majority. As David Vogel explains, this provided an alternative means of "enacting environmental legislation, one which deprived any single member state of the power to block approval."[49] The SEA also expanded the role of the European Parliament in shaping EU legislation. This is significant because the EP has been stricter on environmental regulations than the Council of Ministers.[50] Finally, after the Chernobyl disaster in the former Soviet Union and a massive spill of toxins into the Rhine River in 1986, citizens' concerns about the environment placed ever-increasing pressure on EU leaders to respond to these challenges.

The fourth EAP (1987–1992) reflected these concerns; it was a more comprehensive proposal with a greater emphasis on environmental management. This program emphasized urgent action in the use of agricultural chemicals, treatment of agricultural wastes, protection of animal species, and general guidelines for product standards throughout the EU.[51] In order to stimulate action around these policy concerns, the European Environment Agency (EEA) was established in 1990. The original task of the EEA was to collect data and publish reports on environmental issues and to publish a report on the state of the environment every three years.

The EU measures in environmental management became far more explicit in the fifth Community Action Program (1992–2000). The program specified a holistic approach to sustainability and development and included the following components[52]:

INSTRUMENTS. This section outlines funding and guidelines for implementation of the various parts of the program. It includes technical aspects such as ecolabeling, the Community system of environmental management, and auditing. The EEA serves as an advisory body in these matters. For example, the EU is considering the introduction of environmental taxes on the "polluter pays" principle.

WASTE MANAGEMENT. This includes eliminating waste at source by improving product design, encouraging the recycling and reuse of waste, and reducing pollution caused by waste management.[53]

The EU's approach has been to assign more responsibility to the producer. For instance, the 1997 draft directive on end-of-life vehicles provides for the introduction of a system for collecting such vehicles at the manufacturer's expense. At the international level, this approach was also adopted at the first Conference of the Parties to the OSPAR Convention for the Protection of the Marine Environment of the North-East Atlantic. One of the tasks of this conference was to negotiate the dismantling and disposal of offshore oilrigs and natural gas platforms. The Parties to the Convention adopted the position supported by the European Commission, that the dumping of such installations at sea should be banned and that the costs of dismantling and disposing of such installations should be borne by their owners. The EU is also a Party to the Convention on the Control of Transboundary Movements of Hazardous Wastes and Their Disposal (the Basle Convention), which has been signed by more than 100 countries. The EU has already ratified the amendment to this Convention, banning exports of hazardous wastes from the OECD countries, the EU and Lichtenstein to non-OECD countries, regardless of whether such waste is for disposal, recycling, or use.[54]

NOISE POLLUTION. Noise has been a long-term concern of the Commission. The goal is to reduce noise emissions at the source, develop exchanges of information, and give greater force and consistency to EU programs to combat noise. In its 1996 Green Paper,[55] the Commission proposed extending this strategy by reducing noise emissions at source, developing exchanges of information, and giving greater force and consistency to EU programs to combat noise.

WATER POLLUTION. Since 1976, several directives have set common standards for surface and underground water, drinking water, and the discharge of toxic substances. The current proposals for directives are aimed at further improving the ecology of surface waters, introducing EU action on fresh waters and surface waters, and protecting estuaries, coastal waters, and groundwater. The EU is a party to various international conventions aimed at protecting the marine environment (the OSPAR Convention, the Barcelona Convention for the Protection of the Mediterranean Sea against Pollution).

AIR POLLUTION. The EU has been adopting stricter directives on air pollution by cars, large combustion plants, power stations, and machines since 1970. The EU signed the Kyoto agreement, calling for reducing greenhouse gas emissions by at least 5 percent of their 1990 levels between 2008 and 2012. In November 1998 the EU also participated in the Buenos Aires conference on implementing the Kyoto accords and became a strong supporter of the action plan adopted under this agreement.

NATURE CONSERVATION. Since 1982, the Community has introduced a number of measures to conserve wildlife (protection of certain species such as birds and seals) and natural habitats (protection of woodlands and watercourses). Moreover, the EU has signed a number of international conventions—for instance, the Bern Convention on the Conservation of European Wildlife and Natural Habitats, and the Bonn Convention on the Conservation of Migratory Species.

ENLARGEMENT. Enlargement to Central and Eastern Europe involves serious environmental difficulties, as the candidate countries' Cold War–era industrialization policies paid little or no attention to the environment. Before they can join the EU, the candidate countries will have to incorporate into their national legislation all existing Community environmental law as part of the *acquis*.

In its work program for 1999 [OJ C 366, 26.11.1998] the Commission identified environmental protection as one of the fundamental challenges facing the European Union. It stated that growing industrialization, food hazards, and the rapid degradation of the natural environment require a strategy of sustainable development, involving balanced resource management. As stressed by the European Council in Vienna, the only way that such a strategy can succeed is to make environment and sustainable development an integral part of all Community policies, as provided for by the Amsterdam Treaty. Thus, the European Council called on its members to finalize strategies to take fuller account of the environment in transport, energy, and agriculture policy; to focus on this side of its development, industrial, and internal market policies; and to put emphasis on cross-sectoral issues such as climate change and the environmental dimension of employment and enlargement. The latest Sixth Action Program, which identifies sustainable development as top priority for the EU, includes these considerations.[56] It proposes five priority avenues of strategic action: improving the implementation of existing legislation, integrating environmental concerns into other policies, working more closely with the market, empowering people as private citizens and helping them to change behavior, and taking account of the environment in land-use planning and management decisions.[57] Furthermore, the Sixth Environment Action Program focuses on four priority areas for action: climate change, biodiversity, environment and health, and sustainable management of resources and wastes. In climate change in the short term, the European Union's aim is to achieve the objectives of the Kyoto Protocol, that is, to reduce greenhouse gas emissions by 8 percent by 2008–2012 compared to 1990 levels. In the longer term, by 2020 it will be necessary to reduce these emissions by 20–40 percent by means of an effective international agreement. The objective in biodiversity is to protect and restore the structure and functioning of natural systems and stop the loss of biodiversity both in the European Union and on a global scale. The remaining action areas emphasize the need for protecting the environment, educating the citizens about sustainable economic growth, and pressing ahead with zero-waste environmental policies where recycling of all waste products becomes a long-term goal.

The Sixth Program also addresses external implication of EU's environmental policies. With regard to eastern enlargement, the program suggests that there should be an extended dialogue with the administrations in the candidate countries on sustainable development and the Commission should establish close cooperation with the nongovernmental organizations (NGOs) and businesses in the candidate countries. Also, the program strongly encourages application of international agreements on the environment to EU and candidate country policies.

CONCLUSION

The overall assessment of the EU's regional, social, industrial, and environmental policies is that Europe has made significant gains in these areas. Despite different national standards between the 15 member states, EU-wide policies have been adopted or initiated on a voluntary basis. Regions stand to benefit from the recent reforms that permit multiregional development projects. The Social Charter provides the early blueprints for harmonizing social benefits across the EU based upon the EU's strong self-perception as a welfare state. Although early British opposition to the charter represented an obstacle for its adoption as official policy, the future of these efforts seem promising since the UK government accepted the social policy clause of the Amsterdam Treaty. However, implementation of the EU directives through national legislation is often slow in coming.

ENDNOTES

1. Loukas Tsoukalis, *The New European Economy: The Politics and Economics of Integration* (New York and London: Oxford University Press, 1991), p. 41.
2. Dennis Swann, *The Economics of the Common Market* (London: Penguin Books, 1991), p. 289.
3. Stephen George, *Politics and Policy in the European Community* (Oxford: Oxford University Press, 1991), pp. 192–193.
4. Ibid.
5. Ibid., p. 194.
6. Tsoukalis, *The New European Economy*, pp. 210–211.
7. Judith Tomkins and Jim Twomey, "Regional Policy," in Frank McDonald and Stephen Dearden, eds., *European Economic Integration* (London: Longman, 1992), p. 105.
8. European Commission DG Regional Policy information Web site http://www.inforegio.org/wbpro/prord/prords/history_en.htm, accessed 07/21/02.
9. Tomkins, and Twomey, "Regional Policy," p. 107–108.
10. Ibid., p. 108.
11. Simon Hix, *The Political System of the European Union* (New York: St. Martin's Press, 1999), p. 259.
12. Tomkins and Twomey, "Regional Policy," p. 108.
13. Hix, *The Political System*, p. 259.
14. Tomkins and Twomey, "Regional Policy," pp. 108–109.
15. Hix, *The Political System*, p. 259.
16. Ibid., p. 258.
17. European Union Web site http://europa.eu.int/comm/regional_policy/activity/erdf/erd1b_en.htm, accessed 07/21/02.
18. Ibid.
19. Ibid.
20. Ibid.
21. European Communities, http://www.inforegio.cec.eu.int/wbpro/procf/Stru/prcf1_en.htm# How%20is%20it%20divided, accessed 07/21/02.
22. These objectives are defined in the Maastricht Treaty and in the fifth EAP as preserving, protecting, and improving the quality of the environment; protecting human health; and assuring prudent and rational use of natural resources. In accordance with the environmental directives in force, the fund

gives priority to the drinking water supply, wastewater treatment, and solid waste disposal. Reforestation, erosion control, and nature preservation actions are also eligible.

23. George, *Politics and Policy*, p. 203.
24. Stephen Dearden, "Social Policy," in McDonald and Dearden, eds., *European Economic Integration*, p. 85.
25. Swann, *The Economics of the Common Market*, p. 299.
26. For a detailed discussion of these years see Michael Shanks, *European Social Policy Today and Tomorrow* (Oxford: Pergamon Press, 1977).
27. Beverly Springer, *The Social Dimension of 1992* (Westport, Conn.: Praeger, 1992), pp. 39–41.
28. European Community, *1992: The Social Dimension* (Luxembourg: Office for Official Publications of the European Communities, 1990), pp. 83–85.
29. Ibid., p. 156.
30. "EU Urged to Catch Up with the World," *Financial Times*, December 8, 1993, p. 2.
31. European Commission, Intergovernmental Conference 1996–97: *Commission Opinion—Reinforcing Political Union and Preparing for Enlargement* (Luxembourg: Office for Official Publications of the European Communities, 1998).
32. Hix, *The Political System*, p. 229.
33. Glenda Rosenthal, "Educational and Training Policy," in Leon Hurwitz and Christian Lequesne, eds., *The State of the European Community: Policies, Institutions, and Debates in the Transition Years* (Boulder, Colo. and London: Lynne Reinner/Longman, 1991), p. 273.
34. European Communities, "Education Policy," http://europa.eu.int/comm/education.htm, accessed 07/24/02.
35. Ibid.
36. John Kemp, "Competition Policy," in McDonald and Dearden, eds., *European Economic Integration*, p. 78.
37. Ibid.
38. The members of EUREKA are Austria, Belgium, Denmark, Germany, Finland, France, Greece, Iceland, Ireland, Italy, Luxembourg, the Netherlands, Norway, Portugal, Spain, Sweden, Switzerland, the UK, Turkey, and the EC, represented by the Commission.
39. EC Delegation to the United States, *The European Community in the Nineties* (Washington, D.C.: EC Office, 1992), p. 15.
40. "R&D in a Tussle over EC Funding," *Financial Times*, October 26, 1993, p. 9.
41. "EU Urged to Catch Up with the World," *Financial Times*, December 8, 1993, p. 2.
42. Ibid.
43. Ibid.
44. European Commission, *Fifth Framework Programme, 1998–2002*, http://europa.eu.int/scadplus/leg/en/lvb/i23001.htm, accessed 07/24/02.
45. Ibid.
46. Ibid.
47. John Hassan, "Environment Policy," in McDonald and Dearden, eds. *European Economic Integration*, p. 122.
48. Angela Liberatore, "Problems of Transnational Policymaking: Environmental Policy in the European Community," *European Journal of Political Research* 19 (1991): 292.
49. David Vogel, "Environmental Protection and the Creation of a Single European Market." Paper presented at the Annual Meeting of the American Political Science Association, Chicago, September 3–6, 1992, p. 11.
50. Ibid., p. 12.
51. Hassan, "Environment Policy," p. 124.
52. European Communities, http://www.eurunion.org/legislat/agd2000/index.htm, accessed 07/24/02.
53. European Commission, *Commission Report COM(98)711 final* (Brussels: European Commission Publication, 1998).
54. Ibid.
55. European Commission, *Action Against Noise: Green Paper* (Brussels: European Commission Publication, November 4, 1996), http://europa.eu.int/scadplus/leg/en/lvb/l21224.htm.
56. European Commission, *Sixth Environmental Action Programme 2010: Our future, our choice* (Brussels: European Commission Publication, 24 January 2001, http://europa.eu.int/scadplus/leg/en/lvb/l28027.htm).
57. Ibid.

11

External Economic Relations of the European Union

In this chapter, we will look at the European Union's external economic relations with special emphasis on the United States and Japan, the Mediterranean Basin, and the Lomé (African, Caribbean, and Pacific, or ACP) states. We maintain that the policy packages adopted toward these states are crucial to understanding the EU's competition with the United States and Japan as an emerging world economic power.

MULTILATERAL TRADE POLICY

The EU is one of the key players in multilateral trade negotiations in the world and the world's largest trading bloc, accounting for 21 percent of global merchandise exports in 1998. As the EU becomes a stronger economic union, its voice in multilateral trade negotiations carries more weight. Simon Hix explains that the EU has been a strong advocate of the World Trade Organization (WTO) even when this organization has ruled against the EU.[1] In these instances, the Commission pressed the Council of Ministers to reform the internal market and the Common Commercial Policy (CCP) to adhere to WTO principles. As a matter of fact, since the completion of the single market, the EU's trade openness with the rest of the world has increased significantly. If we take the share of imports of goods and services as percentage of gross domestic product (GDP) as an indicator of how open the economy is, we see that the EU's indicator increased from 10 percent in 1992 to 12 percent in 1999. This figure is very close to that of the United States (13.4 percent) and is better than Japan's (9 percent). When the EU is enlarged, multilateral trade will be an even more integral part of the EU's external policies. With this in mind, the EU approach to the WTO Millennium Round trade negotiations is based on the following policy aspirations:

1. To create substantial benefits for the world economy through trade liberalization of goods and services and better rules in a number of policy areas (in particular, competition, investment, intellectual property, trade facilitation, government procurement)
2. To contribute to harnessing globalization
3. To better integrate developing countries into the world economy by working for a more equitable distribution of the benefits of trade liberalization
4. To further strengthen the WTO multilateral system so that it can become a truly universal, fair, and transparent instrument for the management of international trade relations in support of sustainable development
5. To ensure that the Millennium Round benefits the environment[2]

Furthermore, the EU favors expanding WTO membership to achieve true globalization. One country of concern to the EU is China, with its massive potential as a consumer market. It should also be noted that the EU approach to WTO policy reform is strongly tied to the environment and sustainable growth. Unfortunately, there were serious disagreements between the developed and developing countries over WTO reforms. Furthermore, the EU and the United States also disagree over environmental issues. When WTO talks were held in Seattle in November 1999, the participants failed to reach a meaningful agreement. Among the more serious disagreements were industrialized countries' insistence on improvements in labor conditions in the developing world, the U.S. demand for reduction in EU agricultural subsidies, and the role of the environment in international trade: more specifically how far measures to protect the environment could be pushed without letting them become barriers to trade and whether there should be free trade in biotechnology and genetically modified food.

Since that time, the WTO agreed to launch a new trade round after six days of discussion in Doha, Qatar, to work on opening markets to agricultural and manufactured goods. Moreover, the participants agreed to link trade and the environmental issues in an attempt to boost sustainable economic growth. Although not every participant has the same views on these topics, the decision to launch a new round of trade negotiations is a significant step forward in settling current disputes between members of the WTO. The agreement calls for a new world trade deal by 2005 and will involve issues like the environment, investment, and competition rules for the first time.[3] Under the plan, developing countries have the right to produce drugs cheaply in case of a medical emergency, the EU agrees to reduce some agricultural subsidies, the other WTO members accept the EU's demand that investment, competition, and environmental rules be placed on the agenda, India retains an effective veto (if it gains enough support from other countries) to push EU items off the agenda, and the U.S. agrees to relax some import curbs. All of these items present formidable challenges to WTO countries to discuss, negotiate, and reach a final agreement by 2005.

THE EUROPEAN UNION, THE UNITED STATES, AND JAPAN

Whereas trilateral economic relations between the EU, Japan, and the United States constitute by far the world's largest economic exchange relationship, relations between these allies have been rather rocky in recent years. One major reason for this is that they all have been busy creating their respective zones of influence through regional trade blocs: the EU through the single market and the Economic and Monetary Union (EMU), European Economic Area (EEA), and future enlargement to central and east European countries; Japan in the Association of South East Asian Nations (ASEAN); and the United States in North America through the North American Free Trade Agreement (NAFTA). Table 11.1 provides the breakdown of the EU's global trade in goods and services in 2000 by sectors and by trade partners.

It is important to note that China has become a significant trade partner for the EU as well as for Japan and the United States. During the past decade, we have been observing a growing competition between the EU, the United States, and Japan for shares of the emerging Chinese market.[4] Among the other key trade partners, Poland and Turkey have recently become significant markets for EU products. Both countries

TABLE 11.1   EU's Global Trade and Major Foreign Trade Partners, 2000

Commodity	Imports (% total)	Exports (% total)
Manufactured goods	55.7	66.6
Services	22.5	24.3
Energy	11.6	2.5
Agricultural Products	6.2	5.0
Other Primary Products	4.0	1.7
EU Imports		
1	United States	19.3
2	Japan	8.4
3	China	6.8
4	Switzerland	5.8
5	Russia	4.4
EU Exports		
1	United States	24.7
2	Switzerland	7.5
3	Japan	4.8
4	Poland	3.6
5	Turkey	3.2

SOURCE: European Commission (http://europa.eu.int/comm/trade/goods/stats.htm).

are candidate states for EU membership, and Turkey has a customs union agreement with the EU.

EU–U.S. Economic Relations

The EU and the United States have been each other's important trade partners. Over the years, several trade disputes threatened to disrupt relations between the two allies, but they have maintained close ties and looked for ways to resolve their differences without damaging greater transatlantic security relations. The New Transatlantic Agenda (NTA) and the subsequent declaration of the Joint EU–U.S. Action Plan that was adopted at the EU summit meeting of December 3, 1995, in Madrid, provide a clear joint-action program that commits EU and the United States to collaboration in foreign policy, national security, drug trafficking, migration, environment, health, international crime, and concrete steps toward "building bridges across the Atlantic."[5] For example, the European Commission funded the creation of 10 EU centers at different U.S. universities to promote better understanding of the EU among the American public and to encourage research on topics relevant to EU–U.S. affairs. Ten more centers followed in the second phase of this project. At the EU–U.S. summit, on June 21, 1999, in Bonn, both sides agreed to work as full and equal partners in economic, political, and social affairs. This explicit recognition is a step forward from the NTA in that the document outlined how the two sides would shape their relationship over the next decade while remaining true to the letter and the spirit of the NTA.

TRADE BETWEEN THE EU AND THE UNITED STATES. The EU and the United States are the two largest economies and markets in the world. Taken together, they constitute half the world economy. Trade and investment across the Atlantic roughly equals $1 billion per day. Moreover, the combined foreign trade figures of the two partners equals 40 percent of world trade.[6] Table 11.2 provides recent figures on EU–U.S. trade.

As these figures show, EU–U.S. economic ties represent a very important component of transatlantic relations. However, trade between the two allies has not been smooth or free of disputes over the years. With the exception of the so-called chicken war in 1963 and some disagreements over tax legislation in the 1970s, trade relations were fairly good until the 1980s. Since the 1980s, a series of trade disagreements have often threatened to disrupt relations between the EU and United States. At the heart of most of these disagreements are U.S. complaints over EU subsidies for production and exports in such sensitive areas as agriculture, steel, and aircraft, and the EU's nontariff barriers to trade in building materials, telecommunications, broadcasting, grain, and bananas. The EU complains about unilateral U.S. measures such as section 301 of the 1974 U.S. Trade Act and the Super 301 provision of the 1988 Omnibus Trade Act, which allow the U.S. government to impose unilateral punitive sanctions on goods from U.S. trade partners without consultation with the General Agreement

TABLE 11.2 EU–U.S. Trade, 2000 (€billion)

	EU15 Trade			
	Imports	%	Exports	%
United States	199.0	19.3	232.5	24.7
World	1,032.5	100.0	941.1	100.0

EU Direct Foreign Investment Flows (% total)		
	Inflows	Outflows
United States	68.8	47.5
Canada	8.4	14.3
Japan	0.8	2.2
Australia-New Zealand	0.1	1.3
Rest of the world	21.9	34.7

SOURCE: European Commission (http://europa.eu.int/comm/trade/goods/stats.htm).

on Tariffs and Trade (GATT) (now the WTO) and U.S. policy on steel that resulted in the largest transatlantic dispute in history.

The Super 301 provision requires the U.S. administration to list publicly the countries that trade unfairly with the United States, to negotiate removal of such practices, and to take retaliatory action if negotiations with those countries fail. U.S. trade partners have been highly critical of this policy, and their concerns were echoed in a GATT report in December 1988. They fear that different U.S. administrations could resort to the political use of Super 301 as leverage in gaining an advantageous position in their bilateral trade relations with other countries.[7]

The primary disputes between the EU and the United States have been over Common Agricultural Policy (CAP) and steel industries. The issue of EU oilseed subsidies plagued the GATT negotiations for five years before it was resolved in November 1992.[8] This issue deadlocked GATT negotiations on agricultural trade so badly that it could have brought a halt to the entire Uruguay Round talks. The United States threatened to impose 200 percent punitive tariffs on about $300 million of European Community (EC) agricultural exports, mostly in white wine, starting on December 5, 1992, unless the Community accepted reductions in oilseed subsidies. After painstaking negotiations, an agreement was reached in which the EU would limit the area of land for oilseed production rather than the total amount of oilseeds produced.[9] Under this agreement, up to 15 percent of the area was to be taken out of production during the first year followed by a minimum of 10 percent in future years. In return, the United States agreed that oilseeds could be grown on land set aside for nonfood uses such as fuel for vehicles. Furthermore, the EC agreed to cut the volume of subsidies for agricultural exports by 21 percent from the average of exports during 1986–1990 over a 6-year period starting in 1994. An important sticking point in these agreements was French displeasure.

Other important issues have continued to present problems in EU–U.S. trade in the post–Uruguay Round years. These include the banana import decision of the EU, the EU's ban on the use of growth hormones in livestock and the subsequent ban on importing meat from the U.S., the U.S. farm subsidies versus the EU subsidies, steel industry, and the U.S. Helms-Burton Act, to list some of the key areas of contention.

The banana trade dispute does not directly affect U.S. exports to the EU, but it does affect U.S. companies that grow bananas in Lomé countries (former European colonies in Africa, the Caribbean, and the Pacific). In 1993, the EC adopted a common market organization (CMO) for bananas that was designed to give preferential treatment to banana imports from the Lomé countries.[10]

The United States objected to this decision and threatened to impose punitive tariffs against selected imports from the EU. The case eventually ended up in the WTO when the EU complained about U.S. threats. In 1997, the WTO ruled that the EU banana CMO was illegal. This decision prompted the EU to revise its scheme in January 1999. However, the WTO also found the revised scheme illegal. The United States continued to press for EU reversal of the CMO. When the Commission failed to satisfy the U.S. demand, the Clinton administration imposed trade sanctions on imports from the EU for an annual value of $191 million. This was carried out in the form of punitive tariffs (100 percent customs duties) on an equivalent amount of trade (loss of export income to EU markets by U.S. banana growers in non-ACP countries). Furthermore, the United States chose to carry out these sanctions on a rotating basis every six months by identifying which imports to target.

The EU decision to ban beef and other livestock products that have been produced with growth hormones produced another serious trade dispute. The disagreement between Brussels and Washington has been going back and forth for several years, with no end in sight. The United States initially claimed losses of $202 million annually, but the WTO arbitrator estimated the level at $116.8 million.[11] The reluctance of the EU to lift the ban resulted in U.S. retaliation through a 100 percent ad valorem duty rate on mainly agricultural products. The problem is not likely to disappear any time soon, since the EU's Scientific Committee of Veterinary Measures Relating to Public Health (SCVPH) reported on the risk to human health of six growth hormones in livestock.

Dispute over agricultural support levels resurfaced in 2002 following the adoption of the Farm Security and Rural Investment Act of 2002 by the U.S. Congress.[12] This new U.S. program sets out various agricultural support schemes under 10 titles, notably the commodity (farm subsidy) program, conservation, and trade, and will last for six years. The estimated spending on the programs is between $15 billion and $20 billion and represents a 70 percent increase on the amount previously set at the end of the FAIR Act. The EU argues that the new support level of the U.S. will most likely violate the aggregate measure of support (AMS) agreed upon at Doha.[13] The U.S. counters EU criticism by explaining that the American AMS level is far below the overall European figures and that corrective measures will be taken to assure U.S. compliance with the AMS target of $19.1 billion. In response, the EU accuses the U.S. officials with creative bookkeeping and excluding certain figures, like

$4 billion–$5 billion in price support for sugar and dairy industries, from the overall statistics.

A crucial trade dispute between the EU and U.S. concerns the steel industry, with each side accusing the other of unfair trade practices. Both sides heavily subsidize their steel industries, the United States by use of import quotas and the EU by various policies implemented under the European Coal and Steel Community (ECSC). One episode in this dispute involved the U.S. Department of Commerce's announcement of preliminary countervailing duties on flat-rolled steel imports from six EU countries in 1992 and again in 1994.[14] The Commission estimated that this action cost the EU steel producers sales of some 2 million tons of steel, worth nearly $1 billion, and warned that the EU would retaliate if the United States did not reverse its decision. In a similar fashion, the former U.S. trade representative, Mickey Kantor, announced in May 1993 that the United States would impose trade sanctions worth $20 million against EU firms in retaliation for the EU's refusal to grant the United States full access to the EU telecommunications procurement market.[15] The EU's trade commissioner, Sir Leon Brittan, responded angrily to the U.S. decision, and on June 8, 1993, the EU retaliated. EU foreign ministers agreed on "mirror-image" measures totaling $15 million per year against U.S. firms.

The EU–U.S. trade war in this sector took a turn to the worse in 2002 when the Bush administration decided to impose duties on steel imports to protect domestic industries. The U.S. unilaterally imposed tariffs up to 30 percent on imported steel for three years, claiming that other countries are dumping steel at below the cost of production and damaging its domestic industry. The U.S. claim is bitterly disputed by the EU, Japan, and other major steel producers that argue that the measure is designed to protect inefficient American industry. The EU took its complaint to the WTO and threatened to impose its own counter-sanctions against a range of U.S. products worth $350 million. EU countermeasures would include additional duties of 30 percent on steel, 30 percent on cars and motorcycles, 30 percent on guns, 13–15 percent on fruits, 13 percent on vegetables, 8–15 percent on fruit juices, 8 percent on rice, 30 percent on paper, 30 percent on textiles, 30 percent on optical devices and measurement instruments, and 30 percent on miscellaneous items.[16] The WTO ruled in favor of the EU that the U.S. policy violated the free trade agreements. The EU–U.S. trade war became more complicated when the WTO also ruled against the U.S. for tax breaks provided to American exporters. Acting on EU complaints of violation of free and fair trade, the WTO concluded that the U.S. tax breaks for exporters contravene international trade rules and cost European companies billions of U.S. dollars a year in lost trade. The level of permitted retaliation is up to $4 billion.

The EU also opposes the extraterritorial provisions in the Helms-Burton Act. Helms-Burton was created in retaliation against Cuba, which downed two unarmed U.S. civilian airplanes flying just outside Cuba's territorial waters. The act authorizes U.S. citizens to sue investors who trade with or invest in Cuba. Furthermore, those who do business with Cuba can be denied visas to the United States. The EU, other countries such as Canada, and the World Trade Organization contend that the United States has no right to dictate which countries can and cannot trade with Cuba.

The Iran-Libya Sanctions Act defines Iran and Libya as supporters of international terrorism and prohibits U.S. companies and their subsidiaries, including those in Europe, from doing any business with these countries.

EU–Japan Economic Relations

The EU and Japan represent the two other great economies of the world after the United States. Together, the EU and Japan account for 40 percent of world GDP. Japan, with the greatest national savings rate in the world and largest foreign reserves, represents a rich market for EU businesses. Yet, as any European business would remind us, Japan is a closed market for imports. Similarly, the EU is an important market for Japanese companies. This relationship has not been free of difficulties. The EU's relations with Japan suffer from the quantitative trade restrictions and voluntary export restraints (VERs) that the EU took over from its members as a result of the single market. Articles 113 and 115 of the Rome Treaty have played an important role in this area.

According to the Rome Treaty's Article 113, there was to be a common external tariff schedule for the EU member states by 1969. This was achieved in 1968 as part of the customs union. However, Article 115 provided an escape clause in permitting individual national trade policies as long as relevant parts of the common policy remained on the EU agenda as unsettled.

Protectionist trade policies continue to trouble EU–Japan relations, but the creation of the single market presented an important opportunity for the EU to abolish VERs and other quantitative restrictions on imports from Japan. VERs always cost the consumer, not the domestic producer and foreign exporters of the same products. In an attempt to reduce serious trade friction between the EU and Japan, the two sides reached an agreement on a post-1992 policy in July 1992. This agreement stated:

1. Intra-EC trade will be liberalized by the adoption of an EU-type approval scheme by January 1, 1993, and all national import restrictions will be abolished by the same date
2. Imports of cars from Japan will be unrestricted after December 31, 1999, and in the intervening period will be limited to the level of 1.23 million (approximately the 1991 level of imports)
3. Cars produced in Japanese-owned plants in the EU will have unrestricted access to the EU markets
4. There is an understanding about the levels of Japanese imports to France, Italy, Spain, Portugal, and the UK: a deliberate attempt will be made by Japanese firms to reduce adjustment pressures in the markets from which national import restrictions have been removed[17]

This agreement seemed to allow for better relations in the future, but some outstanding issues remained in EU–Japan trade relations. The first was the continuous Japanese balance-of-payments surplus with the EU. Second, Japan's legal barriers limit EU exports to that country. Third, it is difficult for EU firms to sell consumer goods in Japan unless they have Japanese subsidiaries. The Japanese marketing and distribution system requires close collaboration between the producers, wholesalers, and retailers, which makes marketing and distribution costs higher for EU firms in Japanese markets than they are for Japanese companies in EU markets. Japanese companies maintain close collaboration with each other under the auspices of the Japanese Ministry of International Trade and Industry (MITI). Such collaboration inherently damages non-Japanese firms' access to fair competition. This sort of activity would be illegal in the EU market.[18]

In an effort to overcome such problems, the two parties held a summit on July 19, 2000, to discuss avenues of cooperation. The final document covered all areas of international relations important to both parties. The agreement outlined the need for cooperation, "inter alia: the WTO, international monetary and financial system; improving market access; improving the investment environment, including through promotion and facilitation of investment; competition policy; customs cooperation; information technology, including electronic commerce and telecommunication; business dialogue; dialogue between consumer organizations."[19]

While clearly there are trade problems between the EU, the United States, and Japan, the single market provided an important incentive for all parties to improve their commercial relations. Each side stood to benefit from more open and free trade as well as from a foreign investment regime. One of the driving forces behind the single market is the improved competitiveness of EU firms in the global market. Since the most competitive and technologically advanced industries are found in the United States and Japan, it would be counterproductive to restrict their access to EU markets.

Furthermore, the extent of foreign investment flows between the EU and the United States suggests that protectionism would be counterproductive for both sides despite the current problems that have ended up in WTO arbitration (see previous discussion). The U.S. firms already present in the EU have been in a good position to benefit from the creation of the single market. Some 80 percent of the largest food processors in the EU are U.S.-owned, and other U.S.-owned companies, such as Ford, IBM, and General Motors, are pan-European in their operations.[20] While the Japanese are not as well positioned as the Americans in the EU market, they are rapidly expanding their investments in such areas as banking, cars, electronics, computers, and the information industry. Further progress in these and other ventures would promote better trade and financial relations among all three.

RELATIONS WITH EUROPEAN PERIPHERY COUNTRIES

European Economic Area

The European Economic Area extends the freedoms of the single market (free movement of goods, services, capital, and people) to EFTA countries (Iceland, Liechtenstein, and Norway) but excludes Switzerland. In turn, these countries have adopted relevant parts of *acquis communautaire* and case law associated with the first pillar of the EU.

The EFTA countries have always been important for the EU economically and politically. These countries were members of the democratic and capitalist half of the formerly divided Europe, and their economies are highly developed. Therefore, it is not surprising that Austria, Finland, and Sweden eventually became members of the EU.

With the collapse of communism in Europe, concerns about neutral countries' impact on EU security policies largely disappeared. After 16 months of negotiations the two communities (EC and EFTA) agreed to create the world's largest trading area, the EEA. The original agreement, initially encompassing 19 European states[21] and 380 million citizens, called for the free flow of capital, services, workers, and most goods throughout the EEA as of January 1, 1994. This new trade area accounted for 46 percent of total world trade. At the same time, both the EU and individual EFTA countries maintained their individual tariff schedules for imports from third parties. Furthermore, the EFTA countries remained outside of CAP and maintain their own, even more protectionist, agricultural policies.[22]

Despite initial enthusiasm about the EEA, the agreement suffered some setbacks. First, negotiations broke down because of a reservation registered by the EU Court of Justice. The Court's main concern was the proposed joint EU–EFTA tribunal, which would include 5 of the 13 judges of the EU Court of Justice, to resolve EEA-related disagreements. This raised a question: would these EU judges still be allowed to rule on an EU case if a similar case was already decided by the previous body? The problem ended when the EU foreign ministers agreed to give the Commission more negotiating flexibility with EFTA by dropping the demand that EFTA countries apply EU laws uniformly under the EEA. The EU decided to drop the idea of the joint court envisaged under the EEA accord and proposed an arbitration procedure to settle any future disputes between the two communities. In return, EFTA members agreed to adopt future EU single market legislation.

The second problem with the EEA was the Swiss rejection of the accord. This rejection came after Austria, Finland, Norway, and Sweden ratified the EEA and the ratification process was fully underway in EU member states. Furthermore, the European Parliament had approved the agreement. The Swiss rejection destroyed the chances of the EEA's starting on the same day as the single market and required renegotiation of the original accord to exclude Switzerland from the document. The EU Commission proposed a revised document on March 9, 1993, and the foreign ministers of the member states of the EU and EFTA signed it on March 17, 1993. The revised accord allowed the Swiss to enter the EEA at a later date if they so desired and called for the remaining members of EFTA to cover 60 percent of Switzerland's planned contribution to the Cohesion Fund.[23] Related to this development, tiny Liechtenstein needed to reformulate its own agreements with Switzerland if it intended to join the EEA.

Following these developments, four EFTA countries entered into membership talks with the EU and completed the terms for accession on March 1, 1994 (Austria, Finland, and Sweden) and March 15, 1994 (Norway). The delay with Norway involved fishing rights. On June 12, 1994, the Austrians voted by a 2 to 1 margin in favor of joining the EU. This vote provided a boost to the pro-EU position in other candidate countries. Finnish and Swedish voters adopted the referenda in the fall; however, Norwegian voters rejected membership by a majority of 52.2 percent to 47.8 percent.[24] As a result of these referenda, the EU membership expanded by three on January 1, 1995.

EU's Mediterranean Policy

The Mediterranean countries are collectively the EU's third-largest customer and its fourth-largest supplier of imports, including roughly 20 percent of its energy needs. The Global Mediterranean Policy (GMP), adopted at the 1972 Paris summit, has been the blueprint for the EU's relations with the nonmember Mediterranean Basin countries (NMBCs). This policy aims to promote closer trade and financial relations between the EU and the NMBCs. It represents a crucial shift, from the EC's bilateral relations with each country in the region to a multilateral approach in which the Mediterranean Basin is treated as a single region. The final agreement between the EU and its Mediterranean partners is the 1995 Barcelona Declaration, which represents the most comprehensive approach the EU has taken toward this region. Table 11.3 provides a summary of various agreements signed between the EU and its Mediterranean neighbors.

There were political as well as economic motives for the EC's approach to the Mediterranean Basin. The strategy called for using economic power to promote regional stability, improving trade relations between the Community and the Mediterranean states, and checking Soviet expansionism in the region.[25] However, despite such ambitions, several problems stood in the way of the GMP. First, the economies

TABLE 11.3   Progress of Negotiation on Euro-Mediterranean Association Agreements

Partner	Conclusion of Negotiations	Signature of Agreement	Entry into Force
Tunisia	June 1995	July 1995	March 1998
Israel	September 1995	November 1995	June 2000
Morocco	November 1995	February 1996	March 2000
Palestinian Authority	December 1996	February 1997	July 1997
Jordan	April 1997	November 1997	—
Egypt	June 1999	—	—
Lebanon	2002	—	—
Algeria	2002	—	—
Syria	In progress	—	—

SOURCE: European Commission, *The Barcelona Process, Five Years On: 1995–2000* (Brussels: European Commission, 2000), p. 37.
Bilateral relations with Cyprus, Malta, and Turkey are based on first-generation association agreements concluded in the 1960s and 1970s.

of the EC and the NMBCs were not sufficiently compatible to promote the desired level of trade. Second, while the industrial products of the NMBCs received easy access to EC markets, agricultural goods were not included in the GMP because of the CAP. Third, even in industrial products, key exports of the NMBCs—textiles and clothing, shipping, steel, synthetic fibers, paper and paper products, machine tools, and cars—faced quota restrictions because the EC labeled these as "sensitive industries" that required Community protection. And finally, there was the question of migrant workers from the NMBCs.[26]

The problems of the GMP further intensified with the memberships of Greece, Portugal, and Spain. According to Alfred Tovias, these countries made the EC more Mediterranean-like; they resembled newly industrialized countries (like Israel and Turkey) and had a very strong agricultural base.[27] Studies have shown that the expansion of the Community into the northern Mediterranean and the adoption of various policies for the creation of a single market hampered the NMBCs' trade relations with the EC.[28] The problem is rather serious when we consider the structure of trade between the EU's Mediterranean members and the NMBCs:

> Despite some of the NMBCs' comparative export performance in certain agricultural goods, clothing and textiles, leather products, and footwear, they [NMBCs] have significant levels of export similarity indices with the new members of the [EU]. That is, these products are also produced and sold in [EU] markets by Greece, Portugal, and Spain. To make this issue even worse for the other Mediterranean Basin countries, the commodities involved are in either low or medium demand in EU markets.[29]

This means that the Mediterranean members of the EU have continued to dominate the supply of these products to EU markets, thus reducing the likelihood of the NMBCs increasing their exports of the same commodities.

One other issue creates friction between the EU and its Mediterranean neighbors: migrant workers. When the flow of workers reached its peak in 1980, there were over 6 million guest workers and their families in the EC.[30] The largest number came from Turkey: 714,000 workers and their dependents, of whom 591,000 were located in Germany. At one time, the guest workers were welcomed in the EC states because they were willing to work in manual-labor jobs that citizens did not want. However, after three serious economic recessions in the EC, in 1974–1975, 1980–1983, and 1991–1993, the governments of the member states adopted strict controls on the influx of guest workers and refugees (particularly asylum seekers in Germany). Militant right-wing extremists in the recipient countries began to attack these foreigners, causing many deaths and serious injuries.

On April 25, 1990, the vice-president of the Brussels Commission, Frans Andriessen, stated that there was a need to readdress the GMP because "increasingly closer geopolitical rather than political links will be forged between the Mediterranean countries in the coming decades [and] the European Community will be involved in this process."[31]

To address these policy concerns, the Council called for a four-stage program—a blueprint for the construction of the new Mediterranean Policy. The first stage called for adoption of an EU position paper setting out general guidelines for revitalizing the Mediterranean policy. During the second stage a "Mediterranean Forum," consisting of EC and NMBC representatives, would be established. Its purpose would be to prepare specific guidelines for sectoral policies, launch major pilot development agreements, and coordinate and support member states' policies toward the region. The third stage would involve the establishment of a center or agency, which would provide technical support for the development agreements. And finally, the EU-NMBCs' joint development convention would convene to establish specific institutions for the previously mentioned purposes.[32]

In accordance with the guidelines, the Commission, upon the request of the Council of Ministers, proposed a policy package on the GMP that included economic and technical assistance to the NMBCs, improving nonmembers' access to EC markets, and promoting direct foreign investment in the Mediterranean Basin.[33] But the EU members did not have a cohesive approach to this issue. Spain, Portugal, and Greece actively tried to minimize potential trade competition from the nonmembers in the EU markets. France and Italy also sided with Spain, Portugal, and Greece. On the other hand, the UK, the Netherlands, and Germany favored greater openings for imports from the NMBCs.

In September 1990, the Mediterranean members of the EC, led by the Italian foreign minister, Gianni De Michelis, called for the establishment of a Conference on Security and Cooperation in the Mediterranean.[34] This idea was modeled after the Conference on Security and Cooperation in Europe. The Italian and Spanish officials feared that growing economic and demographic disparity between the EC members and the NMBCs would be damaging to the long-term interests of the EC. While they argued that such a conference should include all of the eastern Mediterranean states, even extending to the Persian Gulf and Iran, the French maintained that cooperation ought to start with a more narrow focus, namely the Maghreb (Morocco, Algeria, and Tunisia). Despite the appearance of some differences in approach to the GMP, it was clear that the Mediterranean Basin has once again become one of the important issues on the EU agenda.

The EU leaders provided some answers at the June 1994 summit meeting in Corfu, Greece. At this meeting, they invited the Commission to draft a new southern strategy for the Mediterranean Basin.[35] The Commission responded by proposing the biggest free trade zone in the world, to include the EU and its North African and Middle Eastern neighbors. According to Manuel Marin, EU Commissioner for Mediterranean Affairs:

> In broad terms, what we would be offering is something like the EEA. . . .
> The main difference would be that whereas four of the seven members of
> EFTA—Austria, Finland, Sweden, and Norway—are poised to enter the EU
> next year, membership would not be on offer to Euro-Med partners [except
> Cyprus, Malta, and Turkey].[36]

The Commission's proposal received support from the EU leaders at the December 1994 Essen summit. At this meeting, the EU reiterated its support for a Euro-Mediterranean partnership with a long-term goal of free trade. The final result came in the form of a bold agreement between the EU and 12 Mediterranean countries (plus the Palestinian Authority), known as the Barcelona Declaration, signed in November 1995. This agreement commits the two sides to create an area of peace and prosperity, improve mutual understanding between the peoples of the region within a free and flourishing civil society, engage in political cooperation to fight international crime, and establish a free trade zone in the Mediterranean Basin by 2010.[37] The financial-assistance program of the EU for Mediterranean partnership is the MEDA program. MEDA 1, which lasted from 1995 to 1999, had a budget of 3,435 million euros plus another 425 million euros for the peace process (aid to the Palestinians).[38] During this period, the European Investment Bank also made loans of 4,808 million euros to the Mediterranean region. Furthermore, the new Mediterranean partnership helped increase trade between the EU and the Mediterranean countries. Mediterranean imports from the EU stand at around 30 billion euros (47 percent of total imports), and exports to EU markets in 1999 were more than 63 billion euros. Finally, the two parties began collaboration on initiatives to protect cultural heritage, youth projects, and civil society.

With regard to the free trade agreements plan, by 2010 four agreements will be in place (Israel, Morocco, Palestinian Authority, and Tunisia). One was recently ratified (Jordan), one has been signed and needs now to be ratified (Egypt), and two have been signed at the Euromed Conference of foreign affairs in Valencia (Algeria, Lebanon). Cyprus, Malta, and Turkey had preexisting Association Agreements creating a customs union with the EU. This means that the association process is nearly completed, as only Syria's negotiations are still ongoing.

As part of the exercise to relaunch the Barcelona process, an informal meeting of EURO-MED Trade Ministers was held in Brussels on May 29, 2001. Despite the eminent trade component of the Barcelona process, this was the first time that EURO-MED Trade Ministers met. Showing a great dynamism, Trade Ministers met again in Toledo, Spain, on March 19, 2002, only 10 months after their first conference, and the ministers endorsed some concrete and important results in the field of rules of origin. This meeting was intended to continue the efforts to reinvigorate the trade chapter of the Barcelona process and create conditions for an improvement in the flow of trade and investments in the area. They also decided to pursue further their strategy of developing concrete measures complementary to tariff dismantling aimed at achieving an effective Euro-Mediterranean Free Trade Area and agreed to hold their next meeting in the second half of 2003 under the Italian presidency.

EU RELATIONS WITH THE ACP COUNTRIES

The centerpiece of the EU–ACP relations is the Lomé IV Convention, signed on December 15, 1989, in the capital of Togo by the EC and 68 African, Caribbean, and Pacific states, most of which were former European colonial territories. The number of ACP countries increased to 69 in 1990. The Lomé IV Convention is in the tradition of the earlier agreements between the two sides: Yaoundé I (1963), Yaoundé II

(1969), Lomé I (1975), Lomé II (1979), and Lomé III (1984). According to Catherine Flaesch-Mougin and Jean Raux, the Lomé IV Convention was "a symbol of continuity, renovation, and innovation."[39] The history of the Lomé conventions resembles that of the GMP in that the initial enthusiasm quickly gave way to cynicism. The conventions neither changed the basic structures of North-South relations nor improved economic conditions of the ACP countries. From the ACP point of view, the erosion of trade preferences through the EU's General System of Preferences (GSP) and GATT, combined with the refusal of the EU to open its markets to more imports from ACP countries, seriously damaged the trade and industrial cooperation agreements of these conventions. Furthermore, according to John Ravenhill, the aid aspect gradually replaced the commercial cooperation as the cornerstone of the Lomé agreements since aid is far cheaper for the EC.[40] This development is clearly different from the experiences of the GMP countries, where commercial relations dominate the agenda.

Problems with the Earlier Agreements

Trade had been a major disappointment in the former conventions. For ACP countries, trade was of crucial importance since the EC was the principal trading partner for most of them. The Lomé conventions granted unilateral free access for ACP products to the EC markets without being subject to tariffs, quotas, or other restrictive regulations. However, there was a serious restriction concerning agricultural products that fall under the Common Agricultural Policy.[41] Furthermore, the EC reserved the right to change trade policies in case of serious economic or trade imbalances of the EC members. Such regulations proved to be detrimental for products like textiles and clothing, when the EC decided to label these industries sensitive industries, subject to special protection. The ACP countries viewed these special clauses as indications of growing protectionism in the EU.

Other issues that undermined EC–ACP trade relations were the extension of the EC's Generalized System of Preferences to all lesser-developed countries and tariff reductions in the EC in accordance with the Tokyo Round of the GATT negotiations. The net result was an increased influx of non-ACP products into the EC markets, which undermined the market share of ACP states. The EC attempted to stabilize export earnings of ACP states through two arrangements: the Commodity Export Earnings Stabilization Scheme (STABEX of Lomé I) and the Mineral Accident Insurance System (SYSMIN of Lomé II).

There is no doubt that the STABEX addressed an important problem of the ACP countries. Most of these countries were exporters of a single primary commodity: in 1975, 50 percent of the exports of 33 of the initial 46 countries to the EC were single-commodity exporters.[42] This meant that these countries were especially vulnerable to fluctuations in commodity prices in the world markets. The STABEX scheme provided funds to exporters of primary commodities in case of shortfall of export earnings due to external factors.

Finally, Lomé I to III provided multilateral funds, mainly through the European Development Fund (EDF) and the EIB, for financial and technical assistance to ACP countries. Lomé I specified 3.5 billion ecus for this purpose. Lomé II raised this figure to 5.6 billion ecus, and Lomé III further increased it to 8.5 billion ecus. Yet, these increases are in reality decreases over time due to high population growth rates and inflation in ACP countries and to the increase in the number of countries signing on to the Lomé conventions. Thus, there is a decline in financial assistance in real and per capita terms from Lomé I to Lomé II and from Lomé II to Lomé III.[43] Lomé IV was an attempt to find acceptable solutions to these problems through a revised cooperation model to encourage economic, social, and cultural development of the ACP countries.[44] The convention's duration is 10 years.

Lomé IV Agreements

Under Lomé IV trade provisions remained unchanged from the previous conventions—that is, ACP countries continued to have free access to EU markets without reciprocity. The trade arrangements, however, were adjusted to provide better conditions for some ACP products.[45]

In addition, the STABEX and SYSMIN schemes were overhauled and redefined. The EU added cocoa derivatives, essential oil products, and squid to the program, and lowered the threshold limit for its implementation. It was also agreed that in the future, the system would cover commodities that make up 5 percent of an ACP country's total exports to EU and other ACP states. This figure would be 1 percent for the less-developed countries. These figures were 6 percent and 1.5 percent, respectively, under the previous Lomé agreement.[46] Furthermore, under Lomé IV, STABEX allocation increased by 66 percent from Lomé III figures to 1.4 billion ecus. SYSMIN, on the other hand, extended product coverage to include uranium and gold.

The financial protocol of Lomé IV provided for 12 billion ecus (10.8 billion from the EDF and 1.2 billion ecus from the EIB) for aid to ACP states. Even though this is a substantial increase from the 8.5 billion ecus provided under Lomé III, it is considerably less than the amount requested by ACP countries (15.5 billion ecus). This protocol also included structural adjustment support for ACP countries in the amount of 1.15 billion ecus. While this figure is rather small, the decision of the EU to include such financing, along with international debt rescheduling, showed that the EU was prepared to assert itself as a principal financial actor in international economic restructuring alongside the World Bank and the International Monetary Fund.[47]

After the expiration of Lomé IV, the EU and ACP successfully negotiated a new ACP–EC Partnership Agreement (ACP–EC PA) that entered into effect on March 1, 2000, for a period of 8 years. This period is shorter than the earlier trade regime, which lasted 10 years. It is a regulatory regime that is designed to help the ACP countries integrate into the world economy through multilateral trade. Due to pressures from the WTO and the United States, the banana protocol of the previous agreement is excluded from the ACP–EC PA.

New ACP–EU Agreement

Today's relations with the ACP are governed by the ACP–EU Partnership Agreement, signed in Cotonou, Benin, on June 23, 2000, and concluded for a period of 20 years. At the same time, the remaining overseas countries and territories (OCTs) continue to be associated to the Community through successive Association decisions of the Council. The new agreement is similar to the Euromed agreement both in scope and ambition and covers five main pillars of cooperation: a comprehensive political cooperation, participatory approaches, strengthened focus on poverty reduction, a new framework for economic and trade cooperation, and a reform of financial cooperation.[48] For this purpose, the EU commits a €13.5 billion European Development Fund (EDF) covering the Agreement's first five years and support for the ACP governments in their attempts to create a balanced macro-economic picture with expansion of the private sector and improvement of both the quality and coverage of social services. €10 billion of this is for long-term allowance, €1.3 billion is for regional allowance, and €2.2 billion is for investment facility. In addition, €9 billion remains from the previous EDF and an other €1.7 billion is available at the EIB.

Political cooperation emphasizes democratic institution building, dialogue, respect for human rights, and peaceful resolution of conflicts. The participatory approaches refer to nongovernmental organizations' and interest groups' inclusion in decision-making process, and creation of such participation channels for them. Economic development is the most comprehensive aspect of the new agreement where the EU commits itself to development of ACP economies, inclusion of women in mainstream economic sectors, elimination of poverty, and reduction of unemployment. With trade and financial issues, the EU provides preferential trade to imports from ACP countries and liberalization of trade regimes and introduction of financial instruments to support development projects (see preceding discussion).

Despite significant improvements in cooperation agreements, ACP countries face an uncertain future in their relations with the EU. As the EU places greater emphasis on the "deepening of integration" and enlargement, the ACP countries' preferential position is likely to be undermined in a way similar to the problem faced by the GMP countries. Furthermore, there are external pressures on the EU from the WTO and the United States to make substantial reforms to preferential trade provisions of Lomé agreements (e.g., the banana crisis).

CONCLUSION

In this chapter we have examined issues that pertain to the EU's external economic relations. The analysis clearly demonstrates that the EU has become a major player in the international political and economic system. Through its enlargement to include Mediterranean and Nordic countries, coupled with special trade and assistance agreements with almost all of the other European periphery states, the EU stands as the most influential economic power in the post–Cold War Europe. Further enlargement of the EU will contribute to this influence. The EU also improved its ties to the non-member Mediterranean countries and ACP states by providing preferential trade agreements and generous aid packages. Over the past two decades, these various programs underwent reforms to reflect the changing needs of the recipient countries. It is clear from the nature of these interactions that the overall impact of such programs is their contribution to the EU's international economic status vis-à-vis the United States and Japan.

ENDNOTES

1. Simon Hix, *The Political System of the European Union* (New York: St. Martin's Press, 1999), p. 338.
2. European Commission, *The EU and the Millennium Round: More Trade Based on Better Rules* (http://europa.eu.int/comm/trade/2000).
3. Steve Schifferes, "Cheers for China's membership after 15 years of talks," BBC World News, November 10, 2001.
4. For a detailed discussion of this development see Chyi Shen, "Foreign Trade Competition Between the U.S.–E.U.–Japan in East Asian Markets". Unpublished doctoral dissertation, University of Missouri—Columbia, 2000.
5. European Commission, *Report on United States Barriers to Trade and Investment, 2000* (Brussels: European Commission, July 2000), p. 1.
6. _____. *EU–U.S. Summit, Trade Relations* (Brussels: European Commission, May 31, 2000), pp. 1–2.
7. For a complete list of EU–U.S. trade disputes and the final settlement clause and/or current status of each case, see the Commission Web site on external trade pertaining to dispute settlement by trade partner and commodity trade at http://mkaccdb.eu.int/miti/dsu.
8. "EC and US Reach Farm Trade Agreement," *Eurecom* 4 (December, 1992): 1.
9. Ibid.
10. European Commission Web site: http://europa.eu.int/comm/trade/, accessed 10/22/02.
11. Ibid.
12. European Commission. http://www.europa.eu.int/comm/trade/pdf/farmbill_qa.pdf, accessed 10/22/02.
13. For a more detailed discussion of the issues involved in this dispute, see European Commission, http://europa.eu.int/comm/trade/goods/agri/pr110702.htm.
14. "EC and US Reach Farm Trade Agreement," p. 2.
15. "US Announces Procurement Sanctions, EC Reacts in Kind," *Eurecom* 5 (June, 1993): 2.
16. Michael Mann, "EU Curbs Raise Trade War Tensions with US," *Financial Times*, March 20, 2002, p. 5.
17. Peter Holmes and Alasdair Smith, "The EC, the USA, and Japan: The Trilateral Relationship in World Context," in David Dyker, ed., *The European Economy* (New York and London: Longman, 1992), pp. 201–202.
18. Frank McDonald, "The European Community and the USA and Japan," in McDonald and Stephen Dearden, eds., *European Economic Integration* (London and New York: Longman, 1992), p. 207.
19. European Commission, *Joint Conclusions—EU-Japan Summit* (Brussels: Commission of the European Communities, July 19, 2000), p. 2.
20. McDonald, "The European Community and the USA and Japan," p. 211.
21. These countries were the EC 12 and Austria, Finland, Iceland, Liechtenstein, Norway, Sweden, and Switzerland. Switzerland, however, later chose to withdraw from the EEA as a result of a national referendum on the subject on December 6, 1992. Austria, Finland, and Sweden later joined the EU on January 1, 1995.
22. "EC, EFTA Create a Larger Common Market," *Eurecom* 3 (November, 1991): 1; and "Lest a Fortress Arise," *The Economist*, October 26, 1991, pp. 61 and 81–82.
23. "EEA Revisions Nailed Down," *Eurecom* 5 (March, 1993): 1.

24. Hugh Carnegy and Ian Rodger, "Outsiders Hit by a Strain of Euro-Fever," *Financial Times*, June 3, 1994, p. 2. "Norwegian PM Warns of Tough Times Ahead as Voters Spurn EU," *Financial Times*, November 30, 1994. p. 1.
25. Roy Ginsberg, "The European Community and the Mediterranean," in Juliet Lodge, ed., *Institutions and Policies of the European Community* (New York: St. Martin's Press, 1983), pp. 161–162.
26. Birol A. Yeşilada, "The EC's Mediterranean Policy," in Leon Hurwitz and Christian Lequesne, eds., *The State of the European Community: Policies, Institutions, and Debates in the Transition Years*, (Boulder, Colo. and London: Lynne Rienner/Longman, 1991), p. 361.
27. Alfred Tovias, *Foreign Economic Relations of the European Community: The Impact of Spain and Portugal* (Boulder, Colo.: Lynne Riener, 1990), p. 2.
28. For detailed discussion of issues surrounding the second enlargement and trade with the NMBCs, see J. Donges et al., *The Second Enlargement of the European Community* (Tübingen: J.C.B. Mohr, 1982); Richard Pomfret, "The Impact of EEC Enlargement on Non-member Mediterranean Countries' Exports to the EC," *The Economic Journal* 91 (September, 1981): 726–729; George Yannopoulos, "Prospects for the Manufacturing Exports of the Non-candidate Mediterranean Countries in a Community of Twelve," *World Development* 12 (December, 1984): 1087–1094; and Birol Yeşilada, "The Impact of the European Community's Second Enlargement and Project 1992 on Relations with the Mediterranean Basin." Paper presented at the Annual Meeting of the Midwest Political Science Association, Chicago, April 5–7, 1990.
29. Yeşilada, "The Impact of the European Community's Second Enlargement."
30. European Communities, *The European Community and the Mediterranean* (Luxembourg: Office for Official Publications of the Communities, 1984), p. 100.
31. Frans H.J.J. Andriessen, "Europe at the Crossroads." Paper presented at the 10th Annual Paul-Henri Spaak Lecture at Harvard University on April 25, 1990, pp. 11–12.
32. Birol Yeşilada, "Further Enlargement of the European Community: The Cases of the European Periphery States," *National Forum* (Spring, 1992): 21–25.
33. European Commission, "EEC/Mediterranean Countries: Refurbishing the Mediterranean Policy," *External Relations*, No. 1544 (November 29, 1989), as cited in Yeşilada, "The EC's Mediterranean Policy," p. 369.
34. "The Second Trojan's Empire," *The Economist*, September 29, 1990, p. 57.
35. "Brussels Urges Wider Trade Zone," *Financial Times*, October 20, 1994, p. 2.
36. Ibid.
37. Birol Yeşilada, "Mediterranean Policy," in Desmond Dinan, ed., *Encyclopedia of the European Union*, (Boulder, Colo.: Lynne Reinner, 1997), pp. 337–339.
38. European Commission, *The Barcelona Process, Five Years on 1995–2000* (Brussels: European Commission, 2000), p. 22.
39. Catherine Flaesch-Mougin and Jean Raux, "From Lomé III to Lomé IV: EC-ACP Relations," in Hurwitz and Lequesne, eds., *The State of the European Community*, p. 343.
40. John Ravenhill, *Collective Clientelism: The Lomé Conventions and North-South Relations* (New York: Columbia University Press, 1985), p. 330.
41. Ellen Frey-Wouters, *The European Community and the Third World: The Lomé Convention and Its Impact* (New York: Praeger, 1980), p. 37.
42. Ravenhill, *Collective Clientelism*, p. 9.
43. For a detailed discussion of this see Ravenhill, *Collective Clientelism*.
44. Cosgrove and Laurent, "The Unique Relationship: The European Community and the ACP," in John Redmond, ed., *The External Relations of the European Community: The International Responses to 1992* (New York: St. Martin's Press, 1992), p. 121.
45. Flaesch-Mougin and Raux, "From Lomé III to Lomé IV," p. 351. For a detailed discussion of the specifics of these trade policies, see Cosgrove and Laurent, "The Unique Relationship."
46. Cosgrove and Laurent, "The Unique Relationship," pp. 351–352.
47. Ibid., p. 130.
48. European Commission, *The Cotonou Agreement: The New ACP-EC Agreement* (Brussels: http://europa.eu.int/comm/development/cotonou/overview_en.htm), accessed 10/22/02.

12

Common Foreign and Domestic Security Policies

$\mathbf{W}$e will now return to the aspects of nation-state responsibilities that are at the very heart of what is called sovereignty. If the European Union (EU) is to become a federation, it will have to take over responsibility for foreign and security policy from the member states. Until that time, the EU will remain a confederation with important economic and social policy responsibilities. It will be confined essentially to the role of serving as a forum where member governments can discuss foreign and security (including internal security) policy. Federalists hope that in time, as integration deepens, the security of the individual states will become less important than the overall security of the larger community. The members of the EU find themselves in a weak security community that is taking on more definite institutional shape. The second pillar of the Maastricht treaty, the Common Foreign and Security Policy (CFSP), represents a major step beyond European political cooperation (EPC), as it merges political and security matters. In this chapter we will examine the EU's attempts to formulate a CFSP, and we will assess how the member states cope with domestic security as borders disappear between them.

COMMON FOREIGN AND SECURITY POLICY

Today in international relations, the EU's powers stem from a transfer of power from member states to the EU. In power relations, the members also know this is a limited surrender of sovereignty to the EU.[1] As a collective body, the EU maintains diplomatic relations with sovereign states and has observer status in the United Nations (UN) and in the various UN agencies. According to Juliet Lodge, some 150 countries have diplomatic missions in Brussels and the EU maintains, in the name of the Commission rather than the EU per se, over 100 diplomatic offices around the world.[2] In these offices, EU representatives enjoy the same diplomatic rights as regular diplomats

211

of sovereign countries and cooperate closely with the EU states' local diplomatic missions, thus serving the purpose of cooperation in maintaining a common foreign policy position among the member countries.

Historical Background

During the Cold War, the security lines between East and West were clearly drawn. Dominant members of the adversary alliances provided the bulk of the capital necessary for maintaining the alliances, as well as leadership in formulating foreign and security policies. According to Peter Ludlow, three major forces contributed to the foreign policy profile of the EU during the postwar era: "the external implications of the EU's internal objectives and achievements; the voluntary agreement of its member states to enlarge their power and influence in the world through common action; and, by no means least, the gravitational pulls of its regional and global environment."[3] The road to a common foreign and security policy has been rather rough.

During the 1950s, the experiment with the European Defense Community (EDC) ended in a disaster, but because this experiment demonstrated how the EU members have viewed collective foreign and security policies, a brief review of the EDC is in order.

After the outbreak of the Korean War in June 1950, Jean Monnet argued that the answer to the increasing Soviet threat in Europe could be found in pooling the military resources of the European democracies. The six members of the European Coal and Steel Community (ECSC) decided to set up a parallel body, the European Defense Community, complete with parliament, joint-defense commission, council of ministers, and court of justice. The EDC Treaty was signed in 1952.

"Now, the federation of Europe would have to become an immediate objective," Monnet had argued.[4] It was clear that this proposed pooling of defense capabilities would inevitably restrict the independent foreign policies of the member countries. Therefore, integration in defense also necessitated some level of political integration. Italian federalist Altiero Spinelli convinced the Italian government that the only way to control a European army was to have federal European institutions. He then persuaded the other five partners. As a result, the six members of the ECSC asked the Assembly, in conjunction with the "co-opted members of the Consultative Assembly of the Council of Europe,"[5] to draft a treaty for a European political community. The outcome was a quasi-federal constitution, drafted in 1953, which would complement the EDC Treaty. According to this plan, there would be one European executive responsible to a European parliament (composed of the people's chamber elected by the citizens and a senate elected by the national parliaments), a council of ministers, and a single European court of justice that would replace the parallel institutions found under the ECSC and EDC treaties.

This development was to be a remarkable deepening of integration among the six members so soon after the horrors of World War II. The parliaments of the Benelux countries, West Germany, and Italy ratified the EDC Treaty, but the idea came to an abrupt halt in the French Assembly on August 30, 1954. Several factors contributed to the French rejection. First was a general opposition to a supranational political community. Second was the French left's opposition to the rearming of Germany. And third was the French right's opposition to placing French troops under foreign command.[6]

Troubles with developing a CFSP followed in the ensuing years. After Charles de Gaulle became president of France, he tried to promote cooperation in foreign policy in the Community on an intergovernmental basis. France proposed the Fouchet plan, which called for coordination of foreign and defense policies outside the framework of the Community.[7] The European Community continued to discuss the plan until de Gaulle vetoed the British application for membership in the Community, after which the Benelux countries refused to discuss the Fouchet plan any further (see Chapter 3).

A decade later, the EC moved to create a mechanism for political cooperation, known as the Davignon machinery, based on a plan proposed by the Belgian foreign ministry. This mechanism consisted of biannual meetings of the foreign ministers, though in practice the meetings have occurred more often. Also, until the 1973 oil crisis, the matters pertaining to the EPC and the EC were kept separate. As Stephen George relates:

> This reached the heights of absurdity in November 1973, when the Foreign Ministers of the then nine member states met in Copenhagen one morning under the heading of EPC, and then flew to Brussels to meet in the afternoon of the same day as the EC Council of Ministers.[8]

When the EC decided to enter into talks with the Arab world in 1974, this separation of EPC and EC matters finally ended. These talks demonstrated that it was no longer possible to separate political matters from commerce. Soon after, the Commission, which had been excluded from the EPC, became involved in coordinating links between the EPC and the Council of Ministers.

The merging of the EPC political and EC economic interests proved to be helpful in promoting the Community's status in the international system and provided a more viable mechanism for dealing with complex foreign policy issues. In 1980, the European-Arab dialogue resulted in the Venice Declaration, by which the European Council made it clear that it recognized the right of the Palestinians to a homeland.[9] Other achievements include:

1. Common EC stances in the Conference on Security and Cooperation in Europe (CSCE) in Helsinki in 1975, in Belgrade in 1977, and in Madrid in 1982
2. A common foreign policy toward South Africa
3. A more harmonious position in UN voting, both in the General Assembly and in the Security Council

The Single European Act (SEA) further emphasized the necessity to coordinate the EPC. It stated "that the EPC could include the 'political and economic aspects of security,' and that the European Parliament should be closely associated with the

EPC."[10] Finally, with the end of the Cold War, a more multilateral approach to security and foreign policy in the EU gained momentum. In this regard, it is possible to identify some important developments in the international system that have affected the EU's CFSP:

- The changing role of the U.S. in the international system, associated with the decline in hegemony
- The collapse of communism in Central and Eastern Europe and the subsequent rise in regional conflicts which have threatened to destabilize the international system (e.g., the Yugoslav crises)
- The unification of Germany
- The Gulf War
- The crisis in Somalia
- The rapid change in the balance of power around EU's eastern front (the Balkans, the Black Sea, the Caucasus, and the Middle East)
- The war on terrorism after the Al-Qaeda attack on the World Trade center in New York City and the Pentagon in Washington, DC, on September 11, 2001
- The war in Iraq, March–April, 2003.

Maastricht and the Common Foreign and Security Policy

The Treaty on European Union (TEU) establishes common foreign and security policy as the second main pillar of the EU and makes the Western European Union (WEU; discussed subsequently) an integral part of the development of the EU while maintaining its autonomy and giving it the task of defining and implementing defense and security issues. When considering the nature and purpose of the CFSP, it is crucial to note that this effort is an expansion of the EU's earlier attempts during the 1970s and 1980s to coordinate external policies of the member countries. The specific objectives of the CFSP are provided in Article J-1 (2) of the TEU:

- To safeguard the common values, fundamental interests, and independence of the EU
- To strengthen the security of the EU and its member states in all ways
- To preserve peace and strengthen international security, in accordance with the principles of the UN Charter as well as the principles of the Helsinki Final Act and the objectives of the Paris Charter
- To promote international cooperation
- To develop and consolidate democracy and the rule of law, and respect for human rights and fundamental freedoms[11]

Furthermore, paragraph 3 of the same article states that the EU, in pursuing these objectives, needs to establish systematic cooperation among its members "by gradually implementing, in accordance with Article J-3, joint action in the areas in which the Member States have important interests in common."[12]

Responsibility for defining and managing the CFSP lies with the Council and the presidency, respectively.[13] According to Article J-3 (1):

> The Council shall decide, on the basis of general guidelines from the European Council, that a matter should be subject of joint action. Whenever the Council decides on the principles of joint action, it shall lay down the specific scope, the EU's general and specific objectives in carrying out such action, if necessary its duration, and the means, procedures and conditions of its implementation.[14]

Moreover, Article J-8 (2) states, "the Council shall act unanimously, except for procedural questions and in the case referred to in Article J-3 (2)."[15] Article J-3 (2) specifies that "when adopting the joint action and at any stage during its development, [the Council shall] define those matters on which decisions are to be taken by a qualified majority."[16] Thus, the Council of Ministers clearly has a major role in defining the scope, the principles, and the objectives of the CFSP. However, the European Council has a decisive contribution to make to this process by providing the general guidelines of the CFSP. All of these policymaking steps require agreement between the member states. When the EU lacks such agreement, the members can follow their own policy preferences and the only restraint on their actions would be the threat of unilateralism (acting in the interest of a single member country rather than the common interest of all members) on the well-being of the EU.

The implementation of the CFSP is entrusted for 6 months to the presidency of the Council, as stated in Article J-5 (2). In this capacity, the presidency is assisted, if necessary, by the previous and next member states that hold the presidency.[17] Furthermore, the Commission is to be fully associated in such tasks.[18]

It should be noted that there is virtually no democratic control over the CFSP, even though the presidency is required "to consult the European Parliament [EP] on the main aspects and the basic choices of the common foreign and security policy and ensure that views of the European Parliament are duly taken into account."[19] This does not mean that the EP plays a major role in formulating CFSP. At times of emergency, there would not be time for the presidency to have prior consultation with the EP. According to Lodge:

> The Presidency will act on its own initiative, or at the request of the Commission or a member state, to convene an extraordinary Council meeting within forty-eight hours or, in an emergency, within an even shorter time.[20]

Thus, consultation with the EP would likely be after the fact and of limited assistance. This is not different from the dilemma faced in democratic countries. Furthermore, it is quite possible for the member states not to honor their commitment to consult each other prior to taking unilateral action. As we will show later, Germany's behavior prior to the Yugoslav crisis serves as an example of this problem. In addition to the previously mentioned clauses, Article J-4 (1) calls for closer cooperation between the EU and the WEU and among the EU countries of the North Atlantic

Treaty Organization (NATO). The same is also expected in the CSCE activities.[21] Nevertheless, such cooperation among the EU countries requires imaginative policy coordination because not all members of the EU are members of the WEU and NATO (see discussion of ESDP in the section "From the WEU to the ESDP/ESDI").

IMPROVEMENT AFTER THE AMSTERDAM TREATY. The Amsterdam Treaty enhanced provisions of CFSP under Title V of the TEU to pave the way for a common defense policy through significant changes. The treaty distinguishes between "common strategies" and more sharply defined "joint actions." Decisions can be taken without strict unanimity; if a member who does not wish to participate in the implementation of a decision is willing to see other members implement it. The European Council may agree on common defense policies while some member countries retain the right to remain neutral.[22]

These developments proved useful during subsequent years as the EU moved to replace WEU with an integrated part of the EU for creating a European Security and Defense Identity (ESDI) framework within the EU.

From the WEU to the ESDP/ESDI

The Western European Union was set up by the Treaty of Economic, Social, and Cultural Collaboration and Collective Self-Defense, which was signed in Paris on October 23, 1954, and came into effect on May 6, 1955. The Paris agreement was a modification of an earlier agreement, the Brussels Treaty, which was signed by Belgium, Luxembourg, the Netherlands, France, and the United Kingdom (UK), and laid the foundations of EDC. The Paris agreement also permitted Italy and West Germany to join the organization. The preamble of the Paris agreement displays the purposes of the signatories:

> to reaffirm their faith in fundamental human rights . . . and in the other ideals proclaimed in the Charter of the United Nations . . . to preserve the principles of democracy . . . to strengthen . . . the economic, social and cultural ties by which they are already united [by cooperating] to create in Western Europe a firm basis for European economic recovery . . . to afford assistance to each other . . . in resisting any policy of aggression . . . to promote the unity and to encourage the progressive integration of Europe.[23]

The subsequent protocols, II to IV, contained further provisions relating to the levels of forces and armaments of member countries and established the Agency for the Control of Armaments. The Brussels Treaty was also very specific about the commitment to collective security of the member states. Article 5 specified that:

> If any of the high contracting parties should be the object of an armed attack in Europe, the other high contracting parties will, in accordance with the provisions of Article 51 of the Charter of the United Nations, afford the

party so attacked all the military and other aid and assistance in their power.[24]

The WEU consists of a council, a consultative assembly, a secretariat, the Standing Armaments Committee, and the Agency for the Control of Armaments. Between 1955 and 1984, the political achievements of the WEU were facilitating the integration of West Germany into NATO and serving as a link between the EU and the UK until the latter became a member of the Community. Otherwise, the WEU was not a major player in the Community's subsequent foreign policymaking, and the organization remained inactive until 1984.

Frustrated with the U.S. nuclear missile and Strategic Defense Initiative policies, France started a campaign to reactivate the WEU in the 1980s. Another important reason for the French initiative was that at the time European Political Cooperation excluded matters relating to defense and security. On October 26–27, 1984, in Rome, the foreign and defense ministers of the member countries agreed to reactivate the WEU. The Rome Declaration reaffirmed the WEU's commitment to strengthen peace and security; to promote the unity and encourage the progressive integration of Europe; to cooperate more closely both among member states and with other European organizations; to make better use of the WEU framework in order to increase cooperation between the members in the field of security and to encourage consensus; and to improve the common defense of all the countries of the Atlantic Alliance since the two institutions were both designed to provide security to the West.[25]

In the years following the Rome Declaration, important developments further strengthened the WEU that paved the way for the European Security and Defense Identity. First, the SEA called for a greater collaboration in political and security matters, and the WEU was the logical place where consensus on security matters could be attained. Second, Spain and Portugal joined the WEU. Third, the Maastricht Treaty provided the most detailed declaration by the EU on the future of the WEU in EU affairs (i.e., on the role of WEU and its relations with the EU and NATO, and on expansion of WEU).

Following the signing of the Maastricht Treaty, the WEU Council of Ministers for Foreign Affairs and Defense held a meeting in Bonn on June 19, 1992, and issued the Petersberg Declaration regarding their views on European defense and security matters.[26] This declaration emphasized the importance of the CSCE in promoting peace and stability in Europe and called for strengthening the CSCE's capabilities in conflict prevention, crisis management, and peaceful settlement of international disputes. It specified that the WEU would support implementation of conflict prevention and crisis management measures, including peacekeeping operations of the CSCE or the UN Security Council. Furthermore, the declaration reaffirmed the members' commitment to strengthen the European leg of the Atlantic Alliance and to invite other EU members and European members of NATO to join the WEU.

In accordance with these developments, nine WEU members held a meeting with six candidates for WEU membership (Denmark, Greece, Iceland, Ireland, Norway, and Turkey) in Rome on July 16, 1992. After a series of negotiations, the WEU decided on November 20, 1992, to admit Greece into its ranks. At the same time,

Iceland, Norway, and Turkey were given associate membership in the WEU, and EU members Denmark and Ireland were admitted as observers to WEU.[27] Further developments followed soon after the expansion of membership. During the defense ministers' meeting of the 13 countries in the Independent European Program Group (IEPG) in Bonn on December 4, 1992, the participants agreed to transfer the IEPG's function to WEU. The WEU's Council of Ministers approved the transfer at its Rome meeting on May 19, 1993, and established a new structure within WEU, the Western European Armaments Group (WEAG), which inherited the previous work done by the IEPG.[28] A follow-up agreement allowed Denmark, Norway, and Turkey to participate in the new institution even though they were not full members of WEU. The significance of this development was that the new institution and its operating agreements with the nonmembers helped promote "the objective of WEU's 1984 Rome Declaration—to provide political impetus for European cooperation in the field of armaments."[29] Finally, during the Council of Ministers meeting in Luxembourg on May 9, 1994, the WEU issued the Kirchberg Declaration, which gave Bulgaria, the Czech Republic, Estonia, Hungary, Latvia, Lithuania, Poland, Romania, and Slovakia associate partnership in the WEU.[30] While this move was aimed at improving ties with the former Eastern Bloc countries, the particular association status granted to these states was not as comprehensive as those with Iceland, Norway, and Turkey. According to the Kirchberg Declaration, the previously mentioned Central and Eastern European countries (CEECs) might participate in the meetings of the Council and "associate themselves with decisions taken by the member states concerning humanitarian and rescue tasks, peacekeeping tasks, tasks of combat forces in crisis management, including peacekeeping."[31] Iceland, Norway, and Turkey, on the other hand, could nominate officers to the Planning Cell in order to "increase WEU's planning capabilities and to enable WEU to draw more easily on the Associate Members' expertise and resources."[32] At present the composition of different categories of WEU members and associates are shown in Table 12.1.

With the Amsterdam Treaty the WEU has been drawn closer to the EU. In this regard, the role of WEU in providing the EU with access to an operational capability was confirmed, the Petersberg tasks were incorporated into the EU treaty, and the possibility of the integration of WEU into the EU, should the European Council so decide, was mentioned. In 1998, the EU launched a new debate on European defense and security. At Saint-Malo, in December 1998, France and the UK adopted a joint declaration:

> The European Union needs to be in a position to play its full role on the international stage. . . . To this end, the EU must have the capacity for autonomous action, backed up by credible military forces, the means to decide to use them and a readiness to do so, in order to respond to international crises. . . . In this regard, the European Union will also need to have recourse to suitable military means (European capabilities pre-designated within NATO's European pillar or national or multinational European means outside the NATO framework).[33]

TABLE 12.1 The WEU States

Members (Modified Brussels Treaty 1954)	Associate Members (Rome 1992)	Observers (Rome 1992)	Associate Partners (Kirchberg 1994)
Belgium	Czech Republic	Austria (1995)	Bulgaria
France	Hungary	Denmark	Estonia
Germany	Iceland	Finland	Latvia
Greece (1995)	Norway	Ireland	Lithuania
Italy	Poland	Sweden (1995)	Romania
Luxembourg	Turkey		Slovakia
Netherlands			Slovenia (1996)
Portugal (1990)			
Spain (1990)			
United Kingdom			

SOURCE: WEU Web site, http://www.weu.int/eng/index.html (membership).

Later, at the Washington summit in April 1999, when NATO allies met to celebrate the fiftieth anniversary of the founding of NATO and to recognize formally its most recent expansion, the leaders acknowledged the resolve of the EU to have the capacity for autonomous action, confirmed its willingness to build on existing WEU–NATO mechanisms in the creation of a direct NATO–EU relationship, and declared its readiness to "define and adopt the necessary arrangements for ready access by the European Union to the collective assets and capabilities of the Alliance, for operations in which the Alliance as a whole is not engaged militarily as an Alliance."[34] Furthermore, the European Council decided to commit itself to establish the necessary capabilities to meet a full range of conflict prevention and crisis management tasks in Europe at the Cologne European Council of June 1999. In this context, the WEU Luxembourg ministerial meeting in November 1999 reaffirmed its readiness to allow EU Council bodies direct access to the expertise of the WEU's operational structures. This marked a significant movement for closer ties, if not full integration, between the WEU and EU in formulating a European Security and Defense Initiative (ESDI). Finally, at the Helsinki European Council in December 1999, the EU agreed on the specifics of the political and military bodies necessary for ESDI:

1. By the year 2003, member states will be able to deploy within 60 days and then sustain, for at least one year, forces capable of the full range of Petersberg tasks, including the most demanding, in operations up to corps level (50,000–60,000 persons).
2. New political and military bodies to be established within the Council: a Political and Security Committee, a Military Committee, and a Military Staff will be established within the Council.

3. Modalities will be developed for full consultation, cooperation, and transparency between EU and NATO, taking into account the needs of all EU member states.
4. Appropriate arrangements will be defined that would allow, while respecting the EU's decision-making autonomy, non-EU European NATO members and other interested states to contribute to EU military crisis management.
5. A nonmilitary crisis management mechanism will be established to coordinate and make more effective the various civilian means and resources, in parallel with the military ones, at the disposal of the EU and the member states.[35]

Since then, the EU and NATO have been trying to work out the details of how ESDI could be established as a partner of NATO and have access to the latter's intelligence, planning, and transport capabilities. At the December 2000 Nice summit of the European Council, the members agreed to establish a rapid-reaction force by 2003 to meet this goal. However, the members had differing views on the nature of this force and its relationship to NATO. France wanted the force to be independent of NATO's integrated military command. The UK, being the key U.S. ally in NATO, insisted on close ties to NATO while maintaining autonomy. The United States warned, "NATO would become a 'relic' unless the European Union's plans for an autonomous military capability were closely linked with the 19-member transatlantic alliance."[36] In reality, however, there is no threat to NATO, at least in the short run, from the establishment of the ESDI: the new European defense force would have to rely on NATO heavy-lift equipment and intelligence capabilities to function. Given this fact, it would not be possible for the European force to act independent of NATO's integrated military structure. The EU's response to these developments requires careful balancing of the member states' and the EU's roles in the ESDI, renamed the European Strategic Defense Policy (ESDP), and NATO. Table 12.2 provides the membership status of the EU states in these institutions.

The EU recommendation, known as the "Berlin Plus" arrangements, that received support from the United States called for NATO to provide equipment and intelligence for the European-only missions as long as the former did not undermine the Atlantic Alliance by creating its own bureaucracy and independent capabilities.[37] However, Turkey, which felt left out of the accession talks at the Nice summit, feared that anything short of being included in the ESDI decision-making mechanism (even when NATO troops are not needed) would simply result in Turkey becoming further distanced from Europe. At the NATO foreign ministers meeting in Brussels on December 14, 2000, Turkey refused to give the EU, which it is trying to join, assured access to NATO planning skills for missions in which NATO as a whole is not involved.

The solution to the Turkish veto emerged, known as the Ankara Agreement, after an extensive British campaign, where Turkey received assurances from NATO that the new EU force will not be used against Turkey's geographic and security interests. The new agreement required EU approval but ran into a Greek objection at the Seville summit in June 2002.[38] Greece objected to the Ankara document and informed other EU members that it wanted similar assurances as a matter of reciproc-

TABLE 12.2 Overlapping Commitments

NATO	NATO and EU	EU
Czech Republic*	Belgium	Austria
Hungary*	Britain	Finland
Iceland	Denmark (opted out of ESDP)	Ireland
Norway	France	Sweden
Poland*	Germany	
Turkey**	Greece	
Canada	Italy	
United States	Luxembourg	
	Netherlands	
	Portugal	
	Spain	

* Indicates candidate status with ongoing accession talks.
** Indicates candidate status without accession talks.
SOURCE: "The Many Tricky Ways of Widening Europe," *The Economist*, December 9, 2000, p. 55.

ity. Turkey, in turn, told the EU and NATO that the agreement had to be accepted as formulated in Ankara. At the time of writing, this issue remains unresolved and threatens the EU's ability to take over peacekeeping mission from NATO in Macedonia (campaign Amber Fox). The impasse promoted some EU countries, notably Belgium and France, to suggest going ahead without access to NATO since Amber Fox does not carry a high military risk. France would like to see ESDP operate independently from NATO, but that idea is opposed by Britain and Germany because independent action of the EU threatens to weaken the transatlantic alliance.

There is one additional issue that could affect the future partnership between the EU and NATO. In 2002, the U.S. Defense Secretary Donald Rumsfeld proposed creation of a NATO Rapid Response Force at the Warsaw defense ministers meeting of the alliance.[39] The proposal envisages a joint force, drawing on a pool of combat forces, headquarters, and support elements, and other capabilities that would be determined at the Prague 2002 summit of NATO.[40] On the surface, the plan closely resembles the ESDI and raises questions over duplication.

Testing CFSP

In recent years, important international crises have put to the test the EU's efforts to promote a common foreign and security policy. These crises were the Gulf War and the civil war in former Yugoslavia (including the Kosovo crisis). In the next sections we examine the EU's response to these challenges.

THE GULF WAR. After Iraq invaded Kuwait on August 2, 1990, the President of the WEU Assembly issued a communiqué condemning the Iraqi aggression and demanding prompt withdrawal of Iraqi troops from Kuwait. He also called upon the

WEU countries to respond to the crisis and asked the UN to take all necessary steps to defend the sovereignty of Kuwait. Yet, despite the urgency of the situation, it took the WEU countries 19 days before they met to discuss the situation. By that time, the United States had initiated its own diplomatic and military efforts to remove Iraq from Kuwait and asserted American leadership within the UN and NATO.[41]

The WEU Council of Ministers agreed to take all necessary steps to comply with the embargo on Iraq in accordance with UN Security Council Resolution 661. On the basis of their experiences in the Persian Gulf during the 1987–1989 operations, the WEU established an ad hoc group of foreign and defense ministry representatives to provide cooperation between the member states' capitals and the forces in the Gulf. By the end of 1990, the WEU had deployed 45 vessels (destroyers, frigates, corvettes, mine sweepers, and amphibious vessels) to the Gulf region. These vessels came from seven of the nine member countries. Only Luxembourg, which does not have a navy, and Germany, whose constitution prevented deployment of German troops outside of Germany, did not participate in the Gulf operation.

The WEU also coordinated its members' response to the second operation in this crisis. On September 18, 1990, another meeting of the Council of Ministers decided to "strengthen the WEU coordination and to extend the coordination at present operating in the maritime field to ground and air forces and, within this framework, to identify the forms that these new deployments will take, to seek to ensure that they are complementary, to harmonize the missions of the member states' forces and to pool their logistic support capabilities as required."[42] When Desert Storm began on January 16, 1991, WEU members France, Italy, and the UK participated with aircraft. The next day, the WEU Council of Ministers held an extraordinary meeting and decided to provide full support for the operation. Parallel to the operations in the air and sea, ground forces from the WEU participated in the massive UN buildup in Saudi Arabia. Following the successful operations in Kuwait, the WEU decided to continue to play an active role in implementation of the UN Security Council resolutions pertaining to the protection of the Kurds in northern Iraq and the Shiite Arabs of Basra.

THE YUGOSLAV CRISIS. The breakup of Yugoslavia and the subsequent civil war in Bosnia-Herzegovina and Croatia represented potentially a very divisive issue for the WEU members. This crisis shows that WEU and the EU were not prepared to deal with a problem of this magnitude, and the subsequent disagreements among the Community's members over how to respond to the problem highlights the member countries' inability to coordinate their national foreign policy priorities. Disagreement over how to stop the bloodshed in these areas also strained relations between the EC and its partners in the other major security communities, the UN and NATO. The crisis in the former Yugoslav republics was perhaps the most damaging test of the EC's ability to respond to security problems in the new Europe. In this regard it is important to assess the EC's relative success or failure in resolving the crises in Slovenia, Croatia, and Bosnia-Herzegovina.

In Slovenia, the EC-sponsored mediation succeeded because the Serbs concentrated their attention on Croatia and Bosnia. Initially, Lord Carrington, representing the EC, organized a series of meetings with the warring parties. Yet, in late 1991, Germany went ahead of its EC partners and pressured the Croatians, the Slovenians, and the Bosnians to choose between independence from the Yugoslav federation or staying as part of Yugoslavia. The German move came before the rest of the EC countries were prepared to undertake such an important responsibility. Soon after the German declaration, Croatia and Slovenia broke away from Yugoslavia and, subsequently, received full diplomatic recognition from the EC. According to Catherine McArdler Kelleher, "Foreign Minister Genscher, himself a convert to the recognition strategy pressed by German domestic sources, argued that recognition would allow comprehensive Community oversight over the pace and costs involved in the disintegration of the former Yugoslavia."[43]

Soon after, the Bosnians voted in a national referendum, which was highly divided along ethnic lines, to secede from Yugoslavia. Bosnian Croats and the Muslims favored independence, whereas Bosnian Serbs voted to remain part of Yugoslavia. The EC immediately recognized the independence of Bosnia-Herzegovina. The EC's recognition of these former Yugoslav republics was aimed at achieving two goals: to maintain a common policy among the EU countries toward Bosnia-Herzegovina, Croatia, and Slovenia; and to oversee the breakup of the Yugoslav federation in a peaceful manner. However, their efforts proved to be futile as civil war immediately broke out in these countries, though only briefly in Slovenia. In Croatia and Bosnia-Herzegovina, ethnic Serbs pushed to gain territories that could be joined to Serbia. In each case the rebel Serbs received substantial support from the former Yugoslav army and quickly made territorial gains against the Croats and the Bosnia Muslims. Subsequently, the world witnessed numerous wartime atrocities—genocide, mass rapes, and massive destruction of villages and towns—as the Serbs attempted to cleanse territories newly acquired from the Croats and the Muslims. The problem worsened as the other sides retaliated against Serbian populations in their respective areas and later when the Croats and the Muslims fought against each other over the control of central and southern Bosnia.

During these crises, the main international security organizations—the UN, NATO, and the WEU—attempted to bring about an end to hostilities by coordinating their political and military efforts. While they were partially successful in Croatia, the civil war in Bosnia-Herzegovina proved too difficult for the Allies to reach a common position. Several factors contributed to this failure.

First, the EC and the UN, and later NATO, failed to provide a common and effective position on the crisis. Time after time, these organizations failed to respond to Serbian actions in Bosnia even when they followed strong ultimatums from the West.

Second, the EC sponsored the London peace process in the fall of 1992, which included the participation of the UN. In this setting, conflict management became an issue that required cooperation between the EC and the UN.

As the war worsened, it became quite apparent that the WEU lacked the necessary military structure to intervene effectively to stop the bloodshed. When human suffering reached new heights, the UN agreed to send peacekeepers, mostly from the WEU countries, to safeguard humanitarian assistance to the civilians. However, the only organization that had the military power to stop the war was NATO. No other organization had the integrated military structure, hardware, and logistical planning and operational capabilities to deal with a crisis like Bosnia. NATO's intervention, directly or indirectly, meant involvement of the United States. Under normal circumstances, this would not be a problem for NATO. However, at the time, the Clinton administration's inconsistencies over its Bosnian policy worried the Allies. When the UN decided to impose an embargo on Yugoslavia and the former Yugoslav states of Croatia and Bosnia-Herzegovina, and to sponsor Operation Deny Flight and Operation Sharp Guard, NATO was asked to oversee these military operations. Once again, the success of the operations depended on cooperation between the UN, NATO, and the WEU.

Among these undertakings, the arms embargo was criticized for punishing both the aggressors and the victims. The Bosnian government continually asked for the lifting of the arms embargo so that it could acquire the means to defend its people against the Serbs. The Bosnian Serbs, on the other hand, continued to receive supplies from Serbia and, at least on one occasion, from Russia. This policy resulted in tensions between the U.S. and the WEU countries with peacekeeping troops in Bosnia, as the Americans occasionally pressured the UN to end the embargo on Bosnia.

Operation Sharp Guard's mission was to conduct operations to monitor and enforce compliance with UN sanctions, particularly against Serbia, in accordance with the UN Security Council Resolutions (UNSCRs) 713, 757, 787, and 820. A combined task force was given the responsibility of preventing unauthorized shipping from entering the territorial waters of the Yugoslav Federal Republic. The operation was equipped with surface warships from Canada, France, Germany, Greece, Italy, the Netherlands, Norway, Portugal, Spain, Turkey, the UK, and the United States. In addition, eight fighter aircraft from Italy and maritime patrol aircraft from Canada, France, Germany, Italy, the Netherlands, Portugal, Spain, the UK, and the United States, supported by NATO Airborne Warning and Control systems (AWAC), provided air support for this operation. By the end of March 1994, this operation had challenged 17,000 merchant vessels in the Adriatic Sea and on the Danube, halting 1,700.[44]

Operation Deny Flight, on the other hand, had a fourfold mission:

1. To conduct aerial monitoring and enforce compliance with UN Security Council Resolution 816, which bans flights by fixed-wing and rotary-wing aircraft in the airspace of Bosnia-Herzegovina
2. To provide air cover (close air support) at the request of and control by the UN Peacekeeping Forces in the Former Yugoslavia (UNPROFOR) under the supervision of UN Security Council Resolution 836
3. To be ready to carry out, in coordination with the UN, air strikes on heavy weapons if they fire from outside (or inside) the 20-kilometer exclusion zone into Sarajevo or if they return to the exclusion zone
4. To be ready to carry out air strikes at other locations to aid UNPROFOR in humanitarian relief operations as authorized by the North Atlantic Council and in coordination with the UN[45]

The aircraft for this operation came from France, Spain, the Netherlands, Turkey, and the United States. In addition, almost 4,500 personnel from 12 NATO countries (Belgium, Canada, Denmark, France, Germany, Italy, the Netherlands, Norway, Spain, Turkey, the UK, and the United States) were deployed in Italy and the Adriatic.

The Serbian testing of NATO and UN resolve continued during the autumn of 1994. The Serbs launched a massive attack on the Muslim enclave of Bihac after the latter had a brief military success that resulted from a surprise offensive against Serbian positions. The Serbian counteroffensive also included attacks on Bihac from Serb-controlled areas of Croatia. When the subsequent UN and NATO threats against the Serbs failed to stop the Serbian attacks, the international media and influential political figures began to question the role of the UN peacekeepers and NATO air power in Bosnia. In December 1994, UN Secretary General Boutros Boutros-Ghali and the British and French governments went so far as to suggest the withdrawal of UN peacekeepers from Bosnia. During this time, the world witnessed a serious divide between some of the allies. For example, as the Clinton administration considered providing logistical support for UN withdrawal from Bosnia, key Congressional leaders in the United States openly criticized British and French policies and called upon the U.S. administration to unilaterally lift the arms embargo against the Bosnian government. Senator Robert Dole argued that maintaining the arms embargo against all of former Yugoslavia amounted to nothing more than punishing the victims, the Bosnian Muslims, since the Serbs had access to heavy weapons.

The inability of the WEU, NATO, and the UN to coordinate an effective policy over Bosnia also affected the European Council summit in Essen. At this meeting, the British and French leaders stated that there was a good chance of withdrawing UN peacekeeping forces from Bosnia within weeks, unless the Serbs agreed to the UN–EU peace plan.[46] The host of the summit, Helmut Kohl, on the other hand, expressed a strong interest in maintaining a consensus within the EU in favor of a diplomatic solution.

These developments showed that the WEU and the UN lacked the necessary integrated military command structure and the logistical means to cope with the crisis in Bosnia. The job had to be carried out by NATO. Whereas such close consultation between NATO, the WEU, and the UN meant slow reaction to Serbian actions in Bosnia, the military undertakings of the allies were not without some limited success. First in Sarajevo, and later in Gorazde, NATO ultimatums, followed by close air support, resulted in lifting the Serbs' siege around these cities. Yet, in Bihac, the UN and NATO failed to stop the Bosnian Serbs.

Under these circumstances the United States decided to take a decisive action to end the crisis and coordinated its efforts with Britain, France, Germany, and Russia. Together these countries became known as the Contact Group and facilitated the signing of the Dayton Agreement on November 21, 1995, thus ending the war in Bosnia-Herzegovina. The Republic of Bosnia and Herzegovina, the Republic of Croatia, and the Federal Republic of Yugoslavia signed the agreement, and representatives of the Contact Group nations and the EU Special Negotiator participated as witnesses. According to the terms of the agreement, a sovereign state known as the

Republic of Bosnia and Herzegovina would consist of two entities: the Bosnian Serb Republic and the Federation of Bosnia. In addition to diplomatic recognition of each state's sovereignty, the Dayton Agreement called for a peacekeeping mission under the command of NATO. The terms of the mission specified that a multinational military implementation force (IFOR) composed of troops from NATO and Russia, under the command of NATO and with authority granted by the UN will have the right to monitor and help ensure compliance with the agreement on military aspects and fulfill certain supporting tasks.[47] The IFOR was to have the right to carry out its mission vigorously, including with the use of force as necessary, and to have unimpeded freedom of movement, control over airspace, and status of forces protection. In addition to the military agreement, the Dayton accords called for an economic restructuring of Bosnia-Herzegovina that relied heavily on the European Union.

The EU's assistance to Bosnia-Herzegovina has been extensive. It covers a wide range of activities: assistance with ethnic reconciliation, the establishment of functioning institutions to promote democracy, economic aid, and efforts to bring the country closer to EU standards and principles. Since 1992, EU assistance has amounted to over 2 billion euros. Some of the large projects include integrated reconstruction projects involving buildings, houses, water supply, energy distribution networks, and transportation. Also, the Sarajevo and Mostar airports have been completely rebuilt with EU funds and assistance.[48]

KOSOVO. The Kosovo crisis in Yugoslavia involved the demand of ethnic Albanians, about 90 percent of the population, for autonomy, and the brutal response of the Slobodan Milosovic government in Belgrade. By 1998, the Serbian riot police and military units carried out attacks against Albanian civilians and a small, armed resistance group known as the Kosovo Liberation Army (KLA). As Serbian atrocities against civilians mounted, more and more young Albanian men joined the ranks of the KLA to fight the Serbs. This resulted in an all-out Serbian attack on Kosovo to drive out the Albanians from the province. As tens of thousands of refugees fled into neighboring countries, Western powers, led by the U.S., warned the Milosovic government to stop its military campaign or face NATO retaliation. When Milosovic refused, NATO warplanes began massive air attacks against Serbian military and strategic industrial sites. NATO strikes lasted for 78 days and caused severe economic damage in Serbia. The Milosovic government agreed to pull its troops from the province and accepted a NATO-led international security force in Kosovo.

The response of the Western Allies and Russia to the Kosovo crisis is an example of cooperation between NATO, the WEU, and the Organization for Security and Cooperation in Europe (OSCE). On June 10, 1999, Kosovo came under UN administration, and the UN mission in Kosovo—known as UNMIK—was set up under UN Security Council Resolution No. 1244. In addition, the allies imposed extensive sanctions on Yugoslavia to force the Milosovic regime into resignation. This goal, however, did not materialize until he lost the presidential election in 2000.

The EU has been present since the very beginning of the international effort to build a new future for Kosovo. As the single largest donor the EU is currently playing a prominent role in the reconstruction of Kosovo. In 1999, the European Commission provided 378 million euros in emergency humanitarian assistance for the victims of the Kosovo crisis, and a further 127 million euros for reconstruction programs. In 2000, the EU continued to support Kosovo with funds totaling 400 million euros.[49] The funds went to finance infrastructure development, housing, institution building, environmental cleanup, education, and other human development programs. In addition to development assistance, the EU is also a key participant in peacekeeping operations in Kosovo. Some 36,000 soldiers from EU nations are currently serving as members of the Kosovo Force (KFOR). This is about 80 percent of the total force. Furthermore, 800 civilian police from EU member states serve in Kosovo. On a related matter, the WEU began a security surveillance mission in the region following a request from the EU. The initial focus of the general security surveillance mission was to gather information for the EU as well as the NATO and OSCE missions on the implementation of the Belgrade agreements as well as on the situation of refugees and displaced persons. With KFOR troops and other international representatives in the region, the mission of the Satellite Center has concentrated on creating a digital map of Kosovo for use in reconstruction and removal of field mines.[50]

Following the democratic transition in Serbia on October 5, 2000, EU foreign ministers announced the lifting of sanctions and the immediate repeal of the oil embargo and the flight ban. They declared the extension of the European Reconstruction Agency to Serbia and Montenegro and promised to help with the clearing of the Danube. Following these decisions, member states of the EU began to normalize their relations with Serbia. Finally, at the October 2000 Biarritz European Council, Commission President Romano Prodi announced an emergency package totaling 200 million euros, and in November the Commission agreed to an emergency assistance program for Serbia.

THE MACEDONIA QUESTION. The division among the EU countries over foreign policy coordination toward the former Yugoslav republics was also evident in Macedonia. Following Macedonia's declaration of independence from Yugoslavia, Greece blocked the EU's recognition because Macedonia is the name of one of its provinces. Greece maintained that Macedonia had territorial ambitions on the Greek province, by virtue of its name, its constitution, its bank notes—which have the picture of the tower of Selonika—and its national flag, which bears the ancient Macedonian dynastic emblem discovered in northern Greece in 1975. Despite Greek opposition, six members of the EU (Denmark, France, Germany, Italy, the Netherlands, and the UK) established full diplomatic relations with Macedonia in December 1993 just before Greece took over the presidency of the Council in January 1994.[51] Belgium followed suit in early 1994. The crisis over Macedonia worsened in February 1994, when Greece moved unilaterally to impose a trade embargo against the former Yugoslav republic. This ban politically isolated Greece, which at the time held the presidency of the EU, and presented a major setback for the common foreign policymaking process foreseen in the Maastricht Treaty. Moreover, Greece's action appeared to have violated the Maastricht Treaty because under the treaty, member states cannot impose unilateral commercial sanctions except in cases of national security. Whereas Greece maintained that Macedonia represented a national security problem, the EU Commission rejected this argument and referred the case to the European Court of Justice to force a reversal of the Greek decision. The worsening of this crisis was prevented when Macedonia agreed to be known as the Former Yugoslav Republic of Macedonia, thus ending Greece's opposition to this state.

THE WAR ON TERRORISM AND IRAQ. Following the terrorist attacks on the Pentagon and the World Trade Center on September 11, 2001, the EU leaders rushed to align themselves with the U.S. The NATO members of the EU, led by Britain and acting on the Alliance's collective security charter, provided military assistance to the U.S. war effort in Afghanistan. During the first six months of 2002, Britain led the international peacekeeping mission in Kabul. Following Britain, Turkey took over the command until February 2003, when a joint command of Germany and the Netherlands replaced the Turks. Furthermore, the intelligence agencies of the transatlantic allies closely monitor suspicious activities and assist each other in tracking suspected terrorists. To that effect, the U.S. Justice Department issued a long list of organizations with ties to terrorism and requested assistance in shutting down their operations and freezing their financial assets.[52] The EU's response to American requests was positive, and the two transatlantic allies have been collaborating in the war against terrorism ever since.

However, since "9-11," the Bush administration's saber rattling toward Iraq over Saddam Hussein's violation of U.N. Security Council resolutions on Iraqi disarmament and U.S. policy toward the Israeli-Palestinian conflict soured relations between the U.S. and some of its EU allies. The EU members, with the exception of Britain and Spain, opposed unilateral American military action in Iraq unless it was backed by a UN resolution on weapons inspection. Even in Britain the public opinion (52 percent opposed to 34 percent in favor) was against a military campaign in Iraq[53] The Europeans believed that the U.S. had the military capability to enforce its will over others. However, they also pointed to the fact that the Americans needed international law and consent more than they may realize. Moreover, the Europeans argued that failure of the U.S. to address the widening crisis between the Israelis and Palestinians was likely to fuel terrorism and more division of opinions in the transatlantic alliance.

Among the European critics of U.S. policy, France has been the most outspoken. When President Bush spoke of the "Axis of Evil" in the world, referring to Iraq, Iran, and North Korea, the French Foreign Minister quickly called this simplistic and dangerous. The French worried that an American military campaign in Iraq would engulf the region in a larger war and draw in both Iran and Turkey with wider implications for NATO.[54] Furthermore, France has been critical of unconditional U.S. support for Israel.

Germany is both uncomfortable with U.S. policy toward Iraq and eager to improve its relations with the Bush administration following Chancellor Schroder's statement during the September 2002 German election campaign that "he has categorically rejected any German support for an American-led attack on Iraq, even if backed by a United Nations mandate."[55] Despite these reservations, even the French admitted that the EU was incapable of stopping a U.S. military action in Iraq. The crisis took a new turn following the UN Security Council's unanimous adoption of a new resolution on Iraqi weapons inspection on November 8, 2002. The U.S. sponsored new UN Security Council resolution gave inspectors sweeping new rights and Iraq 30 days to submit a detailed list of its weapons. It also gave the Security Council a key role before any possible attack but did not force Washington to seek authorization for war. Under the terms, Iraq had until November 15 to respond to the UN, and inspectors traveled to Baghdad on November 18 to set up communications, transport, and laboratories.[56]

Following these developments, the Iraqi government permitted the UN inspectors to begin their inspections for weapons of mass destructions (WMD) in Iraq. However, the slow pace of these inspections coupled with repeated delaying tactics of the Iraqi government caused serious discomfort in Washington and London. The Bush administration, supported by the Blair government in the UK, continued to mass troops in the Persian Gulf, and asked Turkey to permit placement of American troops in Southeastern provinces of that country for a possible northern front in the pending war in Iraq. At the same time, the Bush administration asked NATO to send patriot missile defense systems to Turkey against any possible missile attack from Iraq.[57] The Bush-Blair strategy caused severe rift within the EU as well as NATO.

On the transatlantic front, France, Germany, and Belgium refused an American request for stationing of NATO patriot system in Turkey even after the Turkish government invoked Article 4 of the NATO Treaty. While the American administration and NATO secretariat criticized this decision, the French-German-Belgian bloc argued that they would come to the defense of Turkey if that country were attacked by an outside force. For them, placing of the missiles in Turkey would have amounted to accepting the war plans of Washington. However, other European members of the Alliance (Britain, Denmark, Italy, Portugal, Spain, the Czech Republic, Hungary, and Poland) sided with the U.S. and infuriated the French president Jacques Chirac. Eventually, NATO agreed to place the missiles in Turkey but the anti-war members of the alliance, notable Belgium and Germany, warned that if the Turks entered Northern Iraq or provided active military support to the U.S. they would withdraw Belgian and German assistance to Turkey. The problem within the EU worsened as it spilled over in to intra-EU domain when 10 ex-communist countries forming the so-called Vilnius group awaiting EU membership signed a letter supporting the US-UK position on Iraq.[58]

Relations between the US-UK and France-Germany-Belgium further became strained when the former abandoned all diplomatic efforts to resolve the Iraqi standoff and launched a military campaign to topple the Saddam regime on March 20, 2003. The war started after the U.S., Britain, and Spain abandoned their quest for explicit authorization to go to war from the UN Security Council.[59]

THE ISRAELI-PALESTINIAN PROBLEM. The conflict between the Israelis and Palestinians continues to divide the transatlantic alliance. At the heart of the current U.S.–EU divide is the unconditional support the Bush administration has given to Israel. According to William Wallace, the transatlantic divide reflects a "broad difference of understanding about western interests in the region and about relations between the industrialized democracies and the Arab and Muslim world. The immediate focus is on Israel and occupied Palestine; but the broader differences extend across Iraq through Saudi Arabia to Iran."[60] Wallace argues that for the past 20 years, the EU and the U.S. collaborated well in the region with the Americans defining the Western priorities toward the Middle East and the Europeans providing economic assistance. However, in recent years, the dominance of the U.S. military power coupled with close ties between Washington and the Israeli governments have left the Europeans with little influence in the region.[61]

JUSTICE AND HOME AFFAIRS: DOMESTIC SECURITY

The third pillar of the Maastricht Treaty (Title VI, Article K) contains provisions on cooperation in justice and home affairs. According to these provisions, member states' interior ministers are required to work together on asylum, immigration, frontier rules, crime, customs, and police cooperation regarding terrorism and drug control.[62] Four areas of citizens' rights and internal security fall under the third pillar: the free movement of persons between member states; citizenship rights across the EU (e.g., equal opportunities, individual political and civil rights); immigration policy; and judicial and police cooperation. The subsequent Amsterdam Treaty, which brought two changes to freedom of movement of individuals, had been anticipated by the Schengen Treaty.

The Schengen Treaty, signed in June 1990, began as a Franco-German plan in 1985 to abolish all frontier controls on the movement of people and goods and services between the two countries.[63] The Benelux countries joined France and Germany in 1985. The provisions relating to the free movement of goods and services became effective with the Single European Act, and the group then focused its attention on issues relevant to the free movement of peoples. However, the signing of the Schengen treaty was delayed until June 1990 because of the insecure borders of the former East Germany. The treaty listed 45 countries whose nationals would be subject to border controls in an effort to curb immigration and to deal with refugee and asylum problems.[64] The Schengen group expanded when Italy signed on in November 1990, followed by Spain and Portugal in June 1991 and Greece in 1992. Denmark, Sweden, Finland, and Norway acceded in 1995. It is clear that the issues covered by the Schengen Treaty are addressed in the TEU. However, it was not clear when all of the EU countries would harmonize their immigration, refugee, and asylum policies. This was one of the main reasons behind the intergovernmental conference (IGC) in 1996 that resulted in the Amsterdam Treaty.

The Amsterdam Treaty states that all EU member states will remove controls on persons, be they citizens of the EU or nationals of third countries, crossing their borders within 5 years of the signing of the new Treaty.[65] The procedure outlined for this goal is a consultative one vis-à-vis the EP, with unanimity in the Council of Ministers. Second, the treaty formally incorporated the Schengen Treaty into the legal framework of the EU. The Cologne and Tampere summit meetings in June and October 1999, respectively, called for the establishment of a charter of fundamental rights of the European Union. A convention comprising personal representatives of the 15 national governments, 30 member state parliamentarians, 16 members of the EP, and the Commission drafted a charter and presented it to the European Commission prior to the Nice summit. The European Court of Justice and the Council of Europe had observer status at the convention. The European Council welcomed the draft charter as the first text that combined civil, political, social, societal, and economic rights of citizens in a single document.[66] It called for the Commission to disseminate the charter to the member states and EU citizens, and deferred decision on the charter's enforcement to the future. The major aspects of rights covered under enhanced home and justice affairs include the following topics.

Individual Civil and Political Rights and the Freedom of Movement

These rights define what it means to be a citizen of the EU. EU citizens are nationals of the member states. They have the right to reside freely in any member state, vote or stand as candidates in local and EP elections where there legally reside, and petition all EU institutions. It is, however, important to note that these rights are not uniform rights across member states. Each country defines its own civil and political rights, and they vary to some extent. That is, there is no EU bill of rights similar to the one found in the U.S. constitution.

Immigration and Asylum

The TEU, as amended by the Amsterdam Treaty, defines the objectives of the EU in the following fields:

1. Removal of any controls on persons—citizens of the European Union or nationals of third countries—when they cross internal borders from any one EU member state to another
2. Standards and methods of control and rules concerning visas when individuals cross the external borders of member states, that is, when they come into the EU
3. The conditions under which the nationals of third countries can circulate freely within the EU for a maximum period of 3 months
4. Requests for asylum (criteria and mechanisms for determining which member state is responsible for considering an application for asylum, minimum standards on the reception of asylum seekers, minimum standards for the conditions to be fulfilled to obtain refugee status and for the procedures for granting or withdrawing refugee status)
5. Refugees and displaced persons from third countries (minimum standards for giving temporary protection and ensuring a balance between the efforts made

by the member states in receiving and bearing the consequences of receiving refugees and displaced persons)

6. Measures against illegal immigration of nationals of third countries, including repatriation of such persons illegally resident in a member state
7. Definition of rights and conditions under which nationals of third countries who are legally resident in a member state may reside in another member state
8. Immigration measures concerning conditions of entry and stay of third-country nationals and procedures on the issuance of long-term visas, including those for family reunification purposes[67]

The Amsterdam Treaty mandates that all these measures be adopted within 5 years of the entry into force of the treaty, with the exception of measures listed under points 7 and 8. There are, however, exceptions to the rule. Title VI of the EC treaty is not applicable to the UK, Ireland, and Denmark.

At a special European Council summit at Tampere, Finland, in October 1999, the EU agreed to establish a European "area of freedom, security, and justice," and further refined the political guidelines in the field of asylum and immigration.[68] The leaders agreed that the European Union needed a comprehensive approach to migration that addressed political, human rights, and development issues in countries and regions of origin and transit. Obviously, this necessitated cooperation with third countries concerned. Therefore, the European Council called for more efficient management of migration flows, in close cooperation with countries of origin and transit; information campaigns on the actual possibilities for legal immigration; and campaigns to prevent all forms of human trafficking. This latter issue is very important because of the loss of life resulting from the underground traffic of nationals from the former Soviet Union, the Middle East, North Africa, and Turkey.

Immigration was one of the heated topics at the Seville 2002 summit. Most member states—led by Spain, Britain, and Italy—favored imposing sanctions on countries that failed to control the flow of illegal immigrants to EU. Such sanctions covered trade and economic cooperation agreements, suspension or limitation of which would have serious consequences for economies of these countries. France opposed this idea and, with the support of Sweden, blocked its adoption at the summit. The sanction plan, though supported by the British Prime Minister Blair, also received the opposition of the UK's development secretary Clare Short, who argued that if the sanctions were to pass, her aid programs would have been used as a form of blackmail to try to prevent the flow of unwanted immigrants from developing countries.[69]

The dilemma facing the Europeans over illegal immigration is best stated by Ruud Lubbers, the UN high commissioner for refugees: "it is irrational for governments to spend millions of euros on reinforcing borders, various deterrence measures, custody and detention centers . . . without simultaneously investing in solutions at the source of the problem."[70] Yet, at this time of economic downturn in EU countries coupled with the rise of anti-foreign right-wing political forces, it is far too optimistic to assume increased European economic assistance to nonmember countries in Asia, the Middle East, and North Africa. But there are policy complications in this matter stemming from intergovernmental and supranational characteristics of the EU.

When one examines the EU's policymaking in everything from asylum and immigration to drug trafficking to cross-border crime, it becomes clear that we are dealing with two "aspects" of the EU decision-making processes. Police and judicial cooperation on crime is entirely intergovernmental. On the other hand, EU institutions partly decide asylum and immigration policy. In this second policy area the Commission and member state governments share the right of initiative for new measures. While they share competences, the member states retain their national right of oversight in issues pertaining to asylum and immigration. They need only consult the European Parliament in these matters. As long as this division of authority remains, problems in EU-wide asylum and immigration policy will continue to be a divisive policy issue.

Cooperation of Police and Customs Matters

The Amsterdam Treaty outlines the goals and procedures for cooperation between the police forces and the customs authorities of EU member states (Title VI, Articles 29–42). The goal is to provide EU citizens and others with a high level of safety within an area of freedom, security, and justice because international crime, cross-border smuggling, and trafficking in drugs, arms, and people recognize no national frontiers. In the post–Cold War era, these issues became more urgent as illegal activities, coupled with growing cross-border crime, increased across Eurasia.

The main tools for dealing with multinational and cross-border crime are closer cooperation between the European Union's national and local police forces and between customs authorities on either side of national borders. Europol provides additional support for this cooperation. Europol is the European law enforcement organization that was set up under the Maastricht Treaty. Its purpose is to facilitate cooperation between member law enforcement institutions in combating organized crime, drug trafficking, and terrorism. The Commission works closely with EU member states and the other EU institutions in promoting this cooperation in accordance with the decisions reached at the Vienna summit of December 3, 1998, and Tampere in 1999. The main activities in this field are:

1. Setting up a European police college to train the next generation of police officers and other law enforcement personnel to work and operate in a European context.
2. Establishing a task force of European police chiefs, which had its first meeting in Lisbon in April 2000.
3. Setting up civil-crisis management machinery in the EU. A European rapid reaction force (ERRF) is being set up so it can be sent to hot spots, like Kosovo, to reintroduce civil peacekeeping, law enforcement, and internal security after the military has left.

4. Enhancing customs cooperation in the fight against crime by improving customs authorities' mutual information systems and implementing the Naples II Convention of 1997 on cooperation between customs authorities.

5. Setting up joint police and customs command centers in border regions to ensure that all interested law enforcement forces can work together on either side of national borders.[71]

CONCLUSION

The EU's foreign and domestic security policies are probably the least integrated of all of the EU's policy dimensions. The least unified policy area is foreign and security. Despite efforts at transforming the WEU, the EU's response to foreign policy challenges in Bosnia and Kosovo clearly demonstrated that it lacks the necessary military structure to be an effective alternative to NATO. EU members also have different commitments under NATO, WEU, and the new European Security and Defense Identity. Also, some members remain neutral in foreign security affairs.

On the positive side, the ESDI has come a long way since the inception of the WEU. In recent years, the organization presented a united EU policy in the Gulf crisis, Somalia, and Macedonia. However, NATO still remains the only security organization that has the unified command and military structure to respond to threats to European security. The future reformulation of NATO and ESDI–NATO partnership remains an unknown given diverging views on these subjects. Yet one thing is clear: transatlantic cooperation is needed as much today as it was during the days following WW II.

With regard to domestic security matters, such as free movement of labor and immigration policies, the Maastricht Treaty, as amended by the Amsterdam Treaty, contains specific provisions on cooperation in justice and home affairs. It appears that the member states' interior ministers are working together to establish common EU policies on political asylum, immigration, border controls, and cooperation in police matters. However, these are very sensitive issues, and it will require much cooperative effort over time to harmonize member states' policies.

ENDNOTES

1. Juliet Lodge, "From Civilian Power to Speaking with a Common Voice: The Transition to a CFSP," in Juliet Lodge, ed., *The European Community and the Challenge of the Future*, 2d ed. (New York: St. Martin's Press, 1993), p. 227.

2. Ibid., p. 228.

3. Peter Ludlow, "The Foreign Policy of the EU," in Peter Ludlow, ed., *Setting European Community Priorities, 1991–92* (London: Brassey's for CEPS, 1991), p. 102.

4. Jean Monnet, *Memoirs*, trans. by Richard Mayne, as cited in John Pinder, *European Community: The Building of a Union* (London: Oxford University Press, 1991), p. 7.

5. Dennis Swann, *The Economics of the Common Market* (London: Penguin Books, 1992), p. 8.

6. Henri Brugmans, "The Defeat of the European Army," in F. Roy Willis, ed., *European Integration* (New York: New Viewpoints, 1975), pp. 38–49.

7. Stephen George, *Politics and Policy in the European Community*, 2d ed. (London: Oxford University Press, 1991), p. 32.

8. Ibid., p. 219.

9. Ibid., p. 221.

10. John Pinder, *European Community: The Building of a Union*, (Oxford: Oxford University Press, 1991), p. 193.

11. *Treaty on European Union*. Title V. Article J-1 (2), (Luxembourg: Office for Official Publications of the European Communities, 1992), pp. 123–124.

12. Ibid., p. 124.

13. Lodge, "From Civilian Power," in Lodge, ed., *The European Community*, pp. 244–245.

14. *Treaty on European Union*, pp. 124–125.

15. Ibid., p. 128.

16. Ibid., p. 125.

17. Ibid., p. 127.

18. *Treaty on European Union*, Article J-5 (3).

19. *Treaty on European Union*, Article J-7. Par. 1.

20. Lodge, "From Civilian Power," p. 246.

21. Ibid.

22. Simon Hix, *The Political System of the European Union*. (New York: St. Martin's Press, 1999), pp. 344–345.

23. WEU, "Preamble of the Paris Agreement." October 23, 1954.

24. Ibid., Article V.

25. WEU, Committee for Parliamentary and Public Relations, *Western European Union* (Brussels: WEU, 1993).

26. John McCormick. *The European Union: Politics and Policies*, 2d ed., (Boulder, Colo.: Westview Press, 1999), p. 270.

27. Peter van Ham, "Western European Union," in Desmond Dinan, ed., *Encyclopedia of the European Union* (Boulder, Colo.: Lynne Reinner, 1998), p. 486.

28. Willem van Eekelen, "WEU Prepares the Way for New Missions," *NATO Review* vol. 41, no. 5 (October, 1993): 19–23.

29. Ibid.

30. WEU, *Kirchberg Declaration*, May 9, 1994 (Brussels: WEU).

31. Ibid., Part II.

32. Ibid., Part III.

33. WEU, "A New European Impetus," http://www.weu.int/eng/index.html, accessed 11/28/02.

34. Ibid.

35. Ibid.

36. Alexander Nicoll, "US Warns EU of Need for Close Link with NATO," *Financial Times*, December 6, 2000.

37. "The Many Tricky Ways of Widening Europe," *The Economist*, December 9, 2000, p. 56.

38. Judy Dempsey and Kerin Hope, "Diplomats Press Greece on Deal for EU Force," *Financial Times*, November 21, 2002, p. 4.

39. NATO, *Key to Prague Summit*, (Brussels: NATO Official Publications, 2002), p. 31.

40. Judy Dempsey, "Rumsfeld Presses for New NATO Force," *Financial Times*, September 25, 2002, p. 6.

41. David Garnham, "European Defense Cooperation," in Dale L. Smith and James Lee Ray, eds., *The 1991 Project and the Future of Integration in Europe* (New York: Sharpe, 1993), p. 210.

42. WEU, "Western European Union," http://www.weu.int/eng/weu.html, accessed 11/28/02.

43. Catherine McArdle Kelleher, "A New Security Order: The United States and the European Community in the 1990s." An occasional paper of the European Community Studies Association, 1992, pp. 31–32.

44. NATO/WEU, "Operation Sharp Guard Fact Sheet," NATO/WEU public data service.

45. NATO, "Operation Deny Flight Fact Sheet," NATO public data service.

46. "Britain and France Firm on Bosnia," *Financial Times*, December 10–11, 1994, p. 2.

47. European Commission, "Fact Sheet Released by the Bureau of Public Affairs," December 11, 1995.

48. European Commission, *Facts and Figures: 1991–99 Assistance to Bosnia-Herzegovina* (http://europa.eu.int/comm/external_relations/see/bosnie_herze/index.htm), accessed 11/28/02.

49. _____(http://europa.eu.int/comm/external_relations/see/kosovo/assistance.html), accessed 11/28/02.

50. WEU, "General Security Surveillance Mission in Kosovo," (http://www.weu./int/eng/index.html).

51. "Macedonia Backed by Half of EU," *Financial Times*, December 17, 1993, p. 3.

52. U.S. Department of the Treasury, Office of Foreign Assets Control, *Terrorism: What You Need To Know About U.S. Sanctions* (Washington, D.C.: Department of the Treasury, 2001).

53. "You Can be Warriors or Wimps; or So Say the Americans," *The Economist*, August 10, 2002, pp. 43–44.

54. "Allies at Odds—All Around," *The Economist*, April 13, 2002, p. 49.

55. "Why Gerhard Schroder Has Gone Out on a Limb," *Financial Times*, September 14, 2002, p. 51.

56. "Arab Ministers Welcome U.N. resolution on Iraq," Reuters, November 8, 2002.

57. "A fractured alliance, *Economist*," February 15, 2003, p. 25.

58. "Chirac Vents Over Behaviour of EU Candidates," *Financial Times*, February 18, 2003.

59. "A fight to the finish" *Economist*, March 22, 2003, p. 20.

60. William Wallace, "The Old Argument," *Financial Times*, June 27, 2002, p. 15.

61. Ibid.

62. *Treaty on European Union*, Title VI, Article K. 1–3, pp. 131–133.

63. Swann, *The Economics of the Common Market*, p. 170.

64. Lodge, "Internal Security and Judicial Cooperation," in Lodge, ed., The European Community, p. 321.

65. Hix, *The Political System*, p. 311.

66. European Commission, *Nice Summit: Presidency Conclusions* (Brussels: European Commission, 2000), p. 2.

67. European Commission, Justice and Home Affairs, *Immigration and Asylum: Community Responsibility*, http://europa.eu.int/comm/justice_home/unit/immigration_en.htm, accessed 11/28/02.

68. European Commission, *Tampere European Council Conclusions* (Brussels: Commission of the European Communities, 1999).

69. Quentin Peel, "Europe's Immigration Muddle," *Financial Times*, June 24, 2002, p. 15.

70. Ibid.

71. European Commission, Justice and Home Affairs, *Immigration and Asylum*.

13

■

Conclusion

Throughout this text we have shown that the European Union has followed a continuing, though irregular, course of integration. This course has always found a middle way between integration that is strictly economic in nature and integration that is strongly political, and has, with each integrative step, brought institutional changes representing compromises between the principles of intergovernmentalism and supranationalism. In the 1950s, the effort to achieve a strongly political and supranational form of integration, a European Defense Community, was rejected and ultimately replaced by an important step toward economic integration, the European Economic Community, which assumed a more intergovernmental form. When the principal supranational agency of the EEC, the Commission, took steps in the mid-1960s to increase its own power, it was thwarted by the French president, who had a contrasting intergovernmentalist conception of political integration and who preferred not to move beyond the extent of economic integration envisaged in the Rome Treaty.

By the 1970s the Commission had retreated to a more passive role, while the governments of the member countries, including the new entrants—Britain, Denmark, and Ireland—settled into a more intergovernmentalist mode of agenda setting and decision making, which featured the regularization of summit meetings of the heads of state and government in the European Council, institutionalized in 1974–1975. This was a period of learning and experimentation in the realm of economic integration, especially in the tentative steps taken toward the elusive goal of economic and monetary union. Finally, in the mid-1980s, with another new member, Greece, in place and two new members, Portugal and Spain, about to join, the governments converged on a package that developed the original Rome Treaty idea of a common market beyond the customs union achieved two decades earlier. It also took some modest steps in the direction of greater political union, particularly the extension of qualified majority voting in the Council of Ministers, in order to facilitate the implementation of further economic integration.

In the 1980s the supranational institutions of the European Community, especially the Commission, kicked back into gear from January 1985 under the dynamic leadership of Jacques Delors. It was Delors who spearheaded the public relations campaign in favor of the Single European Act (SEA) and who, in the late 1980s, pushed budget reform, regional and social policy advances, and, ultimately, Economic and Monetary Union (EMU) onto the extraordinary agenda, gaining the support of the European Council. Delors, with the support of Francois Mitterrand of France and Helmut Kohl of Germany, was able to overcome the opposition of British Prime Minister Margaret Thatcher and her successor, John Major, to greater political and economic integration. They could not stop the latest thrust of economic integration; Major succeeded only in getting the acceptance of Britain's right to "opt out" of the Social Charter and EMU.

More quietly, the European Court of Justice, by successfully asserting its authority to interpret the treaties, had strengthened the likelihood that national governments and courts would implement the single market legislation. And the European Parliament (EP) had been gaining power by pressure on the governments to support formal accretions in the Single European Act and the Treaty on European Union (Maastricht). The European Union came into being with the Maastricht Treaty, which made the EP a coequal of the Council of Ministers in many legislative areas and extended EU competence in already existing areas of legislation as well as in some new ones. Most notable of the expanded powers under Maastricht were the planned stages for attaining EMU, and the new "pillars": the Common Foreign and Security Policy, and the Justice and Home Affairs policy areas.

But after the Treaty on European Union was signed, further political integration came under a cloud when the Danish referendum failed in June 1992 and the French referendum commissioned by President Mitterrand nearly failed in September 1992. The British Parliament also refused ratification unless the Danes reversed their vote, which they did in 1993. But by this time Britain had pulled out of the exchange rate mechanism in the crisis of September 1992, and Major was facing fierce opposition to ratification in his own party. Although the treaty was eventually ratified by all 12 countries and the EU moved ahead with the entry of 3 new members—Austria, Finland, and Sweden—there was general dissatisfaction with its outcome, especially in light of the expected enlargement that would take place when 10 or more Central and Eastern European countries (CEECs) became eligible for membership. In order to make the EU ready for such a large influx, another treaty revision was undertaken in 1996–1997, culminating in the approval of the Treaty of Amsterdam. This extended the capacity of the EU to act in foreign and defense policy and internal security matters, but left essentially untouched the veto power in some policy domains, which restricted the capacity of the EU to cope with ordinary agenda items.

The Maastricht Treaty had been significant for the impetus it gave to economic as well as to political integration. Economic and monetary union, with its prospect of a single currency for EU member countries and a single central bank, became a firm EU commitment as a result of the agreement between Chancellor Kohl and President Mitterrand in 1990: France wanted the commitment and made a concession to Germany in the matter of reunification. Margaret Thatcher of Britain did not want either concession. Britain's opt-out at the Maastricht summit indicated that only a portion of the EU members would go ahead with EMU when the third stage began January 1, 1999. Eventually, 11 members did so on that date, and Greece adhered two years later, leaving Britain, Denmark, and Sweden outside as a result of decisions reached through their domestic political processes.

At the beginning of the 21st century the European Union is facing another of its critical crossroads at which it can choose to move ahead toward "a more perfect union," to remain at essentially the point where it was as the old century ended, or to reinforce the dominant features of the late 20th century EU. The latter features would be those in which the governmental heads of the member states not only control the pace of European political integration, but set its outer limits, as they continuously do in pulling up short of decisive steps toward a federal European state. The pressure to change the EU in fundamental ways has produced a constitutional convention, whose work is underway as of the end of 2002, destined to result in recommended treaty changes. Whether the treaty modifications will amount to a decisive step over the boundary between confederation and federation will be known by 2004. This is when the European Council is expected to put a stamp of approval on the work of another intergovernmental conference, whose role it will be to examine the constitutional convention's draft and reach unanimity on a version that the member states can accept unanimously, thus reflecting the extent to which the most reluctant member governments will permit the process of European integration to proceed toward federalism.

While this reexamination of the EU's structure and purposes is proceeding, the final steps are taking place to increase the number of members potentially from 15 to 27. The process of writing a constitution for the EU is heavily affected by this prospect, although the direction that should be taken to accommodate the increased membership is not obvious. Already, the Nice Treaty, agreed in 2000 and fully ratified in 2002, has made adjustments, most notably in the composition of the Commission and the voting weights in the Council, to accommodate a large influx of members. In fact, proposals the convention has considered have run the gamut from strengthening the hand of the leading members of the current EU—especially France, Germany, and Britain—which would be a reinforcement of intergovernmentalism, to removal of the veto in the Council of Ministers over tax measures and immigration policy. These various changes and proposals reflect a concern that the substantially enlarged EU will be incapable of acting coherently in areas of vulnerability, where failure to act as a unitary body could have severely damaging socio-economic and possibly political consequences for the EU members in their relations with one another and with the rest of the world.

In international economic relations, the EU has become a major actor alongside the United States and Japan. On the one hand, competition with Japan and the United States has intensified on several grounds, as shown by trade in "sensitive industries" and the race for economic dominance in Eastern Europe and the Mediterranean Basin. However, despite intense competition, the single market and EMU are likely to promote better commercial and financial relations between the three economic giants. The fear of Fortress Europe does not seem to be founded on rational economic grounds. The extent of direct foreign investment and trade flows supports the argument that protectionism is not likely to be the rule in future economic relations between the three giants.

The EU's relations with its European periphery highlight the inevitability of enlargement for several reasons. First, it is in the strategic and economic interests of EU members to maintain good relations with the nonmember European countries. Second, the EU needs to expand its economic base by absorbing new areas into its framework in order to compete with the United States and Japan—not only in regional terms but also on a global scale. And third, because the periphery states seek the economic benefits of membership in the EU, it promises to reduce the danger of political instability and a return to authoritarian regimes in eastern and southern Europe. In this regard, it is important to note that even those countries that cannot become members of the EU, such as the non-European Mediterranean Basin countries (NMBCs), are interested in establishing free trade agreements with the EU. Such agreements will give these countries preferential treatment over other trade partners of the EU, notably the African, Caribbean, and Pacific (ACP) countries.

At least in the near future, the NMBC and ACP countries stand to lose in the single market as the EU shifts its attention to its near neighbors. Both groups will continue to receive preferential trade and financial assistance from the EU, but the magnitude of these aid packages is not expected to increase substantially. An added problem for the ACP countries is the adverse ruling of the World Trade Organization (WTO) on the EU's preferential trade agreements with them. The CEECs are the targets of an ambitious and complex enlargement scheme, to which the EU has committed itself. Eventually, 13 or more new countries will join the ranks of the EU. However, there are major difficulties along the way: (1) the Cyprus problem, (2) territorial and other issues between Greece and Turkey, (3) Turkey's slow progress in meeting the Copenhagen criteria, and (4) slow reforms in the second-tier CEEC candidates. Yet, leaders of the EU are determined to push ahead with enlargement.

In external security matters, the provisions stated in the Maastricht and Amsterdam treaties suggest that the EU remains a weak security community that requires intergovernmental coordination of common policies. In this regard, the member states are less willing to surrender additional sovereignty to the EU. The various provisions of the treaty do not prevent members from following their own foreign policy preferences. Furthermore, while the members have strengthened ties between the EU and Western European Union (WEU), it is not clear how North Atlantic Treaty Organization (NATO) obligations of some EU member countries will be reconciled. Thus, potential problems exist in formulating common external security policies. The dispute in late 2000 over access to NATO intelligence and transport capabilities and Turkey's veto of an EU–NATO agreement, when added to earlier experiences in the Persian Gulf and in former Yugoslavia, support an attitude of skepticism. During the Gulf War, after the United States had asserted leadership, the EU countries managed to coordinate their policies within the EU and between the WEU and NATO. However, inconsistencies during the Balkans crisis and the Iraq war cast some doubt over the EU's ability to achieve common foreign and security policies.

In domestic security matters, the provisions of the Maastricht and Amsterdam treaties clearly call for cooperation among the member states in the policy areas of political asylum, immigration, border controls, customs, and police cooperation in combating crime. The Commission and the Council have taken steps to improve performance in these areas.

As the successor to the European Community, the European Union at the beginning of the 21st century has not yet assumed a shape distinct from that of its predecessor. The primacy of the intergovernmental bodies, especially the heads of state and government meeting as the European Council, will continue to be true of the EU for the foreseeable future. This is because in today's interdependent world, domestic and foreign policy cannot be separated easily, nor can politics and economics. With the expansion of the EU's functions into areas of once exclusive domestic policy competence, and with the increasing involvement of the EU in the political changes going on in eastern and southern Europe, the highest political leaders of the member countries have compelling reasons to meet frequently and to coordinate their policies. The media and ever-larger segments of the citizenry in the member countries closely watch the deliberations and joint decisions of the EU leaders. This is an inevitable outcome since the public increasingly goes to the ballot box to help settle EU matters. In the commitments made in successive treaty revisions and subsequent steps toward EMU and political union, we can observe that the EU is an emerging political community, but a community unlike the familiar nation-states that have preceded and helped to build it. At the beginning of the 21st century it remains a mix of tightly woven but still separately identifiable intergovernmental and supranational features.

Index